THE
EARLY SESSIONS
Book 5 of The Seth Material
SESSIONS 199-239
10/18/65-03/07/66

THE EARLY SESSIONS

The Early Sessions consist of the first 510 sessions dictated by Seth through Jane Roberts, and are expected to be published in a total of 8-10 volumes. For information on expected publication dates and how to order, write to New Awareness Network at the following address and request the latest catalogue.

New Awareness Network Inc.
P.O. BOX 192
Manhasset, N.Y. 11030

Internet Address: http://www.sethcenter.com

THE SETH AUDIO COLLECTION

Rare recordings of Seth speaking through Jane Roberts are now available on audiocassette. For a complete description of The Seth Audio Collection, write to New Awareness Network Inc. at the above address. (Further information is supplied at the back of this book)

THE
EARLY SESSIONS
Book 5 of The Seth Material
SESSIONS 199-239
10/18/65-03/07/66

© 1999 by Robert Butts

Published by New Awareness Network Inc.

New Awareness Network Inc.
P.O. Box 192
Manhasset, New York 11030

Opinions and statements on health and medical matters expressed in this book are those of the author and are not necessarily those of or endorsed by the publisher. Those opinions and statements should not be taken as a substitute for consultation with a duly licensed physician.

Cover Design: Michael Goode
Photography: Cover photos by Rich Conz and Robert F. Butts, Sr.
Editorial: Rick Stack
Typography: Juan Schoch, Joan Thomas, Michael Goode

All rights reserved. This book may not be reproduced in whole or in part, without written permission from the publisher, except by a reviewer who may quote brief passages in a review; nor may any part of this book be reproduced, stored in a retrieval system, or transmitted in any form or by any means electronic, mechanical, photocopying, recording, or other, without written permission from the publisher.

Library of Congress Cataloging-in-Publication Data

Seth (Spirit)
       The early sessions: volume 5 of the seth material / [channeled] by Jane Roberts ; notes by Robert F. Butts.
       p. cm.–(A Seth book)
       ISBN 0-9652855-5-3
          1. Spirit writings. 2. Self–Miscellanea
    I. Roberts, Jane 1929–1984. II. Butts, Robert F.   III. Title
    IV. Series: Seth (Spirit), 1929–1984 Seth book.
    Library of Congress Catalog Number:96-70130

ISBN 0-9652855-5-3
Printed in U.S.A. on acid-free paper

I dedicate The Early Sessions
*to my wife, Jane Roberts,
who lived her 55 years
with the greatest creativity
and the most valiant courage.
-Rob*

(Tracing of the appointment card used in the 15th envelope test, in the 199th Session, October 18, 1965.)

SESSION 199
OCTOBER 18, 1965 9 PM MONDAY AS SCHEDULED

(In the 198th session of last Wednesday, October 13, Seth stated that financial matters and our kitchen problem would be settled by Saturday, October 16. Jane did hear from the secretary of her publisher on Saturday; she does not regard the situation settled however since the publisher is out of town and could not reply personally.

(The carpenter was to see our landlord last week, and let us know about our kitchen enlargement by last Saturday. We have received no word about their meeting, although it is possible a decision was made Saturday.

(It will be recalled that in the 166th session, of June 30, 1965, Seth told the witness, John Bradley, that "there is one other company in particular with which you could become involved to your advantage. It is situated in the Midwest, perhaps in Minneapolis... presently a small firm comparatively speaking, but it will expand drastically within a short time... you will become involved with this company I believe irregardless, either as a competitor or as a member of the organization."

(John at present is a salesman for Searle Drug. He lives in Williamsport, PA, but has witnessed several sessions. At the date of the 166th session he knew of no drug or pharmaceutical firms in Minneapolis. Visiting us this noon while making his rounds, John told us he had checked up on Seth. He gave us the names and addresses of two drug houses that he learned about in Minneapolis. He had not heard of

them, and they are both small companies.

(*They are the Fuller Pharmaceutical Co., 3108 W. Lake Street, and the Ulmer Pharmacal Co., 1400 Harmon Place, both in Minneapolis. Needless to say, John plans to watch these companies with much interest.*

(*For the envelope test object I used the appointment card for Jane's visit to the dentist last May 5, 1965. This is the appointment that Jane kept while in a trance state, and thus had her teeth cleaned without discomfort. For an account of this episode see the 152nd session. See also my tracing on page 1. The card is on white stock, printed in black ink, with the handwriting in black pencil. I enclosed the card between two pieces of Bristol, then inserted the whole into the usual double envelopes.*

(*This evening's session will see the first of three scheduled attempts for Seth to clairvoyantly tune in on our friends, Bill and Peggy Gallagher, who arrived in Puerto Rico on vacation yesterday, Sunday. We hope that at 9:30 this evening, on Wednesday October 20, and Monday October 25, Seth will be able to pick up something of the activities and/or surroundings of Bill and Peg. They plan to make their own notes at these same times for later comparison.*

(*Jane said at 8 PM this evening that she did not mind if we had an envelope test. I remarked that it was going to be a busy session, what with the material on the Gallaghers and Dr. Instream, a possible envelope test, and the chance that Seth might discuss two very long, vivid, and complicated dreams Jane had while taking a short nap last Friday morning. See Jane's account in Volume 4, on pages 336-38. She believes that at least one of these dreams is a therapeutic dream, resulting from suggestions she gave herself following Seth's material on therapeutic dreams in the last session.*

(*A development that may be of interest is that I had a strong sneezing spell just before this evening's session. It came upon me abruptly at about 8:45, while Jane was reading to me her account of the two dreams in question. For some reason the sneezing made me quite angry and impatient, briefly, and I asked Jane to hold up in her reading. For reasons I was not aware of, I nevertheless felt the sneezing was related to the dreams.*

(*The session was held in our back room. Jane spoke while sitting down and with her eyes closed. Her pace was a little slow in the beginning but soon picked up speed. Her voice was average.*)

Good evening.

("Good evening, Seth.")

My fine sniffler. I do not know which matter to discuss first. Our Ruburt's dreams, or your recent reaction to them, Joseph .

The second dream is an excellent example of a therapeutic dream that results from self-suggestion. Ruburt requested a therapeutic dream from his inner self, and he received one.

I am happy to see that Ruburt tried out the material that I gave on the matter, and that he put it to the test. We will go rather deeply into this dream. However first we shall speak about the first dream, for they are indeed connected.

Indeed, Ruburt is correct in one respect at least, for the first dream, concerning the voices, was meant to be a therapeutic dream. However his own doubts changed the action within the dream, and he reacted to his doubts and ignored the earlier portion of the dream entirely.

The basic action of the first dream involved his reception, his <u>clear</u> perception, of several voices within his head. The voices, though he does not consciously recall their message, the voices spoke words of encouragement. They presented excellent evidence of <u>his</u> own abilities, for they were crystal clear and distinct, and without distortions.

There were four voices, all male. Three of these were the voices of personalities who no longer exist within the physical system, but which were closely allied with Ruburt in past lives. The fourth voice was my own. This was an attempt to build his confidence, and to show him how clearly reception can be if his abilities are fully utilized.

(*Jane has had other experiences, both in dreams and in psychological time, in which she heard Seth's voice but did not recognize it. For an account of an instance occurring during psy-time, involving John Bradley, see the unscheduled 190th session. As it happened John witnessed this session also.*)

Here however there is a drastic change, for the above portions of the experience were indeed <u>no dream</u>, but real experience, occurring while he was in a dissociated state.

The experience however <u>shocked</u> him, hence the shock later on when he <u>turns this</u> into a dream. The experience was to have been <u>remembered</u> however as a dream. He was not to have recalled its true nature, and it was hoped that he would elaborate the experience into a dream which would be composed of the constructive elements which the experience had given him.

Instead the experience frightened him, although only momentarily, for upon immediately awakening his mood was one of joy, and the earlier fear was forgotten. When he heard the voices, rather than becoming confident, he began to rise up to more shallow layers, and the ego ruled the dream sequence that followed.

He would not accept the responsibility that he felt such ability would put upon him, and so he looked for an outside source of the voices, and dreamed the sequence in which the voices came from a radio, and not his head. In the dream he switches the radio off, hoping to still the voices. They continue because he knows that he is picking them up from a channel that is not physical.

But he tries again, and in the dream he discovers another radio on your bookcase, Joseph , where our material is kept. The connection is obvious, for he knows that the Seth material comes from the same system as the voices. Here he reaches out to turn the radio off, and is stopped by a severe and sudden shock. The shock is his knowledge that our material would cease <u>were he to shut off his abilities in such a manner</u>. So the shock, which is one of realization, prevents him.

The connection with yourself is also obvious, since this happens in your room in the dream, for were he to shut off his abilities, you see, as one can turn off a radio, then you would be deprived as well as himself.

(*Here, Jane reached out in front of her as though turning off an invisible radio. Her eyes were closed. Her pace however was now quite fast, her voice stronger, and she was quite restless. She changed her position, to lean forward with her elbows on her knees, her head down.*)

In the dream he then goes into his own room, and this is the part of the dream that he has consciously forgotten, and covers it in his notes merely by saying "unclear here," and a vague reference to an electric storm.

In the dream itself, he goes into his room and discovers that his ability is as much a part of him as his breath, and that he cannot turn it off and on at will, or turn it off as one would a radio. He stands in the room, and there is an electric storm in the dream, and the room is touched by vibrating currents. He is afraid. Nevertheless he realizes that he is part of the storm, and the storm is part of himself, and it is not destructive but creative; and most of all, a simple elemental part of reality as it is.

This realization made the following dream, the second dream, possible. But the following dream would not have been possible without the first. The second dream is a dream of expansion. We will discuss it from two levels. The most meaningful level was one in which the many rooms represented psychic areas of development, endless possibilities that continually opened; but possibilities which were based on previous life experiences, and there are many aspects of reincarnational data in this dream, all reinforcing the healthy aspects of Ruburt's personality.

I suggest a short break. And I will by all means mention your own reaction, which was based on a wrong assumption.

(*Break at 9:30. Jane had been dissociated as usual. Her eyes had remained closed. Her voice had strengthened a bit during the delivery, and her pace had become so fast that my hand was already cramped. Jane said she felt that no more than ten minutes had passed.*

(*We were now due for the material on the Gallaghers in Puerto Rico. During break I jokingly began to speak aloud my own impressions of what Peg and Bill were doing at the moment. I rattled off a string of impressions about them sitting in a long narrow restaurant, and described their surroundings in some detail, including such things as wall lamps, etc. The odd part about this is that I seemed to see pictures of what I was describing, while my eyes were open.*

(Jane laughed with me at first, then asked me to stop, saying that my data might confuse her. At the same time I felt touches of my familiar thrilling sensation that I have often felt during psy-time, or when I see a vision; this gave me the feeling that I might be half right about what I had said; Seth however said nothing about it. Perhaps he will mention it next session.

(Jane's pace now slowed a great deal. As when giving the material for Dr. Instream, she sat with her eyes closed and her head down, usually with her hands to her eyes. Her voice was quiet. She used many pauses, a few of which are indicated. I will also indicate where I used a phonetic version of Jane's utterances, on two occasions. Resume at 9:40.)

If you will give us a moment, we will see what we can do with your Jesuit and the cat lover this evening. *(Pause.)*

These are impressions. A large white, or pale pastel building, they had something to do with today. Flowers here. Iron grillwork. Hacienda... Lucinda *(phonetically; I asked Jane to repeat the word).* They passed here. Bars at the windows of iron, not in jail.

Newspapers sold in front, outside. Later at another end of this same city, they pass shacks. *(Pause.)* This at the northwest portion. A street. Saint Severin *(phonetically.)* A rather high pile of dark dirt. *(Long pause at 9:45.)*

They stay at a pink stucco building, with porch enclosures that are round. *(Jane paused and gestured with her hands.)* <u>The base is not round</u>. The portion between the... *(gesture; groping for words)* what would be the porch railing and the roof is round.

They bicycled. Perhaps in their room there is a rather elaborate lamp on a table that depicts a scene, that glows when it is lit.

Give us a moment again, and we will try to pick them up now. *(Pause at 9:50. Jane, her eyes still closed, wagged a finger at me.)* Ruburt was correct, Joseph. You should not have given your impressions.

Outdoors, on a verandah, nearby suitcases open. A low-scooped blouse, and pale skirt. I believe the owner of the place where they stay is 50 or thereabouts. Name beginning with an M, and ending with an A, and a connection with a dog. They think of an island that sounds like Sumatra, but is not.

It is two words. *(Pause.)* More like San Mutro *(phonetically),* though I do not believe that is exact. An avenue beginning with a B, or San B, period, where they ate lunch. San Beninno *(phonetically)*, or similar. *(Long pause at 9:56.)*

A striped awning, a dinner at 375. I believe this is the cost. A blue blanket on the bed where they sleep? A purchase of an item that is like a small sculpture. *(Pause.)* I get a <u>bear</u> shape. Some <u>rain</u>.

I suggest your break.

(Break at 10:00. Jane was well dissociated, she said—much more so than usual. Her eyes had remained closed, her voice quiet. Again, she had the impression that time had passed quickly.

(While giving the above data Jane had no visual material to accompany it, and said she was just as glad. She took this lack of imagery to mean that her own feelings and ideas were bypassed; she felt free of concern about the accuracy of the material, and thought it might be better for this.

(When she began speaking again, Jane's pace was slow, her voice quiet. As before, she sat with her eyes closed, her head down and her hands to her eyes. Resume at 10:09.)

Now, from Puerto Rico to Oswego *(site of a NY State University)*.

Again, give us a moment. And please be very quiet.

(I had made a noise turning a page in the notebook. Jane took a long pause at 10:10. Because it was a warm night we had a window open. Abruptly I became conscious of traffic noise, and Jane told me later that she did too. This is the 9th Dr. Instream experiment. Each week we send Dr. Instream Seth's material for him.)

A fountain pen, and a desk. A pale yellow handkerchief in a triangle in Dr. Instream's pocket, breast pocket.

If possible he should emotionally think of us. He is thinking of us on an intellectual level now. Concentrating, but trying too hard intellectually. *(Pause at 10:12.)*

If he were to call me an old faker, I should get him more quickly. I get the number 4, but do not know to what this refers.

Ruburt gets the child who is squalling below in the lower apartment, and it is no help. But we shall try harder in our own way.

(I too had just become conscious of the baby below us. Actually the child cried but briefly. Jane had paused at 10:15.)

I see flowers on the dining room table at his apartment. They have been to a movie.

His hypnosis experiments are not doing as well as he hoped, as far as other parties are concerned. They have to do with direct stimuli, applied through hypnosis at a distance; and there is a connection in his mind with myself here, and those experiments.

Something I <u>believe</u> also to do with conditioned reflexes, set up through the hypnotic situation, with himself as hypnotist, and in connection with two other particular individuals.

He will have success with part of the experiment, having to do with an S. What he plans is entirely feasible however, and quite possible. There is a personality quirk, so to speak, that may snag him here, and the word snag has more than one meaning.

(Jane took a pause that lasted for one minute, at 10:22.)

I believe the object has to do with a locket that belongs to his wife, or that belonged to a female child.

He wants a cigarette as this moment *(pause at 10:25)*, though this is far from unusual.

I thank him for his interest and his time.

Do you have a test for me this evening?

("Yes."

(I handed over the usual double envelope, and Jane took it without opening her eyes. I had decided to forget the envelope test unless Seth asked for it, for it would make three tests in a row.

(Jane held the envelope lightly in both hands and paused briefly. This is the 15th envelope test.)

Now again, give us a moment and we shall see what we can do. These are impressions.

A turnabout. Part of a missive. The color yellow. Something swings, or something swinging. The number 5, as in the afternoon.

Two people, as in a negative. Ruburt thinks of his aunt and uncle in New York. This is an associative connection on Ruburt's part. *(Pause.)*

A connection however with a man and woman, not yourselves. Older than yourselves. *(Pause.)* A connection with an afternoon scene, perhaps your parents, Joseph, and an automobile.

A connection with your parents' back yard. *(Pause.)*

A distant connection with a trip by train, and the service. Flowers, and death of a dog. *(Pause.)*

I suggest your break.

(Break at 10:33. Jane was dissociated as usual. Her eyes had remained closed, her voice quiet. She told me she had no idea that there would be an envelope test.

(See the tracing of the dental appointment card on page 1, and my notes about the card on page 2. The card refers to the appointment that Jane kept while in a trance state, to have her teeth cleaned. The test data appeared to contain some far-ranging impressions, but we seemed to be able to connect some of them up without trouble.

(Jane particularly remembered the appointment because it is the first she ever made voluntarily. This she calls "a turnabout" from previous habit. The card can be "Part of a missive." We both saw "something swinging" as the dental drill suspended over the chair. We thought "The number 5" good, since the appointment was for May 5.

(Jane was sure "The color yellow" referred to the fact that she well remembers wearing a new, bright yellow shift while keeping the appointment.

(We regarded, offhand, the data on my parents as probably distortive or associative, as the material on Jane's aunt and uncle. We thought it possible that "a man and woman, not yourselves. Older than yourselves", referred to the parents of Marie Colucci, the dentist's wife. The Coluccis are personal friends of ours. On a visit to their home this summer we met Marie's mother, in Elmira on a visit from New Jersey. Marie had made the trip to New Jersey, to get her mother, by train.

(We thought this connection with "a trip by train" might be the distant connection referred to by Seth, when we remembered that while Marie Colucci's mother had been visiting in Elmira, the mother's husband died of a heart attack at home in New Jersey, while bowling. This would be the connection with "service" and "Flowers," meaning funeral.

(Jane was sure "death of a dog" referred to the last dental appointment she had had previous to May 5, 1965. This would be 3 years ago; Jane said she recalled this vividly because our dog, Mischa, died within two days or so of that long-ago appointment. The appointment itself had also been a painful one.

(Neither of us understood the reference to an automobile, particularly. During break I mentioned that I hoped Seth would take a few minutes to verify our interpretations of his data, or to correct us, before he closed the session.

(Jane had been relaxing on the bed during break, and resumed speaking from there. She lay on her side, her head propped up by one hand. Her glasses were on; because of this I thought her eyes might open eventually. Her pace was good, her voice quiet as she resumed at 10:45.)

We will now end our session. I hope to finish the material concerning Ruburt's dream, however. I would give it now, but I imagine that you are weary.

("Yes.")

Our own test material was only slightly distorted, and quite legitimate.

The appointment was made in the afternoon. The service was a funeral service, hence the connection with flowers, which also reinforced the fifth month.

The appointment was made at five in the afternoon, incidentally.

The older people represented the dentist's in-laws, and the distortion occurred here, for Ruburt picked up correctly the idea of parents, but thought they were your own.

The automobile was the mother's automobile, which was parked outside of the Colucci residence the evening you visited. They drove back.

(*As soon as Seth said this, I remembered seeing the automobile parked before the Colucci's house on the evening Jane and I visited there. Since their home is in the country, and not even close to any other house, the car couldn't be connected to anyone outside the Colucci family. And of course it was not the dentist's car, which we are familiar with. This is the somewhat complicated sequence of events here: Marie Colucci took the train to her parents' home in New Jersey, and drove her mother back to Elmira in the parental automobile. When Marie's father died of a heart attack in NJ, Marie drove her mother back to Jersey in the parental car, then returned to Elmira herself by train.*)

The death of a dog you interpreted correctly, but the death and flowers and service applied, also, all together, to the death of the parent.

There was a very slight connection with your own parents, however, in that Ruburt mentioned the dentist and the trance to them at their latest visit here. And a secondary connection with a car—not close, not a close connection—in which your parents traveled on that occasion.

You may take a break, or end the session as you prefer.

("*We'll end it then.*")

My heartiest regards, and my particular regards to Ruburt, who is following through in good humor.

Did you have a question?

("*It can wait. I was going to ask you to say something about my sneezing spell.*")

You had the particular reaction because you misinterpreted an element of Ruburt's dream, of which you knew, but I believe you had forgotten it.

(*Jane still lay on the bed. Now she groped for her pack of cigarettes, and lit one. Her eyes opened very briefly, and barely enough for her to see, as she struck the match. Then she resumed talking and smoking with her eyes closed.*)

It had to do with the fact that in his dream, the second radio was in your room, and he received a shock when he tried to turn it off.

You interpreted this to mean that you had pushed him, perhaps, that perhaps were it not for you he would not have become as deeply involved as he is, in this endeavor.

You have felt this way fairly often. You felt responsible for the shock of his dream. It is true the sessions would not have been possible without your encouragement and help, and without the reinforcement of your own abilities.

You should be able to see that Ruburt has grown intellectually, emotionally, and psychically, as a result of the sessions, as have you. Not only has his <u>inner</u> self expanded, but his ego has become <u>stronger</u>, even while it has become more flexible. So there is no need for your concern in that regard.

The sneezing was a panic reaction. Naturally you do not want to hurt Ruburt in any way, and you felt somewhat responsible because in his dream he could not turn off the radio which represented his abilities.

(*Jane's eyes opened briefly. They were very dark as she looked at me.*)

Now, I could continue along these lines for quite some time, and I am perfectly willing to do so, for your edification rather than my own. If you prefer that we do this while it is fresh in our minds, then take a break and we shall continue. And if not, do not ask me leading questions, and we shall end the session. I am rather closely allied with you both this evening.

("*I guess we'd better close then.*")

We will indeed let you have your well deserved rest, and I shall say good night, as a talkative old friend might.

("*It's been very enjoyable.*"

([*Jane, after a pause:*] "*It's me again. At least I think I am.*"

("*Good night, Seth.*"

(*End at 11:03. Jane was dissociated as usual. Her eyes were open at the end of the session, her voice quiet, and she was smiling. I might add that while Jane was reading her dreams to me just prior to the session, I was only half listening as I got ready to take the notes. But it seems that actually I listened very well.*)

SESSION 200
OCTOBER 20, 1965 9 PM WEDNESDAY AS SCHEDULED

(*At supper time this evening I voiced my opinion of the tactics of Jane's publisher, Frederick Fell, in no uncertain terms, with the rather obvious implication that Seth could comment upon the situation should he care to.*

(*I planned no envelope test for this session, thinking that the test material on the Gallaghers in Puerto Rico, and on Dr. Instream, would be enough for one session. I was more interested at the moment in having Seth finish his analysis of Jane's two dreams, which he began last session, and made it a point to say so just before the session tonight.*

(*We have not heard from the Gallaghers, incidentally, and do not expect to. The four of us agreed not to exchange mail, leaving any communications up to Seth while Bill and Peggy are on vacation.*

(*Last Monday noon, October 18, our friend John Bradley visited us while making his rounds as a traveling drug salesman. He was too busy to witness Monday's session, but promised to visit us on Tuesday evening, October 19. During the day on Tuesday, John had to attend an important business meeting of his regional office in Binghamton, NY, perhaps sixty miles from Elmira.*

(Remembering her success in clairvoyantly tuning in on Bill Gallagher as he made his business errands on the evening of October 8, Jane decided to try the same thing with John on Tuesday. The difference here was that John had no forewarning of Jane's efforts, since she didn't get the idea until after he left us Monday. See Session 196 in Volume 4 for the Gallagher material.

(At 8 PM Tuesday, Jane wrote down 13 impressions, all dealing with John Bradley's supposed activities. She was ironing at the time, and pleasant music was on the radio. She wrote the impressions in an offhand manner, she said, without straining; she had no idea at the time as to whether any of them were correct. John arrived from Binghamton perhaps three quarters of an hour later. Going over the list with us in the course of the evening, he confirmed 10 of Jane's impressions as correct. Some of them were quite striking.

(Jane keeps separate records of such experiments, and has this one written up in the same manner as the Gallagher experiment that is included in the 196th session.

(The session was held in our small back room. Jane began speaking while sitting down and with her eyes closed. Her voice was quiet to begin, her pace quite slow.)

Good evening.

("Good evening, Seth.")

I will finish discussing the dreams.

First however I would like to speak briefly about Ruburt's attempts at telepathy with Philip last evening. Such exercises are excellent training, and they will boost his confidence, particularly where distance is a factor, as it was last evening.

(Philip is John Bradley's entity name, according to Seth.)

This will help in the Dr. Instream material. The results of the Philip experiment were quite adequate, and some rather specific points were covered.

Now, concerning Ruburt's second dream. Let me say first of all that the many rooms and apartments to be explored all represented various facets of psychic realities, hence his anticipation in the dream. The shop within the apartment had to do with the physical dimension and various physical abilities which are based on past-life experiences.

He thought the clothing was on sale, that it was cheap at the price, but it only seemed so because he did not know that he had already paid for it. Here he found an excellent jacket which he realized was his own from a previous season.

The jacket was green and warm. It represented what will seem like a new ability to him, when he will shortly discover it in himself.

He will however then realize, or he should realize, that this ability was his in a past life, but unused, and is now awaiting him. It will bring both warmth and confidence, and will give him protection.

In his dream he is also aware that these people like him, and that in some manner he has been acquainted with them in the past. This also brings forth feelings of rediscovery and joy that accompanied the dream. The persons involved were good friends indeed in a past life. They were images of the men whose voices spoke to him in his earlier dream, when he was so frightened; and when he leaped so gracefully from the banister, I was the one who extended an arm to assist him.

(*Jane smiled, her eyes still closed. Her pace had picked up and her voice had now grown somewhat stronger and deeper.*)

In the dream however I was a young man with olive skin, from a previous existence. That is, it was myself in a previous existence. There were the other men whose voices were also heard in the first dream. This time however the intended vote of confidence was given emotionally, through smiling gestures and so forth.

The separate building of apartments represented possibilities in the more distant future. Ruburt is not ready for them yet. The one room into which he looked for example was not vacant, or ready for him in other words. The ability represented by the jacket however represents the fairly immediate future.

His dancing and high spirits are self-explanatory. His excellent mood upon awakening showed that the import of the dream was clear to him on a subconscious basis.

I do have a few more remarks, very few, on this second dream. However now I suggest a brief break.

(*Break at 9:20. Jane had been dissociated as usual for a first delivery. She kept the deeper voice and fast pace until break.*

(*Jane said she hadn't consciously connected the voices in the first dream with the olive-skinned males in the second dream. She well remembered the young man who gracefully assisted her off the banister in the second dream. He had, Jane said, exceptionally beautiful and smooth olive skin. He was not very tall, but short, slim and well proportioned, with dark hair. Jane doesn't recall this young man's features specifically, nor for that matter the features of any of the other males. She remembers the fact that they were all smiling, and their smooth olive skins.*

(*It was now time for the second clairvoyant test with the Gallaghers in Puerto Rico. Jane began speaking while seated and with her eyes closed. Her voice was now quiet, and she used many brief pauses. Resume at 9:30.)*

Please give us a moment.

Your friends, my friends, the Jesuit and the cat lover, are sleeping in a different room than they were at our last session.

It is close to water, and further west, and in a different town or location. *(Pause.)* It is to the <u>rear</u> rather than the front of the building, to the side and rear. With a tree immediately outside the window; a bushy sort of tree with something like spikes on it. *(Pause.)*

Some sort of theater. They have visited or it is close, and they passed it on their way to this place.

There is a phone in this room. They saw a motion picture about a woman with lovers, and a cripple, or perhaps a dwarf. They purchased a crucifix, I believe, small, to be worn on a chain. *(Pause.)*

They ate at a place with wide windows and blinds, closed because of the sun. One extremely long window at the front, the entire length of the building, covered with this blind.

They ate with Peggy's sister and husband, or they talked about them during the meal, in an immediate fashion, thinking of them very strongly. Perhaps making an appointment with them for this evening.

(Peggy's sister had been married on the Saturday before Peggy and Bill left for Puerto Rico. The oddity here is that the sister and her new husband also went to Puerto Rico on their honeymoon; however they left for the island Saturday night, whereas Peggy and Bill left for Puerto Rico the next day, Sunday. As far as Jane and I know, the two couples had made no plans to meet down there, nor did they particularly want to.)

The sister's husband has a squat build, and uses his hands often in work.

(Jane and I have not met the husband or sister. Jane now took a long pause at 9:41.)

Let me see if we can pick them up at this moment.

A connection with dice. An old man, and jewelry. A minor disturbance. I think of a pack of cigarettes, not American brand, though neither of them smoke. A shawl, as a gift. A particular dead-end street that should be significant to them on their return.

I have the impression: clor-ra-door *(my phonetic interpretation)* but do not know to what it refers. Also an interior lake.

I suggest your break, and then we shall pick up your Dr. Instream. Figuratively speaking, of course.

(Break at 9:46. Jane was dissociated as usual. Her eyes had remained closed, her voice average. As in the last session when dealing with the Gallaghers, she had no

visual images to accompany her delivery.

(When she began speaking again her pace was slow for the most part, with many pauses. She sat with her eyes closed. Resume at 10:00. This is the 10th Dr. Instream test.)

I have an additional impression here, on our friends. It is of a small, light wooden object. *(Pause.)*

I believe this evening our Dr. Instream is a little late. In any case he is not ready for us yet. *(Pause.)* A car stops, and he gets out of it.

Give me a moment.

He has been with other people, rather formally dressed. He has had drinks at a public establishment this evening, perhaps the Howard Johnson's which you visited; and an affair at the college.

I think the car is a Buick. *(Pause at 10:05.)* He makes an evening visit to his office, and perhaps has coffee in the cafeteria. He speaks to a man in the hall outside the cafeteria. There is some confusion in his mind as to whether or not he can be with us in time, and his thoughts dwell on the matter.

The man he spoke to in the hall is somewhat of a nuisance to him, in some way acting as some kind of impediment.

(Jane now took a pause lasting for a minute, from 10:09 to 10:10.)

Dr. Instream also thinks of a telephone call he is expecting. He is in his office late. The phone call may have to do with his wife. She drives him home, I believe. He is inside his house.

(Pause at 10:12.)

He smokes on the verandah. There is a brief disagreement between his wife and himself. He goes to his room and tries to contact us. He thinks of a knife.

Do you have a test for us, Joseph?

("No. I thought you might like to finish up on Jane's dream material.")

We will then have a very brief break, and I will finish that discussion.

(Break at 10:14. Jane was dissociated as usual. Her eyes had remained closed, her voice quiet. She had used many short pauses, other than those noted.

(While giving the data involving the car at the beginning of the test, Jane said she had a feeling of unsureness at to the location of the car. She didn't know whether it was at Dr. Instream's office or at his home. She also didn't know whether the unsureness referred to Seth or herself.

(Jane resumed while seated and with her eyes closed, in a stronger voice and a more rapid pace, at 10:20.)

It is interesting to see how the second dream was intertwined with events and concerns having to do with everyday realities.

They formed the outer framework for the second dream. At the same time the dream generated sufficient energy to lift Ruburt and his moods from a slavery to physical events. That is, the dream allowed his native good spirits to return in force, and to operate in a healthy fashion regardless of physical events.

Your Mr. Fell is indeed a different sort of personality than yourself, Joseph, but his omissions are not deliberate. Merely the result of lack of discipline and an avoidance of details; and indeed, a meeting between the three of you would be beneficial, indeed.

Believe it or not, Ruburt's letter <u>was</u> a surprise to him. He will feel hurt, but cover this with a cosmopolitan manner.

(*Jane took a long pause at 10:27.*)

He has been away because of family difficulties.

(*Jane had been smoking since break. She now opened her eyes briefly and put out her cigarette.*)

The therapeutic dream cut short Ruburt's poor mood by a good two weeks, and the same tactics can be utilized in the future most productively.

Your own dreams just written down have to do with a change of pace on your part.

(*This surprised me. Seth here referred to two rather brief but vivid and colorful dreams I had written down just before tonight's session began. Jane came back to the studio just as I finished. I told her I was noting a couple of dreams down, but did not describe them to her since time was getting short.*

During our daily life we do not take the time to describe in detail each dream we have to the other, unless obvious connections arise in future events, or the dream happens to be unusually vivid in some way. My two short dreams mentioned above were a little more vivid than usual, but otherwise not unusual, I thought. I now tried to lead Seth on.)

("*I didn't tell Jane anything about those dreams.*")

I realize that you did not. The change of pace may be in connection with two people, your relationships to two people.

(*Jane now took a rather long pause.*)

The colors have to do with quickening intensity of an inner nature. The quickening intensity could seem to involve a chase or pursuit. You are close to achieving a goal, having to do with your work.

An unknown, or not seen, man has to do with that portion of your goal which you are about to reach, but have not yet reached.

(*On the spur of the moment I began to concentrate on having Seth tell me more about this man. I was not sure whether he referred to this man as being part of my dreams, of whether he meant this unseen man existed physically.*

(*At the same time Jane did something she has seldom done since she began speaking while sitting down. Her cigarettes lay on a bookcase out of her reach. Her eyes opened very slightly; she got up, reached the cigarettes, lit one and sat back down.*)

The symbol of a road involves the distance from one life to another, and the change from one set of parents to another. The aggression can be channeled into the pursuit of your goals. There was something to do with a child in the dream somewhere.

("*I don't remember that.*")

We will now take a break, or you may end the session as you prefer.

("*We'll take a short break.*"

(*Break at 10:40. Jane was dissociated as usual. Her eyes had remained closed for the most part. Her voice had been quiet, her pace slow.*

(*Copies of my two dreams in question follow. I am quite sure that I remembered but parts of both dreams. At any rate there follows what I wrote in my dream notebook.*

(*Dream # 1; Monday night, October 18: In color. I was showing a young man in his early twenties some things about drawing. He was blonde, a man I did not know. Deep voice, straight hair, white shirt sleeves. He had a drawing board to which he had fastened a sheet of rough watercolor paper, and carried this around with him. I saw that he had covered the paper with fine-line figure drawings and portraits, in pencil and pen. This is an unusual way to work on watercolor paper. Good drawings, and I still remember one profile head in line, quite clearly.*

(*Dream # 2; Tuesday night, October 19: In very bright and vivid color. Had to do with our Ford station wagon, which is blue. In a big old garage with Jane, I was ready to drive the car away, but then seemed to look up at it on a hoist. I saw that the radiator was pulled away from the rest of the motor, that hoses and other connections dangled, and that the oil and water had drained away. I realized the car hadn't been used in a long time.*

(*Then I saw that the car sat on a steep grassy bank, beside a river I believe, and that another old jalopy had somehow been moved in front of our car so that we couldn't move it. The bank was covered with brightly colored high grass and weeds. Jane and I tried to walk along a path toward the car. The path was worn down to the bare earth. We were barefoot, and now I saw that the path was littered with pieces of broken glass. I think I backed up, telling Jane something to the effect that we had already gone too far. Neither of us were cut or injured.*

(*At break I did not tell Jane anything about the contents of either dream. I thought that what Seth had said so far was related to the dreams in most cases, without being very specific, and was especially interested in his remarks about the intensity of color; this is true of the second dream especially. I also thought the material on my being close to achieving a goal good, in that I have had definite feelings along this line lately. Nor had I said anything to Jane about this; it is my habit to see how things work out instead of making predictions.*

(I did mention to Jane at break that I was concentrating on a question. I then added another question, I told her, but said no more other than that. I wondered whether Seth could answer the two questions. The second question was merely whether Seth could tell us anything about the blue car featured in the second dream.

(Jane said she wished Seth had not taken a break, but had continued with the dream material. I did not know whether I had said too much myself or not. Jane resumed in the same quiet manner, with her eyes closed, at 10:44.)

I have been rather enjoying myself with our last material.

Ruburt's ego reared its rather belligerent head during break. However, even this head is more kindly of late.

A road, a highway or a railroad, a group of people and something pulls away. A landscape, quite vivid, and yourself. Two other people, a clump of trees.

Ruburt wants to say a whistle, so we will let him say it. This is a result of the train connection on his part. He is doing very well.

("Yes.")

(Jane now took a long pause.)

A lake. A chase. You are after something, and fear it gone or unattainable.

("I don't remember that.")

(Jane raised a finger, her eyes still closed.)

You should not comment, for when you do so you leave us open, because you give clues; and these clues do help in any case, my dear friend.

The lake however was in the early part of the first dream.

You may take a short break, very brief. Then ask any questions that you prefer, and we shall end the session. Questions having to do with the dream, incidentally.

(Break at 10:53. Jane was dissociated as usual. Her eyes had remained closed, her voice quiet. She said Seth's admonishment to me hadn't bothered her. Neither of my mental questions had been answered.

(During break Jane again lay on the bed, or half reclined, while she smoked. She began to speak from this position. For part of the delivery at least her eyes were open. I found it a little hard to tell when they might be partially open since she left her glasses on, and reflections interfered. Her voice was quiet, her pace rather fast. Resume at 10:58.)

The failure perhaps was my own. The dream material should have been continued without a break. However I felt that Ruburt might need one. Still we have done well, as you should discover when you read your dreams over once more.

Had you asked the two questions mentally without letting Ruburt know they were significant, you should have received your answers. This is simply because this sort of thing is fairly new with him, and so he was on guard. Later it will not matter.

We will therefore close our session. My best regards to all. And from what our Mr. Gallagher is doing at this moment, I must say that I think he would make a poor Jesuit indeed.

I am quite prepared to continue. However I realize that you must be weary.

("We're getting there.")

(Jane, after a pause, with her eyes wide open: "It's me.")

("Good night, Seth.")

(End at 11:01. Jane was dissociated as usual. I believe her eyes were closed most of the time. Jane said she didn't know, that during the session she wasn't concerned one way or the other.

(Jane was very curious as to what new abilities lay in store for her, especially the one that Seth said she would shortly discover. We speculated that Seth's method of interpreting my dreams in this session might have something to do with it.)

SESSION 201
OCTOBER 25, 1965 9 PM MONDAY AS SCHEDULED

(I planned no envelope test for this evening's session, thinking its place could be taken by the third and final Gallagher clairvoyant test.

(Jane has now settled all matters pertaining to her ESP book with her publisher. In the 198th session, Seth said she would receive a letter from her publisher by the next Saturday. Jane did receive a letter then from his secretary, but not a definitive one. It is thus interesting to note that she received the information she wanted by the next *Saturday, however; October 22, Friday, to be exact. We have yet to receive any word on our kitchen enlargement, which Seth also predicted would be settled by the Saturday after the 198th session.*

(There follows a copy of my dream of Thursday night, October 21, as taken from my dream notebook: "I dreamed briefly that the first of the two short stories Jane has sold has now been published—The Big Freeze, I believe—and that as a result Jane can now get paid for it." I hoped Seth would comment on the dream.

(Saturday, October 23, Jane learned that her short story, The Big Freeze, *was on the stands, in* Dude Magazine. *She had not been notified by the magazine that*

it would be. She is also to be paid on publication, rather than acceptance of the material. The magazine had appeared on the stands Friday, October 22.

(In the 200th session, Seth said Jane's publisher, Frederick Fell, would be hurt by Jane's demands for action, but would cover it with a cosmopolitan air. In his letter of October 22, the publisher certainly did write a cosmopolitan letter, in our opinion.

(The session was held in our back room and was free of interruptions. Jane spoke while sitting down and with her eyes closed. Her voice was quiet, her pace quite slow in the beginning.)

Good evening.

("Good evening, Seth.")

Your dream was an excellent example, Joseph, of a clairvoyant one, in which definite new information was received. The information was specific, and you retained most of the identifying data.

You were given the precise title of the dream content; that is, you knew the particular story was called *The Big Freeze*. It is true that you forgot that the title itself was a part of the dream, yet you did remember enough so that you were sure of the particular story. You knew it was the first, rather than the second.

There was also a rather humorous translation here. When you awakened you felt chilly; although you could not remember having been given the title, *The Big Freeze*, this information was translated into bodily sensation. You were consciously concerned over financial matters. You were wondering when any additional funds would be received, and this gave impetus to your abilities. You asked a question and received an answer.

The sensation of cold was a clue to the title of the story, but one you would not have recognized on a conscious level. There is no reason for you to worry about financial matters. You are hardly in any difficulties here, nor will there be any.

(*Oddly enough, I remember waking up chilly in the morning last week, but do not know whether this followed the dream. I made no conscious connection with the dream in any case, and it seems to me I might have woken up chilly on more than one night last week also.*)

Ruburt did well in regenerating his energies these past few days. The outlet was excellent for him, and in this case incidentally the energy was far from lost, though it was used. You were both wise in your decision to make some purchases for your apartment. The objects were bought in high spirits, with money well earned, and they will retain to some rather strong degree the psychic exuberance which has become part of them, and will therefore add to the overall constructive climate of your dwelling.

I am speaking again of quite practical connections here, for as energy forms matter, matter and energy are inseparable and objects obtain their character from their owners, and from the circumstances surrounding them.

(*We think this passage helps explain some of the results Jane has been obtaining in her envelope tests.*)

I wanted to make a note here, that the tape recorder should work very well as Ruburt plans to use it in connection with collecting dream data.

I have used a portion of this session to deal with rather personal matters, and of course we discussed particular dreams at sessions immediately previous. This is fine, but we will shortly return to our material.

I will now suggest a brief break before we deal with our friends. And incidentally, Ruburt's experience in psychological time was quite legitimate.

(*Break at 9:19. Jane was dissociated as usual for a first delivery. Her eyes had remained closed, and her voice quiet; her pace had picked up considerably as she spoke along.*

(*Jane knew which psy-time experience Seth referred to. I'd made the quick diagram following her directions. From her psy-time notebook:*)

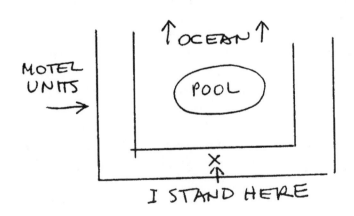

(*Friday, October 22, 11 AM-12 Noon. I was doing so well when the alarm rang at 11:30 that I set it for another half hour beyond my usual time.*

(*None of what I saw was very clear. I felt I stood on a long narrow porch or verandah with a railing. On either a double-story motel, or a motel of one story that was raised up higher than usual. I looked over and down at a pool, and felt that beyond this either the ocean or a large body of water was visible. Doors opened off the long narrow porch which extended full length, and I wondered whether Bill and Peggy Gallagher were staying here. I thought their room might have the door near the center of the porch. I had an impression of Peg sitting by the pool, with Bill in it.*

(I kept telling them I was standing nearby, just in case they could see anything of me. I still knew I was lying on the bed however, while I tried to project myself to their location.

(After I reset the alarm I tried to wander to the other side of the motel to find a name sign. Instead I watched a man from above and behind; dressed in suit, hat, carrying a bag or briefcase. He crossed a blacktop expanse of some kind by a large bulky building. Bill?

(As to sensations: First I achieved a partial projection of some kind, and thought I might complete it but didn't. Strong thrilling sensations, feelings of being swept away. Odd movements of some sort. I could feel the blanket over me and my pillow at neck move in odd fashion as if my physical body was making unaccustomed movements, but thought I was motionless. Very strong momentary feelings of being swept away, though these are poor words to describe this. Extreme lightness, weightlessness.

(Once thought I saw mountains, as though floating. Then feeling of change of direction, more straight upward, yet still retained bedself. Once I was aware that I was looking up at treetops against a gray sky. When alarm rang second time some lightness remained. I did exercises, lightness vanished as soon as I turned thoughts to daily matters. End of account.

(It was now time for Jane to attempt to tune in on Bill and Peggy Gallagher for the last time while they were on vacation. We were not sure but thought they might be on the way home from Puerto Rico by now. Jane began speaking with her eyes closed. Her pace once again became quite slow, with many pauses; although she would give a paragraph of material rather quickly at times between pauses. Resume while sitting down at 9:29.)

Ruburt did indeed pick up some material for his own writing today, and the complete break from his normal activities was very beneficial.

Now, give us a moment.

An airplane. Directly behind our friends *(pause)*, there is a female in blue. Directly across from our friends, there is a couple of middle-aged.... *(Pause, at 9:30; Jane shook her head in vexation.)* We will try to clear this up. The couple come from Daytona or Dayton. The man has a connection with the paper business, but not a newspaper. The production of paper itself.

(Both Jane and I have been to Daytona Beach, Florida, but neither of us has ever been to Dayton, Ohio.)

Arrive New York eleven, perhaps 11:05. *(Jane shook her head.)* There is something, a gate or a runway with the number 3, 5; 35, possibly the number on their luggage ticket. But one of these is a 35. *(Pause.)* The woman directly behind our friends' seat may have a child with her. If so a female child, but there is no man in that seat. *(Long pause.)*

They walk through a large building, most likely a terminal, for there are counters of a sort to the right. Our friend's ulcer may show a slight twinge here, as he passes through the terminal. There is a short discussion concerning where to go next. *(Pause at 9:40.)*

Some place during their journeys they met a white-haired gentleman. I believe the name begins and ends with an A. His age about 62, perhaps older. *(Long pause.)*

The interest was of a business rather than a social one, in connection with this man.

At this time, that is now *(9:44),* our cat lover is reading. Our Jesuit is studying people, and they are flying.

A dress or coat of many buttons. A small boy several seats ahead. *(Long pause, at least one minute.)* I suggest your break.

(Break at 9:48. Jane was dissociated as usual. Her eyes had remained closed, her voice quiet. Many of her pauses toward the end of the delivery had been long.

(Jane said she had a very vague impression of what she took to be the interior of an airplane while she was speaking. She could not describe it in so many words, and had no idea if she was correct to begin with, since she has never been inside an airplane. She appeared to have no memory of pictures of airplane interiors.

(I was busy writing down the above paragraph when I realized Jane had fallen silent. To my surprise I saw that she was leaning back in her chair with her eyes closed once more. She resumed in a very quiet voice at 9:51.)

Also a cab ride. Our cat lover laughs. A three-dollar fare, which seems large. An old, rather than a younger cab driver *(pause)* with a stubby neck.

A direction that is mainly to the right, after one turn. *(Pause.)* A room on the fifth floor or higher, but not lower. They eat a meal here also. I pick up some connection with the word M—

("M?")

<u>Elm</u>, and this building. You had better break.

(Break at 9:57. Jane was dissociated as usual. She said she "knew Seth was going to do that," that he had some more to say.

(Jane said her attitude has changed quite a bit by now, in that she lets "anything through now, at least to a degree." Otherwise we wouldn't be learning anything about distortions, she said. Jane added that when Seth mentioned the right turn, or direction, she had a very definite inner sensation of turning to the right, after traveling in a straight line.

(Once again Jane's pace was slow when she began speaking again. She sat with her eyes closed, her hands to her face. Her voice was quiet. Resume at 10:06, with

the 11th Dr. Instream test.)

Give us a moment.

A cloth, like a handkerchief, laid upon the table, and a candle. Red I believe. *(Pause.)*

He concentrates, and he is thinking of a number, perhaps a zero. He sits at a straight-backed chair. I have the impression of a tall piece of furniture near him. *(Pause.)* Extremely tall, as an upright, rectangular shape, and it is dark. I believe it is behind him.

The room does not seem to be well lighted, for this piece of furniture is in shadow. The table is a round one, with other straight-backed chairs nearby. Some also in shadow. *(Pause.)*

The backs of the chairs are of an open type that is not completely solid or filled in. Perhaps glass doors *(long pause; at least one minute),* but an expanse of glass.

An identification by number. He wears something checked, small checks, but of a darkish rather than light, or bright, overall color. He makes a fist. *(Pause.)* Now I think of two candles, and the piece of cloth is white, the cloth on the table.

An M, S. *(Pause.)* A disagreement today between Dr. Instream and a man with a mustache, over money and a policy, having to do with how funds should be used. Some connection with a fortification *(pause)* or government training program of military nature.

A dispersal. Two coins on the table. 1930. One of the coins is dated 1930. I suggest your break. Do you have a test for me?

("No.")

I thought I would be polite and ask.

("We're taking it easy on you tonight."

(Break at 10:24. Jane reported that she had been very well dissociated during the delivery. She sat quite still while giving the material in a quiet voice, with her hands to her face the whole time, and used many pauses.

(Jane resumed in the same quiet manner, but at a little faster pace, at 10:32.)

We will now bring our session to its close.

Ruburt will have some additional short-story sales in the near future, partly as a result of this story. At least one before the publication of the other story that has already been sold.

There will be word concerning the sister of Ruburt's mother. Not of a fortunate nature.

My heartiest regards to you all. You embark upon a most productive season, that will be important for you both. I anticipate it for you with affectionate regard.

Approximately four days from now, I believe your Dr. Instream will receive an important letter, for which he has been waiting, and that he will receive confirmation concerning his own hypnosis experiments.

Possibly in New York your <u>other</u> friends eat turkey. It is better to eat turkey than crow.

("Good night, Seth."

(End at 10:41. Jane was dissociated as usual. Her eyes remained closed, her voice quiet. She remembered most of what she had said.

(In the 104th session, Seth said that Jane would sell some of the short stories from the group she was working on at the time of the session. The two sales, including the one just published, are from this group; in addition Jane missed out on other sales from the group because various publishers wrote her that although they liked her material, they already had similar ideas in inventory. Jane has now begun work on another group of short stories. Enough time lapses between her short-story work so that it is easy to keep the groups separate. See Volume 3.

(Jane's aunt, mentioned by Seth, lives in New York City. Jane has not seen her for some years, but keeps in touch via the aunt's sister, Jane's mother.)

(Xerox copies of the name cards used in the 16th envelope test, in the 202nd session for October 27, 1965.)

SESSION 202
OCTOBER 27, 1965 9 PM WEDNESDAY AS SCHEDULED

(Jane talked with Peggy Gallagher briefly on the telephone this morning and learned that the Gallaghers returned to Elmira yesterday, Tuesday, from vacation in Puerto Rico. Jane learned little about their trip other than that the Gallaghers took many notes to use in checking against Seth's notes; and that Bill found himself involved in a "strange experience" with a piano player and what he thought was telepathy. The four of us get together this weekend to hash over all the notes.

(For the envelope test I used a pair of name cards made by our friend Bill Macdonnel for his art studio, the Cameron Gallery. Bill gave us these cards perhaps a year or so ago, shortly after he opened his gallery. Each card is handmade and thus somewhat unique. More than anything else, I was interested in seeing if Jane could distinguish that the test involved two objects. I placed the cards between two pieces of Bristol board, then sealed them in the usual double envelopes.

(Jane has been working hard these days, and before the session tonight she remarked that her eyes were tired. The session was held in our quiet back room. Jane spoke while sitting down. Her eyes were closed, her voice somewhat deeper than usual, although not loud; and her pace was rather slow in the beginning.)

Good evening.

("Good evening, Seth.")

I would like to discuss the inner senses in connection with some of the other material that you have been given more recently.

First however I have a suggestion for Ruburt along the following lines. He is now at the point where he can greatly improve the condition of his eyes, and his vision, through consistent self-suggestion. The following phrase should be beneficial: I am relaxed and at ease, and confident. I can see easily and well.

Now. As you know, the inner senses belong to that part of human personality that is not physically materialized. At various times I have spoken concerning the reality of what you refer to as the astral body. You must remember that over a year ago we discussed tissue capsules. The astral body is of this nature. It is composed of electromagnetic components. It is simply the unseen self.

(Seth began discussing the inner senses in the 20th session; by the 50th session he had gone into some detail on nine of them, with more to come. By the 59th session he had also included eleven basic laws of the inner universe, plus three properties of physical material.

(The 7th inner sense is: Expansion or Contraction of the Tissue Capsule. In Volumes 1 and 2 see the 39th, 40th and 43rd sessions among many others.)

This does not mean that it cannot be seen on occasion, but it cannot be perceived through use of the unaided physical senses. It is that indeed which contains the memories and experiences, in codified units, of the present individual. It is that part which survives physical death. It is that part which in physical life is intertwined with the physical image.

The basic consciousness is never physical. Yet within your system it must collect experience within the physical system, hence the physical body. But <u>experience itself is not physical</u>, and cannot be contained within physical matter. Therefore this experience, collected within the physical field, is held in codified form by this inner self or astral identity. It is only by understanding the connection between the physical and nonphysical self, and the communication systems that operate here, that the true nature of human personality can be studied

While we are dealing now with your own species, it should be realized that all consciousness also possesses its own astral identity. The inner senses are part of this nonphysical self. They allow the personality to retain its relationship with nonphysical reality, permitting the material self to focus within its earthly environment.

The inner senses collect information of which the conscious self may not be aware. The astral identity of course <u>is</u> aware of communications from both the inner and outer environment. The astral identity is therefore actually a more complete representation of the whole personality, and its abilities are far-reaching. The inner ego of which we have spoken is the director of this astral identity. You should see now how this fits in with some of our older material.

(Seth began discussing the inner ego along with the inner senses, so material on it is woven through the sessions. A few recent sessions dealing with the inner ego are: 94, 151, 162, 173. See Volumes 3 and 4.)

When the physical self sleeps the astral image may indeed wander. It <u>always</u> returns to the physical body during physical life. Its telepathic and clairvoyant abilities are not hampered in any way by the ego when that self sleeps. In waking hours the communications system is more or less closed on the ego's side, but in sleep the barriers are lifted and knowledge from the inner self has a freer flow.

Obviously then so-called astral projection occurs frequently in the sleeping state. It also occurs however in the waking state, although the ego is not aware of such projection as a <u>rule</u>. When through training there is greater communication between the inner and outer selves, then it is possible for the ego to realize what has happened.

I have told you that dreams are a <u>continuing</u> process, whether or not the ego wakes or sleeps, and whether or not it has, or retains, any knowledge of the dreaming. So also the astral self journeys often, whether the ego wakes or sleeps.

I suggest a brief break, and we shall continue.

(Break at 9:27. Jane was dissociated as usual for a first delivery. Her eyes had remained closed. Her voice had been somewhat deeper than usual, her pace quite even after a slow start. Jane spoke almost as though she were reading aloud, with an occasional emphasis.

(Jane's pace was again slow, her eyes closed and her voice quiet, when she resumed at 9:36.)

The inner ego is then the "I" of the astral body.

The inner ego is then this inner identity. It is closely allied with the entity, and connects a reality that is purely psychic, the reality of the entity, with a reality that is mainly physical, the reality of the physical self.

The inner senses perceive the psychic reality and transmit messages from it. We speak of these as separate, again, only for convenience, for we have but various abilities and various aspects of a self. The divisions are arbitrary. This is very important.

Now. Regard the inner senses in connection with the nature of action and electromagnetic reality, for the perceptions of the inner senses are themselves action, and as such they change both the perceiver and the thing perceived. You can see then that even this astral image is always in motion and never static, and its condition alters the physical self even as the physical self acts upon the astral image.

Any dream is experienced differently by these various aspects of the self. There is not <u>one</u> objective dream that is merely perceived in various fashions. The various levels of the self create their own dreams, which do have meanings to all layers of the personality. But you cannot think of a dream as a concrete block that is for example chipped off in pieces that then apply to these imaginary levels. All of these aspects of the self are so intertwined that arbitrary distinctions must be made for you simply to explain them.

Incidentally, suggestion will reach many aspects of the self, and some which are very distant from the ego, for you are setting into motion psychic action, which is behind all realities. Suggestion will reach portions of the self of which the ego is entirely unfamiliar. Suggestion can indeed <u>change experience which has already passed</u>.

It can change the individual's present reaction to the past event, and alter the original implications and meanings that were once connected with such an event. Suggestion can <u>shape</u> future events because any action changes that which existed before it, and that which shall exist after it within your system.

This is different however from cause and effect for basically a specific action will not give a specific effect, <u>only</u>. Within your system, <u>you only perceive certain actions out of an endless variety of actions</u>. So you take these <u>few</u> as inevitable results of a given cause.

Suggestion then can shape the future. Expectation enters in here particularly of course. Suggestion can shape <u>dreams</u>, and the dreams themselves then operate as action. A strong dream can be a more significant psychic action than any physical experience, and it can change the course of the personality completely.

The inner senses will also react to suggestion. If you therefore suggest that you become more aware of their activities, then so you shall. You are giving suggestions, whether or not you realize it, constantly. You are forming your own physical image with all its strengths and weaknesses whether or not you are aware of it.

Suggestion, well used, with training and knowledge, will therefore allow you to alter the very cells of your body. The inner senses can be requested to operate in such a way that the ego will accept their communications. For the astral body is not some distant and alien other self, but it is even now that portion of yourself that you know but cannot see, that you feel but cannot touch.

I suggest a brief break.

(Break at 10:02. Jane was dissociated as usual. Her eyes had remained closed, her pace good, her voice about average.

(Once again her pace was quite slow when she resumed. She sat with her hands to her eyes and her voice was quiet. This is the 12th Dr. Instream clairvoyant test. Resume at 10:10.)

Give us a moment.

Something is turning, like a top, but as it turns it has many colors. It is more straight and slender than a top. *(Pause.)*

There are several people with Dr. Instream, about a table. *(Pause at 10:13.)* There is a crash, audible from the table, but it comes from another room.

His feet are tired. He thinks of an umbrella, and is now in a very small room or enclosure. He holds something up high that dangles, as from a chain or string. It dangles freely, like a pendulum, and he watches it. *(Pause.)*

There is a connection with something that is round as an apple; that is, round like an apple but smaller in size, and it turns perhaps on the end of a chain. It belongs in a box that is small and square. *(Pause at 10:19.)*

He has his glasses off. His left foot has been bothering him. He wears a green robe with a tassel on the belt ends. The tassel is yellow or gold, or there are bands of yellow or gold by the tassels. He may have a late caller this evening. *(Long pause.)*

I think of five nickels, perhaps in his pocket or on the bureau in a small stack.

    I suggest your break. *(Pause.)* Or do you have a test for me?

    ("Yes."

    (It was 10:24, and too late for an envelope test in my opinion. In the 197th session, Seth had suggested I give Jane these tests unannounced during the middle of the session. I had forgotten to do so, and when I realized this at last break had assumed it would be better to wait until next session.

    (Jane took the double envelope, her eyes still closed, and sat quietly holding it in both hands. Her pauses were rather brief. This is the 16th envelope test.)

    Give us a moment and we shall see what we can do.

    These are impressions. The shape of a star. A connection with a particular event, with some unpleasant connotations.

    The number two. I think of green, the color that is of grass on summer afternoons. A representation. Two people. Yourself a year ago.

    A connection with music, and somehow a more distant impression of a seesaw. That is, not here *(Jane held the envelope up, shaking it, her eyes still closed)* but connected with what is here; as a children's game. Brown and gray.

    Four, six *(pause)* a location with much space, and a steeple shape. An incident to remember, and a connection with F E B, as in February.

    I suggest your break.

    (Break at 10:31. Jane had been dissociated as usual. Her eyes had remained closed, her voice quiet. She said she had been surprised to hear herself ask for the test.

    (We discussed the test results and made some connections. We did not think Seth would clear up the doubtful points, at least not all of them, because of the lateness of the hour. This I regretted, though thinking the test was a good one. Jane was now tired.

    (The design on Bill Macdonnel's handmade name cards can be "The shape of a star" as far as conventional symbols go. At least it can to me, as an artist; Bill is also an artist. Jane and I drew a blank on "a particular event, with some unpleasant connotations" at the moment.

    (We could make many interpretations of "The number two." My personal idea is that "The number two" refers to the fact that two items comprise the test object. We did not know what to make of the color green impression. Any painting in Bill's gallery could be "A representation." "Two people" is also open to many interpretations. "Yourself a year ago" I regarded as valid, since I had paintings of my own on exhibit at Bill's gallery on the occasion for which he made these cards; and the event took place around a year ago, although I do not know the exact date offhand.

    ("A connection with music" can result from the fact that Bill played jazz on a phonograph at his gallery during the exhibition in which I participated last winter;

he plays music also at each exhibition he presents.

(The "impression of a seesaw... as a children's game," is quite interesting to us, and we believe a good example of the way associative memory can work while also being accurate. At the time of the exhibition I participated in at Bill's gallery last winter, he had not had the gallery open very long. Building was still going on; in the back room were <u>sawhorses</u> he had borrowed from a carpenter, plus many other tools, scraps of wood, etc. Note that the sawhorse shape and the support for a child's seesaw would be practically the same. Jane is very attached to playground accoutrements; she has especially fond memories of children's seesaws and swings. Indeed, playgrounds have an almost mystical significance for her and she uses them often in her paintings.

("Four, six" did not ring a bell with us. Bill's gallery, which takes up the entire ground floor of a downtown store location, is certainly "a location with much space." We are not sure of the "steeple shape," unless it may apply to some of the modern sculpture also on exhibit in the gallery last winter.

(We wondered whether "An incident to remember... as in February," might be connected with the first impressions given, "a particular event, with some unpleasant connotations."

(Jane resumed in a quiet voice, with her eyes closed, at 10:37.)

We will now end our session.

The unpleasant event had to do with several errors in introduction, made by Ruburt at that location during a reception.

My heartiest regards to you both.

("Good night, Seth."

(End at 10:37. Jane was dissociated as usual and her eyes remained closed.

(The unpleasant event referred to by Seth made several pieces of information given in the test data fall into place for us. The errors in introduction made by Jane at the gallery reception were humorous, but also so obvious that their significance could be hardly missed. One involved a cousin of mine whom we hardly see; the other involved the director of the other gallery in town, the Arnot, for whom Jane had worked until a couple of months before the reception at Bill's gallery, which we now believe did take place in February.

(Jane's relations with this man became so acerbic that she left his employ in the fall of 1964. At the time Seth said it was a wise move, and that from that point on Jane would do well with her writing. This has been the case. Seth also dealt rather extensively with the conflict between Jane and the director of the Arnot in the following sessions: 74, 75, 77, 79, 82, 84 and 85. All of Seth's material on the situation has worked out. At the time, we found the psychological information contained in these sessions very helpful. See Volume 2.

(Jane and I encountered her ex-employer at the reception at Bill's gallery last winter. Jane was acting as an unofficial hostess. In introducing this man to another couple, or trying to rather, Jane discovered in mid-sentence that she had forgotten his name.)

SESSION 203
OCTOBER 28, 1965 9:40 PM THURSDAY UNSCHEDULED

(Bill and Peggy Gallagher visited us this evening, and Seth came through later in the evening. Before this however we had the time to go over the three sessions in which Seth dealt with the Gallaghers while they were on vacation in Puerto Rico; these are sessions 199, 200, and 201.

(Seth/Jane scored many hits in the material dealing with Peg and Bill. Some of these are quite startling. There were misses of course, and statements that hinted at, or came close to, events and thoughts involving our friends. It developed that the notes Peg and Bill kept did not often coincide with Seth's material.

(As Seth stated in the 201st session, Jane's psychological time experience of October 22, involving the Gallaghers, did prove to be quite legitimate; along with some less striking psy-time events Jane experienced during the week Peg and Bill were in Puerto Rico.

(The session tonight did not dwell on the recent experiments however, although Seth did express himself as pleased because we were pleased. Jane has made copies of the clairvoyant material from the three sessions involving the Gallaghers; they are to write in their account of what actually transpired after each of Seth's predictions or statements. We will then assemble all of the data into coherent form and include it in an early future session. Jane's psy-time experiments will also be so treated so that we have a unified body of work covering this experiment. We are most grateful for the wholehearted cooperation of the Gallaghers.

(Some quotes from Seth will be given from tonight's unscheduled session, since I did make rather thorough notes. They are not all verbatim, however. Jane was in a fine mood, spoke rapidly as Seth for the most part, and I did not try to record each word. Her eyes were open at times, her voice good but not loud except for one or two brief occasions. She smoked while speaking, and for the most part sat or kneeled on the floor before our long coffee table; these are favorite positions of hers, not at all unusual when we have company.

(Seth came through as we were discussing the rather striking fact that while in Puerto Rico the Gallaghers met a woman physiotherapist from Duke University. I do not have her name at the moment. This woman knows Dr. Rhine well. It seems that her department and Dr. Rhine's are somehow linked at Duke, and that his incoming mail goes through her department. We will obtain more details. The lady told Peg and Bill a good deal about the workings of Dr. Rhine's department; and how, now that he is past 70, the mandatory college retirement age, arrangements have been made for him to continue his work in parapsychology through a foundation which is apparently connected to or with the college.

(Shortly after the session began Seth told us that we would receive another letter from Dr. Instream "within a few days." Seth also suggested Jane and I write to Dr. Rhine. The Duke physiotherapist had told Peggy that Dr. Rhine answers each letter he receives personally, "even those from crackpots.")

(Seth said it was coincidence that the Gallaghers and the woman from Duke were in Puerto Rico at the same time, but not coincidence when they met. There was telepathic exchange between the three of them. Dr. Instream knows Dr. Rhine.

(Quotes from Seth that follow, in caps as usual, are not verbatim for the most part, but close approximations. It will be remembered that Seth refers to Bill Gallagher as the Jesuit, and to Peg as the cat lover. Seth now speaks to them:)

You must know by now… You are pleased enough with our results so that you both are easier with me now… You are good for Ruburt in our sittings. You are permissive enough so that he doesn't become wary.

Through the woman at Duke our Jesuit picked up inner information which he has given to Ruburt… Ruburt doesn't know he has received it… The Jesuit doesn't know he has given it. The Jesuit… has already given Ruburt information about Dr. Rhine, telepathically; this happened at the time.

(Peggy and Bill met the woman from Duke in Puerto Rico.)

There is constant telepathic communication… This operates with you both and Ruburt, and of course with me. And Joseph knows things in a different way; not as direct as a rule, though he picks up other things…

Ruburt is not aware of the Jesuit's messages, but Seth is. The Jesuit sent the information he picked up from this woman telepathically, about the character and nature of Dr. Rhine and his foundation.

(Seth told Peg and Bill there is constant communication between them telepathically. He said the four of us would embark "on excellent circumstances" this winter but did not elaborate. Seth told Bill that he took his problems with him on vacation, especially the ulcer, and Bill heartily agreed. Seth then repeated some general suggestions concerning the ulcer, given in earlier sessions. Bill showed us his Japanese "tranquilizer," a small black wooden carving he had bought in Puerto Rico.

(Seth then launched into a long topic involving Peggy, her job at the newspaper, and another girl there. He stressed many times that the situations he foresaw were not drastic or alarming in any great degree, and that Peg could handle them. This discussion grew out of Seth's remarks concerning a very close call Bill had while skin diving in Puerto Rico. The remarks Seth made about this were to the effect that had we asked specifically about potential dangers the Gallaghers might encounter on their trip, he could have given warnings. As it was no such requests were made, thus no warnings given before Peg and Bill left.

(Seth now began in some detail on the situation at the local newspaper.)

The cat lover should look out for someone... This is not too serious... At your newspaper. A situation may have developed in your absence: You should be advised. This implies a nuisance rather than a momentous event...

Give us a moment.

I think now of a woman who is eager, who intends you no harm, but who could convince herself that she was not harming you one iota while she stabbed you in the back.

([Peg:] "Has she already started working there?")

This is a <u>minor</u> circumstance... Not one to be on the angry defensive about, but merely alert. Indeed this does seem to refer to the young woman Ruburt has met... There is not unfriendliness here, but ambition.

([Peg:] "Is it the new Chinese girl?")

Indeed.

We see your Kimball as new mayor, though I do not usually think in political terms.

(Here Seth referred to the Elmira mayoralty contest. Both Jane and I know Howard Kimball, the Republican candidate. His sister lives in a downstairs apartment. Peg now questioned Seth further about the Chinese girl at the newspaper.)

Her subconscious ideas were developing in your absence. She has no particular designs, consciously, as far as you are concerned... She has strong subconscious energies, and she has a goal, and you are in the way.

(Whereupon Peggy remarked that she was used to that kind of competition at the newspaper. She has been aware for some time that each new woman reporter seems to regard her, Peg, as competition.)

I will let our Ruburt rest, at least for a moment or so. Now and then I do indeed look down at him from my painting. I have at times been more presentable than that. Someday we shall show that face, and this face *(Jane pointed to herself)* for I am a stubborn gentleman, and in my own time we shall indeed give quite adequate proofs of what I am.

I am indeed one of many but not one of a kind. I am simply the only one of a kind that you know.

(Break at 10:20. Jane had been dissociated as usual. She had remained in her position on the floor, shifting about but never getting to her feet. Her voice had been average but lively, and her eyes had been open much of the time. She had been

smoking, her manner quite relaxed and happy.

(*The portrait referred to by Seth happened to hang on a wall facing Jane this evening. In the 168th session, Seth stated the painting represented him, but he did not say in which life. The idea "came" to me one day and I painted the portrait without a model. It is quite successful, and depicts an elderly, rotund, bald man standing by a window through which strong light streams. He gestures toward the viewer. As soon as I began work on it last spring, Jane insisted it was of Seth. I did not know who it represented consciously; merely that I had a very clear mental image of a face and figure to paint. The work progressed with considerable ease. See Volume 4.*

(During break, Bill Gallagher described his narrow escape from drowning while skin diving in Puerto Rico. Bill is an expert swimmer and diver, but got caught unawares between an incoming and an outgoing tide offshore, in choppy water, and nearly perished. Bill said the panic that seized him was as dangerous, if not more so, than the tides.

(Jane resumed with her eyes closed at the start, while sitting on the floor again, at 10:30.)

You know enough to use the trance state very well... The trance would have helped you concentrate and disintegrated the panic, within seconds... You knew enough, and you had the impetus. You would have had to say only: I am now in a light trance state, and I will deal with the problem at hand.

...You can also use this technique whenever you are overwhelmed by the pain of an ulcer, or a business problem. You know enough now to use it....

(Bill now asked Seth if an Indian village had ever been situated over the spot where he had done most of his skin diving in Puerto Rico. He had heard talk while there that this had been the case perhaps two hundred years ago, before that section of land had settled beneath the water. He thought the village there, if there had been any, would have belonged to the Carib Indians.

(Note that in the unscheduled 192nd session, Seth and Bill also had an interchange concerning underwater artifacts, Indians, Vikings and Jesuits in this section of the northeastern USA. If what Seth said in that session can ever be verified, some history books will have to be rewritten. Again, see Volume 4.

(Jane, as Seth, listened to Bill's question, then shook her head. Her eyes were closed.)

It was Inca, your village... Their main cities were in Peru. They traveled by sea then, but also over the land. Their journeys are responsible for many artifacts that cannot be explained... They reached Florida, but not inland in this country... The seacoasts. They set up small villages for outposts, for inland explorations...

They also set up two cities in particular, which were highly developed.

Their remains have not yet been discovered...

One of these is in another portion of South America. The place you refer to was just a village base to explore from... They expected other ships from Peru which did not come. They died, and their home city was never aware of their location.

I am having difficulties here with the location... of the second city... around a place called Cape Horn, I believe. But those were not local Indians in your location.

(Bill now commented on his interest in reading recently of the ancient Viking map which Yale University now possesses. The map has recently been authenticated, and purports to show the Vikings in the New World several centuries before Columbus.)

It is interesting... I am more interested in that you are like Joseph, always trying to lead me on... I am simple and quiet and peace-loving... And I will get to our cat lover yet... We shall dissipate this fear of our feline friends.

Your ego is fearful and set up in arms about cats.

(An amusing exchange now developed between Seth and Peg concerning cats. As if to help matters out, our cat got up from his perch on the TV set and jumped down. He walked over to Peg; I picked him up and deposited him in another room. In doing so I missed part of the exchange between Seth, Bill and Peggy, but I heard laughter. I returned to my chair in time to hear the following:)

... fear with a funny face.

(Seth remarked that our weather neither excited or concerned him, and that personality affects weather. He then threw out the God concept as a question for general discussion. He was greeted with a large silence momentarily. Seth asked for ideas from Bill and Peg; it will be remembered that in past sessions he said he would go into this question when they witnessed sessions.

After a moment Bill said he thought his beliefs regarding religion were more or less traditional.)

I don't like the sound of this... We shall here let Ruburt open his eyes... Let's have better ideas.

(I asked Bill to elaborate on his previous statement. Bill's answer included the idea that he believed a god would have to appear to the human race in humanoid form so that we could understand it.)

...The humanoid God idea? I appear to you as Ruburt, but I am not primarily Ruburt...

(Bill remarked that in terms of our existence our Christ was a supernatural being.)

Your Christ had abilities which I still do not have... and he did appear in your form, but he was not of your form... Your people saw but a small fragment that they could understand... a fragment that was part of a larger reality they could not understand...

We have discussed this to some degree in our sessions... I speak of psychic gestalts. You see but portions of these pyramids of intelligences... what we are able to see at any one time.

(See the following sessions for material on the God concept, psychic and pyramid gestalts, and related questions: 51, 81, 95, 97, 115, 135, 146-9, 151, 177, among others, in Volumes 2, 3, and 4.)

There will be a change in 100 years... when you will be able to see more... You will see through a growth of ability and consciousness... an enlargement... that has been growing for 500 years... the change began in the Middle Ages, existed briefly, died, then began again...

It will involve an expansion of consciousness, not physical knowledge... You will directly and simply perceive more... I cannot make Ruburt find all the words. Your God is part of a larger reality. We see what we can see... This larger reality is also a part of our dreams: it is more important and vital than breath, for <u>you</u> are all part of this individually. There is a give and take between you and the stars on a physical basis, just as there is also a connection between selves and what you call a god.

There is no real division between you and God and I... only a unity that you cannot as yet understand.

(Bill asked Seth what he thought of the direction in which the writings of Father Teilhard de Chardin led, and Seth enthusiastically agreed these writings are valid. Jane, her eyes open, looked at Peggy sitting quietly on the couch.)

Our cat lover is so silent.

([Peg:] "I don't understand enough about it.")

Your finger is a part of your physical organism... It does not know what your brain is doing. Prayer is very important... Your toenail is also a part of you... In the same way we are related to God.

You are part of God in that you are part of the consciousness that is, but you are not apart from a god who looks down on you and speaks... There is indeed as you conceive of it no hell or heaven. These ideas have been distorted through the ages... You could call hell a separation from the main stream of consciousness called God, but this is impossible actually...

(Peggy asked Seth what religion, in his opinion, came closest to God as defined by Seth.)

I do not want to puncture idealistic balloons. Buddhists are perhaps closer, but no religion comes close really... The man or woman feeling identity with each day that passes comes close.

(*In the following passages Seth hit his high point as far as feeling and emphasis are concerned. At times his delivery became passionate. I did not get it all down. Jane spoke from her position on the floor, with her eyes closed, her voice strong but not shouting.*)

Sentiment is practical. The idea of birth and death each day is close. Those who cry when they hurt a flea come close... Those who appreciate the consciousness in every rock, tree, bird... come close. Fools and idiots are often wiser than the wise man. Hatred is death. All things are sacred, and every thought is a reality and has its own potential for creation and destruction.

Experiencing every moment comes close. I myself am not known for humility. Nevertheless my existence is dependent upon many things of which I know not. I learn through many existences, but I do not set myself up as many of you set yourself up, and I do not determine what shall be destroyed or who or what shall remain... Such actions... are based on cowardice... Any idea of a God, no matter how distorted, will triumph, for He exists in everything that you know. And when you kill so much as an ant, so do you kill part of Him in most practical terms.

When you kill in thought, you kill indeed.

(*End at 11:06. Jane had been well dissociated. Her eyes had remained closed during the last part of this delivery; her voice had strengthened considerably and she had become quite impassioned. She said she "gets embarrassed when Seth talks like that."*)

SESSION 204
NOVEMBER 1, 1965 9 PM MONDAY AS SCHEDULED

(*No envelope test was held during the session.*

The session was witnessed by John Bradley. John is from Williamsport, PA; he is a salesman for Searle Drug and has witnessed quiet a few sessions. He has also been the subject of some of Seth's material. Jane, incidentally, felt strongly that John would witness the session, so she was not surprised when he visited us unannounced at 8:30 PM. John told us he could stay only until 10 PM. In the meantime he had a little story to tell us.

(John spent last week making the rounds of doctors' offices in Williamsport. One day while driving about town he felt strongly that he should return home. He felt that mail awaited him, that the letter was from his district manager, and that it concerned a raise for him. Ego-wise, John doubted the whole thing, especially so since

he had not been getting along too well with his superior recently.

(But he did drive home. As he walked out to his mailbox he felt certain the letter was there. It was; it did confirm that he had been given a raise by the company. The raise was totally unexpected, he told us. John wondered whether Seth would comment upon the experience.

(See also page 11 of the 200th session for notes on the clairvoyant/telepathic experiment, involving John, that Jane conducted successfully the last time he was in this territory. This concerned John's business trip to Binghamton, NY. Jane wrote down 13 impressions; and John later confirmed 10 of them.

(The session was held in our front room, and was free of interruptions or distractions. It was obvious that Jane was in a good mood before the session, and Seth reflected this. Jane began speaking while sitting down and with her eyes closed; her pace was quite fast, her voice definitely stronger and more active than usual. She began speaking actually at 8:58.)

I bid you all a fond good evening.

("Good evening, Seth.")

My particular welcome this evening to our friend Philip. As he knows his experience was indeed legitimate, and he can expect more of them.

(Philip is John's entity name.)

His familiarity with our sessions has made it possible for him to become more aware of the constant communication that exists between the inner and the outer selves.

I wish this evening that you had your recorder going, since I feel somewhat hampered by the slow pace that is necessary otherwise. All due regards, Joseph, for your limitations.

Now in the affair of the raise, you picked this up, Philip, first of all telepathically from the mind of your superior. You were also aware of it however clairvoyantly. In your mind's eye you literally saw the letter and read its contents, though you were not aware of the actual action as it occurred. The original decision however was made somewhat previous to the meeting which you attended, but it was at that time not yet definite. And your behavior at the meeting reinforced your superior's decision, and made it certain.

(This is the Binghamton meeting referred to here. John attended it on Tuesday, October 19, and it was while he was engaged in this endeavor that Jane tuned in on his activities. John clashed with his superior at the meeting, and because of his outspoken actions had no thought of getting a raise.)

It was not however your <u>general</u> behavior that made this difference, but a particular remark which was addressed I believe to the meeting at large; and which was a tip-off to your dissatisfaction, and which in some way was aimed particularly, he believed, at your immediate superior.

Perhaps we can get the specific remark, perhaps not, but if we do we will slip it in.

("Not too fast."

(Jane was in a good mood and speaking rapidly for Seth. I had been writing practically at top speed since the session began. At break John confirmed that he had made a remark of dissatisfaction to the meeting at large. It concerned expense-account allowances for gas and oil, and John's superior took this as aimed at him personally; the two men clashed on the floor, verbally.)

There will still be a connection however with another company, as I mentioned previously. And there is also an affair which will come up shortly, that will take your attention and time.

(Again, see the 199th session, in which Seth's information on drug companies in Minneapolis is confirmed by John. John now laughed at Seth/Jane's amusing reference to an affair.

([John:] "What kind of an affair, Seth?")

I indeed anticipated that you would ask.

I am not here referring in particular to any affair that might prove embarrassing. I am referring to an affair... Give us a moment... of a family nature that has not yet developed, but that will develop shortly.

I believe this has to do with parents rather than with your wife or children, and also that it involves a financial nature. We will see what else we can get through on this.

(Jane now took a pause that lasted a minute. She sat quite still, her eyes closed, her head down.)

Give us a moment, and we will play around a bit.

We have to work this way with our friend Ruburt, though he is indeed improving. In regards to your raise, the number 3 comes up. I am trying to loosen Ruburt up here, for he is always afraid of wrong results, and this hampers me.

We will however do what we can, and explanations can come later.

(Briefly, Seth now burst out in a loud, deep and humorous voice.)

This is a test. Testing, one, two three; if you will indeed forgive my attempts at humor. The number three in regard to the bonus. This is not very clear. 3 or 300. <u>30</u> or 300. I want to loosen <u>him</u>, Ruburt, up in regards to you, however, for I intend to indirectly look in on you, with your permission, during some of our sessions.

I assume from the earlier conversation that we have your permission.

([John:] "Yes you do.")

Permission, and a very airy attitude indeed. I am however enjoying myself. I will let you all take a break. No one is tired but Joseph, for I have kept him going at a steady rate indeed.

(*Break at 9:15. Jane reported that she had been dissociated as usual for a first break. Her eyes had remained closed. Her voice had been stronger than usual, the pace indeed fast.*

(*John Bradley told us that when Seth mentioned his becoming aware of more inner communications in the future, he felt a twinge of fear. John said one of his favorite expressions has been that he had never wanted to be able to read tomorrow's paper today. I answered that perhaps John was beginning to change his mind at least subconsciously.*

(*John now delighted Jane by telling her that the figure 30 is the correct one, exactly, concerning his raise—thirty dollars a month.*

(*John wasn't sure what financial venture involving parents could mean, although he described a complicated tax and property and business transaction that his father-in-law is involved in at the moment in Bradford, PA. The father-in-law has a great deal of money tied up in the venture and is trying to extricate himself.*

(*Before the session Jane and I asked John if he would cooperate in some telepathic/clairvoyant experiments like those involving the Gallaghers recently. John would make a good subject, we thought, because he lives some distance away and Seth could tune in practically whenever he pleased.*

(*Jane resumed in the same good voice, with her eyes closed and at a little slower pace, at 9:25. She spoke to John.*)

I believe you have another appointment.

We could have done fairly well this evening with you were you here, or were you able to remain for the full session. On another occasion we will see more fully what we can do.

The situation to which I referred was not the one regarding your father-in-law, though that will be resolved.

The conversation had to do with policy on the company's part. But not only generally on a high level, but policy as it filtered down through the hierarchy; and a particular policy, a way of treatment.

You see, in a full session dealing with an individual, I can interweave material. Ruburt cannot follow me then and he cannot block me then. He does not indeed block me on purpose, but the results would be the same.

The situation however in the family does involve your own parents. I would say specifically your mother. The conversation of which you are thinking is the one to which I refer concerning the raise.

There will be others if you remain with the company, for much of your superior's income is dependent upon your own, and he has only at the most two other salesman in his territory which are lucrative for him. One is a short man, already beginning to bald. And your superior himself worries about his own position.

This is a general-enough statement, but at the last meeting he had cause to wonder about it even more.

(*Jane now took a long pause, sitting quietly with her eyes closed. Her pace was now, again, quite fast.*

(*To avoid too many notes at break, I can add some comments as the session progresses. At next break, John confirmed Seth's statement that his superior was worried about his job. John also agreed with Seth that only two other salesman are selling well in the division. The short man who is already beginning to bald, John knows as Bill Driscoll; John told us he is a very good salesman and the only one in the division fitting that description. Driscoll is not old, John said, merely balding prematurely.*

(*As stated before, the floor clash between John and his superior involved expense accounts. John agreed that this was high-level company policy that filtered down to the local level.*)

The family situation is not immediate, this week for example, but it is developing.

I told you that you would have other telepathic or clairvoyant experiences. I did not say however that you would be able to read tomorrow's headlines today, so you need have no such fears. Your ego is a sufficiently well-developed one so that you need not worry but that it will set up acceptable blockages, and shield you.

Does that make you feel better?

(*Seth delivered this material in a very amused manner. John laughed.*

([John:]) "It's my turn to catch it tonight."

(*Jane's voice boomed out briefly.*)

When your turn comes you will know it, and tonight is not the night.

When you intend to leave in the middle of a session, there is hardly time for me to light into you adequately, or to answer the questions that I think we could answer. I am not harsh with you. Indeed, I have been harsh with no one, though I have been tempted at times. And I am always hampered both by time and because of mechanical difficulties, and because we must be so still and silent.

([John:]) "I have a question. A month ago, when I was talking to a female, a voice definitely said to me: 'No, no.' What's the significance of that?")

The voice was a male voice, was it not?

([John:]) "I believe so."

And you did not recognize it.

([John:]) "No."

(Seth/Jane, smiling, eyes closed:)

Then I shall not tell you. I shall not indeed.

([John:]) "Was it your voice? It happened so suddenly I didn't have time to think. It was very unexpected."

You see you put me, as you very well know, in a strange position. For if I say it was my voice, then I was where I was not invited to be.

([John:]) "It was in a public place, and it was perfectly all right for you to be there."

Well, I try to be gentlemanly. While I do not try to tune in indiscriminately with those with whom I am acquainted, nevertheless my range is wide, and at times I pick up information, and I am projected to places. And so it was, and it was my voice.

But then, Ruburt has heard my voice and did not recognize it. For I do not speak like this under normal circumstances. I did not mean to intrude.

I suggest you take a break for the sake of Joseph's fingers. If you have time we shall explain this evening. If not we shall explain another time.

(Break at 9:43. Jane was dissociated as usual, she said. Her eyes had remained closed as far as I had noticed. Her voice had been good, her pace very fast toward the end of the delivery.

(John had to leave to make a telephone call regarding business. He had decided to see if he could postpone his business appointment until tomorrow. Before he left however, he described to Jane and me a plan that he had broached to his brothers and sisters, concerning the care of his invalid mother in Philadelphia. John said this could be the family situation that is developing, and that Seth referred to.

(I might mention here a situation that John, Jane and I, and Bill Gallagher have long been aware of. This is the fact that John, Jane and Bill all have mothers who were, or are, bedridden with arthritis. Bill's mother has died. Quite a while ago Seth remarked that this fact is one of the reasons John and Bill were drawn to the sessions; but he has not elaborated.

(John was still talking when Jane spoke up as Seth abruptly at 9:55. She was sitting down; she looked directly at John, her eyes wide open and very dark. Her voice was deep.)

My friend, you had better leave now. And if you can return by eleven, then do so.

([John:]) "Okay, Seth."

(John had his hat and coat on, and left at 9:56. Jane said Seth was extremely

well tuned in on John tonight; she hoped that he would be able to return this evening while things were going so well. Jane also said she felt that Seth had more information on John's mother, but that she had blocked it.

(John hadn't mentioned the episode about hearing the voice in the bar to us previously, and at break Jane and I asked him to say no more about it to us; we hoped to see if Seth could say more about the circumstances instead, should John make it back to the session.

(John did tell us the event happened about a month ago. This places it in time a couple of weeks before we saw John last time, during the Binghamton meeting affair. But then John hadn't witnessed a session, and the voice episode had slipped his mind, two weeks ago. John heard the voice in a dancing establishment called The Elms, in Elmira Heights, which is a small town adjacent to Elmira. Jane and I have been there once, many months ago.

(As far as we know, this is the first overt experience we have encountered where Seth has spoken to another party while separated, in our time and distance, from Jane. It raises many questions if it is a legitimate experience; if legitimate, it would seem to be a most significant development. We are well aware that it could be said Seth was merely taking credit for another person's psychic experience.

(If genuine, does this experience imply an expansion of Jane's abilities, along with Seth's, or does it merely mean that once others accept the possibility of psychic expansion, they too become receivers? This would imply the separate existence of Seth; he has claimed all along to be an "energy personality essence."

(This thought comes to me: Quite a few sessions ago Seth remarked that an event would occur which would bind John, Jane and I together. I searched briefly for the remark but did not locate it.

(It was now time for the 13th Dr. Instream clairvoyant test. Jane resumed speaking with her eyes closed and while sitting down. Her voice was good; her pace was much faster while giving this material than in any of the previous sessions. She used but a very few brief pauses. Resume at 10:01.)

Now please give us a moment. (Pause.)

Our friend Dr. Instream is thinking about a book. It is from his bookcase, or it has been on his bookcase.

I see a page number, 375 I believe, and a passage brings to mind <u>hooded</u> figures. Connotations of the Middle Ages, and of a female with a headdress that is <u>pointed</u>, and then a veil. I do not know, perhaps a connection here with the heroine of an opera, or medieval novel. And still speaking of the passage, a room of medieval surroundings such as a castle. These are impressions connected with the page. (Pause.)

Again a candle, but a tall one, and a floor with many designs, as of diamond shapes. I am sorry Joseph that the recorder is not going, as I feel restrained and could speak more quickly.

Perhaps this is a scene from the novel or an opera, for now there are two very tall candles, with golden holders and many shadows. *(Pause.)* And the entrance of a male character. Perhaps a deathbed scene, but I do not hear music, and it would seem that music would be connected with an opera. But the scene is macabre.

Is he perhaps at a play, or theater production? *(Pause.)*

The hypnosis experiments have not been productive these last few days for Dr. Instream, though they may have seemed so. Again a snag develops, which may or may not yet appear to him. There is something that holds him back, that he knows but does not realize that he knows.

(Jane had been speaking as rapidly as I could write. She still sat with her eyes closed, her hands raised to her face. Her voice was average in volume.)

Now, separately, I sense a framework, as of a house that is not yet fully constructed. It may have to do with a young relative of his *(pause)*, or close friend, or someone connected with him. The house is on a hill. The framework is there but it is open, with the walls not yet constructed completely. *(Pause.)*

They suggest matchsticks. I sense a turnabout for him. *(Pause.)* An intermission now, I sense. He speaks with many people. *(Pause at 10:11.)*

I think his Dr. Snygg has two daughters.

I suggest your break.

(Break at 10:12. Jane reported that she was very well dissociated—far-out, as she puts it. Her eyes had remained closed. She was aware that she had given much material on Dr. Instream, comparatively speaking, in a short time.

(As break arrived we heard John Bradley returning up the stairs. He had succeeded in postponing his business appointment until tomorrow. We asked him to say no more about his voice experience yet, to see what else Seth could pick up on it. Instead the conversation turned to the fact that last week Jane was offered a part-time job as a dancer in a local supper club. Both of us like to dance, and Jane is an expert dancer. Now during break we amused ourselves discussing some of the humorous aspects of such a potential situation.

(Jane resumed at a good pace, her voice average, her eyes closed, at 10:26.)

I do indeed find the conversation very interesting. As you know I make no attempt to regulate Ruburt's activities, and I should find it highly hilarious to find him in such a position, or positions. We will leave the matter there, with one addition: I do not approve personally. This does not mean however that I would go so far as to caution him against it.

I spoke as I did when I did, Philip, because of what the woman had in mind, which did not specifically enter your conversation.

She did not make her ideas plain in words.

I did not like the implications of her background. I am not speaking of a social background, as you should know. I am speaking of a psychic background and environment that were, and are, unhealthy and detrimental, and with which you should not become involved. I am speaking of a psychic environment only, and of a home situation on her part which has deeply colored her activities, and which regulates her relationships.

For she is grasping in a way that is gluttonous and disastrous for those with whom she comes in contact. There is a reaching out, but a reaching out which is not for the good. Again, I am not speaking in terms of any kind of morality as it is socially understood. I am speaking of emotional health, and of demands.

There is a child in the background here also, and many situations which mold the child.

My comments made you wonder, as they were meant to. There is also a man in the background here, involved with the woman, and a legal paper.

When I spoke you listened. You did not say something that you would have said otherwise.

(*Jane now took a pause that lasted at least one minute.*)

It would appear that all bars are long and narrow. There was a particular decoration however at the center of the bar. <u>Ruburt</u> now thinks of his Green Pastures, but this is <u>his</u> idea not mine. We will mention it in passing. It clears the air.

(*The Green Pastures is the name of another bar in town. Jane and I have been there a few times, but not recently. As stated earlier, Jane and I visited The Elms, the scene of John's adventure, once some months ago. We did not enter the bar however, but stayed in the dancing room of the establishment; thus we have no knowledge of the bar, what decorations it might have had, etc.*

(*At break John confirmed that there was a child in the woman's background, and a legal paper. He heard both mentioned in a general way during his conversation with the woman, and cannot recall more details at the moment. He had not told us this consciously. John said another man was with the woman when he talked to her, and that actually he spent as much time talking with her male companion as he did the woman. John was unable to say whether, in his opinion, the male companion is the man referred to by Seth. John had not told us before this that the woman had had a male companion.*

(*John said the conversation he was involved in was innocuous enough, at least on the surface, but that when he head the voice speak to him within he became more cautious. He has not seen the woman or been to The Elms since.)*

We will say no more concerning the family situation for several reasons, which you shall undoubtedly know in good time. The sister of which you spoke is indeed involved, but not in the precise manner in which you imagine.

You have been coming to sessions off and on now for some time, and I appreciate your interest, and we shall do what we can for you; and we have made headway on Ruburt's part.

I will suggest a short break and we shall continue. How can you want to know the future so badly, and be so afraid of knowing it at the same time?

([John:] "Curiosity, I guess, and then knowing I will be following a certain course—")

This is not the case, for your own expectations are the actions which mold what you call the future, and it is never static and never definite; for you can change it at any moment, as any action changes any other action. You are always free to act, but every action changes that which is acted upon, and you constantly change your so-called future; and the events that I see may indeed be changed at any time.

("Not too fast."

(Once again Seth was racing along, as far as my writing speed was concerned. Jane's eyes had, I believe, opened briefly a few times; her face was turning more toward John much of the time here. She gave no notice that she heard me.)

We shall go into this, for it affects you deeply, and it worries you deeply.

I do however suggest your break.

(Break at 10:43. Jane was dissociated as usual. Her eyes had been closed for the most part, her voice had been good, her pace fast.

(John thought he agreed with Seth's statements on free will. He said he has been concerned for some years with the conflict between the idea of predestination and free will, theologically speaking, and believes his questions stem from his early school days.

(Reiterating, John told us the talk he engaged in with the woman and her male companion at The Elms, about a month ago, seemed innocent enough on the surface. The two warning words he heard so clearly within, "No, no," had no direct bearing on the conversation of the moment, he said; yet they were so definite, so emphatic and even urgent, that he paid heed to them. The adjectives are John's.

(John was now considering trying to locate the woman, to check up on Seth. He was joking, yet perhaps serious also. He was curious however, and was talking about whether he should really make the attempt when Jane resumed in a good voice, and with her eyes closed at 10:50.)

—like a child who is about to be burned.

([John, laughing:] "Correct, Seth.")

There was indeed an unhealthy effect that came from the woman's personality, and <u>you</u> my friend were in immediate danger.

In some way she saw you as a <u>solution</u> to problems, and could have latched upon you had your interest at that point shown itself in any fashion whatsoever.

There is a house, not in the western section of town, the third or fourth house in the middle of a block, in which she dwells. She would have used you quite unconsciously. But in many ways she is very strong, and you would have been driven to return. My words were a warning, and I do not warn without reason, and I do not cry wolf.

(*Jane paused.*)

I am unsure here. I believe she was a Catholic, and that to some extent this had something to do with her own difficulties.

(*John told us at break that he wasn't sure either, but that he thought the woman was a Catholic.*)

The situation of which I spoke concerning the family may occur in February, perhaps the beginning of the month, perhaps the second.

Now, when you speak of free will you automatically think in terms of your own time sequence, for you are caught within it. Those who are not within it can see past, present and future, and the interchange of action.

Let us suppose that you are watching a movie production.

You have nothing to do with making the movie, nothing to do with the plot or the characters, yet you can see the ending, and from the action you know what the developments will bring. You in no way affected the developments within the action; nor were they predestined, but worked out by the characters involved.

You are merely apart from them, and able to switch backward or forward as you wish. Now we are speaking of a planned movie, with a plot. Now however consider another analogy, where action envelopes and changes within a different dimension. I can look in on it and see its progress, but the action develops as it will, and is free.

<u>One dream</u> can change the development of a personality, and change his physical course. To those of us not within your system, we can turn into that dream, pick it up in other words. But the dream is not predestined, and the dream develops because of the personality involved.

(*Seth's remark above, "turn into that dream", involves the fourth inner sense: the Conceptual Sense. He discussed this to some extent in the 37th and 38th sessions. See Volume 1: "The fourth inner sense involves cognition of a concept in much more than your usual intellectual terms. It involves experiencing a concept completely, to the* extent of being a concept completely. You do not leave what you call yourself behind; you merely change what you are into a different pattern. Concepts have what we call electrical and chemical composition. The molecules and ions of the consciousness change into the concept, which is thereby directly experienced. You cannot truly understand or appreciate any other thing unless you can become that thing. You can best achieve some approximation of an idea by using psychological time...")

You have more free will than you imagine, for you have not only your present personality with which to work.

Do I go too swiftly, Joseph?

("A little bit.")

But you have on a subconscious level <u>all</u> the knowledge and experience of your previous selves upon which to build. Your dreams are free from the restrictions imposed by your ego, and your dreams affect your daily life much more than you know. For situations appear in them that affect your actions, and these are elements from your own previous selves. This is a large subject; but though I can tell you some things about your future, the future is not predestined, and subconsciously you are well aware yourself of what will happen, and all human beings are.

It is only the ego which seems to make such questions important, because of the restrictions of its nature.

I will here suggest a break again, out of deference to our Joseph's diligence; and if you have any questions, Philip, I will do my best to answer them. And if you resented my intrusion, I am indeed regretful.

([John:] "Absolutely not."

(*Break at 11:07. Jane was dissociated as usual. Her eyes had remained closed for the most part. Her voice had been good, her pace quite fast. Surprisingly enough, in spite of all my writing my hand felt little fatigue.*

(*John now told us that he knew the name of the woman in question, but did not give it to us; we requested that he wait on this.*

(*The Elms is actually in Elmira Heights, which is like a suburb of Elmira to the northeast. We were discussing Seth's location of the woman's house as he gave it on page 47, when Jane came through as Seth, briefly at 11:18.*)

The house is in the northeastern section, but to the west of the location in which you met the woman.

(*Break again at 11:19. The above information is correct, as John Bradley verified the day after this session. John occasionally has free time between his visits to doctor's offices, and on November 2 he used some of it to check up on Seth, and give us the information. Without seeing the woman in question again, he located her house. He did not tell us how he did this, or give us the name of the street on which* she lives. He drew a map of the location of the house in relation to The Elms, however; a copy of the map is included at the end of this session, and it can be seen that the house is in the northeastern section of Elmira Heights, as well as also being northeast of Elmira, and is west of the location of The Elms.

(*Jane resumed, with her eyes shut and in a good voice, at 11:22.*)

She would have used you as a buffer between herself and another male, and as a bargaining point. I was referring to her subconscious energies when I spoke of force. I was not referring to the personality which she exhibits. She would have exaggerated the slightest interest you showed in her, and an unpleasant situation would have resulted; an unfortunate one involving yourself and the other male to whom I referred. Therefore I spoke out.

Again, you see, you did not have to hear me, and you did not have to listen. But because you heard me and because you listened, the <u>probable</u> future was changed.

It is possible, Joseph, that there could be this evening a change in Ruburt's features, and we shall let this go at that, for we know him too well to say more.

(*Both John and I had been watching Jane as usual as she spoke; neither of us observed any unusual feature changes in her throughout the session.*)

Now the man involved has something to do with mechanics. I am not sure of the age. Between, I should say, 27 and 37, though this is not precise, I know. I have the feeling she may be older.

(*John told us later that the male companion with the woman was a car salesman; hence Jane's possible associative connection with mechanics. Still, as said before, we do not know for sure whether the woman's male companion of that evening is the male referred to by Seth.*

(*John also told us later that he felt the woman herself was the one who was 27; certainly not over 30, in his opinion. Her male companion was older, John said, but he did not know by how much.*

(*Note by John Bradley, June 8, 1966: "Companion at bar with woman was a car salesman and about 24-26 years old. He is not the man involved with the woman. This man is 38-39 years old."*)

Now, Philip. Indeed when I speak of the future I do see possibilities, and speak in terms of trends of activities that may change. This is why, often, our specific dates do not materialize as given, or why events foreseen do not occur as given. For at no time are any events predestined. There should be no such word in your vocabulary, for with every moment you change, and every heartbeat is an action, and <u>every action changes every other action</u>.

I am able to look from a different perspective, but still I see only possibilities. And on that particular evening I saw a possibility that was not attractive.

You and I changed that possibility, and what I <u>foresaw</u> therefore will not come to pass; and your own action in allowing yourself to hear me speak helped change that action.

We shall try to put the session on a more informal basis, and I will be glad to answer any questions that you have, within reason.

([John:] "Can you tell me about the other man in my division who's selling well, besides Bill Driscoll?")

An older man than the one I described.

([John:] "What does he look like?")

Give us a moment. Bigger than the man I described, with more hair, though he is older. I believe he wears glasses.

([John:] "With more hair?")

With more hair, though he is older. One of the men I believe is precisely 37. The second man occasionally wears glasses. His hair is a shade of brown, though not a definite well-defined color.

([John:] "What specific sports is he interested in?")

Which man?

([John:] "The second one.")

I think of a game like hockey, though I do not precisely see how hockey could be involved. Perhaps it is golf, then, with an instrument of this sort. *(Jane, her eyes closed, gestured as though stroking or swinging, her arms stiff.)* If however there is a connection, perhaps in younger years, with skating, as on ice.

There may be a secondary interest in a game like tennis, but I do not see anything else in that line. I feel a connection with bowling, but believe this to be a mistaken conception, perhaps on Philip's part.

I will give you all a brief rest.

(Break at 11:39. Jane was dissociated as usual. Her eyes had been closed, her voice good, her pace fast. See the Bill Driscoll material on page 41.

(John identified the second man described by Seth as a Mr. Dudley, and said that like Bill Driscoll, Dudley is a good salesman. Dudley has brown nondescript hair, is older than Driscoll but not bigger, and plays tennis and handball. Dudley used to play golf, John said, hence Seth's gesturing as though acting out a sport which required some kind of hitting or swinging instrument.

(John thinks Mr. Dudley's sales are on the way up, also, but has seen no actual figures on which to base that estimate specifically. Dudley also sometimes wears glasses. Jane felt Seth had wanted to give this information earlier but that she blocked it.

(Neither John or I observed any feature change in Jane.

(Since the hour was late, John told us the name of the woman discussed by Seth: Judy Fuller. Later we found a June Fuller in the phone book, but this Fuller

does not live on the correct street, either. Either Judy Fuller does not have a telephone or it is under another name.

(Note by John Bradley, June 8, 1966: "Girl's name is Judy Fuller. Judy Fuller is listed in phone book under her old address."

(Jane resumed at an average pace, with her eyes open part of the time, at 11:51.)

I will indeed, because of the expression upon your face, my dear Joseph, bring our session to a close.

We have done the best we could this evening. We could have done better, perhaps, without the interruption. Nevertheless we did well enough indeed.

There is more pertaining to our friend Philip, but for several reasons we shall let it lie for now. The reasons have to do with my judgment rather than any fear of distortion.

However our friend has developed his abilities in ways that he will not be able to close off, and that is after all not so terrible indeed. He shall not be reading tomorrow's newspaper today, but he shall be more receptive to communications from the inner self, and his own ego shall be better informed, though this will not necessarily make it any happier.

Now we think of an episode—I will avoid the word affair—a particular episode occurring a while back in connection with Philip's daughter, in her bedroom or by her bed. I believe late at night, perhaps when she was ill, but in connection with strong feeling on his part.

I hesitate to use the word oath or vow, but something along these lines. Perhaps a promise would be more fitting as a word to describe what I am thinking of.

Now as to the session, Joseph. I leave this to your discretion. We shall end it when you prefer. *(I nodded yes.)*

We then bid you all a most fond and affectionate good evening. We may indeed end up with another session before Monday, but if so we shall see to it that you do not write up all our notes. I do my best in my own way to look out for all of you, and yet I am also limited as to my actions within your system. You must often read between the lines when I speak. Subconsciously you pick up more than you realize, and subconsciously you make preparations for events of which you may be consciously unaware. I cannot spell all things out, and I would not do so if I could.

("Good night, Seth.")

(End at midnight. Jane was dissociated as usual. She said she thought Seth interrupted the material on John's daughter, which Seth intended as another display of telepathy, because he realized the hour was late and the material too long and involved.)

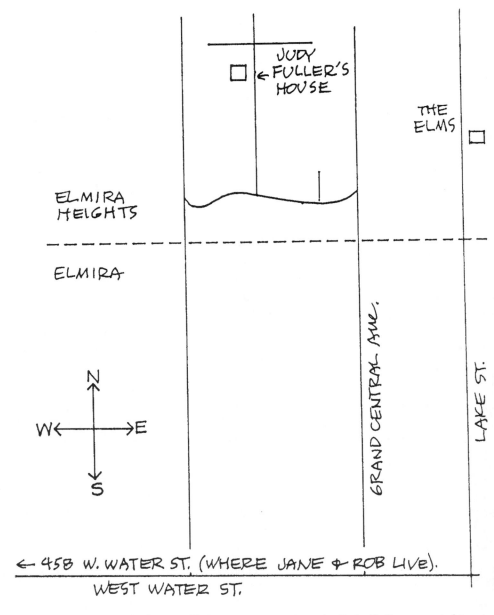

(Copy of John Bradley's map, concerning the Judy Fuller material.)

SESSION 205

(I was in my studio at the back of our apartment, putting the notes for this session away, when Seth came through again briefly as Jane and John talked in the front room. The exchange was finished by the time I walked back to them. It was to the effect that within three years Jane and I would have our own house.

(Seth came through with this, we believe, because he had expressed a wish that we had our recorder going this evening, and because he evidently wanted to sound out strong and loud and could not do so in an apartment house. Seth told John our house would have privacy.

(Jane and I do not usually use the recorder for sessions because it doubles the time involved in transcribing notes. We realize spontaneity is important, but our time is limited. We have considered holding just one longer session a week, in which the recorder could be used. Jane prefers two sessions a week personally, however, and many sessions ago Seth also said he preferred more than one session a week.)

SESSION 205
NOVEMBER 3, 1965 9 PM WEDNESDAY AS SCHEDULED

(No envelope test was held during the session.

(In the unscheduled 203rd session of October 28, Seth told us we would shortly get another letter from Dr. Instream "within a few days." On November 2, four days later, we received a short letter from Dr. Instream in which he asked that Jane and I "simply continue as we are going." This noon Jane told me she thought Seth might have something to say tonight about the attempts at communication with Dr. Instream.

(Also in the 203rd session, Seth said Howard Kimball would be elected mayor of Elmira. On November 2nd, Howard did win the election though of course there is a fifty-fifty chance that guessing could produce the same prediction.

(John Bradley witnessed the last session. In it Seth mentioned developments to come within John's family, involving his mother particularly. Jane also felt she blocked some of this data. The next day, yesterday, Jane had a most unusual experience for her. It involved a peculiar heavy sense of premonition of some kind, as of us personally, or our families, but might be related to John's family. We have not seen him since Monday, and probably will not for at least two weeks. The sense of premonition lasted for about three hours with Jane, then lifted. She has the experience written up elsewhere.

(The session was held in our back room and was a quiet one. Jane began speaking while sitting down and with her eyes closed. Her pace was quite slow at times, her voice quiet.)

Good evening.

("Good evening, Seth.")

Now. May I personally thank our Dr. Instream for his recent letter. I have a few comments that I would like to make here.

We have been progressing, actually at a good consistent rate, considering the fact that no tests of any kind have ever been attempted before we became acquainted with Dr. Instream.

In our tests with the Jesuit and the cat lover, we hit on several specific points. The one that comes to mind right now, though there were others, concerns the three-dollar cab fare, which they considered too high, and the right-hand turn, all of which were given here, and which proved out exactly.

Ruburt's own experience was also specific, in that his description of the place at which the Gallaghers stayed was highly accurate.

(See the 201st session.)

In our recent session with Philip, otherwise known as John Bradley, we also hit some specific points. The raise was one, the description of another salesman was another; and there were more in that session.

Now there is an emotional rapport, set up of course within some time, that exists between these persons. Ruburt is therefore able on his own to pick them up, so to speak, when conditions are good. This is a big help to me.

The intellect is highly important. It has little to do however with the framework within which our tests take place. The idea of a game will indeed work more to our advantage, for this is not an intellectual exercise. The intellect can be used most handily in tabulating our results, but it will not help us to get our results, unless it is utilized as a means toward discovering how best to harness the emotions for communication purposes.

(Jane now took a pause lasting at least one minute.)

If you dislike the term emotions in this context, the word vitality may be substituted. I personally appreciate your interest, Dr. Instream, and we shall indeed succeed. Again, do not concentrate on an intellectual level, if possible. When Ruburt tries too hard, he often blocks material by losing spontaneity; and when you try too hard, you interrupt any communication, or at least make it more difficult.

(Jane took another long pause.)

While we are still developing, the specifics that we have picked up in these tests with others show me that Ruburt is developing as I would like. There is still of course much more to be done before we can operate with a predictable accuracy.

Nevertheless what we need in our work with you is an emotional rather than intellectual attempt, and from your letter I believe that we see eye to eye here.

I will suggest a short break.

(Break at 9:21. Jane was dissociated as usual for a first break. She had been smoking when she began this evening, and put out her cigarette without any trouble as she continued to speak. She also sipped wine. I assume her eyes were at least slitted open for her to perform these tasks, but if so I could not tell. Her voice was stronger than usual, her pace quite slow by break time.

(Jane was again smoking when she resumed, and this time I could see that her eyes were narrowly open. Her pace was again slow, her voice fairly strong. Resume at 9:30.)

Now. Some of this rapport business will take care of itself through the natural course of events, in your letters back and forth for example. And if you yourself have a more flexible, easier, less intellectual attitude toward our tests, this will make our task easier.

This is difficult to put into words. Feel toward us rather than think at us, and let us see how we do. Self-suggestion may be most beneficial when possible, when used to put you in this more intuitive frame of mind. Turn your emotions towards us, and I think we'll be able to pick up your objects.

If the objects used are those to which you are emotionally attached, this will also be of some considerable help. I realize that this would seem to limit the choice of objects which have a meaning for you, and still allow for a variety that is wide.

At least a significant object of some sort. It need not belong to you, but it should have some meaning for you, to get the <u>best</u> results. Keep the object in mind, but do not concentrate upon it so intensely that you block out your own <u>emotional</u>, (underlined) vitality.

I am mentioning these points here, as they can help us. I <u>may</u> try varying a few conditions from this end. We shall see. Ruburt has himself gained some confidence as a result of our own tests, and also as a result of tests that he has tried on his own. One in particular that involved again Philip, or John Bradley.

(See page 11 of the 200th session.)

I have been endeavoring to build up his confidence at this end, and am glad to see that we are succeeding to some extent, since this is as necessary as anything else with which we have to deal. My heartiest good wishes to you, sir.

There is some material I would like to give concerning the examination of dreams, and some instructions that you should find of interest. There may be some slight inconvenience involved. However you can take your time about this, Joseph and Ruburt.

It is an experiment concerning the recorder, somewhat along the lines which Ruburt had planned, but with certain innovations. There is no need to try the experiment night after night in succession, however. Three nights out of a week for a certain number of weeks should be sufficient.

However, I suggest a break so that we pick up our friend on time.

(Break at 9:44. Jane was dissociated as usual. Her eyes were closed for the most part, her voice subsiding to average, her pace on the slow side. She resumed in the same manner at 10:00.)

Ruburt's confidence, or lack of it, was a stumbling block at our end.

While this is not completely overcome by any means, we are certainly on our way to overcoming it, and this will help matters. I do want to have on record my own comments concerning my warning to Philip, or John Bradley, and the implications that are involved. This and the dream material will be our next subjects of discussion.

Now however give us a moment.

(As usual, Jane now sat with her head down, her hands raised to her eyes. She took a pause lasting at least one minute. Her pace while delivering the material on Dr. Instream was the slowest yet, I believe. This is the 14th test.)

He is more relaxed. He looks at a watch, a round one. It seems to be the kind to which a chain was once attached. *(Pause.)*

He has a white shirt on. The collar seems to be open, and the sleeves rumpled somehow toward the cuffs in a noticeable fashion. Not completely rolled up for example, but perhaps partially.

He has just taken off a suit jacket, and he sits down by a dark desk. *(Long pause at 10:07.)* A wastepaper basket with wires, perhaps crisscrossing wires. The top of the basket coming out in some sort of an arrangement that resembles the top of a flowerpot.

The room is an office. *(Pause.)* I think of the word wisteria. *(Long pause.)*

He seems to be asking me a question. *(Pause at 10:12.)* Does it have to do with music? Again I pick up wire. *(Pause.)* An ornament that is heavy, dark green, almost greenish black.

His hypnosis experiments have a unique effect or success, that should be meaningful to him by the time he reads this material.

4 and 4 are 8. I do not know to what this refers. An oval mirror. <u>Oval</u> rather than absolutely round. Long and oval.

I think of a missionary. *(Pause.)*

I suggest your break.

(Break at 10:18. Jane was dissociated as usual. Her eyes had remained closed; her voice had been quieter, her pace quite slow. She said she must have been concentrating, because her neck felt stiff at break.

(During break Jane relaxed by laying on the bed. She resumed from this position, her head propped up on one hand, her voice quiet, her eyes closed. She was also smoking as she spoke. Resume at 10:26.)

We will now end our session.

I would continue it, for there is some material that I am anxious to give you, but our last session was a long one.

There will be another short-story sale shortly for our Ruburt.

My best regards to all of you. I feel quite frisky if you two do not.

("Good night, Seth.")

(End at 10:29. Jane was dissociated as usual. She said Seth could have cheerfully gone on, but she didn't encourage it.

(Seth also said Jane would have some short-story sales in the 201st session. This is a possibility of course since Jane has material out. See the notes on page 24.)

SESSION 206
NOVEMBER 8, 1965 9 PM MONDAY AS SCHEDULED

(An impromptu unscheduled session was held last Friday evening, November 5, for a group of young people. No notes were taken, nor were they intended according to Seth, but I want to note a few points.

(The group of four, exclusive of myself, makes the largest gathering Seth has yet addressed. Jane and I knew they were interested in psychology and ESP in general and had encouraged their reading on the subjects. They did not know about Seth but were somewhat familiar with our work in ESP, and of course would learn of Seth's existence when Jane's ESP book is published. Probably we would have preferred that our friends, two young men and two young ladies, do more background reading before meeting Seth; on the other hand, with the coming publication of Jane's book we have been somewhat curious as to the reaction of interested friends to Seth. Conditions were good last Friday evening so Seth spoke at some length in a general way.

(Although they were surprised at first our guests did not stay surprised long, and began to bombard Seth with questions. He answered the ones that would make sense to them offhand, and parried others or simply stated the answers would make no sense to them at the moment. Some of the questions were suprisingly acute, and involved aspects of the existence of Seth, and his abilities, that Jane and I had not thought of.

(One question concerned what Seth actually "sees" when he is confronting a witness, and he answers this briefly in tonight's session. I would like to note one physical effect that took place. There was a lighted candle on the coffee table before

the group, and as Seth was speaking the flame increased noticeably in height. I called the witnesses' attention to the effect. All windows were closed since it was a chilly evening, and the air was quite still. The enlarged flame lasted for several minutes, then gradually subsided. The flare-up of the candle flame was sudden, not gradual.

(The same effect took place during the 182nd session, which was witnessed by the Gallaghers. Seth stated then, as he did last Friday, that he was at times able to produce such effects when Jane, or Ruburt, was not alert and consequently on guard.

(No envelope test was held during the session this evening.

(The session was held in our back room and was quiet. Jane spoke while sitting down and with her eyes closed for the most part. Her voice was quiet, her pace fairly good, although with pauses.)

Good evening.

("Good evening, Seth.")

This will be a fairly short session, and I will go easily with you this evening because I have kept you so busy.

There are some matters that I said we would discuss, concerning experiments in recording dreams via your recorder, using suggestion to awaken you after a dream sequence. I also told you that we would discuss some implications arising from the fact that Philip was able to hear my voice, and we shall not overlook these matters.

(Philip is John Bradley's entity name. See the 204th session. Jane and I were certainly hoping Seth would go into John's experience, whereby John heard from Seth, more deeply.)

There is however something else that I would like to take up immediately. It had not entered my mind to explain it to you earlier. In most instances, or at least in many instances, I do not see the particular physical image of a witness to a session; but indeed as you described it, I see what you may call a composite image, an energy reality that is composed of past personalities, and in many cases also of future personalities that will be adopted by the inner self.

I can, it is true, focus exclusively upon the present individual. This merely involves a change of focus on my part, and a narrowing of focus and concentration. There is much more that can be said here, but we shall save it for another occasion. The matter was in your mind, and I am giving you a simple and direct answer.

Now. A word concerning the dream experiments. You may try these at your convenience. Obviously because of your schedule you cannot at this time embark upon any rigorous experimentations in this respect, for your sleep would sadly suffer.

Now we all know that various kinds of experimentation is being done, are being done, concerning the dream state. However, very little work, if any, is being carried on along the lines I am about to suggest.

Ruburt's dream notebook has come along very well. In most cases however he writes down only those dreams which he remembers upon awakening. Suggestion will allow him, or will allow you Joseph, to awaken yourself as soon as a dream is completed.

The dream will be fresh. If your recorder is suitably situated with the microphone easily at hand, then you can speak your dream with less effort than is required to write it down. Of course records should be kept. The simplest part of the experiment will involve the use of self-suggestion in dream recall.

The number of remembered dreams should be much higher than your present system allows. There are some interesting elements however that I want you to look out for. I will not tell you much about them however, since your own minds should be free, and you should come to your own conclusions.

I would suggest however that the first recalled dream for any given evening be compared with the first recalled dream from other evenings, that the second recalled dream from any one evening be compared with the second dream from other evenings, and so forth. This should prove highly interesting, and if such experiments are carried on <u>consistently</u> over a period of years, then the results could lead to excellent evidence for the various layers of the subconscious and the inner self, of which I have spoken for so long.

(Jane had been smoking. Her eyes now slightly open, she put her cigarette out.)

Particular notice should also be taken of characters and settings, and the approximate period of history in which the dream action occurs. If a dream seems to occur in no specific location and in no particular time, then these facts should also be noted.

Unknown characters within the dream action, persons unknown to you in everyday life, should be given careful attention also, and the <u>roles</u> which they play within the dream drama. The primary colors of a dream should be noted. It certainly goes without saying that all remembered dream events should be checked against reality, as you have been doing, so that any clairvoyant dreams are clearly checked and recorded.

Of course telepathy within dreams also occurs, as you know. I am sure you realize the difference between these, but basically such dreams are the same. The distinctions are you own. All attempt also should be made through correspondence to check such details.

I will now suggest your break.

(Break at 9:20. Jane was dissociated as usual for a first delivery. Her voice had been quiet, her pace fast enough. Her eyes had been open slightly for some of the time.

She resumed in the same manner, but with her eyes closed, at 9:38.)

You see, I am giving you good breaks this evening.

There are many ways that you can approach these dream experiments. You may if you prefer <u>begin</u> by suggesting that you will awaken after each of the first five dreams. If possible we want to get the continuity here.

You have many more than five dreams a night, however. I believe Ruburt's top number of recalled dreams for one night was thirteen. Now there is something else here that must be considered. The very self-suggestions that will enable you to recall your dreams may also change their nature, to some extent, for any action changes any other action.

(Seth dealt with this problem to some extent in the 194th session, when he spoke concerning the article on dreams in The New Yorker *magazine for September 18, 1965.)*

This is all right, and the effect will be minimized when the newness has worn off. Again, if preferable we want to record the dreams in the sequence in which they occur, so that the self-suggestion should always include "I will recall the first three dreams," or the first five dreams or whatever number you arbitrarily chose to begin.

You may try two different wordings for a start, and now I am speaking of the precise wording. The first: "I will wake up after <u>each</u> of my first five dreams, and record each one immediately."

Now the second alternative wording would be the same as the one I have just given you, but the "wake up" could be omitted. That is, it is possible you see, for you to record these dreams, speaking into the microphone <u>without</u> awakening, in your terms.

(Jane's eyes were now open again, wide this time and very dark. She was again smoking, and speaking rather quickly.)

This is definitely not only possible but certainly the most convenient. You should however try both methods, and discover which works the best for you. By all means, if at all possible, the recorder, Joseph, should be in your bedroom. It is the immediate dream recall we are after. We want you to record the dream at the instant of awakening, or at the instant that the dream is about to dissolve.

The time involved in going from one room to another could result in the loss of dream content and vividness. The very motor responses demanded on the part of the body, and the extra arousal tendency, would force you to lose a great deal of valid material. I would much rather that you work less, if necessary, using the recorder in the bedroom, than work more intensively leaving the recorder in another room.

For it is the dream we are after, the dream experience itself in all the vividness that we can capture, and if you are going to get a watered-down version in any case, then you might as well continue with your present method of dream recording, and not lose any sleep.

You will experience the vivid realization of your own dreams in this manner, and with some training you will record as much of the whole dream experience as any investigators manage to record when the training is done by a mechanical device, or another individual. And you will also be gaining, additionally, excellent discipline and training over your own states of consciousness, and this in itself you see will be an important yardstick of progress for you both.

(Jane's eyes were now closed.)

Now mankind uses but a portion of his capabilities, and when you are along in these experiments, properly set up, you will find that you handle them very well, with no draining of energies or difficulties. Your sleeping hours are already productive. We shall also use them to give you training in the utilization of various stages of consciousness, that will result in time with excellent control over various aspects and stages of your own awareness.

And added to this, the training will give you valuable information regarding the nature of dreams in general, the stages of the subconscious, and the inner life of the personality when it is dissociated from its physical environment to some considerable extent.

I now suggest your break.

First here a small note. Much later there will be other suggestions for you, in which you will direct your sleeping self to perform various activities in sleep, visit certain locations, bring back information and so forth. This is obviously still very much in the future, but it is well within the abilities of human personality, and within the realms of your own abilities.

(Break at 10:00. Jane was dissociated as usual. Her eyes had remained closed since last noted. Her voice had been quiet, her pace fast.

(It was now time for the 15th Dr. Instream clairvoyant test. As usual Jane spoke now with her eyes closed, except for one instant when she put out her cigarette. Her voice was quiet, her pace not too slow for the most part except for a few long pauses. Resume at 10:07.)

Give us a moment, and you may relax a moment longer while we try to pick up Dr. Instream... who sits at a desk or table that has a lamp on it. Not a table lamp type of thing, but a desk lamp variety, perhaps of brown metal. *(Pause.)*

I believe that the light is concentrated directly in front of him upon the desk or tabletop, and that he sits more or less like this, with the light falling in front of him.

(Here Jane, her eyes still closed, leaned forward in her rocker and took a position as though she were sitting at a desk with her elbows on it, her hands raised toward her head.)

There may be something white, a piece of paper perhaps, in front of him, upon which the light falls.

I think of a letter from another university, of three or four very brief paragraphs, not taking up the whole page.

(Jane now took a long pause.)

This may be the sheet of paper to which I referred. It may well be a letter that you have written him, and he concentrates on my name; and thinks *(pause)* of a picture in a frame, of his wife I believe, but not one just taken.

(Jane took a pause lasting about a minute, at 10:13.)

Now he switches off the light and tries without it. I believe he has on a white shirt, and loose collar, and he thinks, "Well now, Seth, well now. What about it, huh?" *(Pause.)*

The picture may also have flowers in it. She has a hat on; and you may take a break, or end the session as you prefer.

We'll take a short break then.

(Break at 10:19. Jane was dissociated as usual. Her pace had been very slow toward the end of the delivery.

(Once again Jane relaxed on the bed during break. Again she began to speak from the bed, propped up on one elbow, her eyes closed, at 10:21.)

The conditions simply happened to be excellent the evening that Philip heard me speak to him.

There is no particular reason why others could not hear me, but practically speaking the ego is usually on guard to prevent such communications. The ego regards anything but itself as an alien, even the portions of the individual's own subconscious. Since these are so often denied by the ego, it is no wonder that voices such as mine only infrequently break through.

If Philip did not already have a familiarity with me in these sessions, it would have been very difficult for me to have made my voice clear to him. It also happened that I was speaking in warning, and therefore his own subconscious was willing to let the contact take place.

Philip was not consciously thinking of me, and his ego was not on guard. His subconscious mind however did consent to the contact, because I impressed upon it the fact that I considered the situation potentially dangerous to him.

Now we can as you prefer, Joseph, go more deeply into this now, or at our next session.

("We'll make it next session then.")

I will indeed wish you all a good evening. My heartiest regards and good wishes.

("Good night, Seth, and thank you.")

(End as 10:29. Jane was dissociated as usual, her eyes closed, her voice quiet, her pace about average.

(Once again, Philip is John Bradley's entity name. In a general way, we believe contact between John and Seth took place between four and five weeks ago. We did not quiz John about this when he witnessed the 204th session, but will do so next time we see him.

(Jane feels the voice John heard within can have one of three explanations: It was Seth; it was a subconscious creation on John's part; it was a telepathic communication, on a subconscious level, from Jane to John.)

SESSION 207
NOVEMBER 10, 1965 9 PM WEDNESDAY AS SCHEDULED

(No envelope test was held during the session.

(It will be remembered that during the 199th, 200th and 201st sessions Seth conducted clairvoyant/telepathic tests with the Gallaghers while they were on vacation in Puerto Rico. Jane and I have now received from them their checklist, made against Seth's predictions and statements, and as soon as it is typed up the material will be inserted into a session.

(Before the session I mentioned that I hoped Seth would say more about John Bradley hearing Seth, as related in the 204th session. Seth gives us at least a little more information on this in the following sessions.

(Just before the session Jane read an article in Fate magazine for December 1965, entitled Radiesthesia; Science of Tomorrow. Seth comments on the article.

(The session was held in our back room and was a quiet one. Jane spoke while sitting down. Her eyes opened narrowly at times during the session. She was smoking as she began speaking, at a slow pace which grew faster as the delivery progressed.)

Good evening.

("Good evening, Seth.")

We will cover some of the points that you have in mind.

Let me first make a few comments concerning the article which Ruburt has just finished reading.

I told you many sessions ago that the most healthy conditions could be achieved for the human organism if the body when sleeping lay in a north-south position, and I repeat this remark now.

(Seth made this statement well over a year ago, saying I believe that the reasons had to do with earthly magnetic fields.)

The reasons do indeed have to do with electromagnetic realities which we have mentioned earlier. I have in mind some experiments that can be done in the future, but I do not suggest them now as you are busy enough. The suggestions have to do with the growing of plants under various conditions.

Now. It is not likely that I will be heard by anyone for some time in the way that Philip heard me speak. Again, the condition simply happened to be favorable. I have told you that all action is psychic action, but the terms used make little difference. All action does have an electromagnetic reality, which is usually not perceived by the physical senses.

The various levels of the self possess this sort of reality. They are actions which are aware of themselves as identities, whether or not such distinctions are made by the ego. They are sensitive to other realities which fall within their particular range, and they repel actions which do not.

For a psychic communication to take place the communication must fall within the particular range of electromagnetic reality that can be picked up by the receiver, and by that particular level of the <u>receiver's</u> self that is able to translate it into meaningful terms. If, that is, you want any kind of proof. Otherwise the communication is simply received and acted upon automatically without leaving a trace. It merely becomes part of a new action, giving no evidence of its source.

For all my humor concerning the particular communication to Philip, I wanted him to be conscious of <u>hearing</u> me. Actually this caused an interruption of action, in order to make the source of the communication stand out in his mind. Otherwise he would have merely automatically recorded my warning, and reacted to it smoothly without any realization on the part of the ego.

(See page 41 of the 204th session.)

The sort of things with which we are involved then often imply an interruption of action of this kind, and a translation or transformation of data from one range of electromagnetic energy to another. On those occasions when Ruburt has heard me more or less directly in his psychological time experiments, there has always been on his part a sound quite independent of himself, from outside of himself, of static. If you recall, on several occasions he was so certain of the static that he checked to see if he had left the radio on by mistake.

The voice seemed to finally be formed, or to rise above this static, and on one occasion the voice was extremely loud.

(This occasion was June 17, 1964, was a psy-time experience of Jane's, and also involved her receipt of information about John Bradley. See the notes in Volume 4,

on page 274, for a summary given during the 190th session. Jane says she has had this experience of static from which a voice emerged three times, all during psy-time.

(Note also that Jane had this experience during what she first thought was a dream on October 15, 1965. See the 199th session and the notes on her two dreams. Seth at the time told us the first "dream" was not a dream.)

This was the result of my attempt to give the voice an independence, to form sound within your physical system without working through Ruburt's vocal cords, but to impress your physical system kinetically.

In these instances the electromagnetic components were made to change range, so that they could be picked up by the physical ear. The static was the coming together of the components before the words were formed from them.

In Philip's case, in one way, my job was easier, since the words were not picked up from the outside. He heard them, but clearly, from within.

They could not have been received by the physical ears because the necessary transformation of components had not been made within that range. Now, Ruburt helped me, though consciously he was not aware of this, because of the peculiar circumstances.

In a trance state the electromagnetic aura that surrounds and is a part of the physical body, changes. The changes can be perceived through the use of several instruments, and by some individuals without instruments. A certain instability is set up electromagnetically that allows the individual to handle greater frequencies and ranges.

In a fully ego-oriented state of consciousness this is not so, for the ego constantly tries to maintain a rigid electromagnetic balance. This is obviously impossible, but in the attempt egotistical identity is helped in its efforts to maintain a more or less closed system of perceptions.

I suggest your break.

(*Break at 9:31. Jane had been dissociated as usual for a first delivery. Her eyes had been open at times. Her voice was average but her delivery had become quite fast.*

(*When Seth is speaking rapidly I find that I write rapidly in order to keep up, often without much awareness of what I am putting down as far as meaning goes. Because of this I occasionally miss out on asking what may seem like obvious questions. A case in point in the above delivery would be the passage where Seth states: "Now Ruburt helped me, though consciously he was not aware of this, because of the peculiar circumstances." I would have liked this explained at the time. As it is it must wait for the next session.*

(*I had planned a question to mention aloud at break, however, and this was simply whether it would have been possible for me to hear the static and the voice at the same time Jane has on her few occasions, had I been present and close to her.*

(Jane resumed speaking, with her eyes closed and in an average voice, at 9:43.)

It should be clearly understood that the physical system with its physical objects are, the objects are, composed from the electromagnetic realities behind them.

All of these realities are not physically materialized, and some are materialized physically to a stronger or weaker degree than, say, an object regularly accepted as physical.

A dream for example again does not have the solidity of a chair, but a dream does have reality in physical terms. The planets and the stars are materialized more fully than a chair, or similar physical objects. A thought has a particular electromagnetic identity which will fall within a certain range of intensities, and therefore indirectly as you know can be received by another individual who is simultaneously open to that particular range.

(See the sessions from 122-130, in Volume 3.)

Now, various men in this country and abroad are indeed experimenting quite scientifically with various instruments, and within ten years much of this will be accepted within scientific circles.

(Jane now paused and smiled, her eyes closed.)

Your question is a <u>nice</u> one. That is, not as simple as you supposed, nor as easy to answer indeed, but we shall have a try at it.

In the particular instances when Ruburt heard me, I simply do not know whether or not <u>you</u> would have heard me, and there are several reasons for this. I impressed or affected Ruburt's ear rather directly because this was the easiest procedure. In other words the actual sound effects, had <u>you</u> been listening, might have appeared as a loud whisper.

The volume in Ruburt's case was caused by proximity, among other things, and if I set up a small sound very close to him, so that it has an explosive and loud effect; but it was directed in such a manner that it was in a large measure closed off. That is, I affected the physical system but only a small portion of it, but then directed the effect purposefully in one direction.

Now if you had been <u>present</u>, I could have formed a larger effect which you could have heard clearly.

("Could you do this sometime during a session?")

We shall see, we may indeed.

(During the 68th session Seth stated that eventually, as Jane's abilities grow, it should be possible for him to speak to us from different locations in the room, independent of Jane's position, and that it might also develop that he could speak to us from his own apparition. During this session an apparition was seen by a witness.

The phenomenon lasted for upwards of an hour, and we have the drawings of it, made by the witness, Bill Macdonnel, on file. See Volume 1.)

There are some matters here involved difficult to explain. It is as if I sealed a portion of your physical system off, so that the voice did not travel outward from it. An invisible cabinetlike effect, if you prefer, within which energies were concentrated and directed.

A small note here: my candle effect was quite legitimate the other evening. This sort of thing will almost always occur without Ruburt's conscious knowledge for a long time to come. The reason is simply that conscious knowledge of such an effect would inhibit him, regardless of his best intentions, and the energy used would block the action or effect that I was trying to deliver.

(See the notes on the unscheduled session of November 5,1965, on pages 57-58.)

Such effects occur when <u>my own</u> energies are high, and when conditions are excellent. So many conditions are necessary that it does not happen often, though it is possible that the frequency may be quickened in the future.

I see no reason to specialize, however. I have used the candle twice merely to show Ruburt that I could affect independent objects, and to show you that I could.

I will suggest your break so that we may tune in on Dr. Instream on time.

(Break at 10:05. Jane was dissociated as usual. Her eyes were closed for the most part, her voice average, her pace quite fast. She gave the impression of being really involved in the material this evening, and I was on the point of asking for a break when it came.

(Once again Jane spoke quite slowly while giving the 16th Dr. Instream data. Her eyes remained closed for the most part, opening only as she put out a cigarette. Her voice was quiet. Resume at 10:10.)

Now give us a moment. *(Pause, one minute long.)*

I do not seem to find him at home, and I think of water, and of his walking near the water. *(Pause.)* In the back, behind his place of residence, and another person with him, I believe a male, though I am not certain of this. *(Pause.)*

I do believe it is a male however. *(Pause at 10:14.)* Perhaps with the initial "R", or "P". A conversation having to do with history, particularly eighteenth-century England.

The other man seems to have a connection with three women in particular. A conventional relationship, perhaps a wife and two daughters *(pause)* or a wife and two sisters. *(Pause.)* The name Erickson is mentioned, and a trip of his, I believe a projected trip.

A conversation, the conversation, turns to statistics. Dr. Instream thinks of us during this time however, and now they walk back toward the house. *(Pause.)* I pick up some connection with a box, a small box, that is in Dr. Instream's possession, and that he may be intending to give to someone as a gift, containing pearls or something of that description. *(Pause.)*

Could it be his wife's birthday perhaps? In any case it seems that he intends to give her the box. *(Long pause.)*

The other man may have papers in a briefcase, in which Dr. Instream is interested.

You may as you prefer take a break or end the session.

("How about giving us Dr. Instream's entity name before we end the session?")

I would prefer that we wait on this for several reasons. When it is given I want to give other material that is connected with it.

I do not mind speaking to your young friends under good conditions; perhaps the recorder can be utilized at such times, and Ruburt can be put to work typing up any additional notes. The <u>number</u> of sessions will never get out of hand, and we shall always be highly discriminating before we speak to anyone, under any conditions.

My heartiest good wishes. I could speak longer, however out of due consideration I shall not.

You will however find a considerable change in your health, though your health is not poor, if you change the direction of your bed as I have suggested.

Good night, my pigeons. I will fly away without flapping my wings, for I am a wise old bird.

("Good night, Seth.")

(End at 10:29. Jane was dissociated as usual. Her pace toward the end of the session was again fast.

(Jane now remembered that as Seth had spoken about her being able to hear the sound of his voice, the left side of her head and scalp, from the top of her head down to her neck, had tingled very strongly for several minutes. She had never had the sensation before, and found it difficult to put into words.

(Seth ended the session upon an amused and pleased note.)

SESSION 208
NOVEMBER 15, 1965 9 PM MONDAY AS SCHEDULED

(No envelope test was held during this session.

(The session was held in our back room. Jane spoke while sitting down, and

at a rapid rate for the most part. She smoked throughout the session, and her eyes were open most of the time; indeed they opened wide before she had spoken for more than a few minutes. Her voice was average.)

Good evening.

("Good evening, Seth.")

I am glad to see such a lively discussion immediately before a session, which shows you are on your toes.

I am aware of several matters that you would like me to discuss, and we shall cover them. There are however several points that I would like to make.

My remark in our last session, concerning the aid that Ruburt subconsciously gave me in connection with the voice effect, did <u>not</u> have to do with the inner voice heard by Philip. I believe this was perhaps an error in your paragraphing.

(See page 65. Philip is John Bradley's entity name.)

Ruburt helped me in <u>producing</u> that voice that he himself heard, simply because of certain electromagnetic alterations that occur within the trance state; and Ruburt was in a trance state upon the specific occasion of which I was speaking.

(See the 190th session in Volume 4 for notes on this. This psychological-time experience of Jane's also involved John Bradley.)

It was easier for me to make certain realignments and adjustments of a necessary nature. The other point that I wanted to make was that while your physical time, or clock time, has no overall basic reality, and is not a <u>primary</u> reality, that runs through various fields or systems, it is nevertheless an electromagnetic reality within your own system, for you have created it on mental terms.

(Jane, her eyes wide open, was now speaking quite rapidly and with much emphasis. She seemed very involved with the material, swept along with it in an enthusiastic, cooperative way.)

It is therefore some force to be reckoned with. If it were a primary reality, you would not escape from it even in the sleeping state. Those realities which are primary and basic you can never escape from. This should give you an idea, for those realities which run through all systems, and which are <u>primaries</u>, are those which exist for you in all conditions of consciousness and under any circumstances.

Those realities however which appear only in certain stages of consciousness, are secondaries. This is perhaps one of the most important bits of information I have given you; for if you are bright enough, and I think that you are, then you have a yardstick by which to measure the nature of primary reality, from which all other manifestations are spun.

I have been leading up to this point in my own way, for the dream experiments that we plan will enable you to accumulate in time a list of primaries. I want you however to come across this knowledge on your own, through these experiments, for you will learn more that way.

If ever in a dream experience you defy gravity, then gravity is not a primary reality, but only a manifestation within your own physical system. If clock time is escaped within the dream state, then clock time is not a primary. What you cannot escape within <u>any</u> range of consciousness, can be called a Primary Condition, and you may capitalize the term.

Incidentally, if it is not now known by your scientists, it will be shortly discovered that the physical organism does not age in sleep at the same rate at which it ages in the waking state. Aging, therefore, is not a primary. Again, this does not mean that secondary conditions such as aging and gravity and clock time, do not have effects within your system, obviously. It is only that these must be recognized as secondary conditions that <u>do not</u> therefore <u>basically</u> (underlined) affect the inner self, <u>which is to a large degree independent</u> of your system.

A recognition of the differences between primary and secondary conditions can however allow you to minimize the effect of the secondary conditions to some considerable degree.

Here now once more, let me repeat that thoughts are definite electromagnetic realities. Therefore, being actions, they affect all other actions, and if I repeat this in session after session, I do so, so that it will never be forgotten. Therefore these secondary conditions are <u>strengthened</u> through the very act, or <u>mis</u>act, of thinking that they are <u>primary</u> rather than secondary elements in action.

Two men for example, of <u>precisely</u> the same physical age, of precisely the same physical condition, will be in completely different states of mind, of competence, of effectiveness and of strength, as a direct result of their inner beliefs as to their relative freedom <u>within</u> the framework of the physical system in which they exist.

The man who <u>does not</u> realize his basic independence from the physical system <u>will not have the same freedom within it</u>.

(*Here Jane's voice deepened and became louder momentarily. Her delivery was fast and emphatic, as indicated partially by the underlined words. Her eyes were wide open and very dark.*)

He will be at all times a prisoner of clock time and of aging, for he will consider these the primary conditions under which he must operate. And the

<u>action</u>, or actions <u>involved</u> in this belief will therefore act upon the physical cells of his body with vengeful force, <u>because he has himself directed them to do so</u>.

You will find it a most rewarding experience, once these experiments have been begun, for you will yourselves discover the difference between primary and secondary conditions. Obviously the secondary conditions are to some extent necessary for your survival as a physical organism, but you are <u>more</u> than a physical organism now, and you shall be other than a physical organism in your future.

And the conditions that are <u>necessary</u>, the <u>primary</u> conditions that are necessary for your existence as other than a physical organism, already exist, therefore, and can be perceived and studied with the equipment which is a part of every individual.

Are your hands tired?

("No.")

(Actually my writing hand was tiring, but I thought Jane was in an exceptionally good mood, and that she might want to continue. Seth must have caught on though.)

We will shortly take a brief break.

I have had several matters to discuss with you; our sessions in general, the matter of spontaneity and discipline, your own fears, rather natural enough, concerning any subconscious effect I might have on Ruburt.

Both of you have been concerned with these questions, and they should be discussed. I would <u>not</u> like the matter of the sessions in general, and the subconscious influence question, to go by the board, and in one way or another we must find time for those matters.

I could have spoken at any time on the question of spontaneity and discipline. It may <u>appear</u> that Ruburt is too easy or too willing to hold sessions. However his ego is very well in control, so well in control that on occasion when I would have spoken on these very matters, I have not been allowed to do so. Of course I realize the time limitations, and others.

One small point: I have <u>never</u> manipulated his subconscious, in any manner. And <u>both</u> of you called me the evening of our last unscheduled session. We will devote some time to this whole matter.

Take your break.

(Break at 9:31. Jane said she was very well dissociated for a first delivery. She felt that Seth came through as a personality to a good degree. She said she could tell this by feeling her features in unaccustomed positions as Seth delivered the material. Jane's eyes were open for most of the session, her delivery very emphatic and fast, her voice about average.

(*The unscheduled session Seth referred to above is the one held on Friday, November 5, for our four young friends. See the notes about it on page 57. Consciously I had not wanted to have the session, since I thought our guests hadn't had enough time to study related material.*

(*Jane resumed in a little slower manner. Her eyes were open part of the time, her voice quieter. Resume at 9:41.*)

Now. If an experience is a part of the waking state, but not a part of the sleeping state, if it is part of the sleeping state but not a part of the waking state, then it is not a primary experience.

This, again, is not to say that it is not <u>real</u>, but that it is not a primary reality that is more or less constant for the inner self. If an experience is a part of all levels of consciousness—this includes the trance state—then it is a primary experience.

Identity of the inner self operates very well within primary conditions. It is dependent upon primary conditions. Its manipulation of primary conditions gives it the knowledge of itself. Identity is retained within the dream state, is it not?

(*"Yes."*)

Yet within the dream state the familiar physical props sometimes disappear. The inner I operates very well without them. In order to manipulate a <u>physical</u> reality however, the inner I needs a self that is acclimated to physical conditions; hence the ego.

As you know therefore we have differentiated between an outer ego, who manipulates within physical reality, and an inner ego who directs the activities of the inner self. Now then, the next step should indeed be clear. In the <u>main</u>, the ego deals with secondary realities, and in the <u>main</u>, the inner ego deals with primaries.

Nevertheless primaries also exist within the physical universe, and secondaries appear often as props within the dream world.

Again, none of these issues are clear-cut, and the distinctions, many of them, are for simplicity's sake. Many primaries will show secondary characteristics. For example, within your clock time there are definite primary characteristics of time as it exists in a primary condition.

Once more, even the word time is misleading, but within the boundaries of your clock reality every individual feels at times—but you see that the use of the word itself binds us—but every individual feels now and then the primary sense of existence that is not arbitrarily divided into moments and hours; and he therefore escapes from a secondary condition into the realization of a primary reality behind it.

A consistent, carefully recorded and extended examination of the dream state will, once more, permit you to compare those conditions and realities which show themselves in both the waking and dream states.

I believe that it is close to our appointment time. I will allow you a brief break.

(*Break at 9:59. Jane was dissociated as usual. Her eyes had remained open much of the time, although her delivery had been slower. She had still been quite emphatic in speaking. She said she had not been conscious of anything else while speaking; that is, Jane heard no other noises, etc.*

(*This is the 17th Dr. Instream test data.*

(*During break I turned on an electric heater that has a fan for circulating the air. It makes a gentle sound we are used to, and I inadvertently left it on when Jane began speaking again. As usual she now sat with her eyes closed and her hands to her face. Her voice was quiet, her pace slow. Resume at 10:06.*)

Now give us a moment.

Simply, Joseph, for our test turn off your machine, please.

(*I did so.*)

Thank you. (*Pause.*)

I pick up a strong connection with Dr. Instream and <u>two</u> other men this evening, with whom he has been particularly involved.

One is some years younger, and one approximately, in any case, of his own generation. One has dark hair, one has blondish or white hair. This second man wears glasses. (*Pause.*)

I will change this—forgive me. The dark-haired man wears glasses.

They have been together today, or are together now, the three of them in an office, I believe; though I am not certain, Dr. Instream's office.

It <u>seems</u> that although this is somehow connected with the university, that their particular conversation has to do with a matter that will be carried on without official university knowledge. (*Pause. Jane's pace was faster now.*)

I believe a woman is involved, though she is not at this meeting, but seems to have something to do with the matter under consideration. One man has recently been on a long trip. The light-haired man.

There is a secondary mention of money, though I do not believe it is directly connected with the main matter. (*Pause.*) I also believe that Dr. Instream had a <u>drink</u> of a liquor which he is not accustomed to drinking as a rule. (*Pause.*) That he would not ordinarily choose, for example.

I see the woman in a connection with yellow or gold.

She is in the background of this matter. I believe there are plans for a future meeting when snow will be on the ground. One of the men has a daughter who is sickly, ailing at present. Perhaps with an illness connected with the lungs. *(Pause at 10:16.)*

An indication here of the <u>possibility</u> of an automobile accident for one of the men within a six-month period. *(Pause.)* On a corner by a large brick building, red building. The accident possibility not applying to Dr. Instream.

It is not a fatal accident, for the man involved, in any case. And again, this is only a <u>possibility</u>, and many circumstances could change this. *(Pause.)*

The light-haired man is the one with which I feel the accident connection, and if it occurs it will be a direct result of his reaction to a letter.

Dr. Instream has been to a store this evening. *(Pause.)* There are some papers <u>due</u>. He is late with them, on a business matter.

I seem also to think of a <u>lease</u>, but do not know to what this refers.

Now, you may take a short break and we will continue, or end the session as you prefer.

("We'll end it then.")

Then I wish you all my heartiest regards and good wishes.

("Good night, Seth.")

(End at 10:21. Jane was dissociated as usual. Her eyes had remained closed during the delivery, her voice had been average, her pace also about average toward the end of the material.)

SESSION 209
NOVEMBER 17, 1965 9 PM WEDNESDAY AS SCHEDULED

(No envelope test was held during the session.

(The session was held in our back room. Jane spoke while sitting down and with her eyes closed for the most part during the first half of the session. Her pace was good for the most part, her voice average.)

Now then, good evening.

("Good evening, Seth.")

This business of primaries and secondaries will concern us for some time, and in more <u>ways</u> than you suppose. For we are outlining the stages of an investigation of the nature and conditions of consciousness.

Whether or not you realize it, you have already begun such an investigation, and Ruburt's careful notes and recordings of his dreams, over nearly a three-year period, and your own dream recordings, are only the beginning.

So far you have analyzed these dreams as best you could, but soon you will begin to look at them in a new way. The dream experiments with the recorder will be much more proficient. These investigations will also deal with a systematic examination into all levels of consciousness.

Autohypnosis <u>then</u> will be utilized in an effort to discover what experiences are common in various levels or trance states, and these shall be examined in a search for primary and secondary conditions. These experiments however are for the future. Some of the data I will give you as a guide, but much you shall do on your own. There is no way to probe the realities of consciousness except that a personality travels through all levels of consciousness open to him, and do so in such a way that he can retain and apply the information that he receives in these inner travels.

The potentialities of human personality cannot be examined as one would crack open a nut to see what is inside. The dream experience is a living, moving action. To some extent it can never be captured, but we shall capture enough of it for our purposes. And the suggestion which I have given you will, after some practice, allow you to awaken and speak the dream into your recorder almost automatically.

And now, if Ruburt worries that he does not carry his share of the work load, because you spend so much time typing our sessions, then the work of typing the dream experiences, both his and your own, shall be his. These dream records shall be kept continually throughout the years, and will yield valuable information. Information, incidentally, that can stand quite on its own regardless of my connection with it, and it shall be added to your life's work.

I now suggest a brief break.

(*Break at 9:14. Jane was dissociated as usual for a first break, and was somewhat surprised that Seth broke his delivery so soon. Her pace had been good, her eyes had remained closed.*

(*Her eyes began to open at times now as the session progressed. First they were narrowly open, then later opened quite wide. Her pace was a bit slower, and she was smoking as she resumed at 9:20.*)

Now. There are indeed common mental experiences that exist in all levels of consciousness, and these are what we shall be after.

Your records must be immaculately kept. The material will indeed serve for several books for Ruburt, and I suggest that serious thought be given to the bedroom setup so that the recorder is easily accessible. An extremely dim light may be used <u>if necessary</u>. As the experiments continue you should automatically be able to switch the recorder off and on in the dark.

I mentioned earlier that with training you can do this in your sleep. You have no idea as yet of the amount of data that can be obtained through these efforts. The dreams will be scrutinized for many elements. Some you are familiar with and some you are not.

The action performed within the dream; the location; the lack of specific location; the time in which the dream appears to occur; the apparent movements through time within any given dream; the emotional content; the surface psychological content; the work done within the dream; the familiar persons spoken to; the unfamiliar persons spoken to; the relation of the dream to past events and to events immediately preceding sleep; the dream events in relation to future events; messages that are given or sent in sleep.

Dreams will be categorized in various ways when enough of them are gathered. You will find I believe that particular kinds of dreams occur with definite seasonal variations. Particular interest should be given to the space that you perceive within a dream. Are you, for example, aware only of the specific location in which the activities happen, or are you aware of a further space extent?

You will learn to take a certain portion of purpose with you through suggestion, so that you can attempt to <u>enlarge</u> the dream space of which you are first aware. You can extend it in other words. The investigation will always be concerned with the search for primaries and secondaries. On many occasions an apparent primary reality will later be seen to be secondary, as a result of experiments with the trance state.

Your psychological-time experiments will serve you well in the future in relation with these endeavors. We shall of course set you about studying the conscious state also. We shall have you using your physical senses to a much higher degree than is normal with you now.

(*Jane's eyes had been wide open during much of the last two pages of material. As in the last session her delivery had been quite enthusiastic and definite. Much of the time she had been smiling.*)

The investigation will allow you to probe into the realities of conscious wakefulness, extending your sensual perceptions so that you can probe further outward into physical reality. This is indeed an ambitious project. We shall proceed as we always do, slowly but steadily; and you shall change along the way, for the very actions involved will change you. I might add for the better.

("*Good.*")

You will learn to deal with primaries, while giving secondary realities their due. Give unto Caesar the things that are Caesar's... I am sure you see what I mean.

("*Yes.*"

Again Seth was very amused.)

All of these projects are interconnected, and they will help both of you in your writing and painting, and greatly increase your capabilities in your own fields. Again, we shall proceed cautiously, precisely but steadily, and always you shall be in control. But when we are finished, and it will not be for a long time, you should be able to travel from any <u>state</u> of consciousness to another and back again, safely, with full awareness of your identity.

<u>For your identity is dependent upon primary reality</u>, which is a certain kind of action, and all of this will lead to heightened consciousness under all circumstances.

As a side benefit, ultimately, recall of past lives may be achieved, and a synthesization, by yourself, of your past personalities.

Hypnosis is not generally understood in its true light. The hypnotist is not necessary except as a director; and indeed in most cases such a director is necessary. But the hypnotic state is simply a level of awareness in which the personality is freewheeling, so to speak, dissociated from physical reality in its usual terms.

He is still dependent upon it symbolically, however, generally speaking. The inner ego however can be utilized in such a dissociated state as such a director of activities, <u>with</u> sufficient training. I must emphasize that indeed years of training are required. But then the experience is <u>ten</u> times more rewarding and informative.

You have what you may think of then as a split action, where one portion of the self, the inner ego, is allowed to travel through the other states of action that compose the whole self, purposefully as a director, and retain the knowledge thereby received.

You may now take another break, as I believe I have been speaking too swiftly for you.

("Fast enough, Seth.")

(Break at 9:47. Jane was dissociated as usual, she said. Her pace had indeed been fast, her voice average, her eyes wide open much of the time. She had smoked almost steadily.

(An overall impression I have is that Seth is very interested in the forthcoming dream-recording project, and that along with various tests this will occupy us for a long time. Jane and I have made a tentative recording setup in the bedroom, and probably will begin experimenting with it soon.

(Again Jane began speaking at a fast rate and with emphasis. Her eyes were open, after closing briefly at the start of the delivery. Resume at 9:58.)

I have only one small point to make here before we have our appointment with Dr. Instream.

This, if I may say so, is an excellent idea. It is this. Once a week to begin with, you will suggest before sleeping that you <u>send a particular message</u>, which you have written down, to another person whose name is also given on the piece of paper, that is of course dated.

This information to be sent by <u>you</u> in the dream state. It will not be restrained by the ego to any large degree. There will be some difficulties here however, since the information, if legitimately sent, will be picked up by the individual in his own dreams, and therefore may escape detection. For this reason an <u>order</u>, may be in order, if you will forgive my pun, such as "come and see me Thursday afternoon."

This idea is not fully developed however, and is in the future, but we should work out a definite plan along these lines. And for curiosity's sake, Ruburt may send you a message in such a manner, which he has of course earlier written out and concealed, and you may do the same, as a warming-up exercise.

Now, give us a moment please.

(It was 10:02. Jane's eyes closed, even though she was smoking. She sat with her head down and a hand to her face. Her voice was quiet. Her pace was fairly good in the beginning of the test but eventually slowed considerably. This is the 18th Dr. Instream test.)

A room with very high ceiling, small, that is almost taller than it is wide. A chair inside upon which our friend sits. A light bulb directly above, and a book in his hands or on his lap. With many pictures.

Copyright date 1903, or 1933, with handwriting inside the first page. *(Pause.)* A bookmark that reminds me of a fabric, of natural color, as of bamboo color. *(Pause.)*

He has told someone else of these particular experiments with us, and that person is particularly aware of <u>him</u> this evening. *(Pause.)*

The <u>other</u> person, a male, is an excellent receiver, by the way, and is partially in contact with Dr. Instream this evening. Whether or not he is consciously aware of this, I do not know.

This <u>other</u> man is at a party of sorts, a gathering. *(Pause at 10:07.)* Dr. Instream's own experiments in hypnosis are now going well, and he received a particular communication yesterday in regard to them. Either then, or the communication was sent yesterday.

(Jane's eyes now opened briefly.)

I get the number 3 4 1, but do not know to what it refers. Also some turbulence in domestic rather than professional affairs for today. Having to do with a relative, and a variation in usual schedules, daily schedules. *(Pause.)*

An annoying physical symptom also, I believe in the left hand. Merely irritating. A nervous reaction of functional nature.

(Jane took a long pause at 10:11, sitting quite still and with her eyes closed.)

He appears unusually tired this evening. He says "Now see here, Seth, let's have something definite," and puts his hand out, like this.

(*Here Jane held out and up her doubled up right hand. She took another long pause at 10:14.*)

I pick up also the number 5. Something to do with a document. He turns to the left now, and reaches up high, and takes down an object. (*Pause.*) Oval, with initials on it, or I am connecting the initials with it. It was given to him by the man with whom he was speaking the other evening, by the water, as we mentioned then.

The man has left now, on a trip I believe.

I suggest your break.

(*Break at 10:17. Jane was dissociated as usual. Her eyes had opened but once as noted, her pace had varied considerably. She resumed at a good speed, her eyes opening and closing, at 10:25.*)

I am giving you a brief session because of our last long one.

On some occasion however I do want to discuss this matter of our sessions, as to when they should and should not be held; and I repeat: in no way do I ever attempt to influence Ruburt's subconscious mind.

(*Jane's eyes opened wide as she looked at me.*)

Now, I do not see you, <u>as a rule</u>, as a series of separate compartments, but rather more in your entirety. It is therefore difficult for <u>me</u> to make distinctions as to your conscious intent and subconscious intent. And in many cases your subconscious intent comes through strongly.

The particular unscheduled session which bothered you both apparently was the one which was requested subconsciously by you both; and it benefited those for whom we gave it to a rather considerable degree.

(*This would be the unscheduled session held on the evening of Friday, November 5, for our four young friends. See my brief notes on this prefacing the 206th session.*)

There is conscious discipline which can be used by Ruburt, that can negate the subconscious <u>permission</u>, if you so determine, and this with practice will come very easily. As <u>entireties</u>—I use the phrase purposely—however, you respond to many influences that may or may not result in a session.

(*Jane and I tried an experiment involving one of the young couples that witnessed the unscheduled session of November 5. We saw them the next Friday evening also, November 12. We answered many of their questions during the evening. During the evening Jane felt that Seth could have easily come through, but in the interests of our experiment she did not allow him to. Seth accepted her decision, she told me at the time, gracefully and did not make any effort to go against her wishes.*)

In any case, there are simply certain circumstances that I have set up myself as a system of balances, so that the number of sessions will stay within reason, within your idea of reason. You are perfectly capable, and Ruburt is perfectly capable, ideally speaking, of holding five sessions a week without ill effects. I do realize that this is highly impractical, so you have no worries in this regard.

I do want to point out however that the only circumstance here, or mistake to make regularity a disadvantage, is the practical, physical inconvenience which would be from your end most annoying. And Ruburt would be the first one to rebel.

You may do as you prefer now. I will end the session or continue along these lines.

("We'll end it then.")

My heartiest regards to you both.

("Good night, Seth.")

(End at 10:34. Jane was dissociated as usual. Her eyes opened at times, her voice was average, her pace rather fast.)

SESSION 210
NOVEMBER 22, 1965 9 PM MONDAY AS SCHEDULED

(The 17th envelope test was held during this session. The test object, sealed in the usual double envelopes, was the insurance slip for the manuscript of Jane's ESP book, dated August 30, 1965. A drawing of it is not necessary since the test data did not coincide by a wide margin. The data, and Seth's explanation of the results, appear in their regular places in the session.

(At 8:30 PM this evening our landlady, Marian Spaziani, and a friend of hers visited us briefly. Marian and her friend, Helen Dyer, both know of the sessions but have not witnessed any. Helen's husband recently died after an operation for lung cancer; this evening Helen described to Jane a recent experience in which she felt her husband was speaking to her while she slept. Helen told us she has dreamed of her husband many times, but felt this particular experience was something other than a dream; she stressed its clarity, its reassurance and simplicity.

(It might be mentioned here that quite a few sessions ago Seth dealt with a similar vivid experience of Marian's, in which she received a message from the father of her husband; the father died perhaps a year ago. See the 100th and 101st sessions.

(The session was held in our back room. Jane spoke while sitting down, in a quiet voice for the most part. Once again she was smoking as the session began; this meant her eyes had to open at least narrowly to find the ashtray, but she was looking

down in the act and I could not actually tell whether or not they did open. Jane's pace was quite slow, with many pauses, in the beginning. I should note here that Marian and Helen left us at 8:55, and that Helen lives just a block from us.)

Good evening.

("Good evening, Seth."

(Jane now took a long pause, quite an unusual procedure after the opening salutation.)

I find myself following the two woman who have just left here. They are on their way, or rather, have just arrived at the home of the woman who lives in this town. They will have a long chat together.

I pick up an incipient malignancy in the woman whose husband recently died. I believe in the abdomen. I say incipient because the condition is momentarily at a point where it can develop cancerous globules; or the condition, a beginning tumor, can retreat and shrink, and entirely disappear, according to the inner climate of the woman's psyche.

(Jane delivered the above paragraph with many pauses.)

She is balanced on a thin line of normalcy at this time. I am speaking organically here. Despair and self-destructive tendencies can so alter the chemical composition that a malignant tumor could develop, again in the abdominal area.

It <u>may</u> not so develop, and subconsciously she is aware of this. I do not intend, particularly, that this information should be passed on at all. I am merely giving you the information because I picked it up during her visit.

The choice is hers to make. It should however be noted here that contact of this type, personal contact, does help. It has nothing to do with the particular abilities that are being used, per se. These operate quite as effectively through distance; and for that matter, though less often, through time.

At Ruburt's stage of development however, he reacts as a result of emotional impetus, which is picked up rather directly, and which acts as additional energy in transmission. It is for this reason that he now and then does enjoy visitors to sessions, because he instinctively feels that he is thereby learning to manipulate and use these abilities oftentimes, and thereby learn the various subjective feelings that accompany valid perceptions, and to distinguish these from subjective feelings that turn out to be based upon <u>invalid</u> perceptions.

In other words, he enjoys the practice, whether or not he knows it. When for fairly long periods there are no witnesses to sessions, then both Ruburt and myself do indeed lean toward unscheduled sessions when informed friends of yours are present. On the other hand when several sessions in a row, regular sessions, are witnessed, then of course I grow impatient because I am anxious to get back to our own material, which is stressed when we are alone.

I meant to mention this earlier, for there is some pattern to our unscheduled sessions which you have not realized. This is why I worked so well with Philip, to make the most of the opportunity while we did have a guest.

(See the 204th session. Philip is John Bradley's entity name. To date 40 sessions have been witnessed out of 210. Jane's eyes were now opening and closing rather frequently as she spoke.)

For training is necessary as with all things, and although Ruburt has excellent abilities he needs also, shall we say, such direct laboratory experience.

We certainly would not want all of our sessions to be witnessed by any means, so you have no fear in that direction. On the other hand again, such experience is necessary and quite valid, and should be accepted certainly as a part of our work.

Now, speaking once more about our primary and secondary conditions, it should be said now that this will not be as simple as it might appear. Many breakdowns and also syntheses will be needed. Ruburt brought up a point, I believe; he observed that the experience of talking occurred in both the waking and the dreaming states, but did not think that these represented primaries.

Talking represents a primary, the primary of communication. Walking represent a primary, the primary of motion. We will have much more to say along these lines, and I give you these as examples only. We shall see if you can work out others by yourselves.

I now suggest your break.

(Break at 9:27. Jane was dissociated as usual for a first delivery. Her eyes had opened and shut often. Her pace had been quite rapid after the slow beginning. She remembered the material concerning Helen Dyer, and now told me she had felt an immediate rapport with Helen when she entered our apartment this evening, and a desire to help her in some way. Helen has been in our place once before, perhaps a couple of years ago.

(In the 185th session Seth dealt to some extent with what he called Jane's healing ability; one point he made was that the desire to help others would aid the development of this ability. Seth of course has given specific data on various physical ills for some witnesses, and for Jane and me. Whenever the advice was acted upon it worked out very well, whether the difficulty discussed was physical or psychological.

(At times Jane gets "feelings" about the physical condition of an individual, whether it is a friend or someone she passes on the street. Sometimes these intuitions involve the approaching death of the individual concerned. She has felt other psychological states also, and now notes them down when they occur. These developments have been quite recent. A recent example involved her sensing the breakup of the

marriage of a friend with whom I work, some two weeks before the friend told anyone. I had suspected nothing amiss personally.

(Seth's malignant diagnosis in this session represents the most drastic to date, and left Jane and me wondering about the best course of action to take in such cases. Jane resumed at a good rate, and with her eyes closed, at 9:39.)

Now first of all, in line with your conversation during rest period. Under no circumstances should this information I have given you be passed on to the woman involved, or to any of her friends.

If this seems to involve you in a problem with morality, then let me add here that such information, on its own, unless handled with utmost care, would immediately involve the negative suggestion that could lead easily to the very condition that we hope she avoids.

She told you of an experience that seems to be a dream, in which her husband spoke to her in terms of encouragement. She will have several other such experiences, for her husband is aware of the situation, and is helping her all he can.

If she accepts the help on an intuitive basis it will indeed change the course of her life in the future. There are sufficient constructive elements about her if she chooses to take advantage of them.

This should not concern you.

(It was 9:45. I placed the test envelope in Jane's lap while she gave voice to the above sentence. She gave no sign that she was aware of my action, other than a slight movement of her legs, but she picked up the envelope almost at once. Her eyes were still closed. She held the envelope in her right hand, making no effort to determine its contents by feeling, twisting, etc.)

We will now see what we can do with your envelope. Please give us a moment. *(Pause.)*

These are impressions. A mist; that is, I believe M-I-S-T, and a long road. *(Pause.)* In parenthesis here, Ruburt's own connection is with the Gallaghers. An afternoon involving three people. A massage. Something like a... I do not know the phrase... like a bandage used to bind wounds at pressure points. *(Pause.)*

Ruburt and dark treetops. A connection with wood, rather strongly, as of many trees, and another connection with a long wooden table, as of a picnic table. *(Pause.)*

Ruburt's own perceptions are somewhat confused here because <u>he</u> thinks of two photographs. One in which he is perched in a tree. This one taken in California, and the other one of the two of you, taken at your New York glen, by a picnic table, in which your images are almost hidden by the trees.

So give us another moment here. *(Pause.)*

We will try and say that a photograph is involved, that it is a fairly dark one, that Ruburt is in it, perhaps also a dog. The dark portions are shadows of trees, or perhaps rocks.

There is a man connected with the photograph. Ruburt's husband. *(Pause.)* But it has to do with the past, at least five years ago.

I suggest your break.

(Break at 9:57. Jane was dissociated as usual. Her eyes had remained closed, her pace had been quite slow. I had the impression as she spoke that she was struggling to sort out what she wanted to say.

(Jane said she was somewhat startled to feel the envelope touch her lap. She hadn't expected a test, and I hadn't mentioned it to her before the session. Actually I had prepared the test envelope some weeks ago.

(Jane said that at the moment she had no idea why she clung to the photograph idea. Although she was a little tired, she didn't feel particularly bad. She now revealed that she had actually seen within three photographs, rather than the two mentioned. She saw these photos quite clearly, she said, and knew that two of them were in our album, and the third in a file of her own. From the descriptions given I recognized them also.

(Since Jane had developed the photograph idea so consistently in the test, we thought something must have happened to put her on that track, and we said aloud that we hoped Seth would deal with the reasons for this before ending the session.

(It was now time for the 19th Dr. Instream test. Jane's pace was now again very slow. Although I could not see her doing so, her eyes must have opened a trifle to find the ashtray, since she was again smoking. She sat with one hand to her face, her head tipped down, speaking quietly. She took many pauses, some of them long. Resume at 10:06.)

Now give us a moment. Then I shall have some remarks to make later. *(Pause.)*

A new interior, or one that we have not seen earlier. *(A long pause at 10:07.)* A neighboring town or village. Three or four people *(pause)* with cards of some kind. Two doors to the room, and old-fashioned furniture.

Many small objects on display, and a chest of large proportions. A beaded framework, as of a beaded lamp. An old bible in which family records may be kept. *(Long pause.)*

The number ten, and the number 375. Also a fee involved. *(Pause.)*

This is all we will attempt on this, this evening, and I will have a few words with you, Joseph.

(Jane's voice was determined, her eyes still closed.)

First of all, I do not want any envelope tests given before the Instream material is delivered. It may be my fault. I neglected to mention this in an outright manner, but in the past I never requested the envelope until after the Instream material.

There is a good <u>reason</u> for this. You always check on the results of the envelope test immediately afterward.

(Jane's eyes now opened wide. She stared at me as she lit a cigarette. Her eyes then closed.)

Therefore, if the results are poor, this undermines Ruburt's confidence for the following tests. This is rather important. I have no objection now to the fact that you check the results of the envelope tests immediately afterward; but <u>only</u> when this occurs after the Instream material.

This fact hampered that work this evening. Ruburt knew the earlier test was poor, and he set up defenses.

Now as to the poor results themselves in the envelope test. Primarily there are two reasons for our unsatisfactory results. He did not want to have the test given to him while the Instream material had not yet been given for one thing, and so this did not work for us. To begin with however he simply was not at his best in any case.

He was shocked by the earlier information that I had given concerning the woman, and this led him to block further information for the evening. He worked, or allowed me to work through, the layers of personal subconscious only, which now and then <u>may</u> yield valid information, but highly distorted <u>as a rule</u>, and unreliable for our purposes.

He put himself back in time, seeing three photographs of himself, progressively further away from the present, in order to separate himself from the sort of information that he heard himself giving earlier this evening. So all in all he was not working at his best, and it can hardly be expected that he do so constantly.

The point about the test envelopes however should be well taken. This is one of the main reasons why, in the Rhine experiments, results were not given until a certain sequence of tests had been completed, or a given series.

I suggest your break.

One point here. I allowed the test to continue because, again, such episodes can teach you lessons. I tried to separate the levels, for a while, of perception; but Ruburt by then would not open up the deeper layers of communication. You may now take your break.

(Break at 10:28. Jane had been dissociated as usual. Her eyes opened slowly. Her pace however had been much faster.

(In the 197th session Seth suggested that I not wait for him to request an

envelope test. *In a recent session also he said it was not wise for such tests to be given at the end of a session, when Jane is tired. Hence I thought I had picked a good time to give her the test envelope. I did not anticipate that it would not be a good test because of previous information, or that it could interfere with subsequent tests.*

(During break Jane relaxed on the bed. She began speaking from there after break, her head propped up on one hand, her eyes closed, her voice quite amused. Resume at 10:30.)

Now. We are going to give you the week of Christmas off, for all students have a holiday sometime. We may even give you a report card. Tonight's performance will not pull your average down too far, but perhaps we can bring it up for you in the meantime.

We will at any time, Joseph, accept envelope tests, as long as they are given to me after the Instream material. There is indeed more that should be said along these lines, and perhaps at our next session we shall make certain points clearer in this regard.

I suggest that we end the session; and I will also discuss the material of a personal nature that you have in mind at a later session. My heartiest wishes and good night.

("Good night, Seth.")

(End at 10:34. Jane was dissociated as usual.)

SESSION 211
NOVEMBER 24, 1965 9 PM WEDNESDAY AS SCHEDULED

(No envelope test was held during the session.

(Bill and Peggy Gallagher were witnesses to the session. As usual the presence of witnesses fired Seth up. His delivery was more active and quite fast from the beginning. Jane's eyes however remained closed. For much of the session she sat on the edge of her chair, leaning forward with her hands clasped together. She began at 8:58.)

Good evening.

("Good evening, Seth.")

I am indeed glad to see that you are all in such high spirits. For a spirit I am indeed in a rather high mood myself.

Of course I welcome our Jesuit and our cat lover, as always. There are however some points that I would like to clear, and I would also like to add to your instructions concerning our dream experiments—since I know, Joseph, that you can't wait to begin them.

(Jane faced me while speaking this last phrase, her eyes still closed, and in good humor.)

Now, I would suggest that two main categories in particular be given special notice. These as you know will have to do with primary and secondary reality. And each dream should be scrutinized first of all with these main points in mind. You must look out for pitfalls, and use your critical faculties. Ruburt uses his critical faculties supremely well in scrutinizing <u>my</u> activities and nature, so I have no doubt that he can also apply them to the job at hand.

You will need to use your wits carefully, for secondary realities will often appear to be primaries. I mentioned earlier that it might seem that walking, for example, was a primary, since it appears that you walk in your dreams. You also walk in the waking state, and you can actually walk, and also <u>appear</u> to walk, in the trance state. Nevertheless, walking is part of the primary of motion.

Now there are several kinds of time, that will appear within your dreams, and you must sort these out carefully. While sleeping in your present time, you may have a dream that concerns your personal past, while the dream is concerned with events that you know to have occurred many years ago. Nevertheless you may experience these events as happening within the present.

The present within which you seem to experience the dream is <u>not</u>, however, the present in physical time, the present in which your body lies upon the bed. There is a fine distinction here, and one that you shall learn through experience for yourselves, for I shall not tell you all.

It should be obvious to you also that within your dreams a spatial location that belongs in present physical time can be experienced in the past or in the future within the dream framework, and there is much more here than meets the eye; and you must be careful so that you catch it. What you do with it will be up to you.

I am particularly interested myself in these projected experiments, and as a preliminary for them we shall have you work with suggestion alone before you attempt to begin with your recordings.

Now I will give you a short break, and again my welcome to our friends, and I do not mean to ignore them. We shall indeed have you, Joseph and Ruburt, working in your sleep, as Ruburt earlier remarked, and you shall be glad of it. For the dream will not be captured in a laboratory by scientists who will not look into their own dreams.

The nature of dreams will only be discovered in such a manner as I am suggesting.

(Break at 9:10. Jane was dissociated as usual for a first delivery. Her eyes had remained closed, her pace had been quite fast and expressive. She resumed in the

same manner at 9:28.)

Now. I will continue. Man will not learn the basic nature of reality by studying the physical universe alone, nor will he learn it by studying the personality as it operates within the physical universe alone.

The nature of reality can only be approached by an investigation of reality as it is <u>directly experienced</u> in all levels of awareness: reality as it appears under dream conditions, under other conditions of dissociation, and as it appears in the waking condition.

Most studies even dealing with the conscious state are extremely superficial, dealing only with those upper layers of egotistical awareness that are immediately concerned with the manipulation of the self within physical reality.

All layers of the personality are indeed conscious layers. They simply operate in the manner of compartments, so that often one portion of the self is not aware of other portions. <u>As a rule</u> when you are awake you do not know your sleeping self; you know your neighbors far better, so your sleeping self appears mysterious indeed. When you are awake, as Ruburt himself has written, you cannot find the dream locations that have been so familiar to you only the night before.

In your sleep you may have greeted friends who are strangers to your waking self. But consider the other side of the coin. For when you are asleep, you cannot find the street upon which you live your waking hours, and when you are asleep you do not know you waking self. The sleeping self is your identity.

Now there are indeed connections between these two conditions. And there are definite realities that exist in both states, and these uniting realities will be what you are looking for. For only by finding these can you discover the nature of the human personality and the nature of reality within which it must operate.

We have also spoken of the dream as a drama, and you must discover the various levels upon which these dramas take place. It will not be as difficult when you are under way as it may seem to you now.

My dear Jesuit, shall I turn my chair around and face you full?

([Bill:] "As you wish."

(Seth broke off his material to introduce this bit of humor because Bill, sitting perhaps five feet away, was leaning forward and staring intently at Jane as she spoke. Smiling, her eyes still closed, Jane now shifted her chair so that she did face Bill squarely.

(A reminder, that Seth's favorite term for Bill is the Jesuit; for Peggy, the cat lover.)

You will also discover, as I have mentioned, that the various levels of the subconscious will <u>yield</u> their own characteristic data, and as your records grow this will become apparent to you. It is obviously necessary then that your suggestion is given precisely as I gave it to you, for we want the dreams recorded in consecutive order whenever possible.

(*See the 206th session.*)

This is most necessary. Certain questions may appear too simple to ask, but you must ask them and you must use your brains here.

Are your muscles tired—

("*No.*"

(*Since Seth paused after giving voice to the question, I answered, since I had been writing at a fast pace. I soon saw that I shouldn't have however, since Jane now turned the same humorous expression toward me that had confronted Bill a few minutes ago.*)

—after a dream of much activity? I was not inquiring after your welfare. However, I am glad that you are in good condition.

I want you to ask questions along these lines, and attempt to answer them through your records and experience.

You see, the work involved in these experiments will of itself allow you to be extremely flexible, and you will discover finally that you can bring a portion of your consciousness with you while you sleep. A portion of the self will be investigating other portions of the self. We shall also have you using suggestion to bring about certain types of dreams in which we may be interested.

I do have here a thought, my Jesuit friend. Surely you can arrange a spotlight, and we could set it here.

(*Again in a jovial mood, Jane indicated a spot just in front of her rocker. Bill had been still peering intently at her.*)

Incidentally, joking aside, some time in the future it would not be a bad idea, if it ever could be arranged, to take Ruburt's blood pressure before, during, and after sessions; also his weight.

You could perhaps learn something from such innocent tests as these. You see, theoretically, you could find out how much I weighed, or if I had physical weight indeed, could you not? Or if Ruburt weighed <u>less</u> during sessions, then you would have a dilemma.

I am going to suggest a brief break, and we shall make our Dr. Instream appointment.

(*Break at 9:48. Jane was dissociated as usual. Her eyes had remained closed. Her pace had been fast throughout, her voice somewhat stronger but not loud by any means.*

(*Our session was being held in our front room. Up until now none of us had* noticed the traffic noise past the front of the house; but now that a test was to come I became conscious of it. Later Jane, Bill and Peggy concurred.

(*This is the 20th Dr. Instream test. As usual Jane now began to speak at a much slower pace. She sat with her head down, a hand raised to her closed eyes. Resume at 9:58.*)

Now, give us a moment. (*Long pause.*)

A company, with four men and three women. A room with a fireplace, so it would seem that this is not Dr. Instream's apartment. (*Pause.*)

A late arrival, another man and woman, who live outside of town. This is, I believe, academic. (*Pause.*)

A clock of an ornate nature. Of gilt color. The clock itself is round.

(*Here Jane began to describe the shape of the clock in the air with her hands, as she spoke with her eyes closed. Since she was so definite about the clock's shape, I made a quick drawing of my version of her description. This of course caused me to miss out on a few words of her verbal account, so I took the chance and asked her to repeat her description. This is the first time I have asked her a question during a test. She responded without a sign of bother or irritation, and her second description was the same as the first, as near as I could tell.*)

(*A copy of my drawing, and of drawings of the clock by Bill Gallagher and by Jane herself, will be included in the notes at next break.*)

Around the clock the gilt shape comes down in this fashion. We are now forming the base. The base of the clock itself is ornate with small pink flowers or figures upon it, and I believe a green felt beneath the base.

It is not an electric clock. (*Pause.*) I believe that Dr. Instream is looking at it.

I also believe that he lost or misplaced an item from his own office at the school today. (*Pause.*) Or he misplaced it earlier and went to look for it today. The item having to do with cigarettes. A holder perhaps, or a lighter, but of that nature. (*Pause.*)

I also am of the impression that he received a letter today from a previous woman student, having to do perhaps with references that she was requesting. (*Pause.*)

One of the <u>women</u> in this gathering wears a large blue or gray brooch (*pause*) that I believe he has noticed. (*Pause.*) He has been or very shortly will be, informed of a change in his teaching schedule that he did not expect or anticipate, having to do with the morning hours of Tuesday and Thursday, I believe, though I am not certain of the precise two days. The change was not expected. (*Pause.*)

You may take at this time a brief break, and that is the end of our Instream material. Except that you may wish the good doctor a happy holiday for me.

(Break at 10:11. Jane was dissociated as usual. Her eyes had remained closed; her pace had picked up considerably toward the end of the delivery. She told me my question did not bother her; also that she saw the clock she was describing pretty clearly. She was aware of the traffic noise.

(Jane and Bill now made their drawings of the clock, without seeing each other's or mine, and my copies of all three are below. It's apparent the three of us agreed pretty closely on what we saw. Note that only Jane points up the uneven gilt surface in her version.)

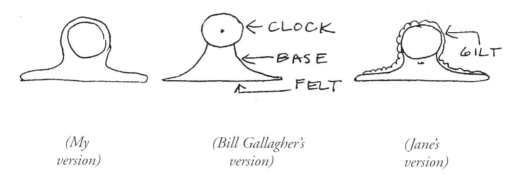

(My version)   *(Bill Gallagher's version)*   *(Jane's version)*

(When Jane began speaking again her pace was once again fast. Her eyes were closed, her voice average. Resume at 10:20.)

Now that our Instream material has been taken care of, we can do whatever you like, within reason of course. We can end our session, I can continue with the material that I have been giving you, or I will be glad to answer questions.

It is indeed up to you. Perhaps you would like merely a social discussion of your own, and if so you are welcome to it.

([My question:] "Have you got a question, Bill?"

([Bill G:] "What significance do you attach to the fact that you seem to be right-handed, but left-handed in sessions?")

Are you referring to Ruburt, or are you speaking to me?

([Bill:] "To Ruburt through you."

(At an earlier break, Bill had mentioned to me, while Jane was out of the room, that he believed Jane was right-handed but that Seth used predominantly left-handed movements. I hadn't noticed this, but told Bill Jane had talked at times of being left-handed as a child; I told him I remembered Jane saying something about being made to write right-handed in school.)

Ruburt, indeed, should give his own answers. Far be it from me to answer for him. I use one hand, and he uses the other, primarily.

([Bill:] "Why?")

I always used one hand, and he used the other.

([Bill:] "I've been wondering why your basic gestures are different than Jane's.")

My dear Jesuit friend. Do I not try to explain things clearly, and am I not grossly misunderstood? I have been saying for some time now that I am myself, and that Ruburt is someone else. It follows that our gestures would therefore be different. Would you not say so?

([Bill:] "I don't know. I've been wondering whether I would think so.")

(The pace was now even faster, and occasionally I omitted a word in the notes to keep up; this did not alter any meanings. Seth was most amused and pleased at the exchange. Jane sat with her eyes still closed; her movements and facial expressions were active.)

I'm glad to see you have had a good think session. Now. If you are thinking in terms of secondary personalities, you can prove nothing one way or another. A secondary personality could indeed use gestures that are different *(with humor)*. Either way, this would be no proof as to my independent nature. I am glad to see that it has been bothering you.

([Bill:] "I was curious as to what you would say.")

My own answer is that I am an energy personality essence, momentarily in contact with your physical system, and that I am allowed to operate through Ruburt.

(See the 63rd and 88th sessions in Volumes 2 and 3 respectively—although Seth has dealt with this problem often before and after these sessions.

[Bill:] "Then you use Ruburt's mechanical equipment, the voice, the eyes and body and so forth, to speak to us.")

I do, and I use them in the manner that I have used mechanical faculties of my own when I had them.

([Bill:] "And does this include Ruburt's facial expressions also?")

It does indeed, though the face does not fully adopt my own expression. First of all, as far as the hands are concerned, to be left or right-handed has to do with inner mechanisms and brain patterns that come first, before the motions of the hands. Characteristically, I operated in certain manners that resulted in the primary use of my left hand, when I was focused within physical matter.

When I am allowed to manifest myself again to some degree physically now, then I manipulate physical matter in my own characteristic fashion.

As to facial expression, this again is somewhat the same matter, for in this case matter does not matter. Physical expression, facial expression, is again the result of the personality's characteristic method of manipulating the physical organism, and when I operated primarily as such I had my own characteristic way of doing so.

Now and then with Ruburt, to a smaller or lesser degree, my own habits therefore show through, for I manipulate his muscles in a different way than he does. But, scientifically again, this would not be proof of my existence as an independent personality who has survived physical death. Not that this concerns me, for it does not.

There is more involved in your questioning, you see, than you imagine. Do you have another?

([Bill:] "Not particularly, I guess.")

(Seth/Jane now turned toward Peggy, who had been sitting quietly by. Jane's eyes were still closed, although she was smiling. It will be remembered that Seth has strong subconscious abilities.)

Our silent cat lover...

([Peg:] "You've said in the past that we would notice changes in Ruburt's features.")

Indeed. On some occasions I can make them very obvious.

([Peg:] "What does it take to make them obvious? You said something about conditions.")

Certain conditions indeed.

([Peg:] "How are conditions now?")

What we need you see are various elements that <u>usually</u> combine spontaneously, but that can be caused to combine when they would not usually combine. This I can usually take care of fairly well. However, I have freedoms that Ruburt does not have, and I am freer to use my abilities than he is.

I work carefully in cooperation with his ego, for we do not want to startle it. When such changes occur in an obvious manner, we shall see that you both are present.

(The most obvious instance of a change in Jane's features occurred in the 68th session, and was witnessed by Bill Macdonnel and myself in full light. This was very definite and easily seen. See Volume 1.)

The conditions are not physical conditions. These would be the simplest. The conditions have to do with the amount which Ruburt is willing to allow me to have of the physical matter of which he is composed, and of which he is naturally jealous.

([Peg:] "Why would this cause him concern?")

His ego is his ego, and because it is his he loves it indeed. All egos fear that which is not ego. A necessary defense mechanism, which is part of each personality.

(*Peggy pointed at a life-sized oil portrait of Jane that I had painted.*

([Peg:] "Wouldn't it be simpler for you to cause a feature change in something like a picture?")

Now we are speaking of something aside from Ruburt's features. When he is off guard, as he was when Philip was present, then we can achieve very much.

(*Philip is John Bradley's entity name. See the 204th session.*

([Peg:] "Well, it seems to us that it's impossible to change the features of a living person. Why wouldn't it be easier to change a picture?")

It would be difficult for me to change the features of a third individual indeed, but far less difficult to change Ruburt's features, since he gives me permission to work through him, and his mental and psychic abilities would help me. A picture would not help me on its own.

No one, you see, wants more proofs than our friend Ruburt, but often consciously he wants so much that he closes the doors through which I can come, and sets down barriers that belong to the ego alone.

I will let you have a break, and you can congratulate me, Joseph, for keeping my voice so well under control. I hear mighty yells when it is out of control, but no comments when it is under control.

("*Thank you.*"

(*End at 10:40. Although Seth indicated a break this turned out to be the end of the session. Jane had been dissociated as usual, and her eyes had remained closed. Her pace had been quite fast at times, and as stated before I occasionally skipped a word in her delivery, or shortened a phrase, etc., without altering any meanings.*

(*Her voice had been well under control, once or twice becoming stronger for a moment or two, and also displaying a trace of the "brogue" it sometimes acquires. I equate this accent with an Irish accent, though the two are not exactly alike as far as I know.*)

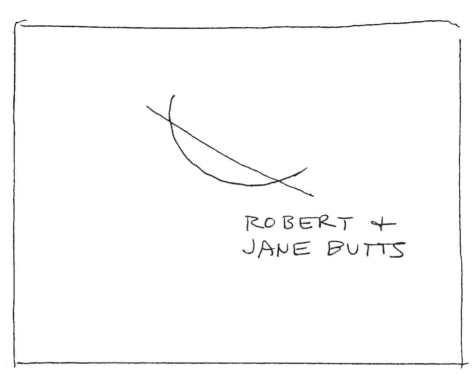

(Tracing of the test paper used in the 18th envelope test, in the 212th session for November 29, 1965.)

SESSION 212
NOVEMBER 29, 1965 9 PM MONDAY AS SCHEDULED

(*The 18th envelope test was held during the session. The test object is simply a drawing in black ink of the same symbol used in the first envelope test, of August 18, 1965, in the 179th session. See that session for an explanation of the personal meaning this symbol has for us. I made the drawing for this evening's test on white paper; the paper was thin and the heavy black ink struck through the paper rather clearly. See Volume 4.*

(*Before tonight's session Jane and I were discussing ways and means of taking her blood pressure, her weight and various other measurements of a physiological nature before, during and after sessions. Seth referred to this in the last session briefly. We know several doctors on a social basis, but for various reasons hesitate to ask one of them to perform these duties; we would also like to repeat these studies regularly,* and could hardly expect a medical man to be available in this respect.

(*The name of Father Martin came up in the conversation. He is a monk in a nearby monastery, an ex-doctor, and knows of the sessions casually. He has not witnessed any. Jane and I like him, but doubted his availability very often. One reason is that he gets up at 4 AM to work on the monastery farm.*

(*Another project we would like to explore is photographing Jane during sessions. I could handle this with a little practice. We talked of illustrating Jane's book on the Seth material, which she is now writing.*

(*Jane has decided that she smokes too much during sessions; as a result she did not smoke while dictating this evening, but did light up at breaks. The session was held in our back room, and was a quiet one. Jane spoke while sitting down and with her eyes closed for the most part. Her pace was quite slow in the beginning, but by first break was up to its usual rather fast state.*)

Good evening.

("*Good evening, Seth.*")

I have been most interested in the topic under discussion immediately before our session. Such medical examinations as you have in mind would be excellent from several standpoints, and we shall have further suggestions on all these lines.

Your acquaintance, Father Martin, will work out well if arrangements can be made. This sort of arrangement is more important than the other matter under discussion, concerning a possible photograph of Ruburt during a session. You may of course do as you like. I have nothing against such a photograph being taken or used.

The presence of a medical man however can stand us in good stead. You are quite lucky in knowing several medical men to begin with. Of course these matters should be handled as simply as possible.

I have another suggestion, incidentally, that you might find most helpful. I would suggest that you purchase a reliable set of scales. Later on, using self-hypnosis, you can experiment to see whether or not you <u>weigh</u> less when you suggest that you will become lighter and lighter.

The scales can also be used for weighing Ruburt before, after, and during sessions. He shall weigh in, as fighters do, though this is indeed a different kind of arena.

I am going to let you find your own answers, but any such tests and examinations will be welcomed by me, as long as they are conducted in such a way so that our sessions are not disturbed. And I anticipate no difficulties here.

It would do no harm to purchase a thermometer, taking Ruburt's temperature before, after and during some sessions. Anything that you learn is to your benefit along these lines, and will serve us all well. The thermometer could also be used of course to test any temperature changes occurring in a regular trance state. These are merely suggestions which I feel may be of benefit.

Again, any changes, or any <u>lack</u> of changes will be significant, and will help you distinguish the differences between various levels of consciousness as they show themselves <u>physically</u> within the organism. You see here that if temperature and pulse is noted before sessions, you may find a correlation that exists between these and specific instances of clairvoyance as demonstrated during a given session, and <u>another</u> given session. Do you follow my point here?

("Yes.")

I could go on for quite a while, mentioning things that you could do. They all would add to your work load, though none of them alone would take much time. You have available, through your television set I believe, data having to do with outside temperature, wind velocity and so forth. For your <u>own</u> records you could note these before a session, and look for correlations.

(Elmira is on a cable TV system, and one channel presents a 24-hour weather report. Constantly, one after another, dials show time, temperature, humidity, barometric pressure, rainfall, wind direction and wind velocity.)

Humidity and barometric pressure would also be helpful. You are functioning within an environment. The psychic and exterior environments are closely connected, and the correlations are available if you know where to look for them.

I would definitely speak to this Father Martin before approaching anyone else, simply because his attitude would enable him to work well with us, I believe that he may be available, though not for any long period. He would be much more apt to be discreet and dependable, and he is more or less outside the regular community in which you live, which could be to your benefit. He is highly intelligent, perceptive and no one's fool.

I suggest your first break.

(Break at 9:25. Jane was dissociated as usual for a first delivery. Her eyes had remained closed; her pace had been fast as break approached.

(Father Martin is well read in ESP and related fields; he conducts a correspondence also with monks in other countries, including a Tibetan monk.

(Jane resumed again with her eyes closed, and at a somewhat slower pace, at 9:33.)

The weather readings from your television station will also be handy in relation to the projected dream experiments.

It will do no harm to note them down before you retire. I believe that you will note some rather significant correlations, if you find the time to carry any of these investigations through with any regularity. And the regularity will be very important.

These will only indicate correlations however, and not basic conditions. They will be correlations <u>between</u> basic conditions, and there is quite a difference here. There is so much that can be done, and I know that you have little time to do them. You see, there are also other circumstances which could be noted, to your advantage, such as the phases of the moon, and others which would be more difficult to ascertain.

All of this does not have to be done at once however, and all in all enough shall be done.

Our last discussion concerning your personal lives helped you both, incidentally. You may insert this into the record or not, as you choose. This remark, that is.

I would definitely suggest that <u>some</u> of the items we mentioned in this session be used in connection with our sessions, for a beginning. There are obviously connections between the psychic and physical self, and there is no reason why you should not begin to investigate these for yourselves.

The physical circumstances which you may discover should never be interpreted as conditions in themselves, under which we operate with varying degrees of efficiency, again, but merely as interconnecting correlations between two sets of intangibles. I will make this clearer at a later time.

(*Jane has not been smoking during her deliveries this evening. However she now took a sip of wine. Though I could not see whether her eyes opened or not, I assume they did sufficiently for her to pick up her glass without fumbling.*)

As far as our dream experiments are concerned, I believe that you will discover definite correlations of a rather important nature that exist between the incidence of precognitive dreams, and data having to do with temperature and weather.

I will see if you can discover these for yourselves, but if not I shall point them out for you when the time comes. I do not believe that it is possible for you to carry your dream experiments far enough to discover certain other factors that do exist between various layers of the subconscious, and falling temperature rates in the physical organism. Therefore I will mention the point here.

It would be necessary to take your temperature many times during the evening, and to correlate the findings with the various levels of the subconscious as they displayed themselves through their characteristic activities within the dream series. Such an experiment would be extremely difficult.

It should be noted however, that with the <u>exception</u> of several other circumstances the various levels of the subconscious can be found to fall within definite temperature ranges. To some extent this fact can be ascertained through hypnosis. However, <u>suggestion</u> as to the effect that the subject's temperature should rise or fall would tend to obscure the effect.

This correlation between the layers of the subconscious and temperature ranges is true, or rather observable, only when the personality is in an inactive state. Suggestions of motion or excitement given to it would change and affect the temperature reading, so that this characteristic temperature range could be unnoticed.

Illness and other factors can also obscure this fact. I am speaking in terms of a healthy, normal individual, in good health.

I suggest your break.

(Break at 9:58. Jane was dissociated as usual. Her voice was average, her pace also. She said she slits her eyes open when she picks up a wineglass, knocks the ashes off a cigarette, etc. Her head is usually tipped down in such movements and I can detect no opening of the eyes.

(It was now time for the 21st Dr. Instream test. As usual Jane spoke in a quiet voice, sitting with her hands raised to her closed eyes. Her pace was not very slow, however, although she took a few long pauses. Resume at 10:03.)

Now. Give us a moment please.

I pick up the impression of a series of confusing circumstances earlier today, for our Dr. Instream. *(Long pause.)*

I am picking up his emotional feeling toward <u>them</u>, the circumstances. Whatever they were, they annoyed him considerably. There may have been a book involved. *(Long pause.)*

A connection with another man who visited him recently, and who spoke of a colleague who is from another state, and in the same field as Dr. Instream. *(Pause.)* A disagreement over, I believe, professional papers and publications, rather the <u>contents</u> of these.

I pick up the initials A. R., but am not sure to what they refer. Now the impression of a small wooden box, quite small *(pause)* with something like medals or buttons in it. The size perhaps of a small box in which file cards could be kept. It is on a shelf, and is of dark wood. *(Long pause at 10:11.)*

I believe Dr. Instream is in a room that is not his own, a different room than he has been in any other time during our appointments. *(Pause.)* A long wall without windows is in it. Adjacent to this wall, a wall with a door. Opposite the long wall, a wall with several windows. The walls of a grayish color.

A shadow passes the door, of a woman I believe, in some outfit of floor length, a floor-length skirt or robe. *(Pause, at 10:17.)*

Do you have a test for me?

("Yes."

(As usual I handed Jane the standard sealed double envelope containing my drawing of the symbol shown on page 95. She reached out for it without opening her eyes, then sat quietly holding it in both hands. Momentarily, she laid her left hand flat upon the envelope. This is the 18th envelope test.)

Ruburt would have preferred that I did not speak out because of our last episode.

Anything you learn however is to your advantage. Give us a moment, if you please.

These will be impressions. Something that is filled on both sides, that is, with neither side entirely vacant. An association with you, Joseph, and an afternoon, either in 1963 or when you were 43. At least these are the numbers that I receive impressions of.

Also a connection with a supper engagement, with two others beside Ruburt. The word congratulations. I do not specifically mean that the word is on the item, but that somehow congratulations are connected with an event associated with the item.

Yellow. Paper; not of course the envelope. A series, as of quickly following events, and a canyon or rock shape.

I suggest your break.

(Break at 10:24. Jane was dissociated as usual, she said. Her eyes had remained closed. Her pace on our own test had been faster than on the Dr. Instream material.

(As stated on page 95, the black ink drawing struck through the thin test paper so that it was visible on both sides of the paper. This could be "neither side entirely vacant." The test object is paper, and is connected with me since my name is on it, and I made the drawing. I was 43 until June 20 in 1963.

(We did not press Seth for an item-by-item interpretation of the rest of the impressions. I had prepared this test envelope for last Wednesday's session but did not use it then; the session was witnessed by the Gallaghers and the test was shoved aside by other developments, notably the impromptu discussion between Seth, Bill and Peg. We ate during the course of the evening, but do not know whether this would be a "supper engagement, with two others beside Ruburt."

(Jane resumed at a slow pace, with her eyes closed, at 10:35.)

Now. If tests of this nature are to be given at all, they should be given with some kind of regularity, so that Ruburt accepts them as simply another part of the sessions.

His confidence will then be maintained through the averages of our successes, which all in all will be quite good. Isolated tests do not work well, for they upset what he considers the normal circumstances of our sessions. When given they should follow our Dr. Instream material.

When the tests are given regularly we will automatically hit those evenings when conditions are excellent for reception. We shall of course also hit evenings when conditions are <u>not</u> so good, but these will not annoy you when you have successes under your belt.

You are investigating these matters, and should be interested in discovering what you can about when we succeed, and when we do not.

I will end the session or continue as you prefer.
("We'll end it then.")
My best regards to you both, and a good evening.
("Good night, Seth."
(End at 10:41. Jane was dissociated as usual.)

(Tracing of the envelope front used in the 19th envelope test, in the 213th session for December 1, 1965.)

SESSION 213
DECEMBER 1, 1965 9:50 PM WEDNESDAY

(*The 19th envelope test was held this evening. The test object was the front of an envelope mailed to us by Jane's father last July. See the tracing on page 101. The writing was in blue ink on white paper. Note the error, 1985, in the postmark; I thought Seth might comment on this but he did not. The envelope front was folded once and placed between two sheets of Bristol, then sealed in the usual double envelopes.*)

(*Tonight's session began at 9:50 PM. After supper this evening Jane expressed a desire to vary the routine, although she did not want to skip the session. On impulse I invited her out for a beer. There were go-go girls at the neighborhood tavern we went to, and both of us enjoyed the break in routine. Jane, very amused, commented every so often that she received little "messages" from a certain party, expressing approval of our actions, and merely suggesting that we do get to the session at least a few minutes before the Instream material was due.*)

(*As mentioned by Seth in the last session, I have begun keeping a record of outside weather data from our television weather channel. This includes humidity, barometric pressure, etc., as detailed on page 97. This record is for session nights only; I do not know whether it is necessary to insert the data into each session. When we begin our dream experiments with the recorder, we will also keep a daily weather record, again as suggested by Seth.*)

(*The session was held in our front room. With the windows closed traffic noise was not a problem. Jane began speaking while sitting down, in an average voice and at a good pace from the beginning. Jane's eyes opened wide immediately after Seth's greeting, which is most unusual. They were very dark. Seth/Jane was quite pleased and amused, and spoke with a smile. Jane was smoking.*)

Now then, good evening my friends.

("*Good evening, Seth.*")

It is perfectly all right now and then to vary your schedule in this manner, and probably all in all most beneficial.

You probably also came to this conclusion by yourselves, and while I would not make the habit of beginning our sessions later than usual, occasionally such tardiness is more than justified. The use of the different room is also beneficial, to vary the routine.

We will of course shortly give our Dr. Instream material, and so I shall not become involved in any complicated matters beforehand. You have both been doing very well however, and shortly we shall be having an anniversary of sorts, I believe.

(Our first regular session was held on December 2, 1963.)

There were a few remarks that I intended to make concerning the Christmas season, and perhaps I shall make them now.

If it seems to you that there is a great gap existing within Christianity, between ideals expressed, and actions, then let me tell you that conditions would indeed be far worse if these ideals had not initially been expressed, and if they were not yearly reaffirmed.

As you both suppose, enough constructive psychic energy is generated during the holiday season to recharge psychic batteries, so to speak, for quite some time. Were it not for this your whole race would be in much more serious a predicament.

One of the reasons, Joseph, for your own lack of festive spirit in the past has been the result of your realization that this gap between idealism and action is great. You could not therefore enter into what you felt to be the hypocrisy of the season. All the more since you have no particular conviction, anymore than Ruburt has, concerning the historic existence of a Christ.

To some extent I have explored some of this, but it will do you well to join wholeheartedly into the very necessary spirit of the time, for it is constructive and most beneficial. And in so doing you help yourself and others.

Now. There was no historic Virgin Birth, and no historic Crucifixion. This does not mean that these do not represent symbolic realities.

I am going to give you a brief break, and then we shall meet with our Dr. Instream; and I shall afterwards discuss this matter somewhat further.

(Break at 10:00. Jane was dissociated as usual for a first break. Much of the time her eyes had been wide open and very dark. Her pace had been good, her voice average, and she had smoked.

(Seth has dealt with psychic gestalts, religion, the Crucifixion, beginnings and endings, etc., under the general heading of the God concept, at various times. See the following sessions among others: 24, 27, 31, 51, 62, 66, 81, 95, 97, 115, 135, 145, 146, 147, 149, 151, 177.

(Seth has referred to my lack of holiday enthusiasm in the past. I have been conscious of this ever since and have been making attempts to improve it. So far this season, I believe my attitude has shown a marked improvement.

(It was now time for the 22nd Dr. Instream test. As usual Jane sat with her hands raised to her closed eyes while giving the data. She used pauses but all in all her pace was not particularly slow. Her voice was quiet. Resume at 10:03.)

Now. Give us a moment.

Again it seems, as I believe one time before, he is in a room that is at least partially below ground level. With chairs, many chairs in it, of the straight-backed variety.

(*Pause.*) Whether or not this is a cafeteria I do not know, but he and others seem to be drinking coffee. (*Pause.*) He is dressed in a business-type suit this evening, with shirt and tie, standing up and talking to two other people.

He finds the conversation in some way inadequate. He is trying to get definite answers from a man who does not seem able to give them. The man is taller than Dr. Instream, somewhat younger, but not in the same department at the university.

The doctor looks at his watch. (*Pause at 10:08.*) He received a book by mail today, a biography sort of book, having to do with a personality of the late 1800's. A medium.

There are four or five people, now, in his immediate party. Two of these are woman I believe. (*Pause.*)

He made a trip to his office, and spoke briefly with one man there. (*Pause.*) Again, some sort of connection with a small black box, very small. The <u>top</u> is black. I do not know about the bottom half.

Cocktails earlier (*pause*), and dinner, with a woman in a restaurant. Your Howard Johnson's. The dinner costing $4.75. (*Pause.*) The dinner was of a business-mixed-with-social affair. (*Pause.*)

Do you have a test for me?

("*Yes.*"

(*It was 10:15. This is the 19th envelope test. As usual I handed Jane the sealed double envelope. She held the envelope quietly, her eyes still closed. She took a sip of milk, then sat with her left hand to her face.*)

Now we shall see, again, what we can do. Give us a moment. A connection with water. One, two, three, or three of a kind. A connection with a commercial venture. A connection again, with an afternoon and two people, yourself and Ruburt.

<u>Ruburt</u> here thinks of a photograph of the two of you, taken at Marathon. (*Pause.*) A border. Horizontal lines that are similar to each other. A late spring, or a spring or summer month.

A strip, and a connection with an event that was not particularly pleasant. Light and dark, with shadow shapes. A connection with another individual, a male.

A photograph, and a connection with someone who visited here.

I suggest your break.

(*Break at 10:22. Jane was dissociated as usual. Her eyes had remained closed except when she had sipped milk briefly. Her pace had been faster than usual for the material on both tests, her voice average.*)

(See the tracing of the test object on page 101. All in all the envelope test results were much superior to the previous two tests, and Jane was pleased. "A connection with water" can be our Elmira, New York address, 458 W. Water Street, or that both Ormond Beach and Daytona Beach, Florida, are on the ocean.

(A later addition by Jane: "I'd say it was referring to the return address—Ormond Beach on the ocean."

("One, two, three, or three of a kind," can be the July 3 postmark date on the envelope. The envelope is addressed to Jane and me, "yourself and Ruburt," but we do not particularly see where "afternoon" comes in. I remember the photograph of Jane and me taken at Marathon, Florida. "A border" regarding the test object does not ring a bell, but "Horizontal lines that are similar to each other," are the postmark cancellation lines. The letter was mailed in July, "a spring or summer month."

(Jane insists that "A strip" refers to the beautiful long beaches at both Daytona and Ormond, which adjoin each other. Without going into personal details, we can say that Seth is correct when he refers to "A connection with an event that was not particularly pleasant"; this involved us and Jane's father in Florida.

(We do not see a connection with "Light and dark, with shadow shapes" particularly. Jane's father, who addressed the envelope, can be "A connection with another individual, a male." Jane's father is of course "someone who visited here," but we do not know what "A photograph" means, particularly, in the test data, since Seth did not elaborate.

(Usually now we do not ask Seth to explain every reference made in a test if we do not see any connection. We list what we see as connections, and have noted that if we are really puzzled about any test data, Seth will say something about the problem after break.

(Jane now resumed with her eyes closed, and at an average rate, at 10:30.)

Now. I am going to give you a brief session, since you do have one coming, and you have been most faithful.

I wanted to have a test, and what I said regarding tests in the last session still holds.

(See page 101.)

This feeling that Christmas represented hypocrisy has been one of the <u>main</u> reasons for your own low spirits during the season, for it represented a rather deep disillusionment with the culture in which you were nurtured.

(Jane's eyes now opened, and for the rest of the delivery they opened and shut often.)

The <u>legend</u> of Christ is of great psychic import however, and is <u>intrinsically</u> true. This does not mean it is based in historical fact. In many ways it is more true than historic fact, for man himself created that which had not been provided. The creation nevertheless happened in quite real terms, and is part of mankind's inner recognition of the pyramid gestalts of which I have spoken.

This was as close as man could <u>come</u> in his imagination to that which is, and this is all right. The basic idea behind Christmas is definitely important, whether or not the intellect is able to see its significance.

Now. <u>Psychologically</u> alone this is beneficial, for it acts against those feelings of despair that can creep up during the winter season. And by reminding men of a birth and a resurrection it hints at the innate abilities of the race to transcend physical time and space.

The <u>getting out</u> of oneself that is involved is excellent therapy, and therapy that does others good, as well as the self involved. There is much more here, however. Culturally speaking, there is a strong connection with pagan intuitions, deep and meaningful, that found newer and broader expressions.

The character of Christ as it is portrayed is an excellent one, since it stressed <u>human</u> rather than specifically male qualities. Or should I say it stressed human qualities rather than those unfortunately considered male qualities. It stressed the best qualities of the race as a whole.

The personality of Christ is an idealization, and a clue to the entity of which each individual personality is composed. And as far as prayer is concerned, though I realize that neither of you pray in those terms, someone does indeed listen. The self who prays listens, and makes necessary adjustments and improvements. For the individual is part of All That Is, and therefore partakes of the abilities of the psychic gestalts of which we have so sketchily spoken.

I will now close our session, with my fondest good wishes to you both, and I believe that we have set Ruburt back on a fairly steady line.

("Yes.")

Sometime shortly we shall discuss some personal material if you wish.

("Yes.")

Your little excursion this evening was quite helpful.

("Good night, Seth."

(End at 10:45. Jane was dissociated as usual. Her eyes had opened and closed frequently, and she had been smoking. She felt good over the test results.)

SESSION 214

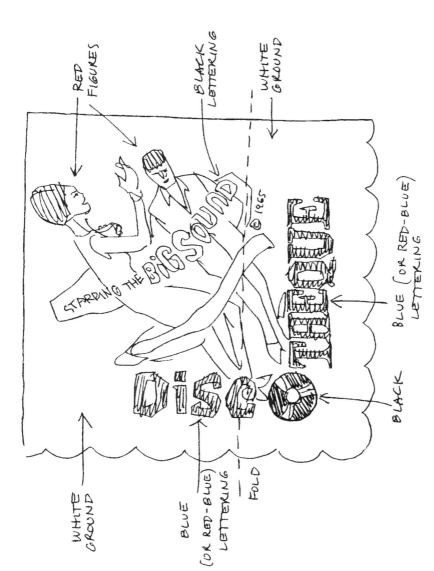

(Tracing of the quarter of a paper napkin used in the 20th envelope test, of December 6, 1965, in the 214th session.)

SESSION 214
DECEMBER 6, 1965 9 PM MONDAY AS SCHEDULED

(*An unscheduled session was held on Friday evening, December 3, 1965, in our apartment. Beginning at about 10:15 PM, Seth spoke at no great length to six people, myself included. The six witnesses comprise Seth's largest audience to date. Bill and Peggy Gallagher were present, and Ann Diebler, and Don and Marilyn Wilbur. The last three named are from the group of young people who witnessed the unscheduled session of November 5, 1965. See the notes on page 57, preceding the 206th session. Ann and Marilyn work with me at Artistic Card Co.*

(*Seth gave Don Wilbur a few lines of information concerning a job change he was considering, and Don has a copy of this material. Seth told Ann Diebler he could not at this time answer her questions concerning a friend in Newport News, Virginia, because he has not yet established an emotional rapport with her. He did willingly answer many other questions asked by Ann, Marilyn and Don, questions mostly based on the material itself and the concepts involved.*

(*Peggy Gallagher, a feature writer for the Elmira Star-Gazette, is in Washington DC for a few days this week on business. Seth volunteered to give information about Peg's activities while she is in Washington, and Jane also plans to tune in on Peg via psychological-time experiments. Both of these methods were used with some success during the Gallaghers' vacation in Puerto Rico last October.*

(*Jane and I have yet to prepare Seth's material on the Puerto Rico experiments, for insertion into the record. We have now decided to present Seth's hits and near misses only, plus Seth's data on the Washington experiment, in one of the sessions falling due the week after this.*

(*Apropos of Peggy's Washington trip, Seth gave predictions when asked to during Friday's unscheduled session. He also asked the Gallaghers not to say any more about the trip to him, once the subject had been brought up. I took no notes Friday evening, but Peggy did. They accompanied her to Washington, and at Seth's request she will also make notes while there. There follows a copy of Seth's material on the trip, as noted down by Peggy:*

("You will meet a woman dressed in green... A clock that doesn't keep proper time... There are three men in particular with whom you will be associated... You will meet a man you do not like... You will have a grand view of an occasion... A turnoff that does not bring you where you want to go... An unscheduled social engagement, not in a private home but a public place... The number 5 and the number 321... Another room besides the one that has been planned.")

(*Since Peggy has now been made aware of Seth's predictions, Jane and I now* wonder what part, if any, suggestion might play in the events that transpire in Washington DC. Is it possible that the recipient of such predictions can influence physical events, either consciously or unconsciously?

(A somewhat similar question arises concerning a dream Jane had on November 30th, and a few lines of the data given for the 22nd Dr. Instream test; see the following lines on page 104 of the 213th session: "He received a book by mail today, a biography sort of book, having to do with a personality of the late 1800's. A medium." This material is dated December 1; there follows Jane's dream of the night before.

("November 30. Dream not very clear now. 'The Mediumship of—1885.' I saw a book with this title. A study of the mediumship of a mother and daughter, it seems. Of the Eisenhower or the Kennedy families? As dream opens I see a house; a farmhouse? Someone is bringing this book to the man or men who live there. This is a country rather than a town house. The man who is given the book startles the man who gives it to him by quoting a line from Dante having to do with (his?) not appointing God. This may have been written inside the book cover, for example. Was the book written by a woman? Woke up finally and wrote this down on scrap paper."

(Another possibility here is that Jane and Seth can work as a team, since Seth has said often that Jane has abilities of her own. If this is true in this particular instance, then the dream would contain elements of distortion. We find the study of dreams more and more interesting. Jane has now begun a book on dreams, to be done concurrently with her book on the Seth material itself.

(Also on dreams, recently I have had two extraordinarily vivid dreams involving my brother in Rochester, whom we usually see about twice a year. Seth said during Friday's unscheduled session that these two dreams are significant, and that tonight's regular session would deal with them. My brother, Bill, is due for a visit here next week; which fact was unknown to us when I had the pair of dreams.

(The 20th envelope test was held during this session. See the tracing on page 107. For the test object I used part of one of the paper napkins Jane and I were given when we varied our routine prior to the 213th session, and visited a local discotheque for a beer. See the notes on this on page 102. The results of tonight's test were very interesting. While we were in the discotheque ultraviolet lights were turned on when the entertainment began; this means the test object was viewed by us in this unusual light, and this fact shows in tonight's test data.

(Tonight's session was held in our back room, and was a quiet one. Jane did not smoke while speaking. As usual she sat down; her eyes remained closed for the entire session. Her rate of speaking was good from the start, her voice quiet.)

Good evening.

("Good evening, Seth.")

Now, I told you that I would discuss two dreams in which you were interested. However, since we are going to devote some time to our cat lover, in Washington, I will not begin the discussion of those dreams now. I could not do them justice in a short period, and would like to devote most of one session to them; and so we shall very shortly. Instead let us speak briefly on time and action.

(Seth's favorite name for Peggy Gallagher is the cat lover, since Peg is afraid of cats; and he likes to call Bill Gallagher the Jesuit, because of his never-ending questions.)

As I have told you, <u>all</u> action is basically spontaneous. Only your perception of it adds the illusion of time to action. You think, for example, that any given action consumes or devours or takes up a certain amount of time. Therefore you think of time as something that contains action.

(Seth has given so much material on action that it cannot be assigned to a few sessions. It was mentioned by name before the 15th session or thereabouts. It has been especially stressed since the 120th session, and so continues.)

The dimensions of action itself have nothing to do, basically, with your conception of time. Instead the dimensions of action have to do with intensities; not only the intensities of the electromagnetic components that compose them, but with intensities as they are translated into psychological terms. Therefore the psychological experience of a particular event or action has little to do with clock time.

It is instead composed of the intensity with which it is <u>felt</u> by a given individual. When you speak in terms of the depth of a river, you speak in terms of distance, physical distance. When you speak in terms of the depth of a psychological experience or action, you mean something else entirely, for this is a depth of intensity. And you travel <u>through</u> an experience only so far as your own experience of intensity will allow you.

(Here Seth begins to elaborate on the material on electrical fields and intensities, given in the 120th to 130th sessions. See Volume 3.)

The psychological feeling of intensity has its own electromagnetic reality. An action is an experienced intensity, and need not involve motion in physical terms. As I have said, <u>every</u> action is a part of every other action, and affects every other action, and is also so affected itself. This is <u>not</u> however your cause and effect theory at all.

For the actions are spontaneous basically, again, and the effects exist so swiftly that it is impossible to say that one occurs before or after the other, or <u>causes</u> another. This could be likened to some gigantic, spontaneous motion that happens very swiftly. When you viewed such a gigantic motion with a slow camera, then you would get the effect that you receive within your system, of a continuous time. Where actually perhaps a sudden explosion had taken place, you would see a slow progression of light and motion.

Your concept of time does not of course <u>change</u> time itself, but it does force you to perceive actions in a certain manner. Much of this is the result of the limitations of the physical organism, but much more is the effect of the development of the ego, which attempts to set itself up and apart from action.

The inner self and the deeper layers of the subconscious are relatively free however from the ego's false gods, and it is for this reason that precognitions are at all possible. For these layers of the self are simply able to perceive a larger portion of action than the ego is able or willing to perceive. As a rule, the ego will not even accept the information that is derived in such a manner, for to do so would be to deny those <u>artificial</u> precepts of continuity upon which it <u>feels</u> its dominance rests.

The ego however is quite secure. It would exist regardless, now, of the particular theories of time which might be held, for it is strongly anchored as a specific manipulator of physical reality. And physical reality, believe it or not, is <u>not</u> dependent upon the theory of time as a series of moments.

Your institutions, both cultural and educational, may be dependent upon time as a series of moments, but physical reality itself is not.

I suggest your break.

(*Break at 9:25. Jane was dissociated as usual for a first break. Her eyes had remained closed, and she did not smoke. Her pace had been good from the beginning.*

(*See the 149th-152nd sessions for the material on moment points and time. Once again, the material on time is woven through the sessions. Seth began discussing time in the 14th session. See the sessions 120-130 for material on the electrical field and time, in Volume 3.*

(*Jane has been reading J.B. Priestley's book,* Time and Man, *recently. She is well aware that Seth often discusses her reading matter. She remarked that tonight Seth had elaborated on a few statements Mr. Priestley had made; that is, Seth was not paraphrasing, but carrying ideas further.*

(*We thought it might be time now for Seth to give some data on Peggy Gallagher and her activities in Washington, DC, since in giving the data on the Gallaghers in Puerto Rico last October, he had done so at 9:30 in each session. Jane now resumed with her eyes closed, and at a good pace. She was smiling. Resume at 9:35.*)

One small note here.

Your physicists know that time does not exist, basically, as a series of moments, one following the other. Therefore my earlier remark that physical reality was not <u>dependent</u> upon time as a series of moments should be obvious.

Physical reality is dependent upon your sensual perception of action, and that is all.

Obviously we have more to say here, and so we shall. For since <u>you</u> are operating still within time as a series of moments, we do not have time for that discussion now.

Please give me a moment—and what happens to it when you give it to me?

(Jane, her eyes still closed, paused briefly at 9:37. Her pace now slowed somewhat, and she held a hand up to her closed eyes.)

Now, we shall see what we can do.

A talk concerning survival of your nation. Our friend the cat lover attends this discussion, perhaps in a room numbered 312.

The speaker is interrupted. A question-and-answer session. Three main speakers in the discussion itself. Survival is a strong issue here, though it may not be the title of the discussion, formally.

A tow-headed man with whom our friend comes into contact. She may not like him overmuch.

(It will be recalled that during the unscheduled session of last Friday, December 3, Seth stated that Peggy would meet a man she wouldn't like. Jane and I wonder what part, if any, suggestion can play in such statements, perhaps unwittingly leading the recipient to react adversely to an individual.)

Something to do with a federation. Pamphlets are given out. Directions to a northeast location perhaps, though I do not know, for tomorrow's lecture.

A <u>particular</u> man with a camera slung over his shoulder, who gets our friend's attention. A handkerchief shows above his breast pocket. Pointed, that is a pointed handkerchief, with an initial, perhaps a C or G.

A grab bag of some kind. Theater-type chairs rather than benches.

Incidentally, our Jesuit's ulcer bothers him this evening, quite strongly.

A <u>measurement</u> of abilities, though I do not know to what this refers. 14,000 in all attend, in all sections, though at various times.

The hotel on a corner. <u>Her</u> room above three floors. A man across the way. The number 421.

I suggest your break.

(Break at 9:51. Jane was dissociated as usual. Her eyes remained closed. Her pace had picked up considerably by the time break arrived.

(Note that in Friday's session Seth had mentioned the number 321 to Peggy. In the material above Seth gives the number 312, which is a scrambled 321, and later the number 421. See page 108: Three other impressions checked out.

(It was now time for the 23rd Dr. Instream test. Once again Jane sat with her

hands raised to her closed eyes. Her pace was not too slow, although broken by many pauses. Resume at 10:04.)

Now. Give us a moment once more, for your Dr. Instream material.

A very smallish crowded room. I believe a cocktail party. A woman seems to be the main hostess, though a man is present with her.

Dr. Instream is present, in an absent-minded way. Something is discussed by Dr. Instream and a man, an event that is to occur in February. The first to the <u>middle</u> of the month, rather than to the end. *(Pause.)*

A fabric. He seems to be thinking of a fabric that is <u>nubby</u>. *(Pause.)* Three late arrivals. One of these someone he has been waiting for, or hoped would arrive. A male of middle age, with a mustache. *(Pause at 10:09.)*

He thinks, or speaks, of Dr. Erickson. Or he and the man who arrived late both have Dr. Erickson as a common acquaintance. Perhaps he introduced them.

Two of the late arrivals are men, and one is a woman.

The fabric is either a wall hanging, such as a curtain, or a woman's dress. I pick up the number 13. Could this be the date in February for the event? Or perhaps there are 13 guests present.

I also think of January 3 as a fairly important date for Dr. Instream. *(Pause at 10:12.)*

Now, do you have a test for me, Joseph?

("Yes."

(I handed over the double envelope, and as usual Jane took it with her eyes remaining closed. She held the envelope in both hands for a moment, then delivered the data with short pauses. This is our 20th envelope test.)

Please give us a moment. These are impressions.

A turn up, something turned up. A photograph. I think of white, snow white. A house. A connection with the past, and with your parents.

Also a connection with another person beside yourself and Ruburt. Purple. Large letters. Something fairly important occurred the following day. A machine such as an automobile, perhaps.

The color yellow as in sunlight, and a gathering. Strongly connected—this item strongly connected with yourself. I see your initials.

I suggest your break.

(Break at 10:17. Jane was dissociated as usual. She said she didn't particularly remember what she had said on the three tests, but could to some degree if she stopped to think.

(See the tracing of the test object, the napkin from the discotheque, on page 107.

(The design on the napkin covers one quarter of the surface area, and it was this quarter which was "turned up" to us when the waitress placed the folded napkins

on the table before us. There was of course no photo involved, or a house or any connection with my parents, or the past.

(Jane felt that "white, snow white," was valid data, even though she was thinking of a certain photo of my parent's house, taken when there was deep snow. She saw this white as very bright. See my notes on page 109. When the ultraviolet lights were turned on in the discotheque, some colors were activated more than others. The light was actually quite dim, but the ultraviolet made anything white appear to be blinding white-paper, socks, white shirts, etc. The effect was very striking. The napkin was of white paper.

(There were two female dancers at the discotheque, and Jane felt that "a connection with another person" referred to one of these, although she couldn't say why. We did not know either of them. One was brunette, one was blonde. Both of us liked the brunette the best, for whatever reason, and certainly she was the better dancer of the two.

(Jane felt good about "Purple. Large letters." See the tracing. The word discotheque on the napkin was printed in a blue that was strongly on the red side, although actually short of being an outright purple. The letters are of course large. "Something fairly important... the following day" did not ring a bell with us. "automobile" could refer to our driving to the discotheque, though there could be other meanings here, we think.

("yellow, as in sunlight," is as interesting to us as the snow-white data listed above. Jane wore a white blouse to the discotheque. When the ultraviolet lights were turned on however, we were surprised to see a large, bright yellow stain on the front of her now brilliantly-white blouse. This stain was invisible in ordinary light. In addition, we discovered more similar yellow stains on both of Jane's palms. We never did discover the source of the stains.

("a gathering" can refer to the crowded discotheque, or bar. I wouldn't say the napkin was an "item strongly connected" to me, although it was my napkin rather than Jane's that I used for the test. Nor were my initials on it.

(Jane said that as she began giving the data, the association she made with Seth's data, "white, snow white," led her to consider the particular photo of my parents' house taken after a deep snowfall. She said that at this stage of her development it is very difficult for her to tell when such personal associations enter in, unless Seth himself notes it by saying "Ruburt here thinks of a photograph," etc. Jane said she saw the photo in her mind's eye, but that as she continued to speak, she eventually received a hazy picture, a "nebulous impression," of a bar. She did not mention the bar in the test data, and indeed had forgotten it until our discussion of the test brought it back to her mind.

(Jane finished her comments by noting that there isn't much she can do at the moment about being sidetracked by such personal associations, except to keep it in mind. She does believe that this knowledge has in itself prevented her from being led astray from Seth's data a few times in the past, and that her ability in separating Seth's data from her own will grow.

(We now hoped Seth would comment on the test before ending the session. Jane resumed in a quiet voice, with her eyes closed, at 10:30.)

Now, we will end our session.

We picked up some valid impressions. The other person was your dancer, upon whom you both were strongly focused.

The important event had to do with some kind of a family nature, and involved one of the two dancers, and their parents, or the parents of whichever girl was involved. I believe the event concerned the other dancer, the blonde.

(There may be an outside chance that we can confirm this data. A friend of ours who lives in our apartment house knows the two dancers, who live together in the neighborhood. But we do not know them, and this was the first time Jane and I had been in the discotheque in over a year.)

The snow white referred to the colors, or to the color, rather, of the napkin in the light. The snow I used merely because the white was so blinding, and this led Ruburt to his own associations, concerning your parents' house, and a particular photograph which was taken in the wintertime. But we managed to continue on after this, to deliver some fairly decent impressions. He is still learning, and it is quite all right.

My fondest wishes to you both, and to our Dr. Instream. I would suggest, incidentally, that you both if possible find time to do the yoga exercises daily, as they provide excellent discipline, and tend to unify various portions of the self. Also, during Christmas week, when I am giving you a vacation, I would suggest that Ruburt rest from psychic affairs entirely.

Now if you have any questions, you may take a brief break, and I will answer them, or you may end the session as you prefer.

("What do you think of Jane's book on dreams?")

Ruburt has a very good beginning, and the book should be very successful; later books on the subject will be more advanced, with experiments to back up theory, but this book will be a very good start. A slight change of title will be beneficial. If you have no more questions, then I shall bid you a fond good evening.

("What title change do you recommend?")

He will think of it.

("I guess that's it, then. Good night, Seth."

(End at 10:42. Jane was dissociated as usual. Her eyes had remained closed.)

(Tracing of the woodblock print used in the 21st envelope test, in the 215th session for December 8, 1965.)

SESSION 215
DECEMBER 8, 1965 9 PM WEDNESDAY AS SCHEDULED

(The 21st envelope test was held during the session. The test object sealed in the usual double envelopes was a woodblock print, made by an artist friend of ours, Roy C. Fox, and enclosed with Roy's Christmas card of last Christmas. It is a black and white print on very thin, almost transparent paper. Once again the test results were interesting, and somewhat different in nature.

SESSION 215

(*We were not sure that Seth would have any data on Peggy Gallagher during the session, since we thought it possible she had left Washington, DC by now.*

(*It will be remembered that on two past occasions Seth has taken credit for making a candle flame grow noticeably in height. See my notes prior to the 206th session, pages 57-58. Both of these sessions were witnessed. Seth told us he was able to do such things when Ruburt's attention was elsewhere, but that as soon as "he", or Ruburt, became conscious of the possibility of such effects they were usually unattainable.*

(*Before the session this evening I wondered what effects Seth might be able to demonstrate, on a consistent basis, if a candle were lit just before each session, as a matter of routine, and then ignored as much as possible. The idea being that if it became part of the regular session routine Jane would forget about it, thus allowing any possible effects to come through without worrying about them. At first I was joking about the idea, but when Jane said it was all right to go ahead with the idea, I took her up on it. When we were set up for the session, I placed a lighted candle on the shelf beside me, behind some books so that Jane could not see it. Since the room was well lighted the candle flame would make no noticeable difference, in the event it flared up while her eyes were open.*

(*The session was held in our small back room. No windows were open, and by measurement I determined that the candle flame burned at a remarkably consistent $3/4$-inch height. Jane began speaking while sitting down and with her eyes closed. Her pace was rather slow, with many pauses, yet her voice was somewhat stronger than usual. She sat much of the time with a hand raised to her face. She was not smoking. She began speaking at 9:01.*)

Good evening.

("Good evening, Seth.")

Now. Let us continue our discussion. I did not say that action was not motion. I want this clear. Action is motion, but not necessarily motion that is perceived in physical terms.

(*See page 110.*)

Your conception of time is dependent upon your perception of action, and that portion of action which you can perceive and appreciate. There is no doubt here that the intuitions can at times perceive action far more completely than can the intellect. And time, therefore, physical clock time, is much more alien to the intuitive self than it is to the intellectual self.

Logic builds its monuments step by step, one thought before the other in a series where each thought or deduction is dependent upon the thought before. The intuitions are of a more spontaneous nature, and less dependent upon such step-by-step movements.

(It was now 9:09. I had been glancing occasionally at the candle flame as I wrote. It burned within a foot of my left hand. The flame had now increased perhaps a quarter of an inch in height, and burned steadily at that level; this meant an increase from ³/₄ of an inch to one inch.

(I was not sure of what I was observing. Jane gave no sign of any kind, and Seth had not even mentioned the candle; I had thought he might smile at the idea. The increase in the flame's height had not been as sudden and dramatic as in the two previous instances noted on page 117. But the candle flame now burned at this new height just as steadily as it had before the increase, and continued to do so.)

The ego attempts to break down action into smaller and smaller units. The intuitions try to perceive action as a whole. The ego breaks down for purposes of examination, the intuitions construct. Both the ego and the intuitions, in performing their functions, obviously create action. The self may of course be considered as a gestalt of action, perceived in a different manner by various levels of itself.

On one hand, basically, the self is <u>limitless</u>, both electromagnetically and because of the nature of action, which affects all other action. The self does not however proceed along straight lines, from a birth to a death. This is only the self that the ego perceives. Action cannot remain inactive or motionless, though the motion may not always be apparent.

Ego's concept of itself as a rock of unchanging identity is highly ludicrous, since its perceptions constantly change it from what it was. It is not a thing proceeding, by any means. This is not to deny the human aspects of the ego, for the ego is also somewhat like a light carried in front of the inner self, a light that gives meaning to the physical universe and to its objects. It enables the inner self to manipulate within physical reality. It translates outer data to the inner personality.

I suggest your break.

(Break at 9:21. Jane had been dissociated for a first break as usual. She maintained the heavier, emphatic voice, even with the pauses.

(The candle flame had maintained its increased height very steadily until close to break time, when I thought it began to fluctuate a bit. At break I thought it was mainly at its original lower height. Jane could not see it, and did not ask about its behavior. We agreed not to mention it during sessions, no matter what took place. I had wondered if the increased height of the flame had resulted from the body of the candle "warming up," since it was a thick one, perhaps five inches tall. When the flame subsided however at break, I did not know what to think, and decided to merely record what I saw without being concerned.

(Jane now sat with her eyes closed and spoke in a slow voice with many pauses,

most of them short. Her eyes remained closed. Resume at 9:31.)

Now give us a moment, please.

A banquet by your cat lover, with long narrow tables. A disturbance of some sort, though not necessarily here. An endeavor to reach someone whom she was unable to contact, the initials perhaps W. B.

Again, a clock that did not work correctly.

(This bit of data was also given to Peggy on Friday, December 3, during the unscheduled session preceding her Washington trip. By now, also, I saw that the candle flame had climbed back up to its one-inch height; it continued to burn steadily at that height. Jane's voice had lost its heavier edge.)

Something with a new format. Ten people in a separate party or gathering, in which she took part. Something having to do with March 10.

A room with a <u>yellow</u> wastepaper basket. Flowers in the room, perhaps roses. But florist's flowers.

An event at eight, last evening, in a different room than the room in which a previous meeting was held, that she attended.

(The candle flame subsided to its beginning ³/₄-inch height for a few minutes, then climbed back up again.)

McNamara. A white taxicab. Identified by a round symbol on it, with a border inside the circle, and some sort of figures. Whether these are people, shapes or object shapes, I do not know. The symbol is of more than one color, however, and fairly dark against the white. I am seeing it in the evening, so the color of the symbol is not very clear. It is in front of a stone building.

An unusual attachment of aides goes with the group which she accompanies. There is some hesitation at a gate while this gathering waits. While clearance is made, but it is a short hesitation.

I pick up something to do with a ballpark, or a park that has been used, or a stadium that has been used for ball games.

Something to do with a pocketbook. Did she misplace it? It is a shoulder variety however. Perhaps it was a camera.

I suggest a brief break.

(Break at 9:45. Jane had been dissociated as usual, and her eyes had remained closed. The candle flame once more subsided to its original lower level. At either the ³/₄ or the one-inch level, the flame burned very steadily, for there was no draft. Nor did it seek out intermediate levels.

(Seth dwelt on the taxicab symbol, and as he did so I found myself hoping that Peggy would notice it. We have wondered before about Seth making statements concerning something that might be in the presence of the subject for the test, only to have the subject fail to notice it. This happened in a test about a year ago, involving

Bill Macdonnel on vacation in Cape Cod. Seth described a certain rowboat with initials and a symbol on its bow; but since Bill failed to notice rowboats in general, we were at a loss as to the accuracy of Seth's information. Seth did insist that this particular boat had been in Bill's close vicinity.

(*During this break Jane said she had the feeling the pocketbook data, given at the end of Peggy's test, might not refer to Peggy at all, but to "something or someone else." As it developed in our envelope test tonight, this could be true. If so it is an example of the "bleeding" of test material from one test to another during the same session. Seth has told us this is a possibility. In this specific case also, clairvoyance enters in, since the envelope test had not been held yet. Telepathy and precognition could also be factors.*

(*Jane said she didn't see anything within while giving the Gallagher data.*

(*It was now time for the 24th Dr. Instream test. As before, Jane sat quietly with her eyes closed, her right hand raised to her face. The candle flame remained at its original ³/₄-inch level. Resume at 10:01.*)

Now. Give us a moment for our Dr. Instream material.

He is in his room *(pause)*, a photograph of his wife on a dresser. Some books or papers on the bed. *(Pause.)* Is he dressing to go out at this hour? Or do I have him earlier? *(Long pause at 10:04.)*

A strained relationship between himself and another, a man. *(Pause.)*

Hypnosis experiments temporarily at a standstill. He is focusing on us, however *(pause)*, trying to send us a message about a round object and a piece of paper, that is written on about a third of the way down, with neat indentation, perhaps five lines or so.

Very even, as if lines from a poem. The indentations are so neat. *(Pause)* But the lines themselves are fairly long.

I believe, though I am not certain, that this is handwritten rather than typewritten. The letters are small. There may be a book, a fairly large one, beneath the paper, with something like dull gold-edged pages, or so it would appear when the book is closed. And brownish covers to the book.

I do not believe it is a new book. I have the impression of worn leather, though I do not actually believe the binding is of leather, but of something allied in appearance. *(Pause.)*

Two candlesticks. I have the impression also that he is discouraged, but affairs will work out well for him.

I pick up quite strongly a discouragement on his part this evening. But again, his affairs will work out. The discouragement seems to be connected with his work, and a lack of confidence that is temporary. By Sunday he will feel much better, partially as a result of intervening circumstances, and partly because his mood will simply have changed. *(Pause at 10:16.)*

Now, do you have a test for me?

("Yes."

(Jane reached out to take the usual double envelope from me. She did not open her eyes. She sat quietly holding the envelope in one hand, with the other raised to her face. Her pauses were brief. This is our 21st envelope test.)

Again, please give us a moment.

I wanted to add something about shipyards to the Gallagher material.

(In the apartment below ours a baby began to cry. The sound was subdued, yet plain enough in our very quiet room. I was afraid Jane might be distracted, but she gave no outward sign. She continued after a pause. The baby soon stopped crying.)

Our own test, then. These are impressions.

Two people at a table with straight chairs.

An item recently purchased. A connection with a February event. A circular object of sun or moon shape. A color green. 1965. A connection with two other people, I believe male and female.

A lack of discretion. A border. The number 3.

Something like ropes, or something tied. A connection with a parent. The color blue. <u>Ruburt</u> thinks of the package that his mother sent him, containing a sweater, and the stamp on the package.

I suggest your break.

(Break at 10:23. Jane was dissociated as usual. Her eyes had remained closed, her pace had been interrupted by many short pauses. The candle flame had remained subdued.

(At first the envelope test data left us at a loss, until memory began to work. To sum up first, we saw that Seth had used the name of the artist who had executed the block print, Roy Fox, as a starting point for data involving Jane and Roy and me, but for some reason had not dealt with the test object itself. We do not know why this happened, since Seth did not discuss the results this evening. Jane's mother and a Christmas present also entered the test data, for reasons we do understand; here Seth tells us that Ruburt thinks of the package that his mother sent him.

(Roy Fox is a personal friend of ours. Last Christmas he arranged for me to have a show of paintings at Harris Hill Inn, just outside Elmira, in February 1965. The show lasted for a month. It opened on February 2, 1965, and on the following Sunday, February 7, Jane and I were guests at the Inn, to discuss the show with anyone interested.

(This brings us to the first item in the test data, "Two people at a table with straight chairs." On February 7 Jane and I spent several hours at the Inn, seated on straight backed chairs at a dining table, ready to answer questions from all and

sundry.

(We see no connection at the moment with "An item recently purchased."

("A connection with a February event," is the show at Harris Hill Inn, arranged by Roy Fox. "A circular object of sun or moon shape" does not mean anything in particular to us, although on the walls at the Inn were various circular objects, such as clocks, a barometer, etc. The same applies to "A color green." Many of my paintings, being landscapes, are predominantly green. The show was held in "1965."

("A connection with two other people... male and female," refers to the fact that Jane and I were scheduled to meet a young married couple, friends of ours, later in the afternoon at the Inn. They did appear: Judy and Lee Wright, who witnessed the unscheduled 129th session, incidentally, that was held that same evening, February 7, 1965. See Volume 3.

("A lack of discretion" is of particular interest to Jane and me, since this is a most apt description of a situation Roy Fox was involved in during that February, 1965, and for several months before and after that month. The situation was common knowledge, so no confidences are violated to say that at the time Roy was keeping company with a woman who was separated from her husband, but not divorced. She had several children. Roy is a man in his sixties, had never married, and since he seemed so completely happy in this situation we had assumed marriage would follow. The woman's husband returned to Elmira last summer, however.

("A border. The number 3," refers we believe to the notice for the show, printed in the local paper on February 6, 1965. It was a two-column notice with a heavy black border, and stated that I would be at the show on February 7, 1965, from 1 to 3 PM.

(The rest of the test data applies to the Christmas package Jane's mother sent her early this week. The package was wrapped with twine, contained a blue knitted sweater, etc. Why this information cropped up in a test we do not know. We can see the connection with the Roy Fox data however, since Roy made the block print; his name is also on the test object. We would like to know why Seth chose to use Roy's name as a springboard, however, instead of sticking to the test object.

(See the notes on page 120, dealing with the data in Peggy Gallagher's test, concerning a misplaced pocketbook of the shoulder variety. As stated, Jane at the time of the Gallagher test said she believed this information did not refer to Peggy. After the envelope test material was in on tonight's test, she then realized an incident involving a lost shoulder-variety pocketbook of her own.

(Harris Hill Inn was closed on Monday, February 1, 1965, and Jane and I met the proprietor there Monday evening and hung the paintings. When we left Jane left her favorite pocketbook behind; she did not realize this until sometime later. The next day the proprietor of the Inn brought Jane's pocketbook to her. If this information

was misplaced in the earlier Gallagher material, then what accounts for it? It appeared in the Gallagher material before the envelope test was held, and of course Jane could not know what the envelope test object was beforehand, by ordinary means. Seth has stated that such terms as telepathy, clairvoyance, precognition, etc., are of but relative usefulness; perhaps this instance is but an example of the ability of part of the mind to dissolve the time barrier.

(It is actually Friday, December 11 as I type this. We have now obtained a written detailed report on Peggy Gallagher's trip to Washington, as compared to Seth's material on Peggy in the last two sessions. Seth scored many hits—Jane's best effort in these tests by far. The material will be incorporated in a very early session, along with the material on the Gallagher's Puerto Rico vacation of last October. I am leading up to the statement that Peggy detected a very clear example of bleeding through of data in the 214th session. She states that the material at the beginning of the Dr. Instream test data, on page 113, applies to a cocktail party she attended in Washington on Monday, December 6. Peggy states Seth's description here of the cocktail party is quite correct, even to the fact that a woman was the main hostess, and that a man, her husband, was present with her. The smallish crowded room data applies also here. More details will be given later. See Session 214.

(And as Seth has mentioned before, such a bleeding through of data from one test to another is a possibility. Nor does the above example mean that Dr. Instream did not attend a cocktail party.

(Jane would like me to add here that she believes the envelope test data of this evening developed the way it did because of the emotional content of events involving Jane, Roy and myself. Whereas Roy's blockprint, while appealing to us both, was comparatively lacking in such emotional content, intrinsically.

(Jane now resumed at an average pace, with her eyes again closed, at 10:33.)

I am not going to discuss our test this evening.

However, we will shortly hold a session where we discuss our tests in general, as this will be of benefit to you. It will help you to interpret our data. Also, I have not forgotten your dreams, and next week we shall have time for them.

Unless you have some questions we will end our session.

("Do you want to say something about the candle-flame test?")

(The candle flame had been burning quite steadily at its original $3/4$-inch level since break at 9:45. Jane now smiled.)

What do you want me to say?

("Do you think this kind of test is a good idea?")

There is nothing wrong with the idea. We shall see what we can do. We have been trying to see what we can do.

("Yes. I wondered.")

(Jane now sat quite still. Her eyes remained closed, The candle was to her right, approximately at right angles to her body as she sat facing forward. Remember she could not see the candle in any event, since it was hidden behind books, and that the room was well lighted. As the moments passed and Jane did not move or speak, I had plenty of time to observe that her eyes did not open. The candle was some three feet away from her, and well away from any draft possibly created by her breath, for instance.

(As soon as I realized that Jane or Seth might be attempting something, I sat very quietly myself so as not to stir the air, and breathed shallowly through my nose with my head somewhat averted. I did not even move my hand to write until close to a minute had passed. The air in the room was very still. Yet soon after this strange interlude began, the candle flame grew quite definitely back to its one-inch height, and remained there steadily.

(Seth broke the silence well after a full minute had passed, according to the sweep hand on our electric clock.)

My best wishes to you, and a fond good evening.

("Good night, Seth.")

(End at 10:36. Jane was dissociated as usual The candle flame remained high, but was not as steady as it had been. Jane said that while she sat silently she felt as though Seth was somehow focusing "sideways" on the candle.

(Jane told me she felt a definite thrust of what she presumed to be energy toward the candle. It was a feeling she had not experienced before. She also had the thought as she sat quietly that Seth wanted to say something about the candle. Jane felt she might distort the information, however, because she realized that whatever she wanted to say was not automatic as it usually is; therefore she said nothing.

(Jane was relaxing on the bed, as she often does after a session, with her head propped up on one hand. She was smoking as we discussed the candle experiment. Both of us stared at the flame. It was now a little higher, and bright and steady, reaching the highest level of the evening. We stared at it for perhaps a minute. Seth then came through again, briefly; Jane was still smoking, and her eyes were closed. Resume at 10:45.)

Now. Do not emphasize the candle. Simply have it present during sessions, and lit. But do not draw Ruburt's attention to it. Certainly not in the beginning, for we want him to consciously forget that the candle is here.

("Yes.")

That is all.

("Good night, Seth.")

(End at 10:46.)

SESSION 216
DECEMBER 9, 1965 8:30 PM THURSDAY UNSCHEDULED

(It will be remembered that in recent sessions Seth has promised to discuss two dreams which have been on my mind recently. Both of these involved my younger brother Bill, who lives in Rochester, NY with his wife and 3 children.

(Actually, I have had a series of five dreams since October 27, 1965, which I believe to be closely related. All of them involved myself in situations of rather drastic physical stress or outright peril. Since the outcome of the dreams left me whole, however, it seemed their symbolic meaning concerned conflicts other than the physical, and I was interested in pinning these down.

(The last in the series took place last night, and since it dealt with extreme situations concerning my own death, Jane and I thought it wise to inquire into it. I had thought of next Monday's session as being soon enough at first, but by now the dreams were on my mind enough so that we thought of an unscheduled session. Also, other material in the regular sessions seemed to push the dream material aside.

(The five dreams occurred on the evenings of October 27, November 19, December 1, December 3, and December 8. Since Seth deals only with dreams of November 19, December 1, and December 8, only these will be presented here from my dream notebook. Seth calls them dreams number 1, 2, and 3. The two dreams not given here are closely similar to the three presented below.

(Dream # 1; November 19, 1965: This was extremely sharp and vivid in detail, and in full color. My younger brother Bill and I were in a very deep mountain valley, with steep rocky brown walls. We were trapped in this valley and knew we might not get out. It was not too large. We were actually in a rickety old house on the valley's slope, perhaps halfway up. There was a sharp drop-off below us. Part of the time I was looking out of a window, and part of the time I stood on the roof or a porch with Bill, our backs pressed up against the side of the house. The shingled roof slanted down and was covered with a fine snow. We were afraid to move because it was very slippery.

(Then I was looking at Bill, off to my left. He was too close to the edge of the porch roof. I hollered at him to be careful. Even as I did he slipped, landed on his backside, then tumbled over the edge as he scrambled for his balance. I heard him hit the ground with such force that I was very afraid he had broken a limb. I then looked over the edge of the roof, and to my great agitation I saw that Dick had not only fallen off the roof and hit the ground hard, but that now he had slipped over the edge of a steep cliff beside the porch, and was saving himself only by grasping a skinny little shrub that was in the process of loosening in the frozen ground. At the same time, Bill looked up at me and I thought he was smiling; or at least he didn't

appear to be worried.

(I then realized that I could go over the edge of the roof at the corner, where there was a drainpipe to use as a handhold, then reach down and save him by lifting him back up with one hand. I also realized that I could move more easily on this slippery roof than I had thought possible.

(Dream # 2; December 1,1965: In color, and sharp and vivid and very detailed. My younger brother Bill and I were in swimming. The water was a beautiful light blue-green, almost like bathwater, and was extremely pleasant and comfortable. We were in a stream above a high and rapid waterfall, with the surface of the water about us broken by rocks. I got the idea of going over the waterfall while holding my breath, yet hesitated.

(Then Bill went ahead, his body curled up into a ball, much like a fetal position. I saw him coast over the edge of the fall. I followed, holding my breath, and felt no shock or fear especially. It was very pleasant. I went deep down into the water at the base of the falls. I let myself float along, knowing that if I held my breath I would rise to the surface. At the same time I somehow knew there was a large underground rock ahead in the stream. It was like a pillar or barrier, dark and rough, reaching up high toward the surface. Still under water, I opened my eyes in plenty of time to see it ahead, and avoided hurting myself against its rough surface.

(I later thought of the pillarlike rock as a phallic symbol; and of the warm water and the fetuslike position of my brother as reincarnational information.

(Dream # 3; December 8,1965: Again in color. A long involved dream; believe part of the beginning of it escaped me as I woke up. The dream had to do with the fact that for some reason I was to be executed, by painless injection. I do not know why. At least part of the time I was in a brick-walled room partially underground. I think my father was to give me the needle.

(To the best of my recall I was not very afraid at any time, yet was sad and concerned. There was an examination table in this room, and I was to lay there while I received the injection. Part of the time I looked out of a window made up of many small panes of glass, and saw Jane on a swing outside the window. She was fully grown, dressed as though in the summertime; someone else was on the swing with her, but I do not know who. She didn't appear to be worried about my predicament.

(I believe that my own feeling was one of sadness that I wouldn't be with her, more than anything else in the dream. Part of the time I was also outside of this brick room. I also believe that I had received the injection, and that it was supposed to take effect hours ago, but hadn't done so. So here I was hours later, wandering around. I thought of Jane but did not see her, and still felt this sadness and concern much more than any fear. I believe the dream ended on this note. At no time in the dream did

I actually see my father; I merely knew he was there, and involved.

(The two dreams not given but very similar to the three here quoted involved myself and cancer and my survival, and my being separated from Jane again, and strongly aware of sadness and concern.

(Jane and I think the following material an excellent example of the way Seth interprets dreams, and it is presented in full. Seth doesn't get all the way through his analysis, but promises to in an early session. However, he told us enough tonight to make me feel much better.

(When Jane expressed a willingness to hold the session, she sipped a glass of wine while we waited for Seth to appear. I sat beside her on our living room couch, notebook in my lap. We listened to music. Nevertheless the start of the session caught me by surprise. Jane took off her glasses, closed her eyes and began to speak in a quiet voice.)

Now, there is no need for a musical accompaniment to this session.

("Just a minute then."

(I turned off the television set. Jane's eyes were closed, but were to shortly open briefly; they remained closed for most of the session. Her pace was fairly fast, although she waited until I sat down again before resuming.)

The dreams are realities on several levels.

Primarily they refer to your own subconscious feelings toward your father. Not only in regard to yourself, but in regard to your younger brother, and to Ruburt. Now this is on one level, and for a few moments we shall speak about the dreams on this level only.

(Her eyes now closed again, Jane wagged a forefinger at me.)

You lose advantage, Joseph, from your recorder. You lose the advantage of your recorder. In sessions such as these it would be most handy for you.

Ruburt could transcribe the notes, and I could speak to you more clearly.

On this level therefore, the three most important of these dreams are related: the two regarding your brother, and the dream that had to do with execution by needle, a painless one, to be carried out by your father.

In the first dream you see your younger brother slipping on an icy roof and falling. You go to his aid; discovering that you can manipulate better than you thought, you jump off the roof only to discover that your brother had also fallen over the edge of the cliff and was hanging on until you could get to him.

The second dream finds you both in water, headed toward a falls. You think of holding your breath and going under, but your younger brother does this before you, and you follow. You are not hurt and you avoid a barrier that is in the water.

In the third dream you face a painless execution which is to be carried out by your father, who will give you the needle. You see Ruburt, who is on a swing, and you are concerned and sad. Later you find yourself unhurt. You wander about, see Ruburt once more, and again you are concerned for him.

(Note that the last line above says I saw Jane again in the dream. My own notes say I did not see her again; that is, I did not remember doing so when I awoke and wrote out my account of the dream. I may very well have actually seen Jane twice in the dream.

(Seth also notes a few other discrepancies, later in the session, between the actual dream events and my written account.)

I realize that I have left some details out, but the details that have been left out belong in other layers of the dreams.

Now. All of these dreams have to do with your subconscious feeling that you and your younger brother could go under, mainly in a financial, but also in an emotional way, because of your father.

The furnace which you are all purchasing for your family is important here. The snow and ice in the first dream represent the fact that your parents were not warm. Dick went in debt to get the furnace. He <u>fell</u> into debt, as he fell off the roof; and on his part the purchase was an emotional and impulsive one.

Although you did not really agree, you leaped in to help him; as you jumped off the roof to go to his aid, you found that he had fallen farther than you thought over the edge of the cliff, and was hanging on. This represented further debt that he has taken on. He had fallen further in debt.

Now you are afraid in the next dream that you both are in over your heads, so you see yourself and your brother in the water. He is still ahead of you, for he is now up to his neck in debt. You are not but you fear that your family situation, your parent situation, could put you in a like condition.

You then project this, thinking that it would happen to your brother first. So he goes under first, and you follow. You come to the surface because you realize that you would never in actuality let <u>that</u> kind of a situation keep you under for long. You do not see your brother because you are not so sure that such a condition could not keep him under indefinitely.

(My account of the dream doesn't mention my actually coming to the surface of the water, but does deal with my holding my breath so that I will automatically rise to the surface; I had no doubt in the dream that I would do so. Nor did I see Dick again after we went over the falls. Seth is correct here.)

I suggest a brief break; and while we are at it, we shall tie these in with the third and most significant dream. I presume your hand is tired.

("A little."

(Break at 8:55. Jane said she had been dissociated more than usual, especially for a first delivery. She thought Seth might have seen to this in order to keep her from blocking. Her eyes had opened once briefly near the beginning of the session. Her rate of speaking had kept me writing rapidly.

(At break I remarked to Jane that she need not hold a session of regular length this evening. Now that we had a little information, I thought we could wait for more if she didn't care to continue. She resumed in the same fast manner, her eyes closed, at 9:00.)

While we are at it, you had better get what you can.

The first dream stated the situation as you saw it at present. Dick you saw as having fallen into debt; and you, by increasing your financial allotment to your parents to help pay for the furnace, had jumped in after him to his aid.

The second dream projected the fears of the first, anticipating what you were afraid would happen in the future.

You would both go under. You thought you could come out all right, but you were not certain of your brother.

Now the last dream looks for the causes behind the situation, and the main key to it is the needle symbol, which on the one hand is a symbol for the penis. But it is <u>not</u> a phallic symbol, which has wider and deeper symbolic and racial implications than this one.

To some extent also the water symbol of the previous dream represented your mother's womb, and was a connection to the penis symbol of the next dream. Now. The execution, which you feared, was a symbol for the death of many hopes, both financial hopes and artistic ones. For you would have to get further work, you feared, to help your parents. And to you this would represent a type of execution.

It was to be painless simply because your father did not mean in the dream to hurt you on purpose. But he would do it nevertheless, so you felt. The puzzlement is obvious. You did not see how he could do this to you.

In the earlier dreams you were certain of your capacity to survive the situation which you feared. In this dream you faced the possibility that you would not survive so easily. Ruburt is in this episode because now you worry about the effect of your own reaction upon his condition in general.

Also, you are not at all certain in the dream that you would not prefer <u>him</u> to find outside employment, rather than increase your own work load, if a situation arose in which money was needed for your parents. Because your parents rather than his were involved you felt sadness and concern, because such a move on your part, you felt, would be unfair.

In the end however you have survived. You are still concerned for Ruburt because you realize that as a matter of survival added funds for your family would have to come from his efforts, since your own painting time is too important to lose. Your father personally did not appear because literally you could not see him doing this to you. So you did not see him give you the needle.

For a very good reason you have forgotten a portion of the dream. At the last moment you simply walked out of the room, and refused to have this done to you. You did not remember this detail simply because it seems to you that you should make every sacrifice for your father. The concern and sadness you felt then, for Ruburt, was false, and added on to hide the fact that you had refused to be sacrificed.

Do you understand this last portion?

("Yes.")

(Jane's eyes had opened once again, rather briefly. They open again within a couple of paragraphs, when she lights a cigarette and sips at a glass of wine. Seth is right; I did forget the above portion of the dream, and my notes bear no reference to it.)

You are subconsciously very concerned with your parents' situation, and also you anticipate financial difficulties because of them. You are also worried about your brother, and all of these have piled up.

The other dream levels had to do with reincarnational material. Your brother is taking too much on as a result of his own impulsive nature, and you recognize that he could indeed go under long before yourself, so to speak, although he is younger.

The dreams very clearly show your fear and concern. There is also some element of distorted clairvoyance, in that your father's death—when it does occur, and it is not imminent—will finally be a painless one.

(Added later: Seth was correct. My father's death was peaceful and painless—six years later, on February 5, 1971.)

You are ashamed to admit that to some extent you resent the payments that you both make, and this is the main reason why these fears were not recognized sufficiently by the ego, but forced into the subconscious where they made themselves known in this manner.

You may now end the session, or take a break as you prefer. I believe I have answered your most urgent questions. There are other dream connections that can be made if you want to pursue them further, however.

("Perhaps you can finish this up next session then.")

As you wish.

("I'd like to thank you very much.")

I stand thanked.

("Good night, Seth.")

(End at 9:20. Jane was dissociated as usual. Her eyes were closed most of the time, her pace quite fast. She said she could have continued, but I thought we had made a good start.)

(Tracing of the child's drawing used in the 22nd envelope test, in the 217th session for December 13, 1965.)

SESSION 217
DECEMBER 13, 1965 9 PM MONDAY AS SCHEDULED

(In the unscheduled 203rd session of October 28, with the Gallaghers as witnesses, Seth gave some information having to do with the Incas reaching Florida and building small settlements. Whether this is established historically Jane and I do not know. We would merely like to note here the appearance of an article in the New York Times for December 5, 1965. This had to do with a team of anthropologists launching a four-year study to assess the culture of a wandering tribe of Indians in South Florida. The Indians came from Central or South America. Some remains have been found. The article did not say these Indians were Inca. Interestingly enough, one of the three anthropologists heading the expedition is Dr. John M.

Lonyear 3d, of Colgate. Serious digging begins next month.

(The 22nd envelope test was held this evening. The test object was a ball-point pen drawing of a dog; my four-year-old nephew made it while my brother Bill's family and Jane and I visited my parents last Sunday. I thought David's drawing good for one his age, and added notes of my own. I intended to file it for the future, but today decided it would make a good test subject. Jane had not seen it. The drawing is on paper the weight of this page. A drawing on the back doesn't apply here. I sealed it in the usual double envelopes, between two pieces of Bristol.

(As suggested by Seth in the 212th session, I have been keeping a record of outside weather conditions just preceding each session. Seven categories of data are involved.

(Once again, as described in the 215th session, a candle was lighted just before the session began. As before, it was sheltered from Jane's vision. The room was well lighted. As soon as I lit the candle the flame soared up to a height that was easily two inches, and remained there without interruption for about twenty minutes. This was twice as high as in the 215th session. The same candle was used. Jane knew it was lit of course but we did not talk about it, and she did not see the flame until first break. I could not account for the extraordinary height of the flame. There were no drafts; the session was held in our small back room, and the windows were closed.

(Jane began speaking while sitting down, at an average pace and in an average voice; her pace soon began to speed up. As in the 213th session, her eyes opened as soon as she began speaking, which is quite unusual. Jane's eyes continued to open and close while she spoke.)

You may put this into your records or you may not, as you prefer. And you will have to take my word for what I am saying for the present, regardless of how impatient you may be.

Ruburt's book will do very well. I am not speaking now in terms of riches. Nevertheless your immediate financial worries will definitely be over within a two-year period, when his other books will also begin to show in financial terms. You will be quite comfortably situated.

I suggest that you purchase the Sherman book by all means.

Your holiday plans can be of excellent benefit to you both. Your friend Mark telepathically picked up your attitudes concerning his friend at your last meeting, not this evening's meeting, and he changed some of his plans because of your attitudes.

On that particular occasion he was, contrary to appearances, quite open to suggestion because he was off guard. You did him a service by going out with him that evening, although you may have not realized it. And in some respects he is good for you. Particularly you, Joseph. He stretches you, both your sympathies and your understanding, and you both benefit.

(*The book mentioned by Seth is one on ESP by Harold Sherman.*

(*Mark is Bill Macdonnel's entity name. Bill has witnessed several earlier sessions. The holiday plans concern a party we planned with Bill, to be held at his art gallery.*

(*Jane and I went dancing with Bill and his girlfriend, whom we had not met before, two weekends ago. Bill appeared to be much smitten, and during the evening paid little attention to us, much to our amusement. This evening he surprised Jane and me by telling us he was not seeing the girl anymore. Jane and I said nothing to him about his girl; we liked her very much. She is quite young. Bill is 27.*)

We shall have much to say concerning the interaction of personalities on many occasions, as there is much that is not understood. The interactions are so swift that they cannot be physically measured, and the sort of parties that you are planning are of great psychic benefit from a variety of standpoints.

Now. Let us return to our discussion on action, and tie this in with action as it is seen within dreams. Your own dreams greatly affect the actions that you take within the physical situation, and as you know telepathy operates within dreams.

This material is somewhat of a personal nature. Nevertheless your young brother, this previous weekend, rather suddenly displayed an inclination to say no when he felt that needless demands were being put upon him.

Your parents definitely let him know that they wanted a new television set, and he quite uncharacteristically told them it was impossible as far as he was concerned. His physical action, his refusal, was based upon a telepathic communication with you, in the dream state, on those evenings when you had the dreams which I interpreted for you.

(*See the unscheduled 216th session, the notes on my dreams involving my younger brother Bill, and Seth's analysis.*)

This firmness on his part saved the situation, for your parents clearly understood what could be expected and what could not be expected. There is obviously no way to prove that this communication took place. On those evenings however when you dream of a certain individual, you may strongly suspect that the same individual is dreaming of you. The trouble is that the other individual most likely has not trained himself to recall his dreams, and so we can prove little.

The telepathic message picked up in dreams under such circumstances will of course be interpreted by the dreaming self in its own way, symbolically, so that the dream actions may not appear to be the same. If it were possible to examine two such allied dream communications however, the connection between them would be very clear.

In years to come we may be able to work along these lines, but this will be in the future. It is nevertheless an important point.

Ruburt will benefit by our vacation, and also by Sherman's book. There are some good hints in it. Obviously I cannot tell you everything at once, and the man's abilities are well developed. We are doing quite well ourselves, considering our circumstances, and we shall do better.

Our results with Dr. Instream have been <u>better</u>, by far, than fair. But he is still looking for more specific data, and I believe we can give it to him.

Our tests must be considered in the light of action, for this is what they are. They involve a more immediate and basic action than physical mobility, and therefore we are concerned with manipulations that are not physical. The associations, personal associations on Ruburt's part, when they are directly connected to test objects in our envelope tests, represent to some degree a step forward on his part.

We are not speaking of <u>my</u> part now; for in such cases the connections are becoming specific, you see, and the preliminary connection has been made. The personal associations on his part that do <u>not</u> apply to the test object, do represent the fact that his own abilities have not fully developed.

Within a fairly decent amount of time, Ruburt and I will be able to work hand in hand, so that our own separate perceptions will <u>build up</u> together, to a more or less precise picture of the object involved. But upon many occasions his personal associations now are <u>connected</u> with the object; so he does not fight me, but we work together.

I suggest a brief break. I also suggest that during our vacation you take your own time, extra time, for reading. It will also be to your advantage to make a habit of taking a sketch pad with you to parties and so forth; since you are known as an artist, this will not be considered unusual or strange, and your own work will benefit. You will pick up intuitional data concerning various personalities in action, and this will aid you in your painting.

(*Break at 9:30. Jane was dissociated as usual for a first delivery. Her eyes had frequently opened to some extent, though not fully; they had been very dark. Her pace had been quite fast.*

(*The candle flame had begun to subside about ten minutes ago, and was now down to about a ¾-inch height, from its estimated high of two inches earlier in the session. It now burned quite steadily at this low point, just as it had burned equally steadily earlier.*

(*Shortly after Jane began speaking again the candle flame climbed back up to a two-inch height. Her eyes were now closed, her pace once again good. Resume at 9:40.*)

In actual cash Ruburt will receive approximately $3,500.00 in the following year, though this will not represent all that he will make, and the amount will double in the next two years. From then on you will do very well. Again, you may or may not insert this in the record, as you prefer.

Now. Briefly I would like to return to your dreams, the same ones that we began to interpret the other evening.

(*Again, see the unscheduled 216th session. We hadn't asked Seth specifically to continue with these dreams, but still hoped he would, soon.*)

On another level they represent something quite different. You saw your young brother in a fetus position, for he will be born again within the <u>physical</u> universe, and you will not. You averted the barrier, which was another existence within this field. He did not.

He went first however because he will die shortly before you, and incidentally in many years to come, and not at a young age. He will live to old age, particularly to compensate for an early death in a past existence.

He will take particular joy in watching his own children develop, because he did not develop in that past life to maturity, though this of course was not definitely in your dream.

(*Since I am nine years older than Bill, it appears that we will both be quite ancient at death. I do not believe that Jane would have allowed such data to come through too many sessions ago, although she did permit Seth to say quite a while ago that she herself would live to old age. That data was also connected to dream analysis and reincarnation.*

(*Seth was giving general reincarnational data on my family and on Jane's as early as the 9th session, while avoiding such things as times of death, etc. Actually the concept of reincarnation made its appearance in the first session. Seth began to be more specific on family reincarnational data when he told Jane and me in a very early session that neither of us would be born again on the physical plane; this, he said, accounted for our lack of children and the desire for them. Seth explained that both of us had been parents before, experiencing both the male and female roles. We have a little material on this; we always are intending to ask for more but somehow don't seem to get around to it. See Volume 1.*)

You saw Ruburt outside the window because he was not directly involved with the relationship between you and your father.

The swing represented your feeling that after all Ruburt was relatively free, on the one hand, from the problem. Therefore you saw him as swinging free. This represented part of your feelings. The other part was represented by your concern for him, for although he was not as directly affected as you, he would still be involved.

The waterfall represented physical death on this level, you see, both of you dying, your brother and yourself; but he first and already adopting the birth position, for he will choose another life rather quickly. He is impulsively drawn to things of earth.

(*Jane's eyes had again been opening and closing rather often. The candle flame, now, attained its highest point of the evening; it was well over an estimated two inches in height, rising up to such a height that a thin trail of black smoke escaped from it. Since the windows were still closed and there were no drafts, I could not account for the flame's height. The candle is a large one, with a diameter of at least two inches and with very little taper. As before it sat out of the reach of Jane's breath, and although it was closer to me I took care to keep my head averted so that my own breath could not influence it. Perhaps temperature changes within the candle could influence it after it has burned for a while, although it felt no warmer to me.*)

He will be born in a warm climate. You both started out from a cold one, hence the snow. Much of this is indeed personal, but is involved here. I would like to make it plain that your mother literally prods your father enough to keep him from withdrawing completely, and he has much to thank her for regardless of their differences.

Without her there would be no vividness for him, for he is unable to relate himself outward. It was because she wanted to feel close to you that she called you this evening, more than anything else, although there was a misunderstanding involved.

Your own attitudes toward the family have changed considerably, and have become more tolerant since our sessions. Such tolerance helps <u>you</u> as well as those otherwise involved. Ruburt's own attitude toward his mother has also become less rigid, largely as a result of our sessions. When you are quiet and not condemning others you can see them more clearly, and you are not afraid of them for you become stronger. You will find yourself enjoying the Christmas season, even with your relatives, for you understand now that a basic reality is involved.

You had better take a brief break before our Dr. Instream material.

(*Break at 9:59. Jane had been dissociated as usual. Her eyes had opened and closed quite often, and she had smoked a cigarette. Her pace had been fast.*

(*The candle flame maintained its unusual height until break, then it began to subside somewhat, and continued to do so through the Dr. Instream material to follow. However it did not reach its earlier ³⁄₄-inch low point. Jane said she had been aware of no feeling of energy thrusting sideways out of her toward the candle, as she had been in the 215th session. This is the 25th Dr. Instream test.*

(*As usual now Jane's pace slowed up, though not to a great degree. She sat with her eyes closed, her face tipped down to meet the ashtray beside her. Resume at 10:07.)*

Now give us a moment, please. *(Pause.)*

A somewhat unusual event today for our friend. That is, not an event that is usually within his daily schedule, involving two other people. *(Pause.)* The circumstance having a connection with a letter from the western portion of the country, or <u>west</u> of his location, from a university or large foundation of some sort, or from a man who is connected with such a group.

An occasion also at his home, where five were present. *(Pause.)* Another situation involving a young man and a family connection. He wears a robe with a large pocket, rather unusual pocket. *(Pause.)*

I pick up a connection with <u>cork</u>, but do not know to what this refers. *(Pause.)* Will you put Ruburt's cigarette out for him, please.

("Yes."

(This is the first time I can recall where Jane herself interrupted such test data in this manner. She did not appear to be distracted, however, or to break off in the middle of a piece of information. I put out the cigarette; its smoke had been drifting toward her.)

The unusual event I mentioned occurred I believe about three this afternoon, or he learned of it then.

A succession of numbers in a row, backwards, as of 10, 9, et cetera.

He is feeling better now than he did at our last session.

A connection now with Dr. Rhine, and some arrangements or a letter. The initials, I believe J. B. R., and a letter from a publisher. The initials <u>could</u> be J. R. B..

(J. B. R. of course being Dr. Rhine's initials. And J. R. B. can be the initials of Jane Roberts Butts. Dr. Rhine is also a parapsychologist.)

Do you have a test for me?

("Yes."

(It was 10:15, and time for our 22nd envelope test. Jane took the sealed double envelope from me without opening her eyes. Now she did something new for her in these tests. For several seconds she held the envelope directly against her forehead. Her eyes remained closed. Then she lowered the envelope to her lap.)

Give us a moment, please.

These are impressions. The numbers 1, 2, 3. A room. Round shapes. The number 12. Perhaps the twelfth month, though I am not sure.

A connection with another location, perhaps out of this town. Two people, yet some connection with a summer scene, and water.

A stopwatch, though I do not know to what this refers. An upright composition. A group, but I pick up busts rather than full figures, and a round object. People about a round object, such as a table.

6 as in 6 o'clock. A letter or note. The color yellow. Light tissue paper. 1963 or 1965.

Something missing, and someone who could not come.

I suggest your break.

(*Break at 10:22. Jane was dissociated as usual. Her eyes had remained closed, her pace had been fairly good. She said that nothing she said in either test made particular sense to her.*

(*The candle flame had fluctuated a bit at low ebb during the tests, but had not reached its previous height by far.*

(*Jane said she received a few visual images during the envelope test, but that they were not sensational by any means. They will be mentioned below.*

(*See the tracing of the test object on page 131. During last Sunday there was a family gathering at my parents' home in nearby Sayre, PA. There were twelve people in all: My parents, Jane and I, my brother Loren, his wife and son, and my brother Bill and his wife, and their two daughters and one son. Bill's son is named David, he is four years old, and it is he who drew the test object, with a black ball-point pen on white paper.*

(*As Seth explains on page 134 of this session, some of the test data tonight represents preliminary connections with the test object, just as in the last envelope test with the drawing made by Roy Fox. Thus Jane's personal associations are now often connected with the test object, and she is working with Seth and not against him.*

(*Jane said that Seth's count of 1, 2, 3 was his way—or Jane's?—of leading up to the number 4 that I wrote on the drawing, referring to David's age. "A room" is too general. Also "Round shapes"; although there are round shapes on the drawing. "The number 12" can apply easily enough. Not only is the month of the test the twelfth month, but there were twelve people present in Sayre the day the test object was drawn. And again, the test object was drawn on December 12th, and so dated by me.*

(*At first Jane and I thought that the out of town location applied to our going to Sayre yesterday. Then we saw that it referred to a visit Jane and I made to visit Bill in Rochester last summer, for here "summer scene, and water" enters in. We went swimming with Bill and his family in Lake Ontario. We recall this especially because the usual beaches at Rochester were polluted by hordes of dead fish; we had to drive some distance to find a suitable swimming spot.*

(*"A stopwatch" does not ring a bell with us. We think David's drawing of the dog can be called an "upright composition." The next statement, about "A group... busts rather than full figures... people about a round object, such as a table," is quite interesting, and can apply twice, as the number twelve applied four times. My parents' dining room table is round, and of course we ate Sunday dinner at this table. My parents also have a round mirror-topped coffee table in the living room. It is a low table; often a group of the children would be playing games on the table, and to do this they had to sit on the floor. Thus only their torsos projected above the tabletop, and were reflected in the mirror.*

(6 as in 6 o'clock is not specific enough for easy conscious connection. "A letter or note" can refer to the notes for reference I made on David's drawing. "The color yellow" we think is a strong connection to the drawing of the dog; Dick recently obtained a puppy for his children, and when Jane and I asked David to describe the dog he called it orange at first, then yellow.

("Light tissue paper" may be nebulous. Jane and I gave the children their Christmas presents Sunday, and rather than wait for Christmas they opened the gifts then. They were wrapped in regular Christmas paper; if this is called tissue It can be a connection. The test object was drawn in 1965 of course, not 1963. The thought here is that calligraphically the numerals 3 and 5 are quite similar.

(Finally, "Something missing, and someone who could not come," is also interesting. As soon as the test was over, and I believe before she knew what the test object was, Jane told me that she believed "Something" and "someone" referred to the same thing. Only one member of the family was missing at the gathering Sunday, and this was my brother Loren's daughter Linda, who was at work in Scranton, PA. It was too far away for her to make the trip up to Sayre, and back, in one day.

(Jane also said that Seth was going to say something about lettering on the test object, but she did not give voice to it. I had made notes on it.

(The candle flame was still down when Jane resumed, with her eyes closed, at 10:30.)

We will now close our session, though you may watch the candle for a moment, as I am teaching Ruburt how to use energy. It is a rather simple matter of directing basic energy along certain lines outside of the physical organism. Everyone does this subconsciously to begin with.

(As soon as Seth mentioned the candle, its flame began to grow. Rather quickly, the flame reached up to a height beneath its maximum for the session, which was well over an estimated two inches. its growth now was quite respectable however, perhaps to something just under two inches. Considering the earlier displays by the flame, I now had a question.)

("Were there earlier demonstrations by the flame that weren't accidental?")

There were. We would like to perfect this. Smoothly however, so that we are able to announce it ahead of time, to show that other conditions are not working such as drafts and so forth. Have you been watching the candle as I spoke?

("Yes.")
(*Jane's eyes were still closed, and the flame was still up.*)
Now it should be getting quite a bit higher.
("Yes.")
(*Seth paused briefly. The flame climbed a little more. It was quite steady, but still short of its high for the evening.*)
And now I suggest we end the session.
("Good night, Seth.")
(*End at 10:33. Jane was dissociated as usual. Her eyes had remained closed. She now told me that once again she had felt the peculiar sideways thrust, as of energy, directed toward the candle to her right. See page 124 of the 215th session for the first instance of this effect.*)

(*Jane now relaxed on the bed. Peculiarly now, we saw the candle flame shoot up to equal its previous high, well over two inches. A delayed reaction? Jane now felt no energy thrust.*)

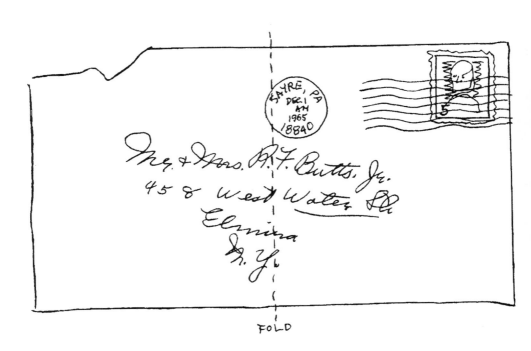

(*Tracing of the envelope front used in the envelope test, the 23rd, in the 218th session for December 15, 1965.*)

SESSION 218
DECEMBER 15, 1965 9 PM WEDNESDAY AS SCHEDULED

(The 23rd envelope test was held this evening during the session. For the test object I used the front of an envelope addressed to Jane and me by my mother. I folded it once as indicated, enclosed it between two pieces of Bristol, and sealed it in the usual double envelopes.

(Today Jane read all day, finishing up J. B. Priestley's book, Man and Time, *which she liked very much. She had read nothing by Priestley before, nor by Dunne, mentioned extensively in the Priestley book. After supper this evening Jane told me she thought Seth had come through twice, briefly, as she went about her daily chores before the session. Both instances concerned the Priestley book, which had excited her.*

(When I lit our test candle at 8:55 PM, the flame at once shot up to an estimated height of three inches; I had not seen it do this before. It smoked noticeably for a few moments. The flame then settled down to a steady height of about 1 $^{1}/_{4}$ inches, and remained there through first break. As usual, the flame was shielded from Jane's vision during her deliveries.

(The session was held in our back room. Jane began speaking while sitting down and with her eyes closed. Before the session she had remarked that she hoped Seth would mention Priestley's book. Her pace was now average to begin, but quickly speeded up.)

Good evening.

("Good evening, Seth.")

Now. Our friend Ruburt has finally discovered the works of Dunne, I see, and he has also been reading Priestley on the subject of time.

Ruburt has not been reading <u>Dunne</u>, incidentally, but Priestley's interpretation of Dunne, which is something else again, but fairly accurate.

I am glad that you did not encounter these ideas earlier, since we cannot therefore be justly accused of having borrowed any of them. Ruburt is amazed at some of the similarities that exist in the concept of time as I am giving it to you, and the concepts held by Dunne and Priestley.

(Jane was both amazed and delighted. She came across the Priestley book while browsing in the library recently. We have heard of Dunne, of course, but have yet to read any of his works; for some reason the library here has none of his books.

(Jane now smiled as Seth began to consider the theories of both men. Before the session she had hoped Seth would discuss them. As it developed, the session proved to be an unusual one.)

Now. Priestley is indeed the priestly fellow, and Dunne is far from done, If you will forgive my jest. Portions of both of their theories are correct.

Sometimes one of them is accurate on one point, and the other one completely off, and sometimes they are both wrong.

All in all however they came much closer to reality than most; and therefore there is an added dimension in their works. This added dimension is simply a result of their intimacy with other dimensions of time, about which most others remain as ignorant as possible.

(Jane's eyes now opened to some degree as she lit a cigarette. Her eyes now alternated often between opening and closing. Her pace was fast. She had finished the Priestley book just before supper, and said she hadn't had time to think it over; but someone had been thinking it over.)

Priestley does not go far enough with his time one, time two and time three, but he is fairly correct up to that point. In a different way he says many of the things that I am saying. I have told you that upon physical death the ego becomes the subconscious in the next existence, and that its conscious knowledge is retained electromagnetically.

(Seth began dealing with these ideas in the very early sessions, mixing it in with reincarnational data. He elaborated to some degree in the sessions on the electrical field and related subjects: In Volume 3, see sessions 122-135.)

Now. Priestley puts it somewhat differently but the results are the same. According to him the consciousness, the individual consciousness of time one, becomes something else at physical death, and the consciousness that is part of time two in physical life becomes dominant in the next existence. There is one large difference here between us however, and I believe an important one. Priestley's individual, after death, with his dominant time two consciousness, has available to him what was time one during physical life.

He can use it, use the knowledge obtained therein, learn from its mistakes, and advance. But this individual as seen by Priestley at this particular point is somewhat limited, <u>still</u>, by this time one. Time one is available to him, though not necessarily as a series of moments, one after another. From this he is free, but he is still somewhat bound by those events, though he may learn from them. According to Priestley, while the individual therefore is free from successive moments, he still does not have easily available, at fingertips so to speak, any information or realizations from time three. I am using Priestley's terms here.

Time three, after the individual's physical death, becomes for him what time two is for him during this existence. It is therefore available only to the same degree that time two is available to him now.

Priestley's concept here becomes more limiting than he realized. At this point Dunne overtakes him precisely where he and Dunne disagree. For once having hypothesized times one, two and three, Dunne continues onward as is the case, and Priestley simply stops here in this particular respect.

I suggest a brief break, and we shall continue along these lines, for we are able to go ahead where Priestley and Dunne were not. We are able to do this, or I am able to do this, precisely because I am from beyond Priestley's time one, two and three, and therefore free of the distortions which even he is unable to avoid.

In concept, again on this particular point, Dunne went further. But in doing so he ended up in a frenzy, losing sight of where he was. And no wonder. It is simply because I am <u>outside</u> of these times that I can see through them more clearly, and there is no particular reason why I should be considered wiser in this respect than they. I am simply in a better position to observe. If Dunne were able to write another book now, on his time theories, he would be able to correct several of his well-intentioned errors.

(*Break at 9:26. Jane was dissociated as usual, she said. Her eyes had opened narrowly frequently. She said that consciously, at the moment, she could not explain what she had just said. Her pace had been fast, and my writing hand was aware of this.*

(*The candle flame had not varied since the beginning of the session. It was not warm to the touch except at the edge of the lip, and even here it was only warm.*

(*Jane's delivery had been quite emphatic, and it remained so when she began speaking again. She resumed at the same fast pace, again smoking and with her eyes closed, at 9:36.*)

When the individual reaches Priestley's time three, then he is left with little individuality. Priestley's vision of the birds and the life spirit is not too much different from nirvana. At least only in degree, and this simply will not do.

It is true that Priestley speaks in terms of consciousness being retained at this stage, but a consciousness devoid of personality is an odd bird indeed. The personality structure changes, it is true, but consciousness of overall identities within any given unit of consciousness is always retained. There is no <u>blending</u> or <u>merging</u>, willy-nilly, into a gigantic ever-rushing-on spirit of life. And the spirit of life in these terms cannot be considered as something apart and separate from, and outside of, those consciousnesses which illuminate <u>it</u>, and through which they are illuminated. And here is our second difficulty with Priestley.

It is one thing to conceive of basic time as being outside of physical time, for the sake of making a point; but it must be realized that Priestley's time one, while only real to the ego, is nevertheless a part or a materialization that exists within this basic time framework, and the life force is at the same time within as well as without.

That is, the life force is constantly renewed by those consciousnesses of which it is formed. The consciousnesses therefore are not simply filled up by a life force which then deserts them to go on its way, for these consciousnesses are themselves portions of the life force, and form its shape, if you will, and continuing existence.

(Seth gave his first lengthy dissertation on the above theme in the 12th session, of January 2, 1964. He places the subject under the general term of fifth dimension. He spoke on the idea for several typewritten pages; this was his longest delivery by a wide margin at the time, and Jane and I were quite surprised. See Volume 1.)

The flame feeds the fire and the fire feeds the flame. Therefore, while this time one of continuous moments is no longer experienced after death, it is still a reality within basic time itself, a reality toward which the personality simply is no longer focused. Because the individual is focused within time one now, you still realize, or should, that the time one is only a small portion of time, and that other kinds of time exist of which you are not aware.

But when you leave time one behind, or because you leave time one behind at death, this is no reason to imagine that time one exists separate and apart from basic time. The same sort of error here exists concerning the life force, as I mentioned. You are merged with the life force now, and no one can deny that you are individualistic.

(Jane's eyes began to open at times now. Her delivery was fast and emphatic. The candle flame remained the same.)

It is a mistake to assume that any future or inevitable merging with a life force is ahead of you, in those terms. This is an error that is precisely due to that which Priestley himself abhors: distortions in thought caused by reliance upon the concept of time as a series of moments.

Priestley cannot help himself here, for it is not possible entirely for him to escape from his own time system, with the best of intentions. And in many respects his theories come very close to explaining the way things are. The idea of reoccurring time is simply off base, practically speaking.

(Jane now took a long pause.)

There are two particular points that I want to make this evening, if at all possible.

One concerns myself and where I would stand in this time framework, and you should find this highly interesting. The other has to do with Dunne, for in one instance he saw further than Priestley, for he carried these times further. But he also fell into an understandable error. For at some point the separate selves of Dunne's, with their separate times, become aware of each other, and merge into the sort of superconsciousness that <u>we</u> have always called the entity.

These times do not go on indefinitely in the precise manner that Dunne thought. Neither do they stop as Priestley believes, at time three. There is a merging of selves into what you may call a superconsciousness, a synthesis; and from then on, dear friends, there is a beginning toward something new, and a something of which I am not prepared to speak this evening, but of which I shall speak in the near future.

I suggest a break.

(Break at 10:00. Jane said she was well dissociated. Her eyes had remained closed for the most part. She had appeared to be wrapped up in the material, speaking rapidly and with much emphasis. The candle flame remained unchanged, burning steadily at an estimated height of 1 ¼ inches.

(We would think in the last paragraph of his delivery above, Seth hinted at the psychic gestalts of which he has spoken very briefly at various times. We gather that he visualizes a chain of such gestalts, with each link one of greater complexity. He has called them "great building blocks of energy."

(It was now time for the 26th Dr. Instream test. As usual Jane spoke while sitting down, with her head tipped down and her hands raised to her closed eyes. Her pace now slowed somewhat, and her voice was quiet. Resume at 10:06.)

Now give us a moment please, for our Instream material.

(Pause.) A fond farewell of some sort this evening. Is someone going on a trip?

Important papers in a briefcase. An upsurge of interest in the doctor's hypnosis experiments. *(Pause.)* Something now turned up, on a desk or table. I believe, again, a piece of paper with a format like a letter.

I pick up the initials R. B.. The letter concerns a particular event, a meeting which has not yet occurred, and it concerns another person also, beside the person who wrote the letter, and beside Dr. Instream. That is, another person in particular, though more may be involved in the event when it occurs. *(Pause.)*

It may take place in March.

The letter is from someone in the south or southwest. <u>Or</u> the other person who will be connected with the meeting resides in the south or southwest. *(Pause.)*

I pick up a rather disconnected or disjointed impression concerning an elephant, or perhaps this is a <u>trunk</u>. I do not know to what it refers. *(Pause.)* Unless it has to do perhaps with the farewell earlier mentioned.

Do you have a test for me?

("Yes."

*(It was 10:15. Jane took the usual double envelope from me without opening her eyes. Reading over the last session, she had been surprised to learn that she had held the test envelope to her forehead for a few minutes, since she didn't remember

doing this. Now, she once again pressed the test envelope to her forehead, this time more deliberately, and with both hands. She continued to hold it there. Her eyes were closed, her voice very quiet. This is the 23rd envelope test.)

Now, give me a moment and we shall see what we can do.

A framework. Two people. An assortment of objects or shapes.

A connection that I do not see clearly, with a missionary. A note. The mention of a time.

Ruburt here is thinking of your monk. Because of my mention of the word missionary, this started a train of his personal associations.

Now. Something square, as a plot. A connection with four other people, and a road, or road shape. Unusual shadows. A <u>cake</u>. Something that two people know, and two other people do not know.

Paper with printing. Your handwriting. A connection with an address that is not your own. Something to which no reply is expected, and a connection with an animal.

I suggest your break.

(Break at 10:23. Jane was dissociated as usual. Her eyes had remained closed for both tests. She sat with the test envelope pressed to her forehead the whole time. The candle flame burned at the same steady height.

(Seth did not elaborate on the test envelope impressions, so what follows are our own interpretations. For his own part, Seth was too eager to get on with his discussion of Priestley's book, it developed.

(See the tracing of the test object on page 140. It is of the front of an envelope addressed to Jane and me by my mother on December 1. The letter contained in this envelope figures in the test results, and will be kept on file with the envelope. The letter would be quoted here except that the contents are rather personal. It is of course available however to anyone seriously considering these tests, should they be that interested.

("A framework" refers to the clear-cut single-line frame that borders Washington's portrait on the current five-cent stamp. The envelope is addressed to "two people," meaning Jane and me. The "assortment of objects and shapes" refers to the words making up the letter.

(Seth's unclear connection with "a missionary" is interesting. My brother Loren is mentioned in the letter contained within the test envelope, and his father-in-law is a retired minister. The letter of course can be "A note".

("The mention of a time" is easily accounted for in the same letter. In it my mother discusses the visit Jane and I were due to make to my parents on Sunday, December 5th. The date was not mentioned, just the word Sunday. My mother then canceled this visit of ours by telephone, and Jane and I then journeyed to visit my

parents in Sayre, PA, on the following Sunday, December 12. It was on this visit that I obtained the test object used in the last session, the 217th.

(The monk mentioned by Seth refers to our friend Father Martin, who is mentioned in the 212th session. Apropos of this, Jane now said she remembered that Seth's use of the word missionary did set up her own chain of association involving Father Martin. She said Seth put her back on the right track by mentioning this.

(Jane said she was sure "Something square" referred to the dimensions of the test envelope when it was folded, although it does not measure out as a perfect square. The "connection with four other people" works out well, since the letter concerns a situation involving both my parents, my brother Loren and my brother Bill, other than Jane and me.

("Road, or road shape," and "Unusual shadows" are too general. There may be a vague connection with "A cake," but it would be several times removed from the test object. We did not have cake for dessert at the family gathering on December 12 for instance.

("Something that two people know, and two other people do not know," is good, since my mother's letter specifically concerned such a situation. Jane and I were the two who did know, and my parents were the two others who did not know. This matter was straightened out on December 12.

(The test object is "Paper with printing," the printing being the machine-applied cancellation, in my opinion, rather than my mother's handwriting. "Your handwriting," meaning mine, does not apply.

(Jane said she was confused while giving the data "A connection with an address that is not your own." She wasn't sure Seth meant an address that was ours, or was not ours, so she tried to relax and let it come through without distortion. And of course the letter came to us from an address not our own. "Something to which no reply is expected," is also good, in that we were due to see my parents within a few days after my mother wrote to us.

(Jane said "a connection with an animal" is also valid, in that while she went for a walk during our December 12 visit to the family gathering in Sayre, she saw a dog, possibly a stray, that aroused in her a strong desire to own a dog. She still misses our dog Mischa, who died three years ago. So do I.

(Jane began speaking in a most emphatic and enthusiastic manner. Her eyes were closed but she was smoking; her eyes soon opened however. The candle flame remained at its steady 1¼ inch height. Resume at 10:37.)

Now. Since you have a vacation coming up, I want to make certain that I cover one point in particular.

(Jane now smiled broadly.)

For Ruburt has a <u>grand</u> idea. A great glimmering of enlightenment has hit him. I hope it did not hurt him; because while his idea is not right in one way, it is not <u>wrong</u>.

Having read Priestley's ideas about Dunne, Ruburt now wonders if I am not a future self of his own, according to Dunne's ideas; that is, if I am not one of those future selves of which Dunne speaks, or if I am not consciousness number two, or three even, of Priestley's concept.

Now. Such thoughts are excellent mental exercise for him, and while he is not precisely correct in either of these suppositions, in a basic manner I cannot say that he is precisely wrong.

<u>Long before he read any notions such as these</u>, I told you that I spoke through the third undifferentiated level of the subconscious, did I not?

("Yes."

(*Jane was again smiling. Seth devoted the 88th session of September 16, 1964, to explaining what he meant by this. He had mentioned it before at various times without elaboration. He also dwelled on the subject to some extent in the 152nd session, the 157th, and others. Again, reincarnation is involved in a basic way.*)

Now. While Dunne and Priestley and myself used different terms often to express the same concept, we also differ in many respects as far as these theories are concerned. <u>My</u> third undifferentiated layer, you see, would correspond to the consciousness of Priestley's third time, which is why I can tell you that at that point individuality is indeed maintained, and personality continues.

Otherwise I should be all life force and no self. Now, I communicate through this level of Ruburt's consciousness. It is subconscious <u>to him</u> or to his <u>ego</u>, but it is <u>not</u> without consciousness by any means. And again, I communicate through that level. At my own level this is not in itself difficult.

The difficulty lies in making this communication, which is direct from me, to what would be Ruburt's time three self, clear to the time one self of Ruburt's, which must speak these words, in what could be called Priestley's time one.

Communications such as these, incidentally, can be explained quite adequately within Priestley's system. Very nicely indeed. Not thoroughly but nicely. Completely, if you do not ask too many tricky questions.

Priestley's theories, although he would not use them in this way, could be used to give some insight along these directions. But because Priestley stopped with time three, you would have to pick up Dunne's, until Dunne himself finally goes wrong.

Now I would be number six self, so to speak, according to Dunne. According to Priestley however, at this point in his theory, I would simply be that life force, or part of it, with no individuality. Priestley is more correct in depth however, though Dunne goes further, only to peter out. Nevertheless I would be a number six self. Using the same terms, however, I will make some distinctions. For as a number six self I have complete knowledge of all the other selves.

<u>Now I could indeed be Ruburt's number six self, you see</u>. I am not, but I could be. It is entirely possible however, using Ruburt as an example, for Ruburt's number six self, to communicate with Ruburt's number one self; these communications sifting through the intervening selves however, and unfortunately. Now these various times of Priestley's and Dunne's have much in common with the planes of which I am speaking in our discussions, and the value fulfillment of our material is akin to Priestley's insistence on depth <u>within</u> any given moment.

I go into particulars however concerning how this depth is achieved, as you know, if you recall a diagram that I outlined for you concerning moment points in the past.

("Yes.")

(*Jane had looked at me for confirmation. See the 149-152nd sessions. Jane made the drawing referred to by Seth immediately after the 149th session. I have always intended to work up a finished drawing on the idea.*)

Now. While I am not Ruburt's number six self, and I should know, this is not to say that I may not be Ruburt's number eight or nine self.

At this point I am at the level, again, that could be compared to Dunne's number six self, as myself. I communicate through the third undifferentiated layer, that could be compared to Priestley's consciousness at number three time.

I repeat myself because I want to make the points plain, and this material is difficult. But things simply do not happen as Dunne supposed they did. He was correct in carrying his times further than Priestley, but he was incorrect in assuming the serialization continued indefinitely along the same lines.

His observations were not complete enough, for there are changes occurring now that he did not perceive. Therefore he did not project them into these other times. The becoming self grows more and more aware of its own portions, and of these various aspects of time in which these portions are or will be focused.

I do not believe that Dunne understood this. There is no serialization as he imagined, after a certain point, simply because this progression of selves through various times in a serial fashion is no longer necessary. The selves reach a point which is not a theoretical point, but a particular mathematically existent point, whereby these times and selves simply become one, or in our terms, an entity.

I must stress that individuality is never lost. But this is too complicated a subject to cover this evening. We have explained it rather adequately in terms of action however, and gestalts of selves do not imply a giving-up of individuality at all. It should be remembered here that reincarnation is simply a fact, and one which is not accepted by Priestley or Dunne.

Reincarnation, considered in this light however, is much more logical indeed than a reoccurring time. And incidentally it is also much more logically a part of these theories, although both Priestley and Dunne would be unable I believe to admit this.

Now. At some point you, Joseph, and Ruburt <u>and</u> myself, are part of the same entity. This entity is that synthesization that Dunne did not foresee, but it in no way implies a loss of individual identities. This is extremely difficult to explain, since when I use the word individual identity, I am not referring primarily to egotistical identity alone. As a matter of fact, I am in one way, and in one way only, a future self—this is extremely simplified—of Ruburt's; that could be compared I suppose to a theoretical number twelve self, according to Dunne.

But we three are <u>all</u> part of another entity, or rather of an entity that exists at that point where Dunne's serialization breaks down and a new synthesis takes place.

Now. In <u>that</u> respect I am closer to Ruburt than I am to you. However I have been connected with both of you in the past, and this is something for another night. And at that point of synthesization we will be part of the same entity.

This is all for the sake of simplicity—

(*Here Jane laughed.*)

—believe it or not. For we are actually, you see, part of the same entity <u>now</u>. <u>Therefore</u>, if you will bear with me, you represent one of the selves through which I must travel in order to communicate. Is this clear?

("*Yes.*"

(*Jane, still smiling, stared at me. Her wide-open eyes were very dark.*)

Would you like a break?

("*Yes.*"

(*Break at 11:22. Jane now said she had been very well dissociated during the last delivery. She had a vague memory of her eyes opening at times. She had smoked a lot, and her voice was getting dry. Her delivery had been fast and emphatic.*

(*Except for an occasional mild spurt, the candle flame had remained at its same level.*

(*Seth began explaining his source and the source of this material in the very early sessions. In the 15th session for example he likened his state to the dream state* of a physical individual. By the 24th session he was dealing with the problems involved in communicating with us. By the 63rd session he was explaining his state as energy not materialized into mass; this after telling us in the 54th session that Jane, Seth and I had been part of the same entity once; he could not tell us this earlier, he said, because Jane and I would have immediately jumped to the conclusion that he was part of Jane's subconscious mind.

(In the 45th session Seth said a little to the effect that I assisted her in drawing upon the energy necessary for these communications. In the 88th and 152nd sessions Seth went into Jane's third undifferentiated layer to some extent, then elaborated a little more on the relationship between us in the 157th session.

(Jane's delivery remained fast and emphatic. Her eyes were open and she was smoking when she resumed at 11:25.)

Now. I will not keep you longer, though it grieves me to stop here.

It is because of the peculiar connection of selves that our communications are possible. It is for the same reason that such communications are relatively rare, for many conditions and circumstances are necessary; and the number one self is made to bear <u>strains</u> unfamiliar to it, and to perceive data which does not make sense within its number one time system.

Because of this I have always leaned on the side of caution. But these strains, and this data, to some extent lift the number one self from the limitations of the number one time, and lends an advancement <u>ordinarily</u> not possible. For the number one time has changed for both of you since our sessions began, and it no longer seems the prison that it did earlier.

The number one time <u>cannot</u> contain other times but the consciousness, with help, can to some extent perceive these other times. And this perception then <u>allows</u> consciousness to escape <u>some</u> of the <u>confinements</u> of that one time. Our spacious present of which I have spoken contains all times, but it is not a <u>thing</u> apart from them, nor precisely their sum. It is ever unfolding and mobile, and changing itself.

I am sorry. I forgot your writing hand, which I suppose is somewhat wilted.
("Yes."

(In the 44th session, Seth began a list of qualities and attributes which are included in the spacious present. To date there are eleven of these: Value climate of psychological reality; energy transformation; spontaneity; durability; creation; consciousness; capacity for infinite mobility; law of infinite changeability and transmutation; cooperation; arrival and departure, meaning physical birth and death; and quality depth, the perspective in which an idea can expand, replacing our time and space.)

Therefore I will regretfully end our discussion for this evening.

I believe it is apparent in our own tests, incidentally, that some preciseness is beginning to show through, for in the general associations connected with the object, identifying points concerning the specific object now appear.

I will be with you during your holidays, even if I am not your idea of the popular Santa Claus.

("Good night, Seth.")

(End at 11:35. Jane was dissociated as usual. Her eyes had opened at times. The candle flame had shown no noticeable change of importance during the session; Jane said she had not been aware of the flame one way or another all evening. My writing hand was tired. Before the session Jane had been tired; she now felt fine. She said Seth could have continued all night.)

(While Bill and Peggy Gallagher were on vacation in Puerto Rico last October, Seth gave impressions concerning them in the following sessions: the 199th for October 18; the 200th for October 20; and the 201st for October 25. No correspondence, phone calls, etc., were exchanged between the four of us during this time.

(The Gallaghers went over Seth's material with us orally a day or two after returning from vacation; this was on the evening of the unscheduled session for Thursday, October 28, and I had time for but a few quick written notes. We obtained this written account from them later, and in the course of checking data with them several times Jane and I soon realized much effort could be saved by getting a written account as soon as possible after any such experiment.

(Thus Jane and I followed this procedure concerning the data Seth gave on Peggy's business trip to Washington, DC in December. A written question-and-answer period was held with Peggy a day or two after her return. Peggy cooperated wholeheartedly and gave much information. I stressed that we did not want to put words into her mouth concerning Seth's data, and she agreed that we did not.

(Seth's statements are presented in full from each session, with the comments from Peggy and Bill just below each statement in italic type. The Gallaghers agreed on each answer, concerning the Puerto Rico material. They arrived in San Juan, Puerto Rico, on Sunday, October 17. We begin with Seth's material on them from the 199th session for October 18, 1965, at 9 PM.)

A large white or pastel building, they had something to do with today. Flowers here.

("Our hotel was white. There were many different colored flowers along the road near our hotel.")

Iron grillwork. Hacienda... Lucinda *(phonetically.*

("No to both.")

They passed here. Bars at the windows of iron, not in jail.

("Yes. Most open windows barred, in Spanish tradition.")
Newspapers sold in front, outside.
("No, but newspapers sold at hotel desk.")
Later at another end of this same city, they pass shacks.
("Yes.")
This is at the northwest portion.
("Generally, north or northeast.")
A street. Saint Severin *(phonetically.*
("No.")
A rather high pile of dark dirt.
("No.")
They stay at a pink stucco building.
("The building had a rough cement finish, but was not pink.")
With porch enclosures that are round. The base is not round. The portion between the... what would be the porch railing and the roof is round. They bicycled.
("No.")
Perhaps in their room there is a rather elaborate lamp, on a table, that depicts a scene, that glows when it is lit.
("There was a rather ornate table lamp of bamboo in our room, decorated with flowers painted flowers.")
Give us a moment again, and we will try to pick them up now. *(At 9:50.)* Outdoors, on a verandah.
("No. But the guest house in which we stayed on Friday had a verandah.")
Nearby suitcases open.
("Yes. In our room on Monday night.")
A low scooped blouse, and a pale skirt.
("No.")
The owner of the place where they stay is 50 or thereabouts. Name beginning with an M, and ending with an A.
("Don't know.")
And a connection with a dog.
("At the guest house where we stayed on St. Thomas a large dog, a family pet, was around most of the time. This again was on Friday and Saturday, October 22-23.")
(Note that this information was given on Monday, October 18.)
They think of an island that sounds like Sumatra, but is not. It is two words. More like San Mutro, though I do not believe that is exact.
("We discussed going to the nearby island of St. Thomas.")

An avenue beginning with a B, or San B, period, where they ate lunch. San Beninno *(phonetically)* or similar.

("No.")

A striped awning. A dinner at 375. I believe this is the cost.

("On Monday night, one of the dinners cost $3.75. On the following Sunday, a restaurant where we ate had a striped awning.")

A blue blanket on the bed where they sleep.

("No. Green and white.")

A purchase of an item that is like a small sculpture. I get a bear shape.

("In St. Thomas on the following Monday, we bought a small sculpture of a bird.")

Some rain.

("It rained a little, as it did nearly every day.")

(From the 200th session, Wednesday, October 20, 1965, at 9 PM. As usual Seth's impressions are in regular type, the written comments of Bill and Peggy Gallagher in italics below.)

Your friends, my friends, the Jesuit and the cat lover are sleeping in a different room than they were at our last session.

("No.")

It is close to water, and further west, and in a different town or location.

("Our hotel was close to water, on the beach. But it was the same hotel we stayed in last Monday.")

It is to the rear rather than the front of the building, to the side and rear.

("Yes. We had a rear corner room.")

With a tree immediately outside the window; a bushy sort of tree with something like spikes on it.

("Yes. It was somewhat like a palm tree, only shorter. The leaves made noise in the wind.")

Some sort of theater. They have visited it or it is close, and they passed it on their way to this place.

("No.")

There is a phone in this room.

("Yes.")

They saw a motion picture about a woman with lovers, and a cripple, or perhaps a dwarf. They purchased a crucifix, I believe, small, to be worn on a chain.

("No to both.")

They ate at a place with wide windows and blinds, closed because of the sun. One extremely long window at the front, the entire length of the building, covered with this blind.

("This is possible. This type is common in Puerto Rico.")

They ate with Peggy's sister and husband, or they talked about them during the meal, in an immediate fashion, thinking of them very strongly. Perhaps making an appointment with them for this evening.

("We ate with them Monday night, October 18. We no doubt discussed them today, since Monday night the four of us made plans to go to the nearby island of St. Thomas, next Friday, October 22."

(See the notes on page 13 of the 200th session. Peggy's sister was married on Saturday, October 16; the bride and groom left immediately for Puerto Rico on their honeymoon. Peggy and Bill left for Puerto Rico on vacation on Sunday, October 17. Jane and I were told that the two couples had no plans to meet in Puerto Rico, oddly enough; we recall Peggy saying for instance that she would not want to honeymoon with relatives close by. But these plans were obviously changed, the two couples soon meeting in San Juan.)

The sister's husband has a squat build, and uses his hands often in work.

("No, as to the husband's squat build. He is tall and slender. Yes, in that he uses his hands in his work. He is a contractor."

(Again on page 13, it is noted that Jane and I had not met the bride and groom. Later we found out that we had met them once, briefly, while they were engaged. Neither of us are acquainted with the other members of Peggy's family, however, and at the time the 200th session was held neither Jane or I were consciously aware we had indeed met Peggy's sister and her fiancé.)

Let me see if I can pick them up at this moment. *(At 9:41 PM.)* A connection with dice.

("Yes. Not on Wednesday; but Thursday night we stopped at a casino where there were dice, and gambling.")

An old man, and jewelry.

("Yes to both. Bill clearly remembers a white man, at least 60 years old by his estimate, who stood next to him at the roulette table at the casino. Bill noticed that the man wore three rings on his fingers; he thought this quite unusual.")

A minor disturbance. I think of a pack of cigarettes, not American brand, though neither of them smoke. A shawl as a gift.

("No to these three.")

A particular dead-end street that should be significant to them on their return.

("Our hotel was on a street that dead-ended at the ocean.")

I have the impression: Clor-ra-door, but do not know to what it refers.

(Phonetically.

("No.")

Also an interior lake.

("Yes. At our hotel, The Americana, there is a very shallow pool that is actually half in and half out of the hotel, on the ground floor, which is one level lower than the lobby. This pool runs inside the hotel from the outside and is decorated with flowers, etc."

(From the 201st session, Monday, October 25, 1965, at 9 PM. As usual Seth's impressions are in regular type, the written comments of the Gallaghers in italics below each statement.)

An airplane. Directly behind our friends there is a female in blue.

("On Sunday noon, October 24, we returned by airplane from St. Thomas, Virgin Islands, to San Juan, Puerto Rico. There was a woman dressed in blue on the plane. But she sat immediately forward of us, and to the right.")

Directly across from our friends there is a couple of middle-aged... *(Jane pauses, shakes her head in puzzlement.)* We will try to clear this up. The couple come from Daytona or Dayton. The man has a connection with the paper business, but not a newspaper. The production of paper itself.

("We don't know. We don't remember such a couple.")

Arrive New York eleven, perhaps 11:05. *(Again Jane shakes her head in puzzlement or vexation.)*

("We arrived in New York on Tuesday, October 26, at 4 PM.")

("However, when we flew to St. Thomas from San Juan on Friday, October 22, our plane left the airport at 10:45 AM.")

(Perhaps Jane's puzzlement while giving the data on this page was caused by her confusing several airplane flights. The Gallaghers were involved in four airplane trips in a space of five days: From San Juan to St. Thomas, and back; from San Juan to New York City; from New York City to Elmira, NY.)

There is something, a gate or runway with the number 3... 5... 35. Possibly the number on their luggage ticket. But one of these is a 35.

("Our luggage ticket number was either 453 or 455.")

The woman directly behind our friends' seat may have a child with her. If so a female child, but there is no man in that seat.

("On our flight to New York City, a woman and child sat across the aisle and a little ahead of us. There was no man with them. We don't recall whether the child was male or female.")

They walk through a large building, most likely a terminal, for there are counters of a sort to the right.

("Yes. We did walk through such a large terminal on our arrival in New York City.")

Our friend's ulcer may show a slight twinge here as he passes through the terminal.

("Yes. Bill's ulcer did bother him then.")

(Bill told us his ulcer bothered him somewhat more than usual during his vacation. He said that usually he has complete freedom from pain on such junkets.)

There is a short discussion concerning where to go next.

("Yes. We decided to look for a place to have a sandwich before the flight to Elmira.")

Someplace during their journeys they met a white-haired gentleman. I believe the name begins and ends with an A. His age about 62, perhaps older. The interest was of a business rather than a social one, in connection with this man.

("No.")

At this time, that is now *(9:44, Monday, October 25)* our cat lover is reading. Our Jesuit is studying people, and they are flying.

("On the plane on Tuesday, October 26, I read during the trip. Bill spent his time studying people.")

A dress or coat of many buttons.

("No.")

A small boy several seats ahead.

("No.")

Also a cab ride. Our cat lover laughs. A three-dollar fare, which seems large.

("Yes. This took place a week before, on the Sunday night we arrived in San Juan, October 17. We paid a $3.00 fare to go from the airport to our hotel. We thought the fare much too high and were both angry; the last time we had visited San Juan the same ride cost less than $2.00; perhaps $1.50.")

An old, rather than a younger cab driver, with a stubby neck.

("The cab driver was younger rather than older. But the back of his neck had a peculiar rough and mottled appearance that did make him appear to be older to us when seen from the rear. His neck could be called 'stubby'.")

A direction that is mainly to the right, after one turn.

(Giving this material during the session, Jane felt the motion, very swift, of the turn.

("Yes. The cab driver did take a sharp right and go in that direction. This happened after the cab driver ran through a red light and frightened us.")

A room on the fifth floor or higher, but not lower. They eat a meal here also. I pick up some connection with the word elm, and this building.

("*Our hotel room was on the fourth floor. We see no connection with the word elm.*"

(*The Gallaghers believe that the following impression, given by Seth in the same session as applying to Dr. Instream, applies instead to them. Jane gave the data after the break which had presumably ended the Gallagher test:*)

A cloth, like a handkerchief, laid upon the table, and a candle. Red, I believe... Now I think of two candles, and the piece of cloth is white, the cloth on the table.

(*[Peggy:] "At a restaurant on Sunday night, we had candles on the table. The tablecloth was white. We had red placemats, giving a checked effect."*

(*At the end of the 201st session, concluding the Gallagher Puerto Rico tests, Seth stated:*)

Possibly in New York your other friends eat turkey. It is better to eat turkey than crow.

(*The Gallaghers said they did not eat turkey sandwiches upon arriving in NYC, but other kinds.*)

(*Concluding the 197th session of October 11, 1965, held a week before the Gallaghers left for Puerto Rico on vacation, Seth stated:*)

I believe a rather bizarre event will occur, regarding the Gallaghers, at approximately five o'clock during their vacation.

(*Bill Gallagher had a narrow escape from drowning while skin diving in Puerto Rico. He hardly lists this as a bizarre experience. Seth deals with it to some degree in the unscheduled 203rd session of October 28, 1965.*

(*Bill did have one experience in Puerto Rico, however, that he said might be called bizarre. He is quite sure he hasn't had any other experience like it, and believes that if he hadn't been somewhat familiar with these sessions that this one too would have escaped his notice; that is, he would not have followed it through.*

(*The experience did not take place at five o'clock, but later one evening while Bill and Peggy were in a restaurant in San Juan. As an entertainer the restaurant had a white Puerto Rican female pianist. During a break she stood next to Bill at the bar. Bill then had the strange feeling that she would at once go back to her piano, on a raised platform, and begin to play. She did so. Bill then proceeded to name, in the correct order, the first three numbers the pianist would play. He has no idea as to how he was able to do this, or why he felt impelled to. After his first three correct calls he felt the ability wane, and began to make errors.*

(*The pianist also sang the numbers she played.*

(*Jane also tried psychological time experiments while the Gallaghers were in*

Puerto Rico. During these she lay quietly on the bed with her eyes closed and tried to contact Peggy and Bill either by acting as a receiver of data, or projecting her astral body to their location. All of the experiments took place in the late morning hours, usually lasting about half an hour. Jane tried five times, from Monday, October 18, to Friday, October 22, 1965.

(The Gallaghers gave their written answers to this material just as they had to Seth's material. This time in the following copy, Jane's psy-time notes are in regular type, followed by the Gallaghers' comments in italics.)

(October 18, 11:30 to Noon, Monday: Jane specifically requested information of the Gallaghers, but she did not list anything they were able to identify.)

(October 19, 11:10 AM to 11:50 AM:)
Music, not from a radio. A spectacular.
("Possibly. People always seemed to be singing.")
San Wano Beach *(phonetic.*
("Yes. Twice we swam at San Juan Municipal Beach."
(Note by R.F.B.: After Peggy and Bill left for Puerto Rico, I quizzed Jane to see how much geographical knowledge she had of the island. It developed that she had but the most general idea, to the effect that it lay south of Florida in the Caribbean. She did not know the name San Juan, for instance; nor had the Gallaghers told her, since we asked them to tell us nothing about their projected trip as soon as it was mentioned.)
Bill wears olive trunks.
("They were blue.")
Peg wears one-piece black bathing suit with a V-neck.
("No. A flowered blue bathing suit.")
Building on high cliff, a stilt-like arrangement built out. Beach below, cove type.
("There were several of that type on St. Thomas."
(Nor did Jane know that both Puerto Rico and St. Thomas are both very hilly islands.)
(Note that this data was received on October 19, and that the Gallaghers did not arrive in St. Thomas until October 22. Seth also gave information pertaining to St. Thomas on October 18.)
Charlie. Or someone calls Bill, Charlie?
("No.")
Now I look up at the bottom of something that is rising, I think like a small plane or boat, maybe.

("*This is possible. Aircraft seemed to be about us all the time.*"
(*The boat reference here makes us think also that it could be a reference to Jane's next data.*)

I see someone male: Bill? Diving, or at least underwater. Flippers, don't recall a tank, seems he has a mask though.

("*Yes. Bill went swimming. Also snorkeling, with the face mask but no tank.*"
(*The snorkeling device enables the diver to breath through a tube to the surface while remaining underwater. Bill said the boat reference above, reminds him of the peculiar look thinks appear to have on the surface of the water when seen from below. Several times while snorkeling he was close to coral cliffs or outcroppings rising above him. Surf breaking over his head appeared to have a "white sideways movement." It had a more or less solid look, like the white ceiling of a room.*)

Peg on shore dries her hair with a white towel. It's wet. Did Bill splash her?

(*[Peg:] "I had a white towel, but used it to sit on sand. Bill didn't splash me."*)
Small white skull.

("*Bill has a definite general association here, but can't recall any details.*"
(*Later Bill told us the skull association may be linked to the skeletons of fish he saw on the ocean bottom while skin diving; but he is not at all sure.*)

Small crucifix.

("*No.*")

(*October 20, 11:30 AM to Noon: Jane tried unsuccessfully to speak to Bill Gallagher. She had a quick clear image of a high sandhill leading down to a beach. The Gallaghers said this is quite possible, but of course could say little else about such a general impression.*)

(*October 21, 11 AM to 11:30 AM, Thursday:*)

Not much. San Quanamo or San Guatamalo Beach? Eating peaches or sitting on beaches.... Impressions were words.

(*The Gallaghers brought back with them a map of Puerto Rico, including a street map of San Juan. It is interesting to note that the U.S. Naval Reservation of <u>San Geronimo</u> lies across a couple of hundred yards of open water from the spot where Bill Gallagher went swimming and skin diving.*)

(*October 22, 11 AM until Noon, Friday. One hour:*
(*In the 201st session for October 25, Seth commented: "...and incidentally, Ruburt's experience in psychological time was quite legitimate." Jane's account of Friday's psy-time experience was included in the 201st session along with our drawing; it is repeated here, with the addition of the Gallagher's comments and Peggy's drawing.*)

I was doing so well when the alarm rang at 11:30 that I set it for another half-hour beyond my usual time.

None of what I saw was very clear. I felt I stood on a long narrow porch or verandah with a railing. On either a double-story motel, or a motel of one story that was raised up higher than usual somehow, from ground level.

([Peggy:] "This is a good description of the guest house where we stayed on St. Thomas on Friday and Saturday, October 22-23. The guest house was two story, and built on the side of a steep hill; it had the feeling of being raised up because of this. It had a long porch with a railing and benches.")

I looked over and down at a pool, and felt that beyond this either the ocean or a large body of water was visible. If the ocean, perhaps part of a bay with shores visible?

([Peggy:] "Looking out from the porch, we saw the bay and the ocean beyond it.")

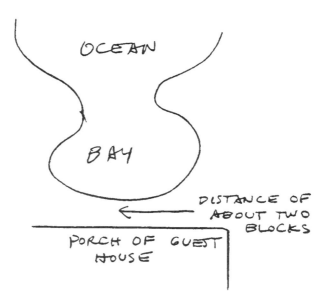

(In Session 201, see the drawing I made following Jane's instructions, after her psy-time experience. Note the similarities between that art and Peggy's drawing above. I added the lettering to Peggy's drawing, as well as to Jane's second version of the same scene, shown on page 162.)

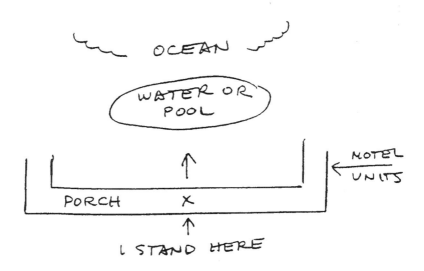

(Jane's second version of what she saw.)

Doors opened off the long narrow porch which extended full length, and I wondered if Bill and Peg were staying here. I thought their room might have the door near the center of the porch.

([Peggy:] *"Yes. Our door opened off the center of the porch."*)

I had an impression of Peg sitting by the pool, with Bill in it. I kept telling them I was standing nearby, just in case they could see anything of me. I still knew I was lying on the bed however, while I tried to project myself to their location.

([Peggy:] *"At no time did we have any awareness of Jane's presence."*)

After I reset the alarm I tried to wander to the other side of the motel to find a name sign. Instead I watched a man from above and behind; dressing in suit, hat, carrying a bag or briefcase. He crossed a blacktop expanse of some kind and walks on sidewalk by a large bulky building.

([Peggy:] *"Yes. Bill watched such a man from just outside the guest house. He was colored. Bill watched this man each morning; he noticed the man because he wore a suit and hat as though for business, instead of the usual tourist attire. He carried a black briefcase. The large bulky building was a post office."*)

Now as to sensations:

First I achieved a partial projection of some kind, and thought I might complete it but didn't. Strong thrilling sensations, feelings of being swept away. Odd movements of some sort. I could feel the blanket over me and my pillow at neck move in odd fashion as if my physical body was making unaccustomed movements, but thought I was motionless. Very strong momentary feelings of being swept away, though these are poor words to describe this. Extreme lightness, weightlessness.

Once thought I saw mountains, as if I were floating.

([Peggy:] "It is very hilly on St. Thomas."

(As stated before, Jane did not know that both Puerto Rico and nearby St. Thomas are very hilly.)

Then feeling of change of direction, more straight upward, yet still retained bedself. Once I was aware that I was looking up at treetops against a gray sky.

(*October 25, 11:30 to Noon, Monday: Poor results.*

(*The map of Puerto Rico, brought back by Bill Gallagher, contains a street map of San Juan and other large cities together with an index of street names. A quick study for names similar to those given phonetically by Seth/Jane during the experiments has yielded no results, with the exception of the apparent similarity between San Geronimo and Jane's psy-time impressions of San Quanamo and San Guatamalo. Any other similarities discovered later will be added to the record.*

(*Peggy Gallagher is a feature writer for the* Elmira Star-Gazette and Advertiser, *a* Gannett Newspaper. *During December 6 to 9 the paper sent her to Washington, DC to attend A Seminar on Poverty, conducted by the Office of Economic Opportunity which is headed by R. Sargent Shriver.*

(*Seth gave data on Peggy's trip in the 214th and the 215th sessions, December 6 and 8. He also gave some preliminary data on the trip during an unscheduled session held on December 3; Peggy took a copy of these predictions with her to Washington. Seth listed nine predictions and Peggy verified three of them. Seth gave them in Peggy's presence; his score in the two sessions held while she was in Washington was much better.*

(*As soon as we realized that Peggy's trip would furnish a good opportunity for another test, we asked her to say no more about it. By then we knew she was going to Washington, but Jane does not believe Peggy told her specifically, for instance, that Peggy was to cover a seminar on poverty. Be that as it may, we were told little in advance of the trip. Peggy herself did not know about the trip until a few days before she left.*

(*She returned to Elmira on December 9 and a written question-and-answer session was held on December 10. Jane and I made an effort to obtain detailed answers to Seth's statements, and Peggy cooperated in excellent fashion. The interview lasted about two hours. Once again, we stressed that we did not want to put words into her mouth concerning Seth's material, and she agrees that we did not.*

(As in the Puerto Rico experiments, Seth's material is presented line by line, in regular type, with Peggy's answers below. These answers are quotes from my notes made during the interview. Begin with Seth's material from the 214th session for December 6, 1965.)

Now, we shall see what we can do. A talk concerning survival of your nation. Our friend the cat lover attends this discussion.

(Peggy did attend this discussion. The talk didn't concern the survival of our nation, but of some individuals within it; it was a seminar on poverty.)

Perhaps in a room numbered 312.

([Peggy:] "The room number began with an 8." Peggy knows this because the seminar was held on the eighth floor of a building occupied by the Office of Economic Opportunity; in an executive conference room of the OEO.)

The speaker is interrupted.

([Peggy:] "Yes. The speakers were constantly interrupted by the various reporters attending.")

A question-and-answer session.

([Peggy:] "Yes. A question-and-answer session was held after each speaker had finished his formal talk.")

Three main speakers in the discussion itself.

(Peggy said either 3 or 4 speakers addressed the seminar in the morning session on Monday, December 6.

(She tried to determine the exact number later, from her own notes, but was unable to do so.)

Survival is a strong issue here, though it may not be the <u>title</u> of the discussion, formally.

(As stated, the title was A Seminar on Poverty. However, the discussions dealt with the survival of the hard-core poor, the deprived, on a strong, even desperate level, Peggy said. The seminar concerned the literal survival of these individuals, and methods of raising their standard of living. Much more than money was involved here.)

A tow-headed man with whom our friend comes in contact. She may not like him overmuch.

(Peggy met a <u>black</u>-haired man whom she found to be "repulsive." She told us she considered this person to be really upsetting to her personally; it was a case of one individual taking a strong dislike to another.

("You will meet a man you do not like" is one of the advance predictions given Peggy by Seth during the unscheduled session of December 3. Jane and I have wondered what part suggestion might play in such a case. Peggy told us she had also been aware of this, and that she could say that her dislike of the individual in question transcended any suggestion that conceivably could be operating.)

Something to do with a federation.

(*Nothing specific here, unless this is a distorted reference to the obvious fact of government buildings, etc., in Washington.*)

Pamphlets are given out.

(*[Peggy:] "Yes." Peggy said the reporters were deluged with pamphlets every day they were present. She herself accumulated a stack of pamphlets seven inches high, weighing several pounds.*)

Directions to a northeast location perhaps, though I do not know, for tomorrow's lecture.

(*The seminar remained in the same building on Tuesday. But on Wednesday, Peggy was in a group taken by bus to Camp Kilmer, which has been taken over by the OEO. Camp Kilmer lies northeast of Washington.*)

A particular man with a camera slung over his shoulder, who gets our friend's attention.

(*Peggy remembers one cameraman, out of several present, who carried his camera slung on a strap over his shoulder.*)

A handkerchief shows above his breast pocket. Pointed, that is a pointed handkerchief, with an initial, perhaps a C or G.

(*Peggy quite clearly recalls a man with such a handkerchief in his breast pocket. She remembers this because the handkerchief had four sharp points showing, which she considered unusual, very much out of the ordinary. She cannot recall however whether this man was also the cameraman. She does not remember any initials."*)

A grab bag of some kind.

(*"No."*)

Theater-type chairs rather than seats.

(*[Peggy:] "Yes. They were folding-type chairs with cushioned seats, as found in theaters. They were very comfortable. These chairs were lined up at long narrow tables. The whole conference except for trips was held in this particular conference room."*)

Incidentally, our Jesuit's ulcer bothers him this evening, quite strongly.

(*Yes, most definitely. This evening, Monday, December 6, Bill Gallagher's ulcer bothered him to such an extent that he called a doctor. This he seldom has to do.*

(*Tests resulting from this upset led to the medical opinion that Bill has two ulcers. However a recheck of old X-rays seems to show that the second ulcer had previously existed, but had not been detected. Needless to say, neither Jane nor I had seen Bill, or heard from him, since the unscheduled session of last Friday, December 3. We saw him later in the evening of December 10, after the interview with Peggy.*)

A <u>measurement</u> of abilities, though I do not know to what this refers.

(*[Peggy:] "Yes." Peggy said a large part of the seminar was devoted to discussing methods by which it would be determined which individuals would be able to take *part in various programs. Their capabilities, intellectual, financial, physical, etc., would have to be determined.)*

Fourteen thousand in all attend, in all sections, though at various times.

(Peggy said that at the seminar many thousands of people were mentioned at different times. She had no idea of the total however, but said the 14,000 figure would not be unreasonable. She thought she might have a total figure in her notes, taken for the series of articles she is to write for the local paper, but a check of the notes yielded no clues here. 14,000 people of course did not attend the seminar.)

The hotel on a corner.

([Peggy:] "Yes.")

<u>Her</u> room above three floors. A man across the way. The number 421.

(Peggy's room, #208, was on the second floor. She doesn't know whether a man had the room across the way, and has no connection to offer for 421.

(Jane took a break at this point, seemingly ending the Gallagher test before she went into the Dr. Instream test. However, Peggy said the first paragraph of the Insteam material applied to her Washington trip:)

A very smallish crowded room. I believe a cocktail party. A woman seems to be the main hostess, though a man is present with her.

(Monday night Peggy attended a cocktail party in a private home in Washington. The party was held in several small crowded rooms, plus a large room. The main hostess was a woman, Judy Carlyle, who is affiliated with the poverty program. Mrs. Carlyle's husband was present in an unofficial capacity, and was introduced to Peggy.

(In the unscheduled session for December 3 Seth said Peggy would meet a woman dressed in green. Peggy met no such woman. After the cocktail party however, Peggy found she couldn't remember the color of Mrs. Carlyle's dress. She checked by phone; Mrs. Carlyle had worn a red dress. Later note by RFB: Red and green are opposites on the artisit's color wheel.)

(We now begin with Seth's material on Peggy's Washington trip, from the 215th session, December 8, 1965.)

A banquet for your cat lover, with long narrow tables.

([Peggy:] "Yes." Peggy attended such a banquet. It was held in the same executive conference room as all the other seminar meetings; as stated, tables were long and narrow, with theater-type chairs. Lunch was also served at these tables each day).

A disturbance of some sort, though not necessarily here.

([Peggy:] "Yes. To wind up the seminar on poverty a press conference was held with Sargent Shriver, director of the poverty program. The disturbance occurred when an incensed group from Syracuse appeared and tried to disrupt the conference

time reserved for the reporters."

(Peggy thought the group was very rude. The group was silenced by Shriver and told to wait for a later meeting with him. The group itself, Peggy said, was obviously very angry. The incident occurred Wednesday at 5 PM.)

An endeavor to reach someone whom she was unable to contact, the initials perhaps W. B.

([Peggy:] "Yes, although the initials are R. D." Peggy wanted to talk with a certain official on the poverty program; his offices were on a floor lower than that of the seminar, in the same building. Peggy went to the man's offices on Tuesday and waited for some time there. Failing to see him, she made an appointment for Wednesday, but did not keep this appointment because of the press of other business.)

Again, a clock that did not work correctly.

(Peggy said she had an experience involving time. At her hotel she left a message with the desk clerk to be awakened at 7 AM Tuesday. The desk clerk failed to call her and she was late getting to the seminar.

(This is, also, one of Seth's predictions given during the unscheduled session of December 3, before Peggy left for Washington.)

Something with a new format.

(Peggy said she has no connection here.)

Ten people in a separate party or gathering, in which she took part.

(Yes, in that Peggy was in the small separate gathering that visited Camp Kilmer, northeast of Washington, on Wednesday. See page 165. Peggy remembered that the bus taking them to Camp Kilmer was far from full; her notes later confirmed that 12 reporters and 2 aides made the trip.)

Something having to do with March 10.

([Peggy:] "No.")

A room with a yellow wastepaper basket. Flowers in the room, perhaps roses. But florist's flowers.

(Peggy has no recollection here.)

An event at eight, last evening, in a different room than the room in which a previous meeting was held, that she attended.

([Peggy:] "No. All meetings at the seminar were held in the same room.")

McNamara.

([Peggy:] "Yes." Seeing the above word in the material caused Peggy to say that it was quite unusual. At the seminar Peggy was surprised to hear the name of Secretary of Defense McNamara brought up rather strongly in connection with Sargent Shriver and the poverty program. The connection being a comparison of the two men's tactics in running their respective departments. Peggy said the point was hammered at more than once during the seminar.)

A white taxicab. Identified by a round symbol on it, with a border inside the circle, and some sort of figures. Whether these are people, shapes or object shapes, I do not know. The symbol is of more than one color, however, and fairly dark against the white. I am seeing it in the evening, so the color of the symbol is not very clear. It is in front of a stone building.

(*Peggy said she took a taxi Tuesday evening, after dark. She cannot offer any information on whatever symbol the cab carried however, but did state the cab was of a "light color." The cab was also in front of a stone building—Garfinkel's Department Store.*

(*Arriving later in the evening, Bill Gallagher told us that the taxicabs of the predominant cab company in Washington are painted white. They carry a symbol on their front doors that is semicircular in shape, the design being based on the Capitol Dome. The symbol is of course in dark color against the white background.*)

An unusual attachment of aides goes with the group which she accompanies.

(*Peggy believes this is a reference to the bus ride to Camp Kilmer. As stated before, two aides accompanied the twelve reporters. Not unusual, then.*)

There is some hesitation at a gate while this gathering waits. While clearance is made, but it is a short hesitation.

(*Peggy said there was no hesitation or delay at the gate to Camp Kilmer, since the military does not occupy the camp anymore. The camp is run in its entirety now by the OEO.*)

I pick up something to do with a ballpark, or a park that has been used, or a stadium that has been used for ball games.

(*Peggy said she attended two meetings at Camp Kilmer that were held in a moderate-sized auditorium.*)

Something to do with a pocketbook. Did she misplace it? It is a shoulder variety however. Perhaps it was a camera.

(*Peggy lost her glasses and a ring at the seminar. She found the glasses but not the ring. No pocketbook of hers was involved.*

(*See page 122. At the time of the 215th session, Jane said she believed the pocketbook data, above, applied to herself, and as it developed a lost pocketbook connection involving Jane did grow out of the 21st envelope test, held in the 215th session.*

(*See also the notes on page 122, concerning the possibility of Seth giving information, in such tests, on something that is not noticed by the subject. A good example here is the taxicab symbol material on page 167-68.*)

(*Before our envelope test in the 215th session Seth added one more line to the Gallagher test material; see page 121:*)

I wanted to add something about shipyards to the Gallagher material.

(At first Peggy saw no connection here. Then she remembered that when she arrived in Newark, NJ from Elmira, she transferred to Kennedy Airport on Long Island by helicopter. During the trip, at an altitude of no more than 600 feet, she thus flew over many of the docks, piers and shipyards lining the Brooklyn waterfront. She thought at the time that Bill would have enjoyed the sight, since he likes ships. The helicopter flight traveled past the Statue of Liberty.)

(Peggy verified three of the nine predictions Seth gave in the unscheduled session of December 3, prior to her Washington trip. Two of the three correct items have been listed in their place in the above material. The third prediction, listed on page 108, is this:)

An unscheduled social engagement, not in a private home but a public place.

(This developed when Peggy spent an unplanned evening, including dinner at a restaurant, with her brother and his family, who live in Washington.)

```
PLEASE RETURN CARD TO INFORMATION DESK

BUNN MISS MARGARET M 3A-6  104674
B E WELLSBORO ST   6-7-65   525P
MANSFIELD PA P #58012  HILLMAN
MANSFIELD 662-310 " 6 7 ' 187 1⁶71




                VISITING HOURS
                            1:00 TO 8:00 P.M.
         1:00 TO 9:00 P.M. AND 7:00 TO 8:00 P.M.
         ARNOT-OGDEN         MEMORIAL HOSPITAL
```

(Tracing of the hospital visitor's pass, furnished by Lorraine Shafer, and used as the test object in the 24th envelope test, in the 219th session for January 3, 1966.)

SESSION 219
JANUARY 3, 1966 9 PM MONDAY AS SCHEDULED

(This is our first session since December 15, 1965. The rest was our longest since the sessions began two years ago, and did us both much good. We were ready to go back to work, although Jane confessed to some feeling of nervousness as session time approached. But she did well. She had no urge to speak for Seth during vacation.

(See the tracing on page 169 for the test object for this evening's envelope test. It was furnished by Lorraine Shafer, who witnessed this session. Details will be presented in the body of the session, as they developed. The last session witnessed by Lorraine was the 195th, of October 4, 1965. See Volume 4.

(The session was held in our large front room. Jane began speaking while sitting down. Her eyes were closed, her voice a little stronger than usual, and her pace quite good. She smiled as she began. Her voice was rather dry.)

Good evening.

("Good evening, Seth.")

After your long vacation, you should be quite ready to plunge into our activities anew. You <u>should</u> be. I do not see any signs however of any great enthusiasm as we resume.

Perhaps your holidays take more out of you than I do.

("Yes.")

My greeting to Marleno, and my sympathy to Ruburt as he struggles to plow through his Dunne.

(Marleno is Lorraine Shafer's entity name. Jane has obtained three of Dunne's book through the state library at Albany, and we are in the midst of reading them.)

I am ready to resume our previous discussion, and look forward to a most effective year, in your time one.

Now. If you will recall our early sessions dealing with value fulfillment, let us now consider what I prefer to call a moment point. This moment point, as you know, refers to any given present instant. If you are thinking in terms of Dunne's theories, then start out with this moment point as it is seen in time one by self one.

(Early in the sessions Seth began giving us lists of the inner senses and the basic laws of the inner universe. Value fulfillment, or the value climate of psychological reality, is the first basic law of the inner universe; Seth presented it in the 45th session in some detail. See Volume 2.

(See the following sessions for details on moment points: 149, 150, 151, 152.)

The ego can perceive only certain portions of any given moment point or present instant, and it sees the moment point indeed as if it were one of a series of lights that approaches the ego from one side, and passes him by on the other side. The ego perceives this moment point, then, very much as if it were a flat cardboard-like object which comes, is flashed before him, and disappears.

The ego cannot see that this moment point is <u>open</u>, so to speak, and represents an opening into many other dimensions. These dimensions may be traveled through; but they may not be traveled through by the ego, for the ego can only perceive those dimensions which it is physically equipped to see, or perceive.

Other portions of the self, on the one hand, are not so limited. It must be clearly understood however <u>that these other portions</u> of the self are incapable of the ego's intense focus within physical reality. Their focus is elsewhere. However, these selves are not limited as is the ego to one main field of perception only, in the manner which Dunne believes. Dunne does leave intervening areas between dimensions which may be perceived by an observer from a neighboring dimension, but all in all his serial selves are to some large degree prisoners of those dimensions in which they exist.

Such is fortunately not the case.

Now. These other selves are more freewheeling. There are indeed limitations inherent within their structure, but in all cases any given identity is more than the dimension in which it finds itself. Its limitations may be great, but the limitations are set not by the identity's nature but by the dimension in which it exists.

(*Consider the whole of the next paragraph underlined for emphasis. Jane was by now speaking more rapidly and with much intent and conviction. She used many forceful gestures, although her eyes remained closed.*)

<u>The identity may, and will, move out of its dimension into another, and it therefore has within it the innate capacity to perceive more than it is allowed to perceive at any given point by the limitations set upon it.</u>

Two of these statements may appear at first glance to contradict themselves, but you shall shortly see that they do not, and you are left for now with a pretty question: for does the self, or identity, then form the perceptive dimension in which it exists, or is it created by the dimension?

Take a brief break and we shall continue.

(*Break at 9:16. Jane was dissociated as usual for a first delivery. She had been wrapped up in the material, speaking fast and with much emphasis.*

(*During break Lorraine asked if we still conducted envelope tests. When we said yes, she told us she had brought a test envelope with her. Moreover, it was one I had given her myself when she witnessed the 172nd session of July 26, 1965. Handing her the two envelopes and the two pieces of Bristol, I had asked her to pick a test object, seal it up, and give it to me the next time we saw her, without telling me what the test object was. She had picked the test object last August, then mislaid the envelope and forgotten it; in addition I hadn't asked her for it.*

(Lorraine handed me her envelope while Jane was out of the room; thus Jane did not see it before the test. It was tightly sealed. I did not mention to either Jane or Lorraine whether I had planned a test for tonight. Lorraine did not tell me the contents of her envelope. Jane didn't comment on it and I let the matter rest.

(Jane resumed in the same fast and active, emphatic manner, again with her eyes closed, at 9:30. Her voice was still dry.)

I am indeed taking it very easy this evening, to break you in again, so to speak.

The vacation has done you both good however, and your energies have indeed replenished themselves. I have some slight trouble with Ruburt when sessions are not regular. However this effect is fleeting, and as always I bear with such things in my usual manner.

(Jane smiled and paused. She cleared her throat rather often.)

Now let us begin again.

We start once more with our moment point. For now this moment point which <u>appears</u> within your physical universe is but a small materialization of larger portions of the spacious present. In the dreaming state, when the ego is released from its idea of time as a series of moments, then other portions of the self can travel <u>through</u> these moment points, and you have here a journey through depths that have nothing to do with <u>your</u> (underline your) concept of time or space.

You journey through <u>intensities</u>, as I have told you. These moment points are like spirals however, and journeying through them these other portions of the self will come in contact with <u>both future and past</u> actions, that have occurred, or will occur, according to the viewpoint of the ego.

To this degree Dunne was correct. But the important point, if you will forgive a pun, is that these moment points are all intensities, electrical realities, and traveling through such dimensions involves a transformation of energy from one intensity to another. The whole self, or the entity of which I speak, is composed of <u>all</u> of these selves, <u>but it must be realized that all divisions between these selves are illusions, basically speaking</u>. For the sake of discussion we separate them, but in doing so we almost manage to change the very nature of that which we attempt to study.

There is nothing contradictory in the overall in supposing that these multitudinous selves exist simultaneously. And any law of physics that appears to make this supposition incorrect is a law that is an illusion, and that in itself leads to false perceptions.

(*Besides the sessions on moment points, see those on the electrical field and on action—too numerous to list here.*)

Such communication between these various selves who compose an entity is natural, continuous. The ego does not perceive the communications, obviously; but the ego, you must understand, is not self one alone, it is only a <u>portion</u> of self one, or the physical self.

Other portions of self one are to some extent aware of these other dimensions. Now you see where we are heading. For now consider what we shall call self A. And we shall say that he is the physical self in the physical universe. He is composed of physical matter, he is composed of psychological matter, a portion of this latter being ego. From your own work you realize however that this individual, or self A, is indeed more than physical matter, even while he exists within the physical dimension.

In the dreaming state and in other states of consciousness, he can indeed to some degree become aware of perceptions which will be neglected by the ego alone. In other words, psychologically <u>there is only one portion of self A that is limited</u> in its perceptions to the physical dimension, and that is the ego.

But self A is <u>not</u> limited to the ego's perceptions only, therefore it may be said that self A's perceptions are not limited, in toto, to the field in which it exists. For it is not so limited in dreams and in other states, yet while consciousness is in these other conditions, self a still exists within physical reality.

If self A were limited to the perceptions of the ego, and if self A were limited then to the dimensions in which it found itself, then my dear friends precognition in dreams would be impossible, and in order to perceive the future self A would of necessity be forced to discontinue existence within the physical system.

I am going to give you a break, and we shall begin then with our material for Dr. Instream, and see what we can do with our time systems.

(*Break at 9:50. Jane was dissociated as usual. Her eyes had remained closed. Her delivery had again been fast and very emphatic. Jane said she "felt" parts of the delivery. She said she could have spoken much faster had my writing been able to keep up.*

(*At break Jane mentioned something that had been on her mind. She was aware of course that Lorraine had brought a test envelope. Jane now wondered whether I would try to be tricky, and perhaps keep Lorraine's envelope for a later test, while giving her the usual envelope that I had prepared. Jane took it for granted that I had a test envelope ready also. I didn't commit myself in any way.*

(*It was now time for the 27th Dr. Instream test. As usual Jane sat with her eyes closed, her left hand to her face, her head down. Her pace was slow at the start, but picked up rather well as the test proceeded. Resume at 10:05.)*

Now, give me a moment, please. *(Pause.)*

These are my impressions. A series of small boxes, as in a post office, though I believe they are connected with the college.

They are rectangular, and fairly deep. *(Pause.)* He has been working there, I believe, on marking grades, or making out some sort of reports which are finding their way into these boxes. He sits now *(at 10:09)* at a table like a card table, I believe alone, with a game of some sort before him, or at least with a board such as a checkerboard. *(Pause.)*

The object before him on the table does have checks upon it. Some are black, and the object is flat and of cardboard. He is in a robe, slippers and pajamas, with a door behind him. I believe to a clothes closet. *(Pause.)*

I pick up once more a connection with boxes, but here in this room. And they are larger, perhaps shoe boxes or that type.

I also pick up a rather uncharacteristic connection with a pipe. Either he has been given one, or he has purchased one; but there is a connection with a pipe here.

(Jane now took a long pause at 10:12.)

A carpeted hall outside the door; and it seems an overnight guest, who has in his possession a leatherlike bag that is not a suitcase, but meant to hold papers. *(Pause.)* Light brown, fairly new in appearance, having I believe about its edges brass or gold colored bands of some sort. The initial C connected with the owner of the bag, and also perhaps a G, though I am not certain of this last letter.

Now do you have a test for me, Joseph?

("Yes. Here you are.")

(I handed Jane Lorraine's sealed envelope. Jane reached out for it without opening her eyes at 10:16. As she has done a few times recently, she held the envelope flat against her forehead while speaking a few words, then lowered it to her lap. Her pace was again broken by pauses, none of them very long with one exception. This is the 24th envelope test.)

Now please give us a moment.

A connection with a turbulent event, or unpleasantness. Four seven. The initial M, a connection with four people, and an afternoon. A location not in this city, that is a connection with a location not of this city.

A connection with a blue saucer, with an event of 1965, winter, <u>and</u> with an event I believe occurring approximately 1947.

A disturbance again, and a storm; whether or not this storm is <u>physical</u> I do not know.

(*Jane took a long pause at 10:20.*)

A miscellany of objects, designs that appear like numbers. A connection with a family record; as a page, <u>for example</u>, from a book.

And a very distant connection with a child's hair ribbon. A wide band sort; this applies to the child's ribbon.

I pick up the number seven, and this could refer to the age, that is, of the child who wore the ribbon.

We have here also the impression of a box once more, and I will tell you later why I have repeated this impression.

A connection also with four numbers, I believe in a row. I suggest your break.

(*Break at 10:25. Jane was dissociated as usual. Her eyes had remained closed, her pace had been slow.*

(*See the tracing on page 169. The test object is a visitor's pass, produced by the Arnot-Ogden Hospital, where Lorraine is a secretary. This particular pass had been discarded; Lorraine picked it out of a wastebasket on the spur of the moment last August.*

(*Since the test object was picked by someone other than me, I had thought that some of Seth's connections might be difficult to trace, and it appears to be the case here. Since the part of the data we can judge is pretty much on the ball, we think it reasonable to assume that the rest of Seth's data may be equally good. Jane was pleased by the test.*

(*This is the first envelope test wherein the test object was picked by someone from outside.*

(*As stated before Jane was somewhat nervous this evening, resuming sessions and tests after the vacation. As soon as she gave the initial M, in the beginning of the data, she thought of Lorraine's entity name, Marleno. Jane caught herself at once, she now said, in order to prevent possible distortions growing out of this thought. She said "To hell with it," to herself, relaxed, and kept on speaking for Seth. She completely cut off her own associations; this ability to discriminate, Seth has told us, is very important, and will grow steadily on Jane's part.*

(*It seems reasonable to describe a stay in the hospital as "a turbulent event, or unpleasantness," and as "A disturbance again, and a storm; whether or not this storm is <u>physical</u> I do not know." We of course realize there might be other connections in the private life of the patient, Miss Margaret M. Bunn. Lorraine does not know Miss Bunn. It is possible the hospital records contain more on Miss Bunn that would be revealing here, but I did not ask Lorraine to try to check.*

(*"The initial M" is a hit. We can offer no connection with "four people, and* an afternoon." "A location not in this city, that is a connection with a location not of this city," is a hit, Mansfield, PA, being the other location.

("Blue saucer" rings no bells, or "winter," or "an event I believe occurring approximately 1947." "An event of 1965" can apply, since Miss Bunn was admitted to the hospital on June 7, 1965.

("A miscellany of objects, designs that appear like numbers," is we think a reference to the words and numbers on the pass. "A connection with a family record; as a page, for example, from a book," is a hit. The visitor's pass contains a number code referring to Miss Bunn's hospital record, Lorraine tells us; and the pass is like a page from a book, in that such passes are kept in spiral books at the hospital.

(We probably will never check on the data referring to a child's hair ribbon, the child's age, etc.

(The numbers "Four seven" are on the pass, and also "four numbers, I believe in a row," if you want to isolate this many from longer groups. On the last line of the data on Miss Bunn some numbers are barely legible; we can see the impression of four numbers in a row here also.

(Jane had no idea as to why Seth referred to a box again. She told us she enjoyed the test involving a more impersonal object, in the sense that I did not choose it. However Jane was as much aware of the emotional charges surrounding this object; she felt that she was quite aware of the emotional disturbances involved in a hospital stay in this particular case.

(I would like to add a curious note. Note that Miss Bunn lives on Wellsboro St. in Mansfield, PA. Mansfield is a college town about seventy miles distant. I was born there. In addition, my father was born in Wellsboro PA., a small town perhaps twenty miles beyond Mansfield. As far as I know Lorraine Shafer doesn't know of my family connections with Mansfield and Wellsboro. She also told us she merely picked the test object out of a group, without paying particular attention to it.

(Jane resumed in a quiet voice, her eyes closed, at 10:50.)

I am not going to keep you. I wanted however to mention one small point concerning the box image that was repeated in both tests.

This has to do with <u>two</u> separate principles. First of all there was a retention of image. Second of all, there was quite separately an association because of the size of the card given as test object. In the second case the association was Ruburt's, for on his own he picked up a file-card image, but he translated this into the image of a box in which such file cards are often kept.

(Jane's eyes now opened. They were very dark. She lit a cigarette, and as she smoked and talked her eyes began to open frequently.)

Now while this association was his own, it was <u>caused</u> by the image retention carrying over from the first test. I want it clear that two rather than one causes existed for this second box image or impression.

Actually it was fairly legitimate, but not carried far enough on Ruburt's part. In this case he did very well in closing off his own associations.

Now when he does so disconnect his own stream of consciousness in this manner, any <u>correct</u> associations on his part will <u>automatically</u> show themselves in the data through attraction. They will become incorporated with <u>my</u> data in a constructive fashion. This is fairly important, and we shall follow it up by examples when possible. For <u>I</u> will perceive certain types of information that are basic, and when Ruburt's abilities, his <u>own</u> abilities as apart from mine, are fully developed, then he will be able to add certain specifics that have direct personal application.

My information will indeed be <u>specific</u> enough, but there are certain human interrelationships that he will more precisely perceive, for they have no particular <u>meaning</u> for me.

I will discuss this more thoroughly, perhaps at our next session so as not to keep you this evening, for I do not believe that I have quite made myself clear.

(*I thought the information clear enough, and quite important. Not wanting Seth to continue in this fashion because of the hour, I picked another question. Sitting across the table from me, Jane appeared ready to continue beyond closing time.*)

("*What about the pair of eyes I saw so clearly last month, while I was in bed? Can you say a few words about this?*")

(*Jane, her eyes open, smiled at me quite deliberately.*)

I did not know that you would tempt me with such a question at the end of a session; and you have no one but yourself to blame, if the session continues longer than you would have it.

("*Well, perhaps we'd better let it go then.*")

You were dealing, indeed, with a legitimate perception into a dimension outside of the ones with which you are familiar, and with a distortion of a <u>sort</u> on your part, as once again you attempted to translate inner data into a form that could be perceived by the physical senses.

(*Jane opened her eyes. Since Seth did not go into my latest vision this evening, I'll save a description of it for next session. The last vision of mine that he discussed took place on August 30, 1965, and is dealt with in the 183rd session. It was of the head of a man I had known centuries earlier in a previous life, according to Seth.*)

Now. <u>I</u> am in fine form. Ruburt is doing well. I realize that the hour has grown late in your time one, so I shall leave it to you as to whether or not I continue a most interesting discussion this evening. You may do as you think best.

("*Will you continue this discussion in the next session?*")

Very well. You must admit that I gave you your money's worth this evening.

("Yes. Thank you.")

My heartiest wishes to you both. And if our friend had been able to stay later we could have done rather well with her, for again our conditions were right.

(Here Seth refers to Lorraine Shafer, who had to leave at last break. He also did well with Lorraine during the last session she witnessed, the 195th of October 4, 1965, delivering quite a bit of information on Lorraine's past; she verified much of it. See Volume 4.)

When we have time I have some remarks, or will have, concerning your Miss Callahan; and also some remarks concerning Ruburt's business matters. For now however I wish you good evening.

("Good night, Seth.")

(End at 11:09. Jane was very well dissociated, she said, even though her eyes had been open at times. She said Seth could have continued indefinitely; Seth had her in a "low" state that seemed to require hardly any of her own energy, Jane said. She now felt very good. The dryness had left her throat; she thought it the result of nervousness at resuming the sessions.

(Miss Callahan is an elderly retired school teacher who lives in the front apartment. Her memory has been affected by a series of small strokes. Seth has considered her in earlier sessions, and she was also the subject of some of Jane's first recorded clairvoyant dreams. These took place at the beginning of Miss Callahan's illness. Seth discussed the progress of her troubles for a while in succeeding sessions, apparently accurately. Jane is still very solicitous for Miss Callahan's welfare.

(In addition, Miss Callahan is the only person we have located who taught Frank Watts' children in grade and high school; Frank Watts was the first personality Jane contacted in these sessions and was soon replaced by Seth. According to Seth Frank Watts had a high regard for Miss Callahan as a person and as a teacher. Miss Callahan however, cannot remember Frank Watts; only that she taught some "Watts children". See Volume 1 for Callahan and Watts material.)

SESSION 220 179

```
EXC...
0.66    21 DEC.65

S. F. ISZARD
DEPARTMENT STORE
    No.32



    02.00 IV

    00.08 IV


    02.08 A

RETURN IN CASE OF
ERROR OR EXCHANGE

  967    21 DEC.65
```

```
    It Pays to Shop
     at PENNEY'S

DEC.28    18.67 ⊄    5338  08
Date Dept.  Amt Clk.   No. Reg.

DEC.18    18.67 ⊄    5338  08
Date Dept.  Amt Clk.   No. Reg.
         J.C.PENNEY CO.
           INCORPORATED
```

*(Tracings of the sales slips used in the 25th envelope test,
in the 220th session, January 5, 1966.)*

SESSION 220
JANUARY 5, 1966 9 PM WEDNESDAY AS SCHEDULED

(*For this evening's envelope test I used two sales slips stemming from Christmas shopping Jane and I did. They are on paper the weight of this page. I put them down between the usual two pieces of Bristol, and enclosed them in the usual sealed double envelope.*

(*On page 177 of the last session Seth mentioned a recent vision of mine, and promised to discuss it further this evening. Since he does so I will now describe it in some detail. It took place in December, as I lay in bed suspended in that pleasant interlude between waking and sleeping; I've had other visions while in this state, incidentally.*

(*I realized on this particular evening that although my eyes were closed, I was staring into another pair of eyes that seemed to be within inches of my own, and had been doing so for some seconds. Conscious realization seemed to be suspended. These eyes were I would say masculine, and very beautiful, and could be human. They were a deep luminous golden brown; I realized I was so close to them that I could see their minutest details in vivid color, even upper lids that fell over the upper portion of the eyeball. At this stage of the phenomenon I encouraged this minute inspection, for I lay suspended below alarm.*

(*I saw the reddish rims of these eyes, and their black lashes with the utmost clarity. The skin about them was a light brown. At the fringes of my field of vision I saw that the face containing these magnificent eyes was quite hairy, covered by long black shining hair almost as though I was visualizing a throwback to more primitive man. But there was no sense of primitiveness here; these limpid brown eyes regarded me impassively; there was no intrinsic threat. These eyes merely stared back at me from beneath heavy black brows.*

(*As soon as I fully, consciously, realized what was taking place, I reacted violently in the manner described below by Seth. Within a very brief period after this unfortunate reaction, I began to regret it, for I knew I had terminated something much too soon. I thought my reaction was a normal one, yet was angry at myself for reacting so strongly. My outcry, my thrashing about in bed and waving my arms, of course startled Jane; I believe she had not yet fallen asleep. I blamed myself for not knowing enough to suspend any conscious judgment; I felt I had enough background knowledge to go along with this vision, to see what developed, yet I had reacted in what I thought a foolish way.*

(*Strange to say, I did not come fully awake as one does when arising in the morning for example. I achieved a state close to waking only, in spite of my momentary panic. Jane began to question me; she told me the next morning that I described the* vision to her while speaking in a sleepy monotone. I was conscious of doing this, and that it took some little time, yet felt no urge to prod myself wide awake. I recall that I felt it urgent that I tell her what had taken place as soon as possible. I thought of getting up to make a drawing of what I had seen, but decided I would not forget. This is certainly true; this vision is as vivid and clear in memory today as it was a second after it ended. I do intend making a drawing, in color, for those who may be interested.

(In addition, Seth has given enough information upon these visions so that I thought I had probably distorted quite valid and alien data into a form I could understand.

(I would add that when I realized I was receiving information for the first time, on a level below that of alarm, I encouraged this flow of data. I believe my perception then sharpened to some degree, and it was at this moment that I saw so clearly the minutest detail of the eyes, the shadow below the lids, the individual lashes, etc. I would say that at this moment of suspended judgment, before the ego exerted its authority, I was perfectly willing to receive this data and to examine it.

(The last vision of mine that Seth discussed took place on August 30, 1965, during waking hours, and was mentioned in the 183rd session of that evening.

(The session tonight was held in our large front room. Jane likes to use this room since it is larger than the back room we have used for the past few months, out of a fear of interruptions. She began speaking while sitting down and with her eyes closed. Her pace was good, her voice average.)

Good evening.

("Good evening, Seth.")

Now. Before I discuss your experience, the image that you saw, let me make a few preliminary remarks.

First of all, you understand from our discussions concerning planes and fields in general, that these are more multitudinous than you can imagine. A proportion of these will be discussed along with the nature of time, since some of these are connected with probabilities that could have occurred within your physical system.

(Seth referred to this bewildering multiplicity very early in the sessions, and dealt with it rather extensively in the 12th session of January 2, 1964, in his first explanation of what he calls the fifth dimension. He has told us we could never cover even a portion of the numberless fields bordering even our own; some will be explained as they impinge upon our own in various ways; Seth also has mentioned his own ability to travel through a few other fields. See Volume 1.)

In your particular state of consciousness on that particular evening, your attention strayed beyond your ordinary fields of perception. You perceived an

<u>inhabitant</u> of another system. There was indeed a quite unusual point of contact reached; most unusual indeed in that you not only perceived this individual, <u>but he also perceived you.</u>

(*Jane's eyes opened. They were very dark. She stared at me and tapped upon the table for emphasis. Her eyes now opened frequently until break.*)

The point of such contact can indeed be mathematically shown, and in the future I shall do just that. Part of your own reaction, I believe, was due to the fact that you realized that this contact represented a personal encounter, that this bizarre apparition was aware of you as you were of him.

("What was his reaction to me?"

(*Jane smiled.*)

First you displayed, if I may say so, a rather unfortunate reaction. You were quite ready to strike out physically at what you could not understand. And <u>this</u> reaction broke the contact.

<u>You</u> did not break it purposely, but the other individual concerned was bewildered, and to some extent frightened, and <u>he</u> withdrew. You were indeed quite willing to strike out physically. It was this <u>emotional</u> reaction that was felt by the other individual, and the other individual had no idea what this emotion was.

Now. The portion of the image that came closest to any semblance of reality was the region about the eyes, and the eyes themselves. There is much to be said here. For this was not imaginary, in that it did have a certain physical reality that existed within your field of reference.

You must understand however that momentarily <u>you</u> had a reality in the reference field of that other individual. The contact was mutual. Now we know what the conditions were at your end. We know that you made no attempt to <u>aim</u> your attention in the particular direction that would allow you to perceive that definite system.

You could just as well have tuned in, so to speak, on any one of the numberless other such systems. The individual within this particular other system, however, has a different sort of psychological makeup than your own. He is not as capable of intense concentration within as large a perspective as that possessed by your ego.

We have spoken, saying that the ego has a relatively small but intense focus. Your friend however has an even smaller <u>specific</u> field of attention, to <u>your way</u> of thinking. The concentration however and the focus is much more <u>intense</u> than that with which you are familiar.

Its <u>general</u> field of awareness however is much larger than any with which you are familiar, and he has a greater control and focus within this larger generalized field than you possess in your comparable generalized field of perception. His dissociated states, for example, make up a much larger portion of his perception, and they are more vivid than mankind's generalized dissociated conditions.

Because his range was so large, your dissociated conditions simply met more easily than otherwise. However, once his attention was centered here, he turned his conscious attention to full focus upon what he perceived. Nor did he perceive your physical form as you know it. But he picked up fully your <u>emotional</u> recognition and fear, and these were translated or perceived by him in his own fashion, so that to him you appeared as a mass of varying colors, and as movement of severe intensity.

The pulsations were caused by the action of your emotional state. And you, my dear Joseph, literally frightened him away. You on your part translated what was inner data into a form that you could, or hoped to, understand. The eyes were the first images that you saw.

I suggest a break and we shall continue.

(*Break at 9:25. Jane reported that she had been quite well dissociated for a first delivery—far-out, as she puts it. Her eyes had been open more than closed, very dark as she stared at me. Her pace had been rather good, her voice average and quite amused at times, perhaps chiding in a gentle way.*

(*She resumed in the same manner, quite emphatic at times, at 9:35.*)

Now. Despite my remarks, your reaction was perfectly understandable.

You should learn from it, for with your particular abilities it is possible that other such encounters will occur, though most <u>improbable</u> that the same system or field will be involved.

(*I have hoped many times for another such contact, with the promise to myself that I would do better next time. I have also used suggestion, although not nightly, to the effect that more such experiences would occur. Nothing has developed to date.*)

The individual was also bewildered however because he was able to perceive you in what you would call both your future and your past, as well as your present.

He perceived that a portion of you was bound, however, within your present time, and this was almost incomprehensible to him.

Such encounters do occur with what would appear to be startling frequency, when those in your system are sleeping; but they are very seldom remembered. What <u>was</u> however extremely unusual was that this contact was recognized as such by two inhabitants of completely different systems.

Such encounters also occur during waking hours, but the ego is not aware of them. I will have some comments later in the session that may enable you to become more aware of other realities beside your own, and also some advice that will enable you to operate within your own system more effectively.

You translated, now, this data into other terms. The alien nature of the individual you translated into an animalistic appearance. This was not to emphasize any lower or base characteristics, but was your way of translating the individual's exceptionally clear, pure and single-minded perception. For the intensity behind the perception reminded you of the unswerving attention often displayed in animals: a complete lack of trickery as it is understood by you.

It will be most difficult to convince others of the reality of other systems beside their own, yet none of this must be taken upon my say-so alone. For once the knowledge is available, others will become aware of their own experiences, and you see here how the conscious self becomes educated and enriched; for the knowledge becomes part of consciousness. In the past the <u>same</u> experience would have remained only in the subconscious, and you have had other such experiences.

(Jane's eyes had now been opening often again.)

You are not alone in this however. You have had no other experiences where contact was recognized both by you and the other individual from the other system, however; and <u>he</u> takes what he learned as part of himself now.

I do not know how it would serve you if I tried to describe the sort of plane which he inhabits. And since we are dealing in words some of the information simply would not make sense to you.

("Well, can you say a little about it then?"

(I was of course much interested, and knew that Jane was too. Jane now closed her eyes and sat quietly for a moment.)

It is a system that I cannot pinpoint for you in terms of physical location within your physical universe; though this location is far beyond your own solar system, it still does not exist as a physical mass however.

It exists within your physical universe but it is not of your physical universe, and it does not deal with physical matter at all. It is an old system, using your viewpoint. It has what I will call an inverted time system, which I will gladly discuss for you whenever you prefer.

There are brain formations, not materialized in physical form. Sensations are perceptions; emotions perceived in terms of color, and directly in terms of intensities. There is no <u>direct</u> relation here to your own system at all, except of course that all systems are ultimately connected. The inverted time system results in a different sequence of experience than that with which you are acquainted.

It is difficult to <u>explain</u> to you in terms you can understand. I will make an analogy, which however will be imperfect. We will take reincarnation as a basis. Imagine that you have had ten reincarnations. These reincarnations all represent portions of your entity, living or experiencing sensation at various times within a physical time system.

The entity has awareness of these ten portions of itself. Consciously however no one of the ten personalities is aware of the others, nor of the entity. Each of the ten egos travels along an egotistical time of successive moments. We understand that <u>subconsciously</u> much more knowledge is available, but not to the ego as a rule.

Now. In this inverted time system individual ten is aware of the experiences of individual two; and individual two is aware of the experiences of individual ten. <u>All</u> of these individuals have access to the experiences of the other. Individual ten may, so to speak, go back without confusion and enter into any experience undergone by any of the other individuals.

(This sounds very much like the use of what Seth calls the third, fourth and fifth inner senses: Perception of past, present, and future; the conceptual sense; cognition of knowledgeable tissue. Material on these senses was presented in the 35-38th sessions.)

There is no time boundary as you know it. This is obviously a gestalt. The <u>experiences</u> however of individual two, for example, are constantly being changed because of the intervention of the other personalities.

We had better take our break, for our Dr. Instream material will begin shortly.

(Break at 10:05. Jane was dissociated as usual. Her eyes had been open much of the time, her pace good, her voice average. She said Seth could have continued in this vein, but stopped because the usual tests were due. Seth had the next thought or concept waiting, Jane said, and all she had to do was give voice to it.

(It was now time for the 28th Dr.Instream test. As usual Jane's pace slowed considerably. She spoke with many pauses, sitting with her eyes closed, her head down, her left hand raised to her brow. Resume at 10:10.)

Now. Give us a moment and we shall see what we can do.

Today, a schedule of events, interrupted, a disturbance. *(Pause.)* Perhaps an illness, and someone in bed.

A late walk, on Dr. Instream's part I believe this evening.

A small meeting this afternoon, with one older and one younger man. Perhaps at five o'clock. *(Pause.)* A wish of Dr. Instream's that is fulfilled, having to do with a project.

Some guests at his office earlier, in the nature of nuisances. A connection here with Ticonderoga. Perhaps one of the visitors was from there. I do not know, but this has application connected with his office today. *(Pause.)*

I believe he lost a scarf, navy blue. In any case, whether it was lost or found, I see a navy blue scarf on the chair by his desk, in his office. Now; that is, in his office now.

(*Jane, her eyes still closed, gestured here as though to make this point clear.*)

A letter today from a man in the Midwest, or a letter <u>about</u> him. The man is on in years. He has two daughters, and is known for grumbling.

Again, I see the image of a clock, with ornate pattern about it, oval rather than round. The impression that it is a lady's watch rather than a man's, or a mantel clock. The decorations are of gold color rather than silver, and the numbers are comparatively small, rather than large.

The disturbance spoken of earlier may possibly have taken place during a class.

Do you have a test for me, Joseph?

("Yes."

(*It was 10:23, and this was our 25th envelope test. As usual Jane took the test envelope from me without opening her eyes. She held it to her forehead for a sentence or two, then lowered it to her lap.*)

Now, a moment again please.

A connection with an arrival, as at the end of a tour of duty. A connection with a view of hills, and with four people. An engagement, as of an appointment or meeting.

A scramble. A connection with the month of June. The numbers three seven, and diagonal marks on the four corners of a rectangular piece of paper, connected perhaps with a photograph album.

A connection with dark hill shapes. A distant location, also connected here.

A dark or darkish brown coat, the color of some uniforms. Crowded. Many voices, dancing.

I suggest your break.

(*Break at 10:30. Jane was dissociated as usual. Her eyes had remained closed and her pace had been slow.*

(*The test results this evening present a case where two separate events are combined in the results, as will be explained a bit later. At the moment I'll list the correct pieces of information that Jane and I can easily identify.*

(*See the tracing of the two sales slips on page 179. The data contain references to both slips, although Seth or Jane did not identify them as such, or refer to the fact that there were two test objects, as I had hoped. Jane said that during the test she was not sure of the source of information, Seth or herself.*

("*An engagement, as of an appointment or meeting,*" applies to the S.F. Iszard sales slip. On December 21 last, Jane and I went Christmas shopping; we parted to get each other gifts, after making an appointment to meet at a certain restaurant downtown when our shopping was over. "A scramble" can apply to either or both slips, since when we went shopping on December 18 and 21 we found the stores very crowded. Some aisles were difficult to get through, there was waiting necessary to get into dressing rooms, etc.

("A dark or darkish brown coat, the color of some uniforms," is a reference to a sports coat of corduroy that Jane bought me for Christmas; this is indicated by the Penny's sales slip for December 18. The coat is a close approximation of the color of the winter topcoat for the everyday U.S. Marine uniform. The Marine connection here will be apparent shortly.

("Crowded. Many voices, dancing," refers to the first time I wore the new coat. This was to a party given by Bill Macdonnel at his art gallery on Thursday, December 30. It was called a New Year's Eve party, was very crowded, and there was dancing. I have yet to wear the coat out of the house again.

(The rest of the test data appears to be all of a piece, and can be connected with a young friend of ours with whom I used to work. Two years ago the friend enlisted in the Marines and was sent to Alaska. He returned to Elmira over the holidays on furlough. I met him twice but Jane did not see him at all. She did listen to me talk about him, of course.

(Our friend wore his civilian clothes, so even had she met him Jane wouldn't have been able to observe his uniform colors. It chanced however that while we were waiting in line at the post office to mail packages, we saw a Marine in uniform. Jane noticed its color—this was not the dress blues uniform—and questioned me as to the soldier's branch of service, etc. Then when we went shopping we picked out my sport coat in a similar color, although I believe neither of us thought of any such connection at the time.

(Jane said that when she gave the data about "diagonal marks on the four corners of a rectangular piece of paper," she saw such a piece of paper rather clearly within her mind's eye, without thinking of it particularly as a photograph.

(Jane also said that when the information "An engagement," etc., came through, it represented Seth's effort to put her on the right track. She had our Marine friend in mind during the test, and he was engaged to be married at the time he went into the service. He is now married and a father.

(Jane resumed in the same rather fast manner, her eyes opening at times, at 10:40.)

Now I will keep you but briefly.

Long enough, however, to make a few comments. Ruburt was not particularly at his best this evening, simply because he was somewhat upset over <u>your</u>

reaction, Joseph, to the car episode.

There is no reason however why tests should be limited to times when conditions are excellent, since we shall be dealing with many conditions. Some valid material did come through however, for I saw that, and the coat was meant to be an identifying piece of information.

Now we simply cannot discuss everything I had in mind, or the session would run too late.

What Ruburt <u>sensed</u> however was somewhat legitimate. When you allow disturbances to upset you, then you become concentrated so deeply within ego time that you close off those very abilities that you need to help you.

There is no use pretending of course not to be annoyed. The point is simply to do your best, so that you gradually learn not to inhibit your reactions to them, but to change the nature of your habitual reactions to them.

Otherwise you concentrate your creative energies, <u>all</u> of your energies, upon the disturbance itself, and interpret all other data in the light of that disturbance. In other words you put yourself into a position where you focus your attention upon very negative influences.

Ruburt does this in his own way also. The one who is at any given time free of such difficulty should indeed help the other when such occasions arise. You actually put yourself in a trance state, and the suggestions take strong hold; and they are rarely constructive ones at such times.

What you need however is additional energy and resources to deal with such problems, and instead often you effectively cut yourself off from the resources within you.

I am taking this incident as an example, but my remarks are to you both, for you both have much room for improvement in this respect. It is true that <u>I</u> am not concerned directly, so you may think that it is easy for me to speak to you both in this way. However it is because I am not directly concerned that I can see the problem and point out ways in which it can be solved. For there will always be such difficulties, and a habit of concentrating upon them could be most disadvantageous.

Now, I will as you prefer give you a break or continue.

("You might as well continue then."

(It was 10:55. I expected Jane to continue, but to my surprise I saw that she had left trance. Evidently there had been a misunderstanding on some level, or I hadn't spoken clearly. Before we had time to discuss it she resumed, her eyes opened often, at 10:56.)

Now. When you react in such a manner, not only do you focus upon the present difficulty, but you <u>project</u> the difficulty and its imagined consequences into the future, turning expectation against you, and therefore bringing about the very conditions which you wish to avoid.

Incidents of this nature may seem trivial. However patterns of behavior are extremely important, and such focus upon disturbances are directly opposed to all I have been trying to tell you. And I am speaking here only of one individual, but such reactions are also picked up by others on a subconscious basis, and the circle can be a vicious one.

You both <u>know</u> this I am sure, as a rule you both do fairly well in following a more healthy procedure. But the lessons must be put into practice or they are worthless.

Again, we come to what is <u>truly</u> practical, as opposed to what the ego may think is practical at any given time.

I have given you both sermon enough for this evening but I cannot emphasize too strongly the importance of what I have said. If you direct your inner self with confidence to steer you through your physical existence, it will do so. If you concentrate upon difficulties you will not allow it to do so. This method of giving yourself room will also help you to achieve a greater freedom in psychic matters. For any <u>negative</u> focus (and underline negative) within egotistical reality will automatically block you.

You will not feel free enough to allow yourself freedom for any psychic adventures. With confidence in your inner abilities however your practical problems will effectively be taken care of when you do not dwell upon them, and greater mobility will be achieved as far as other layers of the self are concerned.

Obviously reason must be used. I am not speaking of indiscriminate Pollyanna hogwash, and yet even that is more practical in the long run than any habitual concentration upon disturbances.

I am not accusing either of you of such habitual activities, but because of our relationship I do feel bound to mention such issues as they arise. You should know, both of you by now, that I have your best interests always in mind.

And <u>now</u> may I wish you a hearty good evening. I would have discussed your friend's inverted time system, Joseph, further, except for the lateness of the hour.

("Good night, Seth."

(End at 11:07. Jane was dissociated as usual. Her eyes had been open at times, her pace rather fast, her voice average.

(A note added a week later: To my great relief, Seth dealt with my car episode in the 223rd Session.)

(Tracing of the drawing and verse used in the 26th envelope test, in the 221st session for January 10, 1966.)

SESSION 221
JANUARY 10, 1966 9 PM MONDAY AS SCHEDULED

(On Saturday January 8 Jane and I received a letter from Dr. Instream, asking that Seth do his best to give data on but one object during tests. Dr. Instream also mentioned his difficulty in attempting to repeat an experiment with ESP cards, involving odds of a million-and-a-half to one. Jane and I mentioned that we would like Seth to say something on both points in tonight's session.

(Over the weekend Bill and Peggy Gallagher agreed to try mutual concentration upon a single object in their home at session times. They would keep a record of the chosen objects for a month, without telling us what they were, then we would compare the list with Seth's data after the experiment ended. We have thought of trying this before.

(We had some reservations however about trying it now, but decided to see what Seth would say. We didn't want to give rise to a feeling of pressure on Jane during sessions, and wondered whether it was wise to try three regular tests. We want room for other material also. For this reason we had let the candle-flame tests go for the moment, even though they appear promising.

(See the tracing of the envelope test object on page 190. It is a humorous drawing made by Ann Diebler, who works in my office at Artistic Card Co.; Piggie, incidentally, refers to pigeon. I had mentioned the drawing to Jane several weeks ago, but not since, and of course she did not know I had brought it home. I put it between two pieces of Bristol and sealed it in the usual double envelope.

(Ann Diebler has heard Seth speak twice during unscheduled sessions, and had read some of the early material. See the notes for the 206th and the 214th sessions.

(The session was held in our large front room. Jane said she was somewhat sleepy before the session began. She began speaking while sitting down and with her eyes closed, but halfway to first break her eyes began to open occasionally. Her pace was good, her voice average.)

Good evening.

("Good evening, Seth.")

Now. First of all, I advise Ruburt along these lines: it is best if he not work at his own writing or records up until the last moment or so before a session.

He should relax, in any way he chooses, the hour preceding a session.

Now. An inverted time system actually presents us with a system that more closely approximates the true nature of time. Time does indeed turn in upon itself, even as it explodes outward from itself. The expanding universe theory applies much more truly to time than it does to the physical universe. You think of a steady progression into the future. However, as you know there is no real <u>progression</u>, moment by successive moment, as you suppose.

(Seth dealt with the expanding universe theory in sessions 42-45, saying among other things that our physical universe is not expanding as is currently thought; he had much to say on the distortive data furnished us by our instruments.)

You think of the past as done with and completed, but on a subconscious basis you travel through the past. The past therefore becomes present. You know that precognition is a fact. The steady line of time does not exist. Inversion in terms of value interwound upon value, energy compressed, contained, working upon itself, contained but with momentum—this comes much closer to reality.

However, the momentum works both ways. I am referring now to your own terms of reference. For if time speeds ahead, my dear friends, or if you <u>say</u> that times speed ahead, which is an entirely different thing, then you must say also that it speeds backwards. For this energy moves in all directions from its core, and the core at times becomes its outer surface.

In an inverted time system the momentum is recognized and it is also taken advantage of, in that it is utilized by individual consciousness, so that your so-called present, past and future can be viewed as existing in a spacious <u>now</u>. Again, this sort of a system is very close to the true nature of time.

I mentioned that the inhabitant of the other system with whom you made contact perceived your existence in both the future and the past. He <u>also</u> was aware however of your own comparative imprisonment in a limited present. For the present as you know it is very limited indeed. He realized therefore, when the incident occurred, how it would end. <u>He</u> can relive the incident at his leisure, and experience it as present if he so chooses.

He can also remember it from any viewpoint in his future, if he chooses. He can give this information about this event to his own image as it existed in time before the contact was made. He can therefore make alterations in any aspect of time as it affects him.

In essence you see the past can be changed. Present actions can change future events that would otherwise occur. But when this is admitted, then we must admit also that present events can alter the past, for there is no element in the past that has a different structure or composition or characteristic, that is not present in the future.

(Seth has referred to the ability of suggestion to change experience which has already passed. See the 187th and 202nd sessions.)

Time does not have certain characteristics when you view it as past, or when you view it as future, or when you view it as present. Any seeming difference between the past and the future is simply due to your own perception. Much of the material that I have given you concerning the nature of physical matter will be helpful when considered in connection with this material on time.

(See the 60-73rd sessions in Volume 2.)

We will try here to give you an example. Take for example then the house in which Ruburt spent his childhood. Now as you know, that was never one definite unchanging object. That house was a conglomeration of atoms and molecules, perceived <u>generally</u> as a house, but perceived specifically by everyone who saw it as a slightly different house. For each observer quite literally created from his own subconscious energy an approximation of a house, a general shape then perceived as a house, and further embellished by personal judgments.

It was, say, in 1943 even then merely a portion of space perceived by all who saw it in their own light. It did not exist devoid or apart from those who viewed it.

Time inversion would merely permit the recreation of a particular perception. The year for example 1943 was simply an artificial collection of events loosely agreed upon. The past exists to the same extent that the present or future exists, and it is only the perception that is limited.

I suggest your break.

(Break at 9:30. Jane was dissociated as usual for a first delivery. Her eyes had opened frequently after the middle of the delivery, although her pace had begun to slow somewhat.

(She resumed at a slower pace, her eyes again opening often, at 9:37.)

Now. Shortly we shall consider various psychological frameworks, for there are endless varieties; though we shall discuss only a few, the few with which I am familiar.

These psychological structures obviously act as stabilizing platforms, so to speak, from which energy can view itself. The psychological frameworks simply are various organizational structures that are equipped to perceive reality discriminately.

They are equipped to focus along particular directions. This material will be extremely interesting when we come to it. It is extremely difficult for a psychological structure to view itself, for in order to do so it must lift itself from the limitations and abilities of its own nature. In many realities such scrutiny is simply impossible, while the structure operates in a given fashion.

Gradually psychological structures are able to focus upon vaster areas, and in order to achieve proficiency in this manner you do indeed begin to build up layered selves that <u>have been</u> independent identities. These varying perceptive abilities organize so that their perceptive powers are pooled in a gestalt that eventually forms a new identity, a more complicated psychological structure that is capable of perceiving larger areas of reality.

Even within a given system however all individuals are not at the same point. Now, in our sessions I am sure that by now you are at least to some extent aware of what would seem to be something quite strange: the emergence of a self that observes the self of which you have been ordinarily aware; a self with a slightly different time system, a slightly different viewpoint of reality, a self with greater control over the physical material that composes your physical image, a self with some quite effective control over your personal future.

I am speaking now of course of both of you. That is, <u>each</u> of you should by now be aware of such an emerging psychological unit. It is the result of your ability to step out of your own system to some small extent, for you cannot do this until you are ready. For the <u>very attempt</u>, or successful attempt, results in an extension of the self out of the system in which you were nurtured.

From the viewpoint of this emerging self you can view to some extent the system in which the earlier self was mainly imprisoned. Now I speak of imprisonment. I do not speak in terms of compulsory confinement however. Your perceptions simply kept you where you were. You could not <u>clearly</u> see even where you were, for the dimensions were not clear to you from the inside. You could not scale the wall, so to speak. You had to grow taller, if you will forgive me for using another analogy.

I will have more to say along these lines, for we shall shortly be considering the psychological structures in terms of action, and in their relationship to time. We will first relate them to this emerging self that you can sense personally, and then we shall go further.

Now, take your break.

(Break at 9:59. Jane was dissociated as usual, her eyes opening often. They had been very dark. Her pace had picked up considerably by break time.

(It was now time for the 29th Dr. Instream test. As usual Jane sat quietly with her hands raised to her closed eyes. Her pace was quite slow, broken by many pauses that ran to 15-20 seconds. Resume at 10:09.)

Now. Give us a moment.

I do have a few words for Dr. Instream. I believe I mentioned earlier that an object will work best if it has emotional significance for him.

Give us a moment. It may be a long one.

(Jane took a pause of 40 seconds.)

You see, at this point we must flow through many legitimate impressions that we pick up in <u>connection</u> with Dr. Instream, before we get at the specific impression that he wants.

If it is an emotionally charged object this will make our task easier. Though he need not concentrate upon it <u>then</u> with too great an intensity, since the object itself will send out information of its own.

Ruburt has progressed very well, but is still learning to <u>pinpoint</u> in a specific manner.

Something round, in the nature of a pin cushion. Red in color, perhaps with green. Round with an apple shape, belonging to his wife.

Now this will be considered as the object. *(Pause at 10:17.)*

I have some impressions concerning the ESP cards. A student with brown hair. I seem to get the initial E, though I do not know if this is a first, last or middle initial.

Also the number six. Six of a group. *(Another 40-second pause.)* That is a particular group. A male student. *(A one-minute pause.)*

There is no reason why the test results cannot be repeated, intrinsically. Dr. Instream however fears that they will not be repeated, and unless this feeling is changed on his part such will be the case. He wants a repeat, but he fears he will not get it, simply because he wants it so badly, and the student reacts to this subconscious inhibiting factor.

I seem to pick up a similarity somewhere between Dr. Instream and the student involved—a similarity in name, I do not know. He believes and expects success in his hypnosis experiments, and that is why he attains success. We shall however achieve what we want.

A stronger emotional contact between you, if it had been possible, would have led to somewhat quicker results. *(Pause at 10:29.)*

Now. I suggest that the experiments with our Jesuit and cat lover wait for a while yet, though the idea is a sound one, and we shall conduct our experiments later. You can tell them when you see them.

In the meantime, for this evening, we shall give the impression of a rock or stone that can be held in the hand, that has a connection with the water, that is speckled, and gray, with an indentation in it.

Do you have a test for me Joseph?

("Yes."

(It was 10:31. I handed Jane the 26th double sealed test envelope, and as usual she took it without opening her eyes. She pressed it to her forehead and continued to hold it there, speaking with many pauses.)

Give us a moment, please.

The word nondescript as applying to the Gallagher object.

Now. We shall see what we can do.

Something to do with money. Ruburt thinks of a money order. This is his personal association, because of your recent activities.

A schedule of events. A connection with several people, two male and one female in particular. The color blue, and a note or letter.

Your brother, pictures. An afternoon. Now a series of impressions having to do with the pictures taken by your brother Loren, of Ruburt.

A connection however with a <u>November</u> event. Special lights. Ruburt's white coat, and last Saturday evening.

I suggest your break.

(Break at 10:40. Jane was dissociated as usual Her eyes had remained closed. When break arrived she discovered that she had left her glasses on while speaking, something she rarely does. Her pace had been slow.

(*See the tracing of the test object on page 190. As can be seen practically none of the data applies to the test object, with the exception of the white coat; the connection here is tenuous, and will be explained. I thought "November" might be correct also.*

(*Jane said she had rather strong images visually of the data; twice she saw her white coat quite strongly. In the test she was unable to tell when she got off on the track of personal associations; somehow the fine discrimination was lacking. Jane said that by the time she approached break she knew the test had been a poor one. But she also* knew *the test was poor, something she wouldn't have been able to distinguish not too long ago. She could, she said, feel herself getting involved with what she knew were incorrect images.*

(*The white coat connection referred to the fact that Jane wore it last Saturday evening, when it was bitter cold. Now the test object contains a poem referring to shivering pigeons and snow—hence the connection. I thought the November reference might be legitimate, since the originator of the test object, Ann Diebler, could have visited our apartment during that month. A check showed this to be so—Ann witnessing the unscheduled session for November 5, 1965.*

(*Jane resumed at a moderate pace, with her eyes opening occasionally, at 10:45.*)

Now. I saw immediately what we were doing here.

However, only by making mistakes can Ruburt learn to distinguish the highly nebulous changes, subjectively speaking, that characterize legitimate hits from failures, and without the experience he would not learn. The coat was a legitimate connection, but I could not get through to him to make it correctly. He was working on the level of personal associations. There is a certain feel to the correct channel, and he will learn to distinguish it.

The November event I believe had to do with an occasion when your Ann visited here, but it is hardly adequate.

Now, I was prepared to go into some other material this evening. However since it is growing late perhaps we should save it for the next session.

This is all a process of learning. Relaxation in the hour before sessions will help. We are trying to work on two levels here. We want success of course, but we also want to know how success is achieved, and so we shall.

Contrary to popular thought, while everyone has so-called psychic abilities, they must be trained in specific areas of accomplishment. This is what we are doing.

Now unless you have any particular questions we shall close the session.

(*"I guess not then."*)

My heartiest regards to you both.

SESSION 222

("Good night, Seth.")

(End at 10:57. Jane was dissociated as usual. Her eyes were closed for the most part. She said that in poor tests she is aware of a slight feeling of strain, mentally, that could be compared to the physical feeling of strain involved when she doesn't do a Yoga exercise quite right, or goes a little too far without adequate preparation.)

```
                    FOLD
                                    Jan. 4, 1965
Dear Bob, and Jane:
        Here are the two slides I took but am sorry to say
neither one is any good as I had to use too slow a
shutter speed to hand-hold the camera, this caused the
blur you can see. There was just not enough light to
do this. The film is Kodachrome II with an ASA rating
of 25, as compared to several that go to 160 and 200.
        With one of these films, I could have done it. After
we got back home my flash unit arrived, again if I had
had this there would have been no problem. I am still
learning to use the telephoto lens and I'll be the first
to admit I have a lot to learn.
        We are sorry that Dad, etc.

        (Note by RFB: The rest of this letter from my
brother Loren is personal, concerning family matters,
and deals with a "disturbing event" that is referred to
in the envelope test data. We will however be glad to
make the balance of the letter available to anyone
studying these results.)
```

(Copy of the letter used in the 27th envelope test, in the 222nd session for January 12, 1966.)

(Tracings of the two Kodachrome transparencies of Jane that Loren enclosed with his letter. They were not used as test objects, but were referred to in the test data.)

SESSION 222
JANUARY 12, 1966 9 PM WEDNESDAY AS SCHEDULED

(This afternoon while doing Yoga exercises Jane gave herself suggestions to the effect that she would do better in the envelope test tonight, than she had done last session. As will be seen, she did do much better.

(See the copy on page 197. For the test object I used a letter from my brother Loren, who lives in Tunkhannock, PA. It is typewritten in black ink on paper the weight of this page, and white. It was folded once between two pieces of Bristol, then sealed in the usual double envelope. My brother inadvertently dated the letter 1965 instead of 1966.

(The session again was held in our large front room, and was not interrupted. Jane began while sitting down and with her eyes closed. Her eyes soon opened, however, and she displayed much amusement. Her pace was good, her voice average.)

Good evening.

("Good evening, Seth.")

Now. I have a few remarks to make. However you, Joseph, have been rushed with your notes, due to circumstances; and if you prefer we can then, after my few remarks, wait until ten o'clock for our Instream material. We are at all times flexible.

("No, I'm all caught up now.")

(*Jane now smiled. Her eyes, very dark, opened briefly. She stared at me from across the table.*)

Then I shall continue. First of all, may I congratulate you for doing something that you do not realize you have done. You did have some help, it is true, from Ruburt, but in the main you did this on your own. Do you have any idea of what I am speaking?

(*Another smile from Jane as she stared at me. I didn't know what Seth was referring to so I began to guess.*

("My dream?")

(*Last night I had had a very vivid dream in which I was levitating, my first of its kind since I began keeping records. Jane shook her head.*)

This is not what I am referring to.

("The dentist?")

(*This afternoon I put myself in a light trance before going to the dentist, then used suggestion. I felt nothing in the chair.*)

That indeed was very good, quite excellent—but it is not what I am referring to.

("Well, the car, then?")

(*Jane smiled broadly and nodded her head. She was much amused. She pointed at me, her eyes wide open.*)

<u>Now</u>—now you are on the correct issue. It was an accomplishment because you started from scratch, so to speak. Consciously the whole affair annoyed you no end. You saw it as a grumpy old machine, with its best days finished. But you put to excellent use the advice which I gave you, concerning the importance of psychological reactions.

On your part this did indeed represent an important level of achievement, simply because you have been in the past more easily given to pessimism.

(*See pages 187-89 of the 220th session for the advice Seth refers to.*)

I want to explain precisely what you did, for you should find it most amusing.

When the trouble initially began, the most recent trouble, you were generally disgusted with the car, and your disgust led to the difficulties. <u>Not</u> in any nebulous symbolic manner, but in very literal terms.

You forgot to buy the gasoline. You had previously not noticed the small red flash indicating that oil was needed, and if the trend had continued you would have continued to ignore this warning light. If your attitude had been strong enough to affect Ruburt, he would not have noticed it either. The general and overall condition of the car was on its way to deterioration.

(A week or so ago I forgot to buy gasoline, and this led to a situation that could have been dangerous. When Jane and I were on our way to the home of the Gallaghers, who live on top of a steep and long hill outside Elmira, the car lost power, then stalled out on the hill. It was after dark, the road was slippery with snow; I had to back down the hill while Jane lighted the way with a flashlight, until I found a driveway. I did not realize I had run low on gas at the time, for the car started as we coasted down hill. We arrived home safely but the car would not start up again.

(Jane and I walked to a nearby station for gasoline but the car still wouldn't start; consequently the garage had to tow the car in for repairs. Seth's information on the oil warning light is also apparently correct, for when the garage checked the oil level it was quite low. I usually make a point of watching this closely, and it is interesting to speculate as to how I failed to see the warning light go on, since it is situated on the dash in front of me. I had the oil checked immediately after I became <u>aware</u> that the warning light was on. Nor had Jane noticed it on.

(The car operated well the day after the garage repaired it, saying the trouble was moisture in the distributor. The next day the car once again would not start. This necessitated another tow to the garage. To our surprise the second tow and repair were free, the service manager telling us there was corrosion on the coil connections, and that the mechanic should have noticed this and corrected it the first time the car was in the garage.

(The 220th session, containing Seth's advice, was held while the car was in the garage the first time. After the session I made a conscious effort to improve my attitude about the car. By then I had the idea that psychological attitudes could affect the car, and had recalled that once before Seth had dealt with the car and our attitudes while on our way to a Maine vacation in August 1964. See the 80-81st sessions. According to Seth, Jane and I had succeeded in altering considerably the car's oil consumption; and as evidence we had before us the fact that the car had used much less oil on the trip than we had calculated. See Volume 2.)

Now when your attitude began to change, it changed first on a subconscious level. Consciously you were not aware of the change. Now. You had already done some damage. The problem was to make it as minor as possible. It was therefore concentrated as corrosion on the coil, and this corrosion was <u>not there</u> when your garageman previously examined it.

The destructive elements were concentrated, given nice, neat tangible form, and therefore remedied in a physical fashion.

Now you can do, that is any individual can do, and <u>does</u>, the same with the physical body. If his reactions cause a generalized overall poor condition, this is much more difficult to treat. But if this energy can be put into a specific form, one pimple, one pain, one ulcer, at least the problem is recognized, localized, and can be treated with somewhat less difficulty.

There was no need for your garageman to think, then, that the trouble had not been noticed, for when he examined the car last the overall condition <u>was</u> poor. But there was no specific physical or localized trouble. I thought that you would find this rather interesting.

(*Jane smiled again. I did find it interesting, especially when I contemplated trying to explain it to our service manager at the garage, who is a personal friend of ours, but does not know about these sessions.*)

I was pleased with the trance state that you achieved when you visited your dentist. And when you can do this under that stress, you see that you can also do it in other situations. With your parents for example you can use this knowledge, so that their actions will not upset you unduly. With them you simply need the suggestion that you will only react to constructive suggestions.

This still leaves you free from ordinary reactions with them, need not close you off from conversation, and yet gives you an immunity from their negative attitudes. In such a manner you can indeed help them while remaining free yourself.

Both of you do this now in relation to your Miss Callahan, so you should understand the feel of it.

You may take your break.

(*Break at 9:21. Jane was dissociated as usual for a first delivery. Her eyes had opened frequently, and her pace had been fast as the session progressed. She resumed in the same manner at 9:26.*)

Now. I have several things to say.

First of all, to give you a rest, Joseph, you may tape any sessions that you prefer, say, tape one week's sessions during which Ruburt could then transcribe the notes to give you some extra time for yourself. He could follow your format and type them now and then for you.

I have much more material on inverted time to give you, but there is a personal matter that I would like to discuss.

Your attitude toward your faithful old car is not based upon the reasons you ascribe it to. An automobile means one thing to you and one thing to Ruburt. Obviously your backgrounds have much to do with this, but I do not believe that you realize what I am about to tell you.

Do you have any idea, now?

("*Maybe.*")

(*I thought Seth was going to say something about my attitudes influencing the actual physical behavior of the car.*)

I am speaking of the relationship in your mind between your father and automobiles. Has this occurred to you?

("Only in a very general, symbolical way."

(Jane smiled, her eyes wide and dark.)

Well then, it is indeed time for these remarks.

First of all, for Ruburt's idea of an automobile. For his ideas are simpler and easier to explain. His mother could not leave the house. He always ran as a child to make sure that he could move at all. To <u>him</u> a car is an extension of that mobility.

It does not matter whether the car is old or new, as long as he has one, and it is for this reason that he fights any of your suggestions that you do without one. The car is also to him a complementary image of his father, who was always on the move, more so than most men, while his mother could not move at all. A lack of a car also makes him fear a return to poverty, since in his neighborhood any car at all was a sign of luxury.

<u>Now</u> your situation is not only entirely different but contrary, for to you a car represents, because of your father, an image on one hand of perfection. Your father insisted, because of his work with batteries, upon perfection. An <u>old</u> car hardly represents this image.

(I am 46. As a young boy I used to watch my father make automobile batteries by hand. He had his own business in Sayre, PA, and took great pride in the excellence of his work. The business began to fail when batteries became mass produced, and the great depression finished it.)

Your father would like to kick at old cars, for he felt that they defied him since they worked improperly. More than this however, both of your parents still feel that a car is a symbol of social status, and you grew up with this. When your cars were new you felt at one with them. But an old car brings back the old struggles between your parents, and it is precisely here that subconsciously you and Ruburt do not agree. He gladly settles on an old car—anything that moves will do. But to you the old car has not meant freedom, but imperfection.

I want to make this clear, for it should help you both to understand your reactions, and to change them accordingly. Some of your most basic feelings toward the automobile grew as a result of the early trip to California, when for days on end as a child you heard your parents bickering. They were uncertain of what they would find, pessimistic, and they blamed each other for having left at all.

This is not the adventurous spirit they told you of, and you heard every word. On the other hand you do have a rather deeply felt feeling for mechanical objects. This has some connection with your position in the service. But the <u>conscious</u> reasons that you have for being annoyed with your automobile, these reasons are rationalizations to hide the deeper causes.

(*I was three years old when my parents made the month-long drive to California, and my brother Loren was two. I have a few vivid conscious memories of the trip. I grew up listening to my parents talk about the trip. When I was drafted during the second World War I was given aptitude tests; to my surprise I did well on mechanical subjects, and ended up as an airplane mechanic and instrument specialist in the Air Transport Command.*)

There is also a lesser connection here with the garage in which your father spent so much of his time, for you picked up your mother's anger that he was so often there. One small remark and you may take your break: Ruburt, for the reasons mentioned earlier, also liked anything with wheels that moved, roller skates for example. Anything that offered hope of mobility.

(*Break at 9:49. Jane said she was very well dissociated this delivery. Her eyes had been open often and her pace had been good. Break had barely begun when she resumed briefly, in a much deeper voice, at 9:50.*)

One note: Your <u>father</u> felt ineffective and a failure when an automobile did not work right, because of his connection with them, and you picked this up. Which is highly ridiculous, as you can see, since your own interests lie in other directions.

(*Break again at 9:51. Jane said she realized of course that she enjoyed having a car, any kind of car, available. But she hadn't particularly associated this with the reasons Seth ascribed to a need for mobility. Nor had she made any great connection with the idea of her father being a traveling man. My idea was that Seth had mentioned these things briefly in much earlier sessions.*

Jane now told me that while speaking last time, she received a message from Seth to the effect that from now on she wasn't to smoke during tests, because of the distraction involved. She didn't have to pause while giving the regular material to get this message, but seemed to receive it on another level simultaneously with the material she gave voice to. She had been smoking so far during the session.

It was now time for the 30th Dr. Instream test. It did not materialize immediately however, and Jane resumed at 10:01 with her eyes opening occasionally.)

I see that Ruburt received my message correctly. This message was given, incidentally, <u>mentally</u> while he was delivering my words on another subject, and this is an accomplishment indeed.

We will give Dr. Instream a moment or two while I make a few other remarks.

(*Jane looked at me now.*)

<u>You</u> are doing very well, much better than you think, generally speaking. Reactions which you would have accepted as natural in the past, you now accept

as being unfavorable, as they are. But the <u>recognition</u>, you see, causes you at times to think you are <u>not</u> making progress when indeed you are. You expect more of yourself now, and you are getting more.

These small episodes of late would have snowed you under in the past, out of all proportion; such is not the case now. You have noticed, I am sure, also, that Ruburt's reactions are of a more steady nature.

("Yes.")

He does not feel the need to change the furniture with such startling rapidity.

("Yes.")

Now. Please give us a moment.

(*Jane paused at 10:10. She sat quietly with her head down, her hands raised to her closed eyes. She was not smoking. Her pace was now slower, with many brief pauses.*)

Something in the nature of a fabric with a wooden framework I believe, for our object. The color blue. The framework is used for support. *(40-second pause.)* Upholstery. Blue upholstery, with something like small tacks in it that are indented. A blue chair. This is our object. *(Pause.)*

Disturbing events today, I believe surrounding our Dr. Instream.

A <u>snag</u>. <u>Perhaps</u> some difficulty in his hypnosis experiments which had been going so well. For some reason however there seems to be better chances in his ESP card experiments, though not of as spectacular nature as those earlier achieved. *(Pause.)*

I believe this change for the better, or this possibility of change, is due to an upspurt on the part of the student, a mood change that can be taken advantage of. There seems to be some connection, to <u>me</u>, at any rate, between the blue chair and this student. *(Pause.)*

Plans that Dr. Instream has been making for a large meeting next spring or early summer will not materialize in the manner that he anticipates. There will be an <u>overall</u> change in them. You may underline overall. *(Pause.)*

A letter from New York mentioning a meeting, the initial P connected with this.

I have specifically given the blue chair as object. *(Pause at 10:20.)* I will ask you, Joseph, for our test, and I will then have a few general remarks to make concerning our tests at this point.

(*As usual Jane took the sealed double envelope from me without opening her eyes. Her head was tipped down; such was its position that when she held the envelope up, as she has been doing lately, she pressed it against the top of her head. This is the 27th envelope test.*)

Now give us a moment please.

These are impressions.

The habit of squirreling away. A connection with four people, I believe men. A studio. A paper item. *(Long pause.)*

A connection with a photograph that was taken along with others, more than one of its kind in other words.

Now this remark leads Ruburt to think of Lois. Such personal connections are important for our purposes, so I mention them.

Now. A square, and a round object, perhaps inside the square. Initials. *(Long pause at 10:26.)* Ruburt's connection: a disturbing event. You may put Ruburt's connections in parenthesis.

I pick up a very distant connection with Wisconsin, which I do not understand *(pause)*, and with objects seen from above.

Also a connection with something like a flag. Horizontal lines and star shapes. Two o'clock.

I suggest your break.

(Break at 10:29. Jane was dissociated as usual. Her eyes had remained closed. She held the test envelope to the top of her head the whole time. She didn't think she had done well in the test, whereas actually the results were very good.

(See the tracing of the test object on page 197.

("The habit of squirreling away" is a good reference to my father, in whose photographic studio my brother Loren took the pictures he refers to in the test letter. The studio is in part of my father's cellar; the rest of the cellar is stuffed and cluttered with odds and ends my father has accumulated over the years. The rest of the family views the overloaded cellar as a fire hazard.

("A connection with four people, I believe men." Three men and one woman were present in the studio when the pictures shown on page 198 were taken, for the correct total of four people: Jane, myself, my father and my brother Loren.

("A studio." Refers to my father's photographic studio.

("A paper item." The test object is a paper item.

("A connection with a photograph that was taken along with others, more than one of its kind in other words." The test object of course is connected to the photos also indicated on page 198, and these particular photos were connected with "other's" since they were the last two exposures on a roll of film.

("Now this remark leads Ruburt to think of Lois." This is a good example of the way personal associations can work. Our friend Lois took some photos of Jane recently, for use on the dust jacket of Jane's ESP book. The photos my brother Loren took were also to be used in connection with publicity for the ESP book.

*("A square, and a round object, perhaps inside the square." This is a good

reference to the color transparencies my brother took. Again, see the tracings of the photos on page 198. What we have is a rectangular area with rounded corners inside the square object. Perhaps Seth/Jane's perception of the rounded corners led to the statement concerning a round object inside the square.

(Initials. The initials "ASA" appear in my brother's letter. There could be other meanings here.

("Ruburt's connection: A disturbing event," is a good reference to the balance of my brother's letter, which is not included on page 197. The contents of this part of the letter are available however to anyone studying these results.

("I pick up a very distant connection with Wisconsin, which I do not understand", puzzled Jane, since she had no idea of what this could mean. I thought it might be a reference to the fact that my brother Loren, who wrote the test letter, is a model railroad fan. The magazine Model Railroader was, I thought, published in Wisconsin. There is a strong connection here because Loren has contributed articles and photographs to this magazine for many years. A trip to the newsstand to check verified my idea; Model Railroader has editorial offices in Milwaukee, Wisconsin. Jane was especially pleased at this because she knows nothing of the hobby, or the magazine or its address. It took me two days after the session to come up with the connection with Wisconsin myself.

("and with objects seen from above." This is speculation: Loren's model railroad layout is built at waist-high level in the cellar of his home in Tunkhannock, PA. Thus while standing before it one looks down upon the small models of trains, etc.

("Also a connection with something like a flag." More speculation: many of the symbols of the various railroads are designed in a flag shape, and Loren has made drawings of some of these symbols for publication, I believe, in Model Railroader.

("Horizontal lines and star shapes." is vague to us, although the test object, the letter, contains horizontal lines of type.

("Two o'clock." would seem to be a reference to the time the photos were taken of Jane. On a Sunday after a noon dinner at my parent's home Jane, myself, Loren and my father went down to the photographic studio.

(Jane said that Seth's reference to Lois put her back on the right track as far as subsequent data went. There was a fine distinction to be made here, since both Lois and my brother were involved taking pictures of Jane for the same purpose: Jane's ESP book. Thus Seth and Jane worked very well together here. Also note another example of cooperation, wherein Jane contributed accurately with her connection to a disturbing event, and Seth said this was Jane's idea.

(As stated earlier, Jane took the time to relax before the session tonight, and feels it was well worth while.

(Jane's eyes once again opened fairly often when she resumed at 10:40.)

<u>Now</u> Ruburt may have his cigarette.

He is doing very well. He will automatically improve. I want <u>him</u> to remember this, for there is no reason for him to blame himself when, as in our last test, we did poorly. There is no blame involved.

The positive suggestions that he used today were excellent, however. This evening I specifically mentioned the incorrect impression to set him straight. This also represents a fine distinction however on <u>his</u> part.

<u>We work</u> in our tests almost as one organism, as a gestalt, and you also have a part here Joseph. We were certainly specific with this last test, but there must be <u>freedom</u> first.

Now Ruburt grows unsure as far as Dr. Instream's tests are concerned, when we are asked for a specific object, and this does hamper us. However this feeling will vanish as we continue, and again, it is a natural reaction on his part so he should not blame himself for it.

We shall end up not only with excellent results on a fairly predictable basis, but your records will form an excellent document that shows how these abilities are used and translated into practical terms.

With <u>many</u> psychics, the ability is so automatic that you can learn nothing about the process as it occurs. Now I shall <u>try</u> to point out impressions that are incorrect when I am able to. You will be able to see how extrasensory perceptions merge with personal associations, and watch the mind as it actually learns to perceive the difference.

You will see when and how Ruburt's personal associations help us, and when and how they do not help us. As result Ruburt will be able, finally, to screen out the incorrect data. This is difficult simply because the data <u>is</u> legitimate to important layers of the personality, and you can see extrasensory perceptions as they merge <u>with</u> other associations.

(Jane's voice now deepened a good deal and became considerably louder. For more emphasis she rapped on the tabletop. Her eyes were open and very dark.)

<u>And this is precisely how dreams are formed, and why they appear so often so incomprehensible—for when you examine them you do so in the light of your personal associations only. You view them with only half an eye</u>.

Now, I am fully prepared to speak on. However I am aware that we have approached the time of our usual closing, and you may continue or not, as you prefer.

("I'm afraid we'll have to close then.")

You may if you like have a session in which you ask me any personal questions that come to mind. I was holding the material concerning your car for such an occasion, but decided this evening that it was important enough to you to take up a regular session.

My heartiest good wishes, and I have enjoyed rides in your car.

("That's good. Good night, Seth.")

(End at 10:55. Jane was dissociated as usual. Her pace had been good. She said she had been quite aware, this evening, of the presence of another personality in the room with us. She had felt as though she were reacting to a third person, one whom she felt rapport with and hated to see leave. She hadn't been as plainly aware of the feeling before.

(Seth's statements on page 207, to the effect that even incorrect test data is legitimate to important layers of the personality, is probably an important one in our opinion. We have been aware of this possibility and plan to ask more questions about it. I do not recall Seth's referring to this point so plainly before, although he may have. Jane and I do not recall reading anything treating with the subject, and wonder whether it could not be quite a valid field for investigation in itself.)

SESSION 223
JANUARY 16, 1966 APPROXIMATELY 10 PM
SUNDAY UNSCHEDULED

(Bill and Peggy Gallagher visited us this evening, and Seth held a rather short unscheduled session. The Gallaghers sat in on the first part of the session. After they left Seth and I had a discussion of moderate length. I made a few brief notes, not verbatim except for the names, which Seth spelled out.

(After Seth announced his presence Bill said that half an hour previously he had wondered whether Seth might speak. Seth confirmed that at that time he had almost come through, and Jane later told me she had been aware of this, without feeling impelled to have a session.

(The exchange was quite jovial among the group. Seth discussed several psychic experiences Bill had noted recently, saying they involved telepathy and precognition. Seth said that as in the case of John Bradley, Bill should become more and more aware of such experiences, now that he is more familiar with these sessions.

(Somehow the conversation turned to the lives Jane and I had led in Denmark. When I remarked jokingly that as yet we didn't even know what names we bore in that life, Seth promptly began to spell them out. Jane and I have always been curious about these names.

(My name in Denmark, in the 1600's, was Larns Devonsdorf. Seth was Brons Martzens. My wife in that life was Letti Cluse. Jane was my son in that life, his name being Graton. Seth has dealt with our Denmark lives in a few early sessions without going into much detail, and has occasionally referred to them in later sessions. In the second session, while still speaking to us through the personality of Frank Watts, Seth told us he had been a merchant who dealt in spices. He now confirmed that data and gave us a little more information. See Volume 1.

(Brotzanin II had been one of the ships with which Seth had been connected in his Denmark life. The II, he told us now, meant that this was the second ship by that name. It had been a Danish frigate—a warship before coming into Seth's hands as a merchantman. Seth owned it in 1631-32, and used it in the spice trade.

(Bill Gallagher doubted that warships were used by merchantmen but Seth told us this was common in those days; all ships had to be armed anyhow as a protection against piracy. The Brotzanin II had not been in very good shape when Seth acquired her. The conversation led to some of the voyages the ship made. Seth quite emphatically reminded us that most of the time he "kept his feet on dry land," but he did talk about a few voyages he made. He stressed that he was a merchant rather than a sailor.

(In talking about his voyages, Seth said that we would have to bear with Ruburt now, because Ruburt—Jane—knew very little about geography; this I can vouch for. Jane now spoke quite slowly, with her head down and her eyes closed, whereas before her eyes had opened often and her manner had been very animated and cheerful.

(Seth told us the Brotzanin II had followed a warm current and that her voyage took 22 days to "our first port, where we added some supplies.... We were then 42 days out before another port. You will have to bear with me here.... 62 days then to our destination. Nutmeg from one shore, cloves from another."

(Bill and I tried to pin down the route of the Brotzanin II, and seemed to get a course that included the Azores as first stop, then around the bottom of Africa at the Cape of Good Hope, up the east coast to Madagascar and Zanzibar. Zanzibar is the source of cloves, I recall from my own reading; Jane said she did not know this. However Seth said the ship did not stop at Zanzibar on all trips.

("Lemons," Seth told us, "we knew about lemons before the English did. We grated lemon skins and drank the juice, and made the skins into a kind of poultice to put on sores. We dried the skins also and kept them in the hold." Lemons were used in those days as a protection against scurvy.

(After the Gallaghers left Seth and I continued to talk. Seth told me I would become a very well-known painter; Ruburt, he said, knew nothing about artists' agents or their locations in New York City, he said for the record, adding that there is an agent on 62nd street who can be of great help to me. This is the correct neighborhood, I can attest from past experience. He did not give me the agent's name. Seth told me I have been working to free my intuitions; I already have enough discipline. With Jane it has been the other way around. Both of us are making good progress.

Seth also said that my work would become known partly because of the source of inspiration for some of it—the visions I have that grow out of these sessions.

(Seth said Jane and I should make a trip to New York this spring whether we are asked by anyone or not, meaning Jane's publisher principally. The trip can be of great benefit to us through the contacts we make. These contacts will grow out of our seeing the following people: Don Wollheim, an editor Jane has previously published with; her present publisher, Frederick Fell; Eileen Garrett; and Dick Roberts, a senior editor at Dell Books with whom Jane has published. We should set up appointments to see these people, and should make the trip whether or not publicity for Jane's ESP book, to be published this spring, is involved.

(Seth told me that as the years passed and these sessions continued both Jane and I would become more and more sure that he is what he says he is—an energy personality essence. The evidence would pile up.

(In the 221st session Seth suggested we postpone our series of object tests with the Gallaghers. At the same time he described the object the Gallaghers were focusing upon in their home outside of Elmira at session time. Jane learned from Peggy Gallagher later in the week that the object was a miniature teapot. At tonight's visit I had Bill draw an actual-size version of the teapot for inclusion in the record, and it is found on page 211.

(Seth's data on this test was this: "... we shall give the impression of a rock or stone that can be held in the hand, that has a connection with the water, that is speckled, and gray, with an indentation on it... the word nondescript as applying to the Gallagher object."

(Without indulging in wishful thinking, Jane and I thought we saw some points of similarity in the above data and a miniature teapot, namely the fact that the test object could be held in the hand, had a connection with water, and an indentation. Since this was Jane's first such attempt with the Gallaghers, I was curious as to what Seth would say. He now told me that the rock or stone impression was his error, and not Jane's, or Ruburt's.

(Seth said he was not careful enough in sorting out his own impressions. He picked up accurately enough that the test object could be held in the hand, had a connection with water and an indentation—the opening in the teapot—but erred in the rock or stone terminology, the color and the word nondescript. Bill indicated the color of the teapot in his sketch, saying the object is anything but nondescript. Seth said Ruburt transmitted accurately enough the data he gave. He also said that we would conduct a series of tests with the Gallaghers, involving objects, and that they would be successful.)

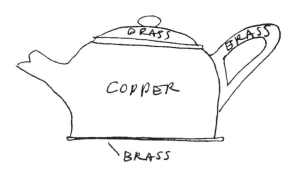

(Front)

(Back)

(Reduced-size copies of the identification card used as test object in the 28th envelope test, in the 224th session for January 17, 1966.)

SESSION 224
JANUARY 17, 1966 9 PM MONDAY AS SCHEDULED

(*See the tracing on page 211. For the test object I used a wallet identification card that I picked up two years ago in an empty house that Jane and I nearly purchased. Both of us had met the owner of the house, Jim Birch, a few times. He had changed jobs and left Elmira at the time we were interested in his house, in June 1964, however. Seth dealt with the purchase of this house in several sessions, saying it would be a good one for us psychically. See these sessions among others: 65, 67, 69, 71, 74, 76, 77, 79, 82. See Volume 2.*

(*The test object was among other papers that we cleaned up at the house, with the intention of mailing them to Mr. Birch's new address in North Carolina; later we learned this wasn't necessary and the papers lay forgotten in my file until I came across them the other day. As far as I know Jane never did see this specific item among the papers. I sealed it in the usual double envelope after placing it between two pieces of board.*

(*It will be remembered that these sessions began two years ago through our contacting a personality called Frank Watts, who was superseded by Seth in the fourth session. Jane and I have made a few sporadic attempts to learn more about Frank Watts; such a man did live in Elmira, we learned, through a resident who knew him. Since the sessions we keep an eye out for the name in the local paper, especially in a section called "Twenty Years Ago This Week," which is printed every Sunday.*

(*Last Sunday, in the death notices in this section for the week of January 9-15, 1946, I noted the name Richard J. Watts. We wondered if Richard Watts bore any connection to Frank, and I made a point of mentioning it just before session time tonight. This technique usually leads Seth to discuss the point in question during the session.*

(*The session was held in our large front room. Jane spoke while sitting down. She was smoking, and her eyes began to open and close often. Her pace was good, her voice average.*)

Good evening.

("*Good evening, Seth.*")

Now. I should like to continue our discussion concerning time.

I made the statement that action in the present could alter the past, and now we shall set about explaining the statement.

The past exists as a series of electromagnetic connections, held in the physical brain on the one hand, but it also consists of the same sort of realities retained in the nonphysical mind. These electromagnetic connections can be changed. The present exists as a series of electromagnetic connections in both the brain and the mind, and this is the only reality which you are justified in giving to your present.

In other words the past and the present are real to the same extent. At times in fact the past can become more real than the present, and in such cases past actions are reacted to in the present. You take it for granted that present action can alter the future, but present actions can also alter the past.

The past is no more objective, no more independent from the perceiver, than is the present. These electromagnetic connections which compose the past were largely made by the individual perceiver, and the perceiver of course is always a participator.

The connections therefore can be changed at any time, and such changes are far from uncommon. They happen spontaneously on a subconscious basis a good deal of the time. The past was seldom what you remember it to be, for you have already rearranged it from the instant of any given occurrence.

There is of course a composite past that is composed of such individual electromagnetic connections, and this composite past is not the same past that once existed, <u>in those terms</u>. The past itself is being continually recreated by every individual, as attitudes and associations change. This is an actual recreation, and not a symbolic one. The child is indeed still within the man, but he is <u>not</u> the child that once was, in those terms. For even the child within the <u>man</u> continually changes, and again I am not speaking of symbolic change.

Now. Difficulties are caused when such changes in the past <u>do not</u> occur automatically. Such difficulties as severe neurosis are often caused precisely because the individual has not automatically changed his past. Once more, the only reality that can be assigned to the past is that granted to the symbols and associations and memory images that exist electromagnetically both within the physical brain and within the mind.

But this is the only reality that can be granted to the present. I am speaking now in your terms only, and this point should be clearly understood, for I am simplifying conditions considerably. A change of attitude, a new association, any of innumerable other actions, will automatically set up <u>new</u> electromagnetic connections, and break others. Now part of this we shall explain later, for these changes obviously affect both the future and the past. But the past, again, is continually changed by you, and by every individual. For basically you see, it is not something done and finished with, as is supposed.

And you are more free than you imagine to completely alter many aspects of your own past. If you say that the future is dependent upon the past, therefore, you must also say that the past is dependent upon the future. Once more, the past was never an independent, concrete object existing apart from the perceiving participator; for he made his past, and its only reality exists in the electromagnetic connections within his own organic and psychic structure.

(Jane now smiled. Her eyes were wide open and very dark.)

<u>Every action changes every other action</u>. We return to our ABC's. Therefore every action in the present affects those actions which you call the past. Ripples from a thrown stone go out in <u>all</u> directions.

(Another smile.)

I am going to go out rather far on the limb right here. Remembering what you now know about the nature of time, you should know that the apparent boundaries between past, present and future are only illusions, caused by the amount of action you can <u>physically</u> perceive. Therefore, it is more than possible to react in the past to an event that has not yet occurred, to be influenced by your own future.

We are not getting involved here in the free will or predestination question, though we have spoken about it, and we shall discuss it thoroughly in connection with time in general. Suffice it to say that it is more than possible for an individual to react in the past to an event in the <u>future</u> which may <u>never occur</u>.

This takes us into the problem of probabilities. I do not want to get too complicated. However I should explain the last statement to some degree. I suggest that you take a break, and I shall continue.

(Break at 9:30. Jane had been dissociated as usual for a first delivery. Her eyes had opened frequently, usually to emphasize a point, and they had been very dark. Her pace had been good, her voice average, and she smiled often. She had also smoked a good deal.

(She resumed in the same manner at 9:41.)

Now. I am sure that you remember the couple that you saw at York Beach.

("Yes.")

I have explained that these were psychic projections, given physical reality and projected subconsciously into the physical world by you and Ruburt. You then reacted to them in present time, at the time, you understand.

("Yes."

(See the 9th, 15th, 17th, 69th and 80th sessions. Jane and I saw this couple, who bore remarkable physical resemblances to us, in the dancing room of the Driftwood Hotel, York Beach, Maine, in August 1963. These sessions began in December, 1963. See Volumes 1 and 2)

Now. This couple <u>also</u> represented a sort of time projection, for quite literally you could have become what they were. This existed in the present as a probability. You perceived this portion of the probable future in that present, reacted to it; and the probable transformation of yourselves into those images did not occur. Because the past, present and future exist simultaneously however, there is no reason why you cannot react to an event whether or not it happens to fall within the small field of reality which you <u>usually</u> observe and participate in.

On a subconscious basis <u>you react to many events</u> that have not yet occurred, as far as your egotistical awareness of them is concerned. Such reactions are carefully screened out, away from conscious awareness, by the ego. The ego finds such occurrences extremely distracting and annoying, and when forced to admit their validity will resort to the most far-fetched rationalizations to explain them.

Now. The inner self exists in quite a different fashion than that seen by Dunne. For the inner self can indeed perceive events that will occur after physical death. It is not, and never was, imprisoned by ego time. Its perceptions of other times are merely inhibited by the ego. The inner self can perceive events that will occur to itself after physical death, and it also can see events that will occur in which it is not involved.

In all of these instances however there are uncertainties, for <u>probable</u> future events can be foreseen as clearly as events that will more actually occur. No event is <u>destined</u> to occur, and it can be changed, not only before and during, but after its occurrence. Again, I do not speak symbolically, and I am leaving myself open to many strong critical remarks which cannot all be answered in one evening.

You have yourself doubtless thought of some, but we shall do our best to make these ideas clear and understandable, and to explain various complications that can be anticipated. There are for example certain limitations set here that must be clearly stated; but within these limitations you will find that events can be changed, <u>and are</u> constantly changed, regardless of the point or the apparent point of their original occurrence.

All of this applies unless for example an individual is taken completely <u>out of</u> the physical time system. A murdered man will not be returned to physical life in the same fashion, whole and intact, as he was before the murder, for example; for he has been taken out of the particular system of action of which we are speaking.

He <u>may</u> return to the system however, as you know, through reincarnation. Many changes may occur however in that same point for the murderer who is still within the system.

I suggest your break.

(*Break at 10:01. Jane was dissociated as usual. Her eyes had been frequently open. She had smoked and her pace had been a little slower, with pauses. She said Seth was going on with this material when he abruptly realized what time it was.*

(It was now time for the 31st Dr. Instream test. As usual Jane sat quietly with her head down and her hands raised to her closed eyes. She used many short pauses, but her pace overall was fairly good. Resume at 10:11.)

Now. Give us a moment.

For our object, a ring. *(Pause.)* I believe a gold one. That is, a gold band. *(Pause.)*

In <u>connection</u> with the ring, I pick up an impression of a past event, a gathering in good weather, perhaps summertime, of youngish men and women. An outdoor affair is what I am thinking of, and I believe that it was near water *(pause)*, and that there was a connection with boats.

An afternoon affair. Disconnected from the northeast. The water was a river, I believe. At least it seems to have been banked on either side, so I <u>presume</u> it was a river. Buildings about that seem to have a Gothic structure. *(Pause.)*

They do not <u>appear</u> at any rate to be private dwellings, and seem to have a connection with a fairly distant past. An outdoor party then. This could have been in another country, perhaps England, and the ring is somehow connected to this event.

I seem to have the impression of the word Avon as being part of the location, or as indicating the location, and perhaps Stratsford. Perhaps the ring came from a shop somewhere about this location, or events began here at this affair which would <u>end up</u> with the giving of the ring. *(Long pause.)*

Some indication that Dr. Instream does not feel up to par this evening, and that a scheduled event did not occur.

Do you have a test for me, Joseph?

("Yes."

(It was 10:22. I handed Jane the sealed double envelope for our 28th test; she took it without opening her eyes, then for several minutes held it against her forehead. She spoke at a somewhat slower rate than she had in giving the Dr. Instream material.)

Now please give us a moment and we shall see what we can do. These are impressions.

An initiation of some sort, the <u>beginning</u> of something.

Cowardly—I do not know to what this word refers. Yellow. A connection with music. Large shapes in the foreground.

A black and white photo. Expressed concern—this is tentative—over the lateness of an hour.

An interior. An indication of green colors. Stubbing of the toe.

(Now Ruburt's personal association with this last impression is of your brother Loren and his wife. You may put this in parenthesis.) *(Jane now lowered the envelope to her lap.)*

Flowers, the odor of flowers as if it is summertime. Either this, or a strong flowery perfume.

Tumult, meaning noise. In parenthesis now for Ruburt's impression: (the interior of a trailer, and the country.)

I suggest your break.

(Break at 10:30. Jane was dissociated as usual. Her eyes had remained closed. Her pace had been fairly good.

(Jane said that while giving the Instream material she had a vague mental impression of an outdoor scene, and of a woman in outdated clothing. This reminded her of scenes in old paintings, as by Degas.

(As will be noted most of the data in connection with the envelope test cannot be checked by us. I expected this when I picked the object. The idea in choosing it was to simulate a test in which an object chosen by a third party was used; then this third party would interpret the data, leaving Jane and me free, so to speak. I got the idea for this approach from the 24th envelope test in the 219th session. The object was chosen by Lorraine Shafer, and to some extent she helped us interpret the resulting data.

(It will be remembered that Jane and Seth noted many valid emotional connections pertaining to the test object in the 219th session. We feel that with practice Jane and Seth will be able to pick such charges up regardless of what individuals they are attached to, or directed at.

(While giving tonight's test data, Jane said she had a few mental impressions, and that she believed she could vouch for a few items in the test.

("Flowers... as if it is summertime." she said, referred to the flower garden at the Birch house we considered purchasing in June 1964. We spent several weekends at the house cleaning up, and Jane weeded the flower garden.

("Tumult, meaning noise." referred, Jane said, to the traffic noise we became sharply aware of while working about the Birch house. Although situated on a hillside, the traffic noise seemed to roll up at us, and we used this as a reason for not buying the house. Seth said this was rationalization on our parts. See the sessions referred to on page 212.

("Country." Jane said she thought the last word of the data referred to the Birch house being located in the country outside Elmira, and not to be "the interior of a trailer."

(I joked that I thought "A black and white photo." meant the wallet identification card had been placed next to a photo in the wallet. There is a "Stubbing of

the toe." incident in my brother Loren's family—one of a humorous nature that has become kind of a standing joke.

(Jane resumed at an average pace at 10:43.)

I will shortly end our session.

As a matter of fact, our own test was a fairly good one. Unfortunately you cannot check up on the impressions with the owner of the card, and there is little reason for me to go into the various episodes connected with the card.

Some of the points did concern your attachment to the house which at one time was owned by the owner of the card.

Unless you have any questions for me I will end the session.

(I now mentioned the Richard Watts death notice of twenty years ago, described in the notes on page 212.)

It was not our Frank Watts. However there was a family connection of a distant nature. They were I believe second or third cousins.

("I guess that's it then for tonight.")

My heartiest wishes to you both.

I will make one small comment here. Ruburt's association with the trailer was caused by the fact that the owner of the card has a male child, who was somewhat unmanageable. And the owners of the trailer, <u>also</u> living in the country, have a child of similar nature.

The large objects in the foreground did refer to the rock ledge, or the ledge of rocks in front of the house.

(I neglected to mention this on page 217. Jane was aware of the connection here.)

The other impressions all referred to situations connected with the owner of the card. The card was carried next to a black and white photograph, incidentally. And now again, good evening. I close our sessions, Joseph, within a convenient hour, for your own benefits. Any time that you wish a longer session for any reason, simply request it; or a shorter session for that matter.

("Yes. Good night, Seth."

(End at 10:51. Jane was dissociated as usual. Her eyes had remained closed. Her pace had been rather slower than usual. She said Seth had been quite prepared to continue on inverted time.)

```
APPOINTMENT
FOR _____
Tues Jan 11   at 2:30 o'clock
DR. ANDREW T. COLUCCI
112 WALNUT STREET          TELEPHONE
ELMIRA, NEW YORK, 14905    4-8055
```

(Tracing of my dental appointment card, used in the 29th envelope test, in the 225th session for January 19, 1966.)

SESSION 225
JANUARY 19, 1966 9 PM WEDNESDAY AS SCHEDULED

(For the envelope test tonight I used my appointment card for my visit to the dentist earlier this month. As Jane did last time she visited Dr. Colucci in May 1965, I put myself in a trance state as an experiment, and was very comfortable. I also used Jane's appointment card of May 5, 1965 as the test object for the 15th envelope test in the 199th session. I picked the card for tonight's session because I thought it would be loaded with strong emotional charges of a personal nature, whereas the identification card used in the last test belonged to a person almost unknown to Jane and me.

(I placed the card between two pieces of card and sealed it in the usual double envelope. To the best of my knowledge Jane had never seen it, since I carried it in my wallet from the time Dr. Colucci's nurse gave it to me.

(The session was again held in our front room, and was not interrupted. Jane began speaking while sitting down and with her eyes closed. Her pace was a little slower than usual. Her manner was most amused, and she smiled often. She hadn't been speaking long before her eyes began to open frequently; they were very dark. She was smoking as the session began.)

Good evening.

("Good evening, Seth.")

I have a few rather humorous preliminary remarks to make, concerning

Ruburt's recent reactions.

There were several causes for them, and these reactions were triggered by the visit of your friend Mark last evening.

(Mark is Bill Macdonnel's entity name. See Session 68 in Volume 2.)

The reactions are beautiful examples. First of all Ruburt was worried, somewhat, concerning your own reactions when you found that you now had a <u>new</u> engagement for Friday evening, after already planning to cancel a previous one, in order to have some free time for yourself, and he felt to blame since he had already made a commitment to Mark—rather unwillingly, by the way. But it will harm him in no way to help Mark in his endeavor.

Next, he discovered that another gentleman had also been invited, the owner of another gallery, and a man whom Ruburt quite actively dislikes. Following this, reacting rather typically as a woman, he discovered that he did not believe enough good chairs were available.

This is highly amusing, for he did not <u>want</u> to have a chair available for the owner of the second gallery. He did not want him in the house. However he felt quite guilty over this, for the man is a Negro, and he feared that his dislike would be taken as discrimination. To prove to himself that this indeed was <u>not</u> the case, he began a nervous, frenzied and altogether desperate attempt to make certain that enough chairs were available.

He was very fond as a child of Edward Briscoe, who was also Negro. Edward was poor and the victim of circumstances. He helped out in Ruburt's household, therefore Ruburt feels that he should be <u>extremely</u> pleasant and helpful to any Negro, for this other boy's sake. And so he felt extremely guilty because he did not welcome the thought of this other Negro into his house.

(Jane's childhood friend, Eddie, died of diabetes in his early thirties.)

He was quite correct in assuming as he did that his upset had little to do with a lack of chairs, since he knew perfectly well that a sufficiency was available. Now, for another piece to our puzzle. The mayor is also to be present upon this occasion, and Ruburt thought subconsciously how pleased her friend, Edward Briscoe, would be in his simple way—in the old days—to be present, and how impressed he would be with the mayor.

So Edward and this Negro owner of the gallery became entwined in Ruburt's mind. He knew that it would be quite an occasion for this young man to visit informally, so to speak, with the mayor, though he would vehemently deny it; and yet Ruburt did not want the man in the house, therefore denying him such a privilege at least in thought.

I decided to mention this since he is at the point now—I am speaking of Ruburt—when he will not accept the superficial reasons given by the ego for many reactions, but seeks to discover deeper causes. There was also some other problem here, in that Ruburt feels, as you do, and quite rightly, that Mark is in over his head, psychologically speaking.

Mark, in attempting to help this other young man, may indeed end up helping himself, for it will turn him outward. But the situation also has other dangers. Because of Mark's background, subconsciously he fears Negroes; and the fear is so great, unfortunately, that it becomes a fascination. He is repelled and fascinated at the same time.

I will not take too much of our session up with these matters. Suffice it to say however that Mark's interest in this state art exhibit <u>can</u> be of great benefit to him. We shall turn to other matters. You may as you wish include the early part of the session in your records, or exclude it as you wish.

Let us get back to time. Now. The idea is current in academic psychological circles that the child exists psychologically intact in the man, that the man contains within him the psychological replica of the child that was.

Such is not exactly the case. The child exists within the man, yes, but he is not the same child. The memories that he thinks are the child's memories are not memories of a particular event that happened to the child. That is, they do not <u>contain</u> a precise picture of any particular incident that occurred. Each incident is <u>recreated</u> when the memory of it arises, but the memory is changed with each recreation, and subtly changed.

The past is, then, continually changed. The electromagnetic connections themselves, that make up any particular event—these connections, even while seemingly intact, have changed. The energy that composes them is not the same, and the past is constantly altered. Nothing can stand still, including the past, and <u>any</u> such appearance of stability is an illusion.

It is as much an illusion to believe that the past has vanished, as it is to believe that the future does not exist. The past does not vanish, for there was no past <u>to</u> vanish, in those terms.

I suggest your break.

(*Break at 9:34. Jane was dissociated as usual for a first delivery. Her eyes had opened frequently and her pace had remained a bit slow.*

(*She said that although she had a good idea of the reasons for her upset this afternoon, she didn't make conscious connections with her childhood friend, Eddie Briscoe.*

(*Jane resumed in the same manner at 9:44.*)

If you two are finished with your little discussion I shall continue.

I would prefer <u>when possible</u>, and without putting too much of a <u>strain</u> upon you both, that you discuss fairly neutral situations in our breaks, and avoid discussions with such emotional overtones.

    Now. The child does not stay in a neat psychological package, enclosed in the past and insulated from the present or the future. It is not as simple as all that.

    There is no point where the child ceases and the man begins, and no point where the young man ceases and the old man begins. These are states happening simultaneously, but perceived in slow motion within your system. Not only are they perceived in slow motion, but they are perceived along one line of focus only. The focus is indeed intense, but so limited in scope that it is relatively impossible for you to keep your attention upon the self except in the most inconsistent and fleeting of ways.

    You no longer perceive the past, therefore you think that it has vanished, and the self that you were has gone. But that particular moment, any particular moment, that you think of as the past, existed <u>before</u> your egotistical perception of it, and is constantly being changed by you, even when you no longer consciously perceive it.

    For the inner self can perceive it, and does change it. The idea of inverted time states that time flows in all directions, and that as each action affects every other action, so time constantly affects itself and continually reacts within itself. The past moment is never completed. <u>Consciously</u> you have simply lost sight of it, and have not followed it through in its endless depths.

    Some systems experience time exclusively in terms of probabilities, in which the self experiences a particular moment most thoroughly, where continuity is achieved not through a continuity of moments but a continuity of <u>self</u>, as it experiences all the various events that exist as probabilities for it in any given instant.

    <u>You</u> merely skip along the surface, and this is all right. But do not regard this hopping from moment to moment, as from stone to stone, as the approximation of time as it actually exists. The nature of perceptions determines the experience of time.

    I suggest your break.

    (Break at 10:01. Jane was dissociated as usual. Her eyes were often open and very dark, and her pace was quite rapid as break approached.

    (It was now time for the 32nd Dr. Instream test. As usual Jane sat quietly with her hands raised to her closed eyes. Her pace became quite slow, broken by many pauses of 15-30 seconds. She had been smoking earlier in the session but did not do so now. Resume at 10:10.)

    Now. Give us a moment for our Instream material. *(Pause.)*

    A box shape for our object. Small, with something like a transparent top, cellophane or plastic, of that nature. *(Pause.)* A <u>filling</u> inside, or lining, as of velvet or silk or some such *(pause of at least one minute),* and perhaps a divider within the box.

Longer than a ring box. It does not seem to have a cardboard cover, nor to be made of cardboard. Perhaps it holds a pen and pencil. I have the impression of a date, 1936 or 7. Perhaps this is when he obtained the box or its contents, I believe as a gift. Somehow connected with achievement, however. *(Pause.)*

A connection with a man as close to him as a brother, so to speak, with sandy hair, who is somehow connected with the object. *(Pause of 50 seconds.)* The object also had to do with an understanding that was reached between the owner and another man.

Do you have a test for me?

("Yes."

(As usual Jane took the envelope, our 29th, from me without opening her eyes. It was 10:30. She sat quietly, holding the envelope pressed to her forehead. Her pace became somewhat faster.)

Give us a moment, please. These are impressions.

Madison Avenue. A trip. A letter or note. (Ruburt thinks of Frederick Fell, in parenthesis.)

A disturbing event in the month of June, '64. A connection with another car, not your own. The number 12. I do not know whether this refers to 12 <u>people</u> or not.

A round object. A letter connected with an older individual.

A symbol. The object connected with an event that happened in the afternoon. The vicinity of another city, and also a connection with an accomplishment.

A long narrow road. A filling station.

I suggest your break.

(Break at 10:27. Jane was dissociated as usual. Her eyes had remained closed. She had no special thoughts about the evening's test data except to say that none of the impressions she heard herself giving made any sense to her.

(See the tracing on page 219. Seth goes over much of tonight's test data, but in order to avoid mixing my notes with his I'll give the usual interpretations Jane and I made first.

("Madison Avenue. A trip. A letter or note. [Ruburt thinks of Frederick Fell, in parenthesis.]" We agreed this data probably referred to Jane's publisher in New York City.

("A disturbing event in the month of June, '64." Jane said she thought this referred to an episode when she should have visited the dentist, Dr. Colucci, but did

not. She keeps a brief daily record of activities, and verified her idea. In her notebook she found a record that on May 31, 1964, she woke up with a swollen lower left jaw. I thought it a bad tooth. At this time, not having practiced self-hypnosis consciously, Jane had a great fear of dentists. Instead of seeing a dentist she visited our doctor next door; he put her on a series of antibiotics that lasted for four days, on into the month of June 1964. The pendulum told Jane the swelling was psychosomatic and not a tooth; the doctor agreed, eventually, and Seth did too, in the 59th session for June 3, 1964. See Volume 2.

("A connection with another car, not your own." When I visited Dr. Colucci on January 11 he told me that about a week previously, probably on Sunday, January 2, 1966, he had been unable to make the climb up the icy road leading to his home outside Elmira. Dr. Colucci lives on top of a long steep hill, yet this was the first time in three years, he said, that he had been unable to drive home. Jane said Seth gave this bit of test data because we ourselves had had trouble making a nearby steep hill in our own car, also this month. Seth dealt with our own car troubles in the 222nd session. Jane said she thought the association between these two episodes was legitimate.

("The number 12. I do not know whether this refers to 12 people or not." Jane said she believed the "12" came from the address of Dr. Colucci's office, 112 Walnut Street, around the corner from our address on W. Water Street, and that Seth speculated about people because of Dr. Colucci's waiting room being a gathering place for people.

("A round object." I thought this referred to the large round light over the dental chair, but it could also refer to many other things.

("A letter connected with an older individual." Jane said this referred to her letter of January 13 to Dr. Instream. In it she told Dr. Instream of my using the trance state on my visit to Dr. Colucci.

("A symbol." Here again there could be many references.

("The object connected with an event that happened in the afternoon." My dental appointment as shown on the test object was for 2:30 PM.

("The vicinity of another city", was a reference, Jane said, to the fact that Dr. Colucci lives in Pine City. Pine City is one of those small suburban communities that border more populated places like Elmira; though their population is small they actually cover many more square miles of land.

("and also a connection with an accomplishment." Jane and I agreed this meant my using the trance state successfully on my visit to Dr. Colucci.

("A long narrow road." We thought there could be association here also in the manner of the previous data about a connection with another car, not our own. Dr. Colucci, as stated, lives atop a hill climbed by a long narrow road. So do the Gallaghers, in the same general area. Dr. Colucci had trouble climbing the road to his home, and we had trouble climbing the road to the Gallagher home.

("*A filling station.*" *We thought there might be a connection here in that our car ran out of gas on the road to the Gallaghers; even so, this data would be too far removed from the test object.*)

(*Jane resumed, her eyes opening and closing, at 10:50.*)

Now. We will shortly end our session.

The June event did refer to Ruburt's swollen gums, which were very painful. He feared most strongly that he would have to visit Colucci, and went to the doctor rather than see the dentist—although Colucci was out in the yard, and Ruburt saw him, as he will now remember.

(*As soon as the session ended Jane said she did indeed remember seeing Dr. Colucci as soon as Seth mentioned that she would. Dr. Colucci's office is but four doors down the street from the M.D. she visited. Seth was quite amused in giving this information.*)

The gas station association, while not particularly helpful for your purposes, was in some ways legitimate. The other car did refer to the dentist's difficulty in making the hill, as he told you at your visit. The gasoline station was Ruburt's personal association derived from this, subconsciously.

For lately you could not make a hill, and as a result later you went to a gasoline station for gas. This was too broad an association for your purposes, but legitimate, and it should give you some idea of how these things work. For often quite legitimate associations such as these must be bypassed for more specific data. Nevertheless this particular impression does show the evidence of clairvoyant data.

The number 12 did refer to the address. However it was confused with people because of the people in the waiting room. There was a merging here, or a scrambling, of valid information.

("*What about the reference to the vicinity of another city?*")

That did indeed refer to Pine City, and connected, you see, the office incident of your appointment with the car incident, which occurred in the vicinity of Pine City.

The note referred to the appointment card. This led Ruburt to think of Fell however, and a trip.

(*Jane and I hesitated to say that the note referred to the appointment card, since Madison Avenue and a trip were mentioned in close approximation, as well as Fell.*)

("*What about the interpretation for the round object?*")

The round object referred to the light. This is my fault. I should have been more specific.

("And the letter to an older individual?")

The letter to the older individual referred to Ruburt's writing to Dr. Instream <u>about</u> your trance, induced during your Colucci appointment.

("The symbol?")

The symbol was a distortion referring to the round object.

I saw at first the object as if it were—the round object which was the light—as if it were on the card.

(Jane and I think this a most interesting bit of information. We also compare it with the number 12 data, wherein the numerals in the dentist's address became scrambled with the idea of people in his waiting room. Only now, it appears, is Seth beginning to get this specific in his interpretation of test data.)

Madison Avenue simply means New York City to Ruburt, and was connected to his Fell associations, which were wrong.

Now, they were wrong, but there was a connection here, in that Mr. Fell had recently had throat difficulties. Ruburt picked up the connection with the mouth, you see.

(Jane's publisher had written her recently that he had had throat trouble.)

As always I could continue. However we shall gracefully dismiss <u>ourselves</u>. My heartiest wishes to you both.

("Good night, Seth.")

(End at 11:05. Jane was dissociated as usual. Her pace had been average, her eyes had opened frequently. As usual, she said, Seth could have continued indefinitely.)

SESSION 226
JANUARY 24, 1966   9 PM MONDAY AS SCHEDULED

(Friday evening, January 21, Jane had some success hypnotizing both Bill and Peggy Gallagher at their request, separately. The experiment was not planned. Peggy has been hypnotized twice—one of these times by Dr. Milton Erickson—but this was Bill's first experience. Dr. Erickson is nationally known.

(Jane achieved partial success with Bill on two attempts. The first try was the best. Bill was unable to open his eyes and developed good amnesia in his left hand, these being the tests Jane used to show him something about the trance state. However he was not able to speak during either session, and came out of the state both times when Jane asked him to answer questions. He did succeed in relaxing very well. This is difficult for him to do; he has ulcers.

(Nor was Peggy able to speak during her first session and left the state when Jane began to ask her questions. On the second attempt Jane succeeded quite well by

using a more authoritative approach. She did not ask Peggy questions this time. Peggy attained a deep enough state to show no reaction when Jane placed our cat, Willy, on her stomach as she lay on the divan. Peggy has a deep fear of animals in general and cats in particular, this being why Seth calls her the cat lover.

(All of us, including Peggy, were amused when she insisted that she tolerated Willy's presence because she thought Jane was touching her, instead of the cat.

(Seth came through briefly shortly before the Gallaghers left, at about 1 AM. He told us he had watched the proceedings with much pleasure and amusement. He explained that Bill had allowed the hypnosis to proceed just so far before his ego called a halt, but that he could progress. Seth said Peggy used rationalization in saying that she stood for Willy's proximity because she thought Jane touched her instead of the cat. Peggy, Seth said in high good humor, had actually achieved an excellent state of deep hypnosis when Jane used the more authoritative approach; otherwise she wouldn't have permitted the cat's presence.

(I was somewhat dubious about Jane's hypnosis attempts since we haven't had time to do much work in this direction lately. But Jane said she felt like it, and the Gallaghers insisted that she try. I didn't think Bill could be easily hypnotized, but he was quite pleased with his results for a first attempt. Both Bill and Peggy said they thought they could have done better had Jane taken more time with her induction, yet Jane's approach had been quite leisurely; thus time appeared to have been compressed for them.

(Seth had the interesting comment to make that he had looked out at us from Jane's eyes during the evening, along with Jane, and that he saw us as individuals instead of composite electromagnetic images embodying our pasts, presents, and futures. On two very brief occasions Seth let his voice blast out to some extent, though not at full volume by any means. The hour was late and I was quite aware of possible reactions from neighbors in the house.

(No envelope test was held during tonight's session.

(The session was witnessed by John Bradley, our friend from Williamsport, PA, who attends a session occasionally. John usually inspires Seth in a telepathic/clairvoyant way, and so tonight some effects were obtained also. The last session John witnessed was the 204th.

(When he first appeared John mentioned that he had attended a meeting for medical salesman in Cleveland OH earlier this month; John is a sales representative for Searle Drug. As soon as he mentioned Cleveland I asked him to say nothing more about it, in the event Seth chose to do so later. Fortunately Jane was out of the room at the moment and did not hear Cleveland mentioned.

(The session was held in our large front room, in full light as usual. Jane began speaking while sitting down and with her eyes closed. As is often the case when witnesses *are present she seemed to draw upon extra energy; her pace was fast from the start, and her voice stronger and somewhat deeper than usual.)*

Good evening.

("Good evening, Seth."

([John:]) "Good evening, Seth.")

My welcome to our friend Philip.

Now. If our exuberant Ruburt has calmed down, and if our friend Philip has put down his paper, we shall begin.

(Jane had been very pleased with some humorous poetry she had written today, and had been reading it to John before the session. John's entity name is Philip. Just as the session began he had been folding a newspaper; as usual Seth wasn't bashful about asking for quiet.)

I would like to give you some more material this evening concerning our inverted time system, for when you understand how it operates then you can begin to take advantage of it more readily.

I will leave it to you, Joseph, to cut me short if I speak too quickly.

When the inverted time system is understood for what it is, then the individual is in contact simultaneously with the experience gained in the so-called past, and is also able to take advantage of events which have not yet occurred within your present. This does not mean that he will be consciously aware of future events, for if you remember these events can be changed by him at any time. He is constantly making his own experience. He is constantly <u>forming</u> the events of the past, even as he forms the events of the present and future.

In many respects the individual is not at the mercy of past events, for he changes them constantly. He is not therefore at the mercy of future events, for he changes these also, not only before but also after their occurrence. I regret that our friend Philip does not have the preliminary background to follow this discussion with clarity.

Now. So-called hunches indeed are often caused by an inner recognition that a given event might occur. As you know, there is no cause and effect as you understand it. Nevertheless there are probabilities. Now basically it is not true to say that an individual's decisions must be based upon concrete events within his own past, nor that he is largely imprisoned by his past, nor that his future actions are predetermined by his past experience. For as you now understand the past is as real as the future, no more and no less. The past exists as far as the individual is concerned as a pattern of electromagnetic currents within the brain, and these connections constantly change.

The individual can change past action <u>within</u> however the limitations earlier mentioned in our last session. Therefore his future actions are not dependent upon a concrete and unchanging past, for such a past never existed.

I would like these points made most clearly. Now. An <u>event</u> foreseen through precognition or clairvoyance, a future event, <u>may</u> or may not actually occur within time as you know it. For you are seeing into probabilities, and the probable event may or may not occur, <u>within</u> your time system.

Such an event <u>will</u> however occur within another time system, for all probabilities become actual, although you may not perceive them. Our friend Dunne was quite correct here.

I shall now let you take a break, and enjoy a brief social discussion.

(Jane paused at 9:16, her eyes still closed. She then resumed briefly.)

For now, just write down 12th Street, and let it go at that. The 12th Street may have a significance to Philip.

(Break at 9:17. Jane was dissociated as usual for a first break. Her eyes had remained closed, her pace had been fast, her voice stronger, deeper, and more emphatic than usual.

(John Bradley didn't say anything about the 12th Street data, as I hoped he wouldn't, and Jane didn't ask him about it. During break we discussed John's company, Searle Drug, which is in the throes of financial difficulties compounded by management problems; Seth has discussed this often when John has been present, and to date his statements have been accurate.

(Just before break ended the conversation concerned some of the new drug products Searle has coming on the market. Jane resumed in a most active and emphatic manner, her eyes still closed, at 9:29.)

I do find the conversation quite amusing, and having no problems of that kind myself I will therefore avoid making any comments.

Now. These probabilities, these <u>events</u> that may or may not occur, are extremely interesting. Let us consider our self one and time one. As a rule our self <u>two</u> can indeed view what may happen in self one's future. However, our self two views probabilities, and some of these probabilities will indeed occur to self one. Some will not, and this is where, again, our friends Priestley and Dunne fall short.

Priestley was right also to some extent here. These probabilities do occur somewhere, but they will occur to a self that Priestley nor Dunne ever imagined—a self who exists simultaneously with any given individual, and who is a part of him; but a self that he will never know while he is within your particular system.

Someday we shall explain this in mathematical terms. However for now we shall try plain English. Every thought is composed of its own energy, and it has an effect within energy. We are not speaking here now of your tired old cause and effect theory however. Every action changes every other action. Any probability is a reality whether or not it occurs within your own system, and I shall add to that early mention.

Reality within some systems other than your own, is experienced not as a series of moments, but as experience into <u>all the probabilities</u> of action that exist within any given instant. A <u>continuity</u> therefore is in terms of the self <u>rather than</u> in terms of a series of moments. <u>Instead there is a series of selves</u>—

(Jane's eyes now began to open wide for emphasis; they were very dark. Her voice was strong, her manner most emphatic and fast. She gestured frequently as she spoke.)

—with the inner ego operating <u>consciously</u> to give continuity.

In such a system therefore <u>your</u> ideas of present, past and future would not exist. Nor would your idea of one and only one event at a time be understood. Now this dimension exists in a reality which Priestley nor Dunne even began to examine.

The whole psychological formation of the perceiver is entirely different, and <u>there is no one event out of all probable</u> events, but there is experience of <u>all the mathematically probable</u> events that could happen <u>to</u> any given individual, within any given amount of time as you know it.

(Consider the whole of the next paragraph underlined, so strong and positive was Jane's delivery.)

<u>The psychological composition of the perceiving participator is therefore entirely alien to your own. In such a system however, as in your own, the perceiver is also a participator and a creator, but he does not work with your conception of time, but with probabilities. In your terms then, he would seem to delve into each moment in all of its probabilities, so that in your time on the one hand many centuries would have passed, and on the other hand only an instant.</u>

The time system is entirely different here. <u>The value fulfillment</u> is quite as valid however within both systems, and in a very loose fashion this probability system could be compared to Dunne's time three.

(Seth said a little on the above ideas when he began to give us the material on the electrical field and on moment points, several months ago. This was some time before Jane began reading Dunne and Priestley.)

There would be many respects however where they would not agree, and I mention this similarity only to make my idea somewhat more clear to you.

We will have a break. I am anxious however to tie in this material on the system of probabilities with dreams, for at times there can be a connection; and something indeed that our friends Priestley and Dunne did not consider—for their self three can indeed wander outside of the dimensions which they assigned to him.

(Break at 9:48. Jane was dissociated as usual. Her voice and manner had been strong and emphatic, her pace fast.

(Just before first break Seth had mentioned a 12th St. in connection with John Bradley. Jane now asked John about it, but John said he wouldn't tell her anything about such a statement yet. Jane said she received this bit of data quite strongly while giving Seth's other material, and that at first she wasn't going to give voice to it because she wasn't sure if it was from Seth or herself. Then she decided to speak it out anyhow.

(Jane's eyes had been open and very dark during much of the above delivery. Since it was now time for the 33rd Dr. Instream test however, her eyes closed and her pace slowed considerably. Her head was down, her hands raised to her face. Resume at 10:05.)

Now, give us a moment for our Dr. Instream material.

I get the impression of glass. He is looking at a glass. The glass is the object. *(Pause.)*

The glass is in front of him. I do not pick up any strong emotional attachment between him and the object.

Now for other impressions. Wisteria.

(John Bradley shifted his position on the divan. Jane spoke to him without changing her position.)

Philip, during the test data please try to be as quiet as possible. Dr. Instream's hypnosis experiments <u>now</u> doing very well. Some slight difficulty in one particular area, caused by a motor malfunction. The malfunction the result of subconscious associations on the part of the subject. *(Pause.)*

The glass which I have given as the object has a connection with roses. A disturbance also. This disturbance is in connection with the owner of the glass.

1934, also in connection with the object.

Dr. Instream's physical condition disturbs him more than usual. A pronounced limp. *(Pause.)* There is a connection with the glass and a note. *(Pause.)* The note from a woman.

Do you have a test for me, Joseph?

("No."

(It was 10:14. Jane retained her position, sitting with her hands raised to her closed eyes, her head down, her voice slow.)

I repeat the short data given earlier for Philip, in a town that is large and not in this location. I think also of a meeting and a fat man.

The number 4, and 8 o'clock. At least I believe the number 8 refers to time. A stuffy place. Also an apartment. Three alternate plans. Two were not followed, and there is a question over the third.

A corner bar and grill establishment in the same town, I believe, though I am not certain, as the 12th Street address. And in connection with this a tall thin man, and a discussion concerning money.

A hilltop address. Two women live together, this is a separate impression. One woman wears a string of beads, and Philip knows her. 1652.

I suggest your break.

(*Break at 10:18. Jane was dissociated as usual. She received no images, she said, while giving either the Dr. Instream or the John Bradley material.*

(*At first John said Seth's material meant little or nothing to him. This is just about a standard first reaction from witnesses for whom Seth has given such material; offhand Jane and I can think of no one who has reacted differently. It takes time for memory to begin to work. As usual I read Seth's data back to John, and as he has in past sessions he then began to make connections. See the 135th, 166th, 190th, 199th, 200th, and 204th sessions for material re. John. A fair amount of the material is telepathic and/or clairvoyant, especially that of the 204th session. Seth expands on this last session in the 205th and 206th sessions, and deals with John's experience in hearing Seth speak to him when he was alone.*

(*John attended a salesmen's meeting, held by his employer, Searle Drug, in Cleveland OH on January 12-14, 1966. He stayed at the Sheraton-Hilton Hotel. The president of the company and his top assistants also attended the meeting.*

(*"12th Street." John now told us that he took several meals in the Manger Hotel—pronounced with a hard G—and had some business engagements there also. This hotel is on either 12th or 13th St. in Cleveland; John was not positive, but felt the address would be 12th Street rather than 13th Street.*

(*"in a town that is large and not in this location." Cleveland is of course some distance from here. As stated Jane did not hear John mention Cleveland to me, although she knew he had been traveling. In any case Seth mentioned no city by name.*

(*"I think also of a meeting and a fat man." At the Sheraton-Hilton John had several meetings with Searle's Washington, DC representative to the government, Mr. McKeown. This man engaged John in conversations designed to feel him out, John said, and did it so cleverly that the meeting in Cleveland was over before he fully realized what had taken place. John is aware that he is being considered for promotion however. Mr. McKeown, John told us, is quite overweight, but is not a truly obese person. John said his own idea of a "fat" man is one who is grossly overweight; this Mr. McKeown is not, even though on the heavy side.*

(*"The number 4," John could offer no interpretation here.*

(*"8 o'clock." John said this could refer to a time in the evening when he was* supposed to make a telephone call, but he doesn't consider it very relevant.

("A stuffy place." This is most interesting, John said, because of the fact that the Sheraton-Hilton was very stuffy during the three nights he was there. Indeed, John said, it was so stuffy at night particularly that he had trouble sleeping, and was out of bed several times.

(I might add another bit of information here, to the effect that on Jan. 8 Jane had a dream in which she saw a strange room, not a bedroom although there was a bed in it. The room, she knew in her dream, belonged to John Bradley, although she did not see him in the dream. In addition the bed had been slept in, and the bedclothes were tossed about as though John had been quite restless. The time was at night in the dream. We do not know if there is a connection here.

("Also an apartment." John could offer nothing here at the moment, although there was a good connection, involving the Sheraton-Hilton and Mr. McKeown. It will be explained later in the session.

("Three alternate plans." John said he didn't see connections here, unless the reference was to his own personal plans. Recently he did have three plans in mind, which Jane and I also knew about, and which Seth had mentioned. These were to leave Searle and buy a restaurant in his hometown of Williamsport, PA; to stay with Searle and in Williamsport; or to demand a transfer of location from Searle, and a promotion. Mr. McKeown is involved with the last of these alternatives, so it is conceivable that "there is a question over the third." as stated by Seth.

("A corner bar and grill establishment in the same town, I believe, though I am not certain, as the 12th Street address." Seth is correct here, John said. The Hotel Manger is situated at a corner location, and the bar and grill in the hotel is on the corner. As stated, the hotel is on either 12th or 13th Street.

("And in connection with this a tall thin man, and a discussion concerning money." John said he accompanied a tall thin man to the Hotel Manger's dining room, which is located next to the bar and grill. The tall thin man also has a position high up in the company, John said. John could look into the bar and grill of the Manger from where he sat while eating supper. He had a long talk with the company executive, but money was not the specific subject of the conversation.

("A hilltop address. Two women..." one of which John knows, and "1652." meant nothing in particular to John, at the moment.

(We were discussing these last points when Seth came through again. Jane resumed at a fast pace, with her eyes closed, at 10:37.)

The two women referred—I am not sure so we shall go slowly—the two women live together and they had reference to <u>one</u> of the two gentlemen I have mentioned in connection with Philip.

Here I also pick up 34. Now I am not certain whether this refers to the age of one of the women, or whether they live on a 34th Street in the same city. One has a connection with jewelry.

("*Not too fast.*")

Perhaps she works in a jewelry shop. I also pick up the name Alfred—an atrocious name—and a Leo.

But I am going too far, for I am thinking now of the bartender, and this will not help us.

An occasion at Philip's home at about three o'clock in the afternoon, in connection with his family. A grievance also.

I will here end our session, with a gentle note to Ruburt, that I have asked him not to smoke when we are dealing with such material. Also a supper engagement, two men, and a <u>paper</u> is shown.

Now, my heartiest regards to you all. And as always I regret leaving, for you grow on me.

("*Good night, Seth.*")

(*[John:] "Good night, Seth."*)

(*End, presumably, at 10:47. Jane's eyes had remained closed, and she had smoked during this last delivery.*)

(*John said he could offer little help, still, on the two women mentioned by Seth. He said that one of his friends sees a woman friend whenever he goes to Cleveland, and that perhaps this woman has a companion, or a roommate.*)

(*During my efforts to get as much data written down as possible, I forgot to ask John whether "a supper engagement, two men, and a <u>paper</u> is shown." meant anything to him.*)

(*John was interested in whether Seth could add anything to the long range material he has given concerning Searle Drug over the past year and a half. This material is somewhat long and complicated, and is covered in the sessions John has witnessed: 37, 54, 63, 70, 95, 135, 166, 190, 204. Searle is going through a financial and management crisis, and this is reflected in the stock market; John is naturally concerned. See Volumes 1 through 5.*)

(*John said his barber in Williamsport, PA, is named Alfred, and that a friend of his who is active in a political organization that John belongs to, in Williamsport, is named Leo. But if these names refer to Cleveland, John could offer no confirmation.*)

(*Nor could John pinpoint any three o'clock occasion in particular at his home, in connection with his family, or with a grievance.*)

(*In reply to John's queries about Searle, Seth came through once again. Jane resumed in a quieter voice, with her eyes closed, at 10:45.*)

The connection should be rather apparent, and beginnings are already known. Events will take place, in the <u>main</u>, as I said that they would.

I pick up in connection with this the initials A J, A G—I am not certain.

At another meeting some other aspects were made known to you, Philip, of which you may not be consciously aware. A vague but definite connection to Dayton, OH, here. A man with connections with Dayton, OH will be involved with a change in your company. We speak in terms of probabilities. Nevertheless no actions thus far have occurred to drastically change any of the predicted events, and unless actions are so initiated events will occur as given.

There is a child, a female, who is seemingly not connected with any of these episodes, who will be important in a man's decision. Now see what you can make of all this.

(Break at 10:49. Jane had been dissociated as usual. Her eyes had remained closed.

(Seth's predictions for Searle include the loss of power for the current vice president, who is the son of the company's founder, although the son may retain a titular chair. There is to be a drastic reorganization, finally, after all else fails. John, according to Seth, would be wise to remain with the company, for eventually things will work out well. Seth told John he could go as far as he desired in the company. John has been sounded out before by high officials, and was again at this Cleveland meeting.

(As stated earlier, the sounding out was quite subtle as performed by Mr. McKeown and the other official, the tall thin man. They sought to learn John's views while not committing themselves in any way, so as to save themselves the embarrassment of being refused. John has since written to Mr. McKeown for further information—this after he realized what was transpiring.

(As John explained company politics to us now, he said he thought he saw a connection with Seth's mention of an "apartment." on page 235. It will be remembered that at first John could offer nothing for this data. Mr. McKeown, John said, had gone so far as to invite him up to his private room at the Sheraton-Hilton, for more secluded talks involving the company. At the time John was somewhat surprised that a high company official would pay particular attention to him. It was during such meetings as this, and those at the Manger, that the sounding-out process commenced.

(John could offer no help on the initials A J, or A G. Seth has given other initials in past data for John, with the same results, and Jane and I believe that this kind of information is probably distorted. Nor could John tell us anything about a female child, or a Dayton OH connection.

(In reference to the apartment data, Seth came through again at 11:00.)

This is what I referred to, and the room is what I was thinking of as an apartment, in that it was private.

The information that was given to you and which you did not understand had to do with this man, and his impression of <u>you</u> had much to do with what I am saying, insofar as the <u>company</u>, and Philip's connection to it, is concerned.

He was sent with a purpose.

(End at 11:03. Jane had spoken quietly, her eyes closed. As stated, John has since written Mr. McKeown for more information, and any additional information related to Seth's predictions in this session will be included in a future session.)

SESSION 227
JANUARY 26, 1966 9 PM WEDNESDAY AS SCHEDULED

(No envelope test was held during the session.

(The session was held in our front room. Jane began speaking while sitting down and with her eyes closed; her eyes then began to open frequently after a few paragraphs of material. Her voice was about average, her pace somewhat slower than usual in the beginning. Her pace picked up considerably however as the delivery progressed, and acquired much emphasis. Jane began speaking at 8:58.)

Good evening.

("Good evening, Seth.")

I was quite pleased with the amount of quite specific material that I managed to deliver concerning our friend Philip, at our last session.

(Jane paused and smiled. Philip is John Bradley's entity name.)

The confidence that Ruburt receives in such circumstances is of great help to us all. We shall have a relaxed session this evening. There are several points however that I would like to make. They have to do with our discussion of time in general.

A part of the whole self is quite aware of the probabilities. Now. This is a portion of the self that exists as a perceiving participator, in the dimension which we discussed in our last session. This is fairly difficult material, and so I am giving it to you carefully.

The ego as <u>you</u> know it, the conscious self within your time system, this ego, let us say, arrives at and experiences event X.

("Wait a minute."

(Our cat, Willy, had jumped up into Jane's lap. As cats will, he began to knead her legs with his forefeet. Jane's eyes did not open up but her delivery became spasmodic. As I got up she lifted Willy herself and dropped him to the floor.

(This is the first time in many sessions that Willy has paid any attention to Jane during a session. In the early sessions he exhibited some drastic behavior at Seth's

presence and/or arrival. At times he would attempt to entangle himself in Jane's legs as she paced about the room while speaking for Seth. At other times he seemed to exhibit plain panic, running to hide just before session time. Seth told us this was because the cat's very acute senses detected his arrival on our plane. Willy, he said, would get used to his presence eventually and show no reaction; this has been the case now for well over a year.)

Now this event X is only one of a literally numberless amount of probable events which the conscious self could experience. For its purposes however the conscious self <u>chooses</u> this particular event X. But again, this event X, until the conscious self experiences it, is only one of <u>many</u> other <u>probable</u> events, different in no basic manner from the others. It becomes <u>real</u>, actual and different from those other probable events, only when it is experienced by our conscious self, or by <u>this</u> conscious self.

(Jane's manner had become faster and more emphatic, and her eyes began to open. They were very dark. She lit a cigarette.)

I am making this discussion as simple as possible, and using the conscious self simply because less difficulties are presented in explanation. It is obvious, for example, that some events are experienced by the subconscious also, that may or may not be experienced by the ego.

This event X becomes real then, in your terms, only when it is experienced or perceived by our conscious self. What about all of these other probable events, however? The only difference between them and event X is that event X was perceived and experienced by our conscious individual. In other words, were it not for this perception of the event X, it would still be as valid, or as invalid, as real or as unreal, as all the other probable events that were <u>not</u> perceived.

This leads us then to an obvious conclusion: if event X were not perceived it would still be a probability only. By the same token, if our individual chose to perceive and experience, say, event Y, then event Y would be the reality, and event X would still be <u>un</u>real.

As I have explained the ego to you, within your system it can only perceive in terms of continuity, in a straight-line fashion so to speak, one event after the other. It can only choose to experience one event out of all the probable events at a time. The ego is however the only portion of the self that is, in the main, limited to follow experience along these lines.

Since your physical time operates as it does, the physical organism does not have time within its own framework to experience <u>any more</u> than one probable event. It cannot focus upon two events at once. It goes without saying, again, that we are simplifying matters considerably, since each physical event is actually a gestalt of many small events.

The underline_package_ of experience that you can focus upon and make sense of, is indeed composed of many small packages, but the whole package of reality is actually much larger than this. There is however a portion of the self that can and does experience events in an entirely different fashion, and this portion of the self goes off on a different tangent. For when our individual perceives event X, this other portion of the self branches off, so to speak, into all the other probable events that could have been just as easily experienced by the ego.

The ego must choose one of all these because of its physical time limitations. But this other portion of the self can, and does, delve into what you could call event X1, X2, X3, et cetera. It can pursue and experience all of these alternate events, and it can do so in the same amount of physical time that it takes for the ego to experience event X alone.

This is not as far-fetched as it might seem, for again, you perceive now more than you realize; although you may not be consciously aware of this, it still falls within the framework of your associated experience. The mere shaking of a hand may be perceived by you as a simple action. You are not consciously aware of the million small actions which make up this seemingly insignificant act.

These actions exist nevertheless. It does not take you time to perceive them one by one. You perceive them in their completed fashion. Now this other portion of the self experiences these probable events, consciously, with as much rapidity as you subconsciously perceive the million small actions that make up the handshake.

You may take your break.

(Break at 9:29. Jane was dissociated as usual for a first delivery. Her pace had become fast but her voice had been rather quiet. Her eyes had opened often and been very dark. She had smoked.

(Jane said she was aware of Willy climbing up into her lap, and that the cat's presence might have interfered with her delivery had he remained there.

(Jane resumed in about the same manner at 9:40.)

Now. These various portions of the self of which I speak are just that—portions of the whole self that simply operate in different dimensions of reality, and within different fields of activity.

There are no ultimate boundaries that divide one from another. They simply seek their experience in separate dimensions. In this particular instance, compare the various portions of the self to the various members of a family.

The man may work in a city. The woman may work in their home in the country. Of three children, all three may attend different schools. They are all still part of the same unit. They all operate out of the same house. There is no reason why any of the children could not spend his day at the office with the father of the family, basically speaking, but he would not be able to understand or perceive many of the events that occurred there.

I am trying to make this analogy clearer. The child would <u>fit into</u> the man's office building, for example. There would be no boundary to keep him out while letting the father enter, physically speaking. The man could also enter the school. In the same manner there is no basic reason why one self, or rather <u>one portion of the self</u>, has its main experiences in one dimension, while other portions of the self experience reality within different fields.

There is within the family a general realization of the experiences of its members, but these are second-handed, <u>except</u> for those experiences <u>which the family shares as a unit</u>. This is an important point, for there is an <u>unspecialized</u>, extremely generalized and intuitional knowledge on the part of <u>any</u> portion of the self, as to the nature of experience as felt by the other portions of the self.

Some experiences or events will be perceived by all layers of the self, though in their own fashion, and experienced as a unit. There are few of these, but they are extremely vivid, and serve as the family's joint experiences serve to reinforce the identity of the whole psychological structure.

The imagination can vaguely perceive, of course, some probabilities, but the physical organism can directly experience but one of these within physical time, and in terms of continuity. The probable events however are precisely as <u>real</u> as that one event which is chosen from them to be a physical experience. And these events therefore become "real", in quotes, within other dimensions. As a sideline here, there are some interesting episodes, not at all understood, when a severe psychological shock, or even a deep sense of unendurable futility, will cause a short circuit, so to speak, so that one portion of the self becomes aware, and begins to experience reality as it exists for another portion of the self.

I am thinking here in particular of some cases of amnesia, where the victim suddenly ends up in a different town, with a different name, sometimes even with a different occupation, and with no memory of his past.

In some such cases the individual is experiencing a <u>probable event</u>. But he must experience it, you see, within his own time system.

I suggest a break before our Instream material.

(Break at 10:00. Jane had been dissociated as usual. Her eyes had been open much of the time. Her delivery had been rather fast and emphatic, she had smiled often, used many gestures, and smoked a couple of cigarettes.

(It was now time for the 34th Dr. Instream test. Jane sat quietly with her head down and her hands raised to her closed eyes. She spoke now with many rather short pauses. She was not smoking. Resume at 10:05.)

Now. Give us a moment, please.

The object has something to do with a desk top. A rather old-fashioned desk top. *(Pause.)* The attention seems focused here. A green blotter, a letter opener, the sort that is in the shape of a dagger, and a letter holder. *(Pause.)*

A lamp on a still <u>higher</u> portion of the desk. This portion is like a ledge. The letter opener is a metal-type one, I believe of a silver color. Also a small round object on the desk, I <u>believe</u> of glass, the shape of a globe, and it is heavier than it looks. *(Pause.)*

For Dr. Instream in general, visitors from out of town today. The initials I believe M W, or W M. The M is part of a name that is fairly long, with two R's in it. *(Pause.)*

An occasion that is rather grim. This is not necessarily connected however with the other impressions.

A studio that he visits in the back of the building. *(Pause, at 10:15.)*

Do you have a test for me?

("No.")

I ask out of a sense of courtesy, and also so that you understand that I welcome them, knowing the spirit in which they are given.

(Jane still sat with her hands raised to her face.)

Now I told you that this would be a relaxed session, and I shall here bring it to a close, unless there are any matters in particular about which you have questions. We got through a bit of difficult material this evening very well.

("I have no questions.")

Then my heartiest good wishes to you both, indeed as always.

Ruburt will find incidentally that his book of poetry, the <u>new</u> and rather swiftly written one, will be published. He recognized the abundance of energy that was available to him as he wrote it.

The spontaneity that allowed him to deviate from his usual schedule is largely responsible for the whole book, for his original intention was merely to write a few humorous verses for out cat lover's birthday. I will have a little more to say concerning this, perhaps, at our next session.

Good evening.

("Good evening, Seth, and thank you."

(End at 10:22 Jane was dissociated as usual. Her delivery picked up a little toward the end, and her eyes opened a few times. She said Seth was pleased when I said thank you.

(It was very interesting to watch Jane produce the above-mentioned book of poetry. It grew out of earlier suggestions, and I would say the end result represented a fine example of spontaneous creative power at its best. The poems are of high quality indeed, and Jane felt certain from the start that they would be published. It is difficult

to publish poetry in hard-cover.

(Wednesday and Thursday nights, January 19 & 20, Jane gave herself suggestions that she would have a great abundance of energy. She usually uses suggestion each night, but this time she wanted a little something extra.

(Jane said she had been working quite happily on the book dealing with the Seth material, and on one about dreams. When she got the burst of energy on the poetry book idea however, she took advantage of it, and felt certain the material would be published. Here is a schedule of events:

(On Friday, January 21, she wrote 10 poems for Peggy's birthday in the space of 2 1/2-3 hours. The poems were of a humorous, social commentary nature, and highly polished. These gave her the idea for the book, which she considered over the weekend.

(On Monday, January 24, Jane wrote 20 poems in the space of 6 or 7 hours.
(On Tuesday, January 25, she wrote 15 poems in 5 or 6 hours.
(On Wednesday, January 26, she wrote 7 poems in 2 1/2 hours. This time span included doing some other work on the book also.

(The book was then finished, and Jane spent part of the next two days typing up the version for submission to publishers. In addition she recorded the 10 poems originally done for Peggy on Tuesday evening, January 25.)

SESSION 228
JANUARY 31, 1966 9 PM MONDAY AS SCHEDULED

(No envelope test was held during the session.

(Watching the blizzard that hit Elmira this weekend in action, I thought it like a disembodied psychic storm. Jane agreed; as session time drew near tonight she said she thought Seth would discuss the storm, and our weather in general. Seth has had something to say about the weather in these sessions: 56, 84, 123 and 175, without going into any great detail. Check Volumes 2, 3, and 4.

(The session was held in our front room. Jane began speaking while sitting down and with her eyes closed.)

Good evening.

("Good evening, Seth.")

Now. For a break from our material on probabilities and inverted time, I will indeed discuss a matter which is in your thoughts: the blizzard of the last few days.

(There came a knock on our door. It was a young neighbor from downstairs, concerned about transportation to work tomorrow. We work together at Artistic Card

Co. but had not tried to get to the plant today. She does not know of these sessions.

(For a time we held sessions in the back of our apartment to avoid such interruptions, but Jane prefers them held in the large front room. The interruption tonight was not any kind of a shock to Jane; she left the trance state easily, although I noticed her eyes were very dark when they first opened. It was Jane who answered the door however. We then engaged in a half-hour's conversation with our neighbor.

(When we were alone again Jane resumed as though the break had not occurred. Her voice was average, her pace average; her eyes were to open after a few paragraphs, and she was now smoking.)

Now. This is a good time to discuss certain interactions that occur within your system, and we can take your winter storm as an excellent example.

There is a constant give and take between psychic and chemical components which actually cause your daily weather, your weather cycles, seasons, droughts and storms. This physical weather then in its turn affects and changes the psychic atmosphere of each individual. The force that causes your weather can be thought of as self-generating.

Ultimately it is not self-generating, but for the purposes of our discussion it may be termed so. The force originates within the psychic or nonphysical aspects of each living creature within your system. This force acts as a balancing mechanism for the psychic structures, and through use of it living forms create and maintain in a most basic manner their own physical environment.

This is not to be taken as a symbolic idea, for I am speaking in quite practical terms. Not only does the human system for example become influenced chemically, electronically and psychically by physical weather, but also the human system electronically, electromagnetically, chemically and psychically affects and creates the climate in which existence is possible.

The chemical connections are the most easily discovered. The discovery however comes about, or is coming about, as a result of studies made concerning the effect of physical weather upon the individual, in chemical terms. It will take longer before it is at all realized that the individual <u>also</u> affects the weather.

Nevertheless some of this is, or should be, obvious. It is known that photosynthesis affects most vitally the makeup of your atmosphere, for example. The biological methods by which each individual utilizes oxygen are well known, but no assumptions have been drawn from this knowledge.

Now I have told you that dreams are caused <u>in part</u>—underline in part—by chemical excesses built up within the human system. Dreams also carry the weight of emotional excesses that cannot be adequately expressed within daily physical action.

(Seth began talking about dreams by the 15th session, then began to give

material on their chemical excesses soon after. See Volume 1.)

Now I shall tell you that physical weather is also caused in part by psychic energy, rushing through the human system and through the systems of all living creatures, and also by an excess, a chemical excess, beyond that which the individual organism can handle.

The word excess may be a poor one. Perhaps the word abundance of chemical energy would be more correct. The chemical energy is <u>above</u> that which is ordinarily needed by the individual physical organism, yet it must be used. The utilization comes about subconsciously.

This blizzard, and the last storm of last week, both of these are beneficial primarily. Now the physical organism simply cannot handle all of the energy that is available to it. It has abundant energy, not only to care for itself but to create a favorable physical environment. Without the outlet, the constructive outlet provided it in the formation of its own weather environments, the physical organism would have little balance or stability.

As emotional storms may be the result of a lack of discipline or of knowledge, or of control of one or more portions of the self, bringing about a corresponding exaggeration or growth of other portions of the self, so also erratic physical storms come from the same causes on a collective basis, but with the energy directed outward <u>and</u> often turned to a constructive purpose. Though this is not always the case.

A physical storm may, as you know, be far more disastrous than an emotional one. But a physical storm is a <u>collective</u> endeavor, and can be compared, if it is disastrous, only with disastrous collective emotional storms such as those that sweep across nations, when all minds seem seized by irrationality.

I suggest your break.

(Break at 9:55. Jane had been dissociated as usual for a first delivery. Her pace had become quite fast, and sometimes emphatic. Her eyes had opened often toward the end of the delivery.

(It was now time for the 35th Dr. Instream test. The blizzard howled outside. As usual Jane's pace slowed; she sat with her head down and her hands raised to her closed eyes. She spoke with many rather brief pauses. Resume at 10:02.)

Now, give us a moment before our Instream material.

First of all—this is not the object—I pick up the impression of a merge of some kind, in which our Doctor is involved.

A connection now, separate from the merge, with a shoe, a man's shoe *(pause),* or a slipper. This is our object. The color of it is brown, but very dark, so that it appears almost to be black. *(Pause.)* It is his own *(pause),* and he concentrates upon it.

I do not know if it is a slipper or a shoe, because while it has laces it appears somehow different from a shoe.

A turn of events for him, in an opposite direction. The events having to do with a doctor of some sort.

I pick up the initial D, but do not know unfortunately whether the D applies to doctor, or if the D is a name initial. *(Pause.)*

The object is the <u>left</u> shoe or slipper, purchased in a shop on a side street, directly off from a main street. The street beginning with a C or G, and with the numbers 1 2 appearing somewhere in the address of the shop. *(Pause.)*

The shoes were purchased on a rainy day. I think of April but am not sure. He drove, or rather was driven, and did not walk there, and he had an appointment immediately after.

There was I believe a birthday about the same time, and the name Harvard somehow connected here. Harvard shoes or oxfords, I do not know. *(Pause at 10:14.)*

Do you have a test for me, Joseph?

("No.")

(Pause.) The D mentioned earlier does apply to a name in the shoe.

(A point of confusion arose here. The last word above, which I took to be shoe, was not clearly pronounced by Jane. I asked for a repetition of the word, whereupon Jane, her eyes still closed, pointed at me rather emphatically.)

<u>Before</u> the shoe data, with the material having to do with a doctor I think of, rather oddly, of a connection to a flamingo, which seems rather bizarre.

We shall, then, take a very brief break for Ruburt's benefit, since I always give him one after this sort of material.

The initials D G may be the ones that I have been after here.

(Break at 10:16. Jane was dissociated as usual. Her eyes had remained closed. Her pace had become good toward the end of the delivery. The wind had been hitting 40 MPH in gusts, and our apartment had been chilly all day. Jane's slower and quiet manner had made me more aware of the storm and I had wondered whether it would bother her, but she said she had been aware of nothing while speaking.

(I explained the confusion over the shoe data to her during break, and asked Seth to clear it up. Jane resumed with her eyes again closed and her hands raised to them, at 10:26.)

Now first of all, the initials mentioned last do not apply to the shoes, but to the data given earlier, as specified.

I also see a wooden chair with some kind of scrolls on it, and some wicker, though the chair is not a wicker chair. This ends the Instream material.

There is much to be said concerning the interrelationships that exist between the human system and the weather system, and these shall be, these interrelationships, shall be discussed most completely at a later time. I do not want to interrupt our data concerning probabilities and time, however, to get involved in any long involvements on other matters. The question was in your minds however, and so we have taken a short while to give you some brief notes concerning it. At our next session we shall return to our previous subject matter.

I will now, according to your pleasure, continue the session for a while, or end it.

("You might as well continue for a bit."
(It was 10:25.)

Then I will speak briefly concerning Ruburt's book of poetry, for this is an excellent example of how suggestion can be used to utilize energy for conscious purposes.

The achievement, the book itself, is excellent. The book was written by other portions of the self than the ego, and it was not written at the ego's wish alone.

Ruburt's ego now contains elements that did not at one time belong to it. It contains portions of the self that are—I hesitate, you see, to say superior, for he is not to get conceited—but portions of the self that contain more abilities than those usually held by the ego.

His <u>egotistical</u> decisions therefore now more <u>faithfully</u> reflect the whole self, or the whole personality. There has been an integration. It is for this reason that his suggestions are taking hold so well, for they do not <u>conflict</u> with other layers of the self.

The abundance of energy met no resistance therefore, and was immediately focused and disciplined according to the desire that he expressed. This is simply a fact. He is simply <u>learning</u>. And he has much more to learn.

You are also learning. You are both <u>beginning, barely beginning</u>, to integrate your personalities in such a way that creativity can be put to positive use, free of negative inhibiting factors, which are <u>always</u> indications of conflicting inner doubts and desires. You will improve if you continue to progress as you have.

This is meant indeed to encourage you. It is not meant in any way to give Ruburt the idea that he is superior to anyone else. You both have the responsibility to use all of your abilities, and this is perhaps the one thing that is required of you.

I should be quite disappointed if you were not showing improvement. Your own psychic improvement, Joseph, is marked. Ruburt, with this book before him as an example, should know that he can now expect more of himself, and should not be satisfied with less. You are both becoming therefore <u>more</u> responsible as a result of your successes.

Now, my friend, I am quite capable and agreeable. I will continue the session, or you may end it and instead take a break. It is up to you. I should suggest however a good night's sleep, and I should suggest specifically that you give yourself the same sort of suggestion that Ruburt gave to himself before retiring.

You are on short time, and such suggestions will allow you to produce in a minimum of physical time excellent work.

("That's a good idea.")

Your energy will be focused where you want it. Ruburt's book ordinarily would have taken him, <u>at the very least</u>, four months with ordinary efficiency. You notice that Ruburt did not specifically request that a book of poetry be produced, nor was a book even mentioned.

The suggestion was given that he have an <u>abundance of energy</u>, and that he would focus and discipline the energy so that he could use it in his writing and in his psychic work. The hows and wherefores and the ultimate product were left to the inner self.

I recommend most strongly that you use the same procedure; success would allow you to do ten times as well in the available time as is usual. You have Ruburt's book before your eyes as proof.

My heartiest good wishes to you both, and unless you particularly wish me to continue I will end the session.

("Good night, Seth.")

(End at 10:47. Jane was dissociated as usual. Her pace had been fast. Her eyes had opened often and a few times her voice had grown stronger for emphasis.

(See page 241 of the last session, the 227th, for the data on the time schedule by which Jane produced the book of poetry. It will be noted that on the four days, January 21, 24, 25, 26, Jane wrote 52 poems in the course of from 16-18 $^1/_2$ hours.

(A recount since last session reveals that the total number of poems should be revised upward, to 63, produced in the same amount of time. In giving me the first set of figures Jane counted the pages in the book of poetry, forgetting that there were two poems on some pages.

(As early as the 6th session Seth told Jane and me that we were living the last of our physical lives, and that both of us had chosen to become entities. Because of this, Seth said, it is very necessary that we develop all of our abilities as much as possible in this life. See Volume 1.)

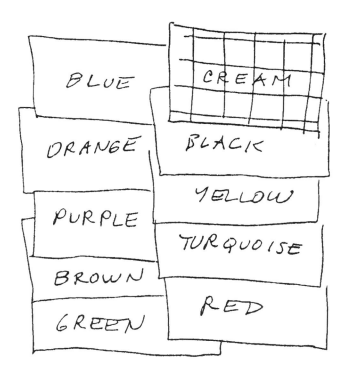

(Tracing of the colored pieces of construction paper used in the 30th envelope test, in the 229th session for February 2, 1966.)

SESSION 229
FEBRUARY 2, 1966 9 PM WEDNESDAY AS SCHEDULED

(The 30th envelope test was held during the session. I cut out ten small pieces of colored construction paper, put them between the usual two pieces of Bristol board and sealed them in the usual double envelope. I was aware that there wouldn't be much emotional charge connected with these, and Seth was too. As is the case also, Jane did not do well on the resumption of such experiments.

(The session is quite unusual, in that all of it is devoted to experimental material of one kind or another. This includes the two usual tests plus the material delivered by Seth concerning our landlord. The landlord data arose out of one of those rather small incidents that keep accumulating emotional charges when most of the people involved turn stubborn.

(Right after the first snowfall two weekends ago, our landlord appeared with

his Jeep and snowplow attached, and cleaned out our long curving driveway and the garage area in back of the apartment house. About a foot of snow had fallen, but this rather small amount still made things difficult for automobiles, and the area involved would mean hours of shoveling by hand.

(After the second foot of snow fell last weekend, the tenants of the house waited as usual for the landlord to appear with his plow. Drifts several feet deep had piled up in the driveway and against the garages. The landlord did not appear. Three days went by. It developed that he had thought we could shovel our own way out. By this time of course recriminations were beginning to fly back and forth by phone, although this did not involve Jane and me. Finally one of the tenants threatened to move, after feelings had been bruised all around. The situation was not without its comic aspects.

(By the time the landlord realized we couldn't shovel our own way out, he couldn't get his own plow into the driveway, nor could he hire help; everyone was busy. I was working overtime at my job also. I felt the brakes on our car needed adjusting so I wasn't planning to drive personally regardless; this made it somewhat easier to be objective about the whole thing. I also decided that I wasn't going to get excited about it in any event. Then yesterday morning it developed that the thermostat on the furnace was not working; we got up to a cold house, and this led to more telephone messages, the calling of a specialist, etc.

(The specialist, actually the man who keeps the house in good running order for the landlord, is a personal friend of his. While talking to Jane he mentioned that our landlord's books had been called in by the Internal Revenue Service.

(The session was held this evening with the chance that it might be interrupted. One of the tenants in the house had finally located a man with a plow, who was due to clear the area at 9 PM this evening. Everybody in the house was to chip in to pay him. We decided to go ahead with the session anyhow, on the chance the man with the snowplow did not show up, or was late.

(The session was held again in our front room. Jane began speaking while sitting down and with her eyes closed. They opened just once briefly when she put out a cigarette. Her voice was average, her pace quite slow by comparison. Neither of us had expected the kind of material that began to come through.)

Good evening.

("Good evening, Seth.")

Give me a moment, please.

Now. There are difficulties arising, of a personal nature, concerning your landlord. He feels now that everyone is against him.

He is indeed in the wrong, but over tax matters, certain falsifications. Also certain procedures on the borderline, concerning the house in which you live.

He is worried that the illegal tax methods in connection with his business will be discovered.

Nor, given his particular personality pattern, could he easily have <u>avoided</u> initiating these practices. He felt driven to them. He is aware of the compulsion with which he acts when finances are concerned. Since he realizes that he did not <u>choose</u>, consciously, to take these illegal steps, then he cannot understand why he should ever be penalized for them.

Nevertheless the fear exaggerates his morbid concern with his heart. He is somewhat like a wounded buffalo, and to some extent at least the wound was not self-inflicted, although he himself has aggravated it.

There will be some legal difficulties for him, with a March 15 date connected here. There will also be an illness for him, unless he makes some inner adjustments. Some difficulties also for his oldest daughter. Papers in connection with the landlord himself now, kept secretly, in a place not often used, within or <u>behind</u> an old desk. Perhaps in a basement, I think having a concrete or stonelike floor.

(*Our landlord, Jimmy Spaziani, is 50 years old. His daughter mentioned here is a junior in high school. We like him and his family very much.*)

Now. The <u>figure</u> 14,378. This refers to dollars, but interest will be added to it. This amount plus interest, I <u>believe</u>, will represent an initial amount due, but will not represent the full amount due.

<u>If</u> he falls ill I believe it will be at a party-type gathering, at least with many people about. A fairly serious but not critical illness, possibly caused by circulation fluctuations. The difficulty showing up in a right leg, though the <u>origin</u> of the illness will not be in the leg. Something of the sort of a blood clot in the leg, that type of illness.

Some private papers hidden, mingled with old photographs in poor condition. Possibly he will have some kind of a visitation from his own father to warn him ahead of time.

I believe also a death of his wife's father by next November.

I suggest your break.

(*Break at 9:20. Jane was quite well dissociated for a first delivery, she said. Her eyes had opened briefly but once. Remember that the above material was delivered with many pauses interspersed. Most of the time Jane sat with her head down and her hands raised to her face, as during the Instream and envelope tests.*

(*The material surprised us, and we had no thought of trying to relay it to anybody. We have no idea as to whether the tax matters referred to are true, and/or will develop. Our landlord is a complex and generous man who has lowered our rent and the rent of some of the other tenants over the last few years.*

(Seth had dealt with Jimmy and his family in other sessions, notably the 100th and 101st. Our landlord operates a restaurant featuring a large party and catering service, so it is conceivable that a falling ill at a "party-type gathering" could refer to an illness occurring on those premises. See Volume 3.

(The visitation-from-his-father reference involves the material in the 100th and 101st sessions. Jimmy's father died in the summer of 1964. Following the father's death our landlord's wife had several vivid experiences involving the deceased father; Seth said these were legitimate experiences involving contact with the father, and not dreams. It appears that our landlord's wife is a good receiver, or relay station. Perhaps she would receive and pass on to her husband any visitations from the dead father.

(Jane had not smoked since putting out her cigarette shortly after the session began, and when she resumed speaking again she refrained from smoking. As before her manner was quite slow. She sat with her head down and her hands raised to her closed eyes. She used many pauses. Resume at 9:31.)

I am trying to see what else we can discover here.

Some connection with a long-term contract. Some irregularity in almost all property arrangements. Bonds, the private papers originally kept at the hill house, then moved.

(This is a reference to a 400-acre farm our landlord owns near Watkins Glen, NY. It is now empty. Various tenants have done much damage to the place.)

One legal irregularity existing for twelve years. Business, an irregularity going back to an early small restaurant. An interesting sideline here: his stinginess in small matters is not so much the result of greed as an emotional attempt to maintain the psychic warmth of childhood, a childhood which was marked by poverty.

(Jimmy was one of perhaps a dozen children. As a child, one of his tasks was to pick coal along the railroad tracks in winter.)

An uncle of his, on his side of the family, to die in the near future.

I am trying to give you some material that you can check. His wife is ignorant in the main of his financial manipulations, and she hides what suspicions she has from herself.

The eldest boy also has suspicions. In many ways he is a severe child.

(The boy is a sophomore in high school.)

There may be bonds of some type, belonging to him but under the names of different people. I am not sure. The people may be members of his family. There are some stocks held on a long-term basis, perhaps in his children's name. I am on unfamiliar ground here. I think of AT&T.

(Jane, still sitting with her hands raised to her closed eyes, took a long pause. Later I asked her if she knew what AT&T represented. After some thought she

arrived at telephone and telegraph; guessing, she thought A might stand for Atlantic. But she did know the initials meant a stock.)

I do not seem to see a courtroom situation however, but a settling up, or an agreement to settle up. An admission and settlement of some kind, through a lawyer. Perhaps a penalty paid, but with no confinement. A lawyer convinces him to settle, and avoid going to court, and through certain manipulations this part of it will be taken care of. *(Another long pause.)* Some money will be borrowed. The hill property will be sold, or used for collateral. Stocks will be sold. He will not lose his own house because of this.

There is some connection with Joe Cernohorsky's wife, though not a <u>direct</u> one, in all of this.

I suggest your break.

(Break at 9:55. Jane was dissociated as usual. Her eyes had remained closed throughout the delivery. Much of the time she sat with her head down and her hands raised to her temples. Her pace had been very slow. She hadn't smoked.

(Joe Cernohorsky is the specialist mentioned on page 248, the man who keeps the apartment house we live in, in running order for the landlord. Joe and the landlord are of an age, 50, and have been friends for years. Jane and I have never met Joe's wife, and have no idea what kind of connection Seth might be referring to.

(It was time for the 36th Dr. Instream experiment. Jane's pace remained slow when she began speaking again, and as before she sat with her head down, her eyes closed, her hands raised, etc. Resume at 10:07.)

Now. Our object is a small framework *(pause)*, small as if made of matchsticks. It is <u>light</u> *(pause)*, and miniature, and formed of squares. I do not believe it is solid all the way through, but with open spaces in it. Some of the square shapes may be open.

Ruburt thinks of a mobile, but that is not precisely it at all. Light in color *(pause)*, mainly <u>vertical</u> in form; that is, taller than it is wide. It may have a connection with an L P. *(Long pause at 10:12.)*

There is something twisted on it. I also seem to pick up a connection with water and the object. The object was given to him rather than purchased by him. It may have a connection with a chain. *(Pause.)*

I believe his mail is late because of the storm, and that he will receive a letter from the Midwest, later than he would have ordinarily. The letter not entirely unexpected. Duplicity, or a dual manner, in connection with a man who wrote the letter.

Now I pick up the word granger, but do not know to what it refers. *(Pause.)*

Do you have a test for me?

("Yes.")

(It was 10:16. I handed Jane the envelope for our 30th envelope experiment, and as usual she took it without opening her eyes. She sat with the envelope held against her forehead.)

Give us a moment, please.

Filling—no, filing. Filing cabinet. These are impressions. From a filing cabinet.

The number 12. Several people who do not seem to be related.

Cloth connection.

A referral. L M, two one. Studious, someone studious. (Here now Ruburt thinks of your niece, and the letter announcing her marriage. You may put this reference in parenthesis.)

The connection with cloth is a good one. Evening. A connection with an endeavor that does not work. A short note. Several trees. This is a note, from someone in another place.

A woman connection with a relative, as well as the earlier-mentioned connection with people who are not relatives.

I suggest your break.

(Break at 10:25. Jane was dissociated as usual. Her eyes had remained closed throughout both experiments, she had used many pauses, and had not smoked.

(As stated earlier the results of the envelope experiment were not high. The first reference, to a filing cabinet, is a good one; the colored paper I used in the test is kept in my cabinet, and has been so for perhaps two years. But after this Jane kept veering toward the letter. I thought someone studious referred to myself, but again there was not sufficient elaboration.

(From what Seth says after break, we saw the connection with cloth, evening, and an endeavor that does not work. Jane and I bought this colored paper to use in an experiment whereby, blindfolded, we tried to determine the various colors by touch alone. This after we had read an article in Time Magazine *about a woman who had been able to do this. Our tests had been held in the evening, and our results reached chance level only.*

(Jane resumed while smoking, and with her eyes opening at times, at 10:29.)

Now. After our star performance, I have a few words to say.

<u>If</u> you are interested in any kind of evidential material, it is good to hold tests fairly regularly. Now. When you want to give Ruburt a vacation from them, this is quite all right. But because of his peculiar makeup the first, or first few tests after resumption are apt to be poor <u>now</u>, at this time, because he is apt to try too hard. He is not used to the touch enough yet. He loses the touch of it, and falls back on other layers of the self which are not reliable for

this sort of data.

One part of his whole personality is able to help me very much at times, but other portions simply cannot. I mentioned specifically Ruburt's impression that the item had to do with a particular letter purposely, to tip him off, so to speak.

A very few legitimate impressions came through. The cloth connection had to do with distinguishing the color of cloth, which was mentioned in an article that you read. The other legitimate impressions I believe you have already picked out.

I like to keep our sessions fairly balanced. It is possible that sometime in the near future, perhaps late spring or summer, we can arrange for a few specific sessions, in which several envelopes are prepared ahead of time. The purpose of such possible sessions simply being the fortification of Ruburt's shaky confidence.

Notice also that little emotional content was contained in the test item. I like something better to get my teeth into.

This is indeed a training period, and at sometime in the future we will have greater opportunity for <u>range</u>. You see how well we do in a spontaneous manner, as with Philip.

(*Philip is John Bradley's entity name. See the 204th and 226th sessions.*)

Now. You may end the session or continue it as you choose.

("*I guess we'll end it then.*")

Then I bid you a most fond good evening.

("*Are we going to get any more snow?*")

(*Jane smiled, her eyes closed.*)

Do you want any more snow?

("*No.*")

I am not a personal weather forecaster. However, you will get no <u>appreciable</u> amount of snow, I believe for ten days or so, though some perhaps this weekend, as Ruburt is fully aware since he heard that on the radio.

("*Good night, Seth.*"

(*End at 10:44. Jane was dissociated as usual. Her eyes had opened occasionally. She said she had been looking forward to the envelope experiment tonight, hoping I would give her one; she had given herself suggestions concerning it this afternoon.*

(*Jane was curious about the Instream object. I thought that perhaps it was a ship model. I then recalled that earlier in the week Bill Gallagher and I had been looking at some of my books on the ships of the 17th and 18th centuries. These books contained plans and photographs. Jane and Bill's wife Peggy had been present but hadn't paid much attention to our talk.*

(We were discussing the material on our landlord when Seth came through again. Jane resumed with her eyes opening at 10:50.)

One note: since much of this session has to do with personal material concerning your landlord, I did not mean earlier to point out to you your own reaction, Joseph, which has been excellent to the situation in general.

Your improvement is noted here more strongly, for you have refused to become very much annoyed, and you have <u>almost</u> automatically adjusted your reaction. The situation is entirely different <u>because</u> of your reaction.

Your reaction has changed the situation for the better. Not only so far as you and Ruburt are concerned, but as far as those others involved. Because of your most sensible reaction, the whole situation is much less bothersome than it would be otherwise. Not only for you but for your neighbors.

In the past you would have allowed it to disrupt your inner life. I wanted you to realize that this was a <u>tangible</u> improvement.

(End at 10:55.)

SESSION 230
FEBRUARY 6, 1966 APPROXIMATELY 10:00 PM
SUNDAY UNSCHEDULED

(A brief but potent unscheduled session was held Sunday night, with Bill and Peggy Gallagher as witnesses. This account is written the next evening from memory, since I took no notes at the time.

(No session was planned. The conversation among the four of us touched upon many things, including the news Jane received from her publisher that her ESP book is set for publication on May 16, 1966. During the evening we played some tapes also, and among these was one of the recordings Jane made of G. K. Chesterton's poem Lepanto; *Jane was in a trance state while reading this, apparently in a close approximation of the voice of her now dead friend, Father Trainor.* Lepanto *was Father Trainor's favorite poem. Jane has experienced this same phenomenon several times while reading this work, and it is dealt with in the 131st and 158th sessions.*

(Bill Gallagher asked Seth about a possible operation for his ulcers, although he has been feeling well. Seth replied that he saw no operation for Bill, should present trends continue, and that Bill should surmount the ulcer problem eventually. Seth has told Bill this before.

(This led rather naturally into a discussion of ages. Seth then told Bill he saw him living until around 85, with Peggy equally old. Seth then told me I would live to be 87. This is the first time he has given me any specific age, although in several

previous sessions, among them the 149th and the 217th, he has mentioned my living to an old age. In the 105th session, among others, he stated that Jane's death was not "to occur for many years." In our immediately past lives, spent mainly in Boston in pre-Civil War days, Jane lived to be 82 or 83 as a woman medium, and I lived to be 63 as an Episcopalian minister. We have received a limited amount of data on the Boston lives, and are not sure of our personal relationship, except that we were not man and wife. See Volume 4, for example.

(*Tonight, Jane then went on to foresee her own death at 67. This naturally surprised us. Seth prefaced this by saying something about "I see a breathing difficulty." He went on to say that Ruburt was upset at this information, and that her relatively early death simply meant she had to work harder in this life. According to Seth this is the last physical life for Jane and me. Seth said he was having trouble getting this information through.*

(*The Gallaghers left shortly after this. Jane was upset, so upset that at first she couldn't let Seth through, even though she wanted to. I urged her to sit quietly, smoke a cigarette, and relax. In view of earlier material I remembered, I thought the 67th-year information was a distortion, and that such a distortion was natural enough when one talked about one's own passing. I also thought that all such predictions, whether favorable or not, depended upon probabilities, in line with the latest material we have been getting. I should add here that the 105th session dealt with the death of Jane's mother, as well as Jane living to an advanced age. The mother's death has not yet occurred, Seth saying that the information was by way of allowing Jane to prepare herself for the shock of her mother's death. The subject had been brought up by several vivid dreams and psychological time experiences Jane had had concerning her mother. While giving this 105th session, Seth had also had trouble getting the information through, ascribing the difficulty to Jane's ego. See Volume 3.*

(*Within perhaps fifteen minutes after the Gallaghers left, Seth did come through. He proceeded to explain that Jane had indeed distorted her personal information. Subconsciously, Seth said, Jane was aware that the death of her grandfather, whom she had loved, was early next month, March. The grandfather had died of tuberculosis, hence Jane producing a distorted reference to a "breathing difficulty." The grandfather had also died at the age of 67. Jane did not know this offhand consciously, Seth said, but had the records to prove it, and subconsciously was well aware of it.*

(*Jane has in her files a family record book going back to the mid 1800's. Consulting this after the session we found that Seth was correct, that her grandfather had been 67 when he died March 12, 1948. Jane was extremely attached to her grandfather; she grew up without a father since her parents separated when she was three years old, and her grandfather did his best to fill in the gap. Seth said the anniversary of his death has been on her mind. Seth dealt with the grandfather rather extensively in the 14th session. This material was the longest at the time, dealing with another personality in such a manner. See Volume 1.*

(Seth also agreed with me concerning my memory of earlier sessions in which he stated she would live to old age. Since our index is not completed for all the sessions, I cannot find as many exact references here as I would like, other than to ask Seth for help in naming particular sessions, and do not know whether this is possible. We may try later.

(Seth also agreed that all such predictions are indeed based on probabilities. By and large, he said, predictions will work out if no major drastic changes in personality and/or behavior occur.

(Seth went on to give us some information that I for one found surprising. After saying that Jane would live into her eighties also, he said that we would be instrumental in offering conclusive evidence for the survival of the personality after physical death. Without naming names, he told me that the one of us dying first would succeed in communicating with the surviving partner in such a way that the results would give conclusive proof "to the masses."

(I tried to question him closely about this and remember what I could. By masses, Seth said he meant the man in the street. I said I though much evidence had been collected already, and that more was certain to be gathered before our deaths forty or so years from now, granting his dates were correct. Seth agreed, but said the evidence might convince scientists and investigators long before it convinced the average man, who knows little about such things now.

(Experiments would be set up in advance of the death of either Jane or I, Seth said, that would furnish this convincing proof once one of us died. I am nine years older than Jane. Seth went on to say that once this proof was made known and accepted, it would change the behavior of every man on earth, for man would have to live his physical life in the face of knowledge of an afterlife.

(This brought the session to a close, somewhere around 11:30 PM, I would estimate. Jane's eyes had remained closed while the Gallaghers were present. After their departure and when Seth resumed, they began to open occasionally. Her voice remained at an average level, nor was her delivery out of the ordinary.

(Before the session, Bill G. told Jane he thought she possessed healing ability—to her surprise. During the session I believe Seth agreed.

(A note added 5½ years later: In July 1971 Bill Gallagher did have an operation for his ulcers. It went very well, and he is free of pain.)

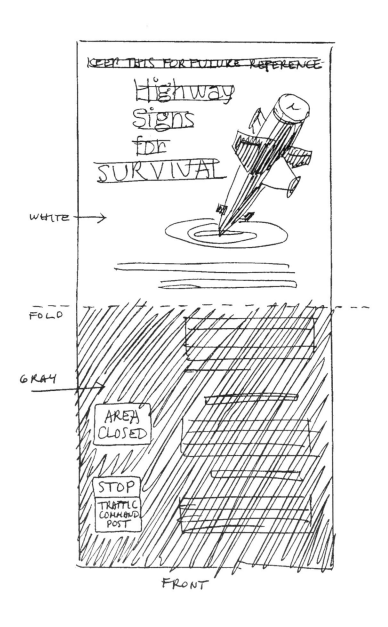

(Reduced copy of the survival literature, front, used in the 31st envelope experiment, in the 231st session for February 7, 1966.)

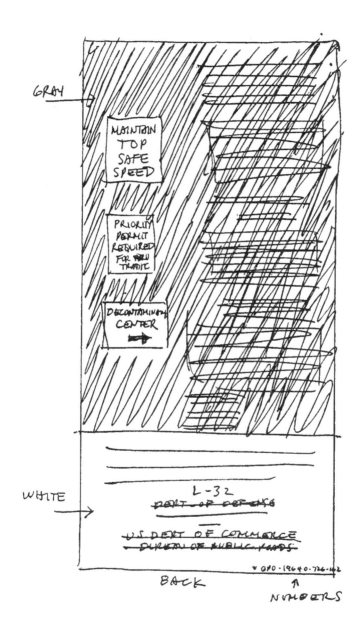

(Reduced copy of the survival literature, back, used in the 31st envelope experiment, in the 231st session for February 7, 1966.)

SESSION 231
FEBRUARY 7, 1966 9 PM MONDAY AS SCHEDULED

(*The 31st envelope experiment was held during the session. The test object is a leaflet concerning highway signs to be used in case of an atomic attack. Jane and I picked it up at our local Bureau of Motor Vehicles the second week in January, when we went there to inquire about the delay in receiving my new license plates. I had ordered them December 3,1965; as will be seen this date plays a part in the test results.*

(*This leaflet had a good emotional connection to Jane, since a very few days before we went to the bureau she had a dream concerning an atomic attack, radiation, contamination, etc.; in the dream she saw a building and a floor plan that were very much similar to the actual layout of the local bureau. The data contained in the leaflet closely paralleled the dream; therefore Jane was quite pleased to discover stacks of these leaflets at the motor vehicle bureau. She had not been inside the bureau for at least a year.*

(*I folded the object once, placed it between the usual two pieces of Bristol and sealed it in the usual double envelope.*

(*The session was held in our front room and was not interrupted. Jane began speaking while sitting down and with her eyes closed, although they began to open after a few minutes. Her pace was good, her voice average.*)

Good evening.

("*Good evening, Seth.*")

Now. I would like to give you some further data concerning probabilities and the inverted time system.

Now when I first spoke of the inverted time system, I spoke of it as if it were apart from your own time system, to enable you to see it with some objectivity. However as you know by now, this system operates within your own. It simply is not the time system recognized by the ego.

There are many implications here, and now perhaps you can understand why I gave you the information on the nature of action before I introduced you to the inverted time system. For action is action whether or not you perceive it, and probable events are events whether or not you perceive them as such.

Thoughts are indeed events therefore. Wishes and desires are events. As you know, wishes and desires also influence those actions which will be perceived by you as actual events in the physical universe. The human system responds fully as much to these events as it does to physical events. In the dream state often portions of these probable events are experienced in a semiconscious manner. This amounts to a bleed-through, and I use the term purposely, for your recorder can serve us here in an analogy.

Imagine the whole self as composed of some master tape. Your recorder has four channels. We will give our master tape numberless channels.

Each channel will represent a portion of the self, each one existing in a different dimension, and yet all part of the whole self, or the whole tape. You can see that it would be highly ridiculous to say that the material on your Mono One was any more or any less valid than your material on Mono Two. Mono One and Mono Two could be compared then to self one and two; self one and two <u>here</u>, however, in the context of the ego as self one and the subconscious as you know it as self two. We are not using Dunne's terms here, in other words.

We will imagine then these various one and two, Mono One and Mono Two, multiplied, literally, an endless amount of times. Now on your recorder I believe you have a setting for stereo. This enables you to unite and combine harmoniously the elements on the various channels simultaneously. I am taking my time here so that we get this clearly, for I do not often come through with the pure clarity of stereophonic.

(*Jane paused and smiled. Her pace had become quite slow.*)

Now. Your stereophonic setting can be compared to what we have termed the inner ego. Now each of these selves experience time in their own manner, and as you should see by now this only means that they build their own realities according to the nature of their own perceptions. <u>But</u> the nature of their own perceptions is not chaotic. The portions of the self are so constructed, so to speak, that when the stereophonic channel is turned on the selves then know their unity. Their various realities merge in the overall perceptions of the whole self.

None of these portions of the self are the whole self, obviously, and until the whole self is <u>able to perceive its own parts simultaneously</u>, then these seemingly separate portions of the self appear to themselves isolated to a large degree, and alone.

There is communication between them but they are not aware of it. The tape is the element common to all the channels. Now. The inner ego is the director as you know, but the whole self must know itself simultaneously. It is not enough that the inner ego knows what is going on. Ultimately therefore the inner ego must itself bring about comprehension on the parts of the various portions.

Each portion of the self must therefore become fully aware of all the other portions. We are not dealing however with anything as simple as a mechanical recorder, for our tapes, in analogy, are constantly changing.

I will suggest a break, and we shall continue this material. I also will have a few pertinent but brief remarks later in the session concerning last evening.

(*Break at 9:26. Jane was dissociated as usual for a first delivery. Her pace had been good and her eyes had opened frequently. Her pace had been quite slow in the middle of the delivery.*

(*When she resumed her pace was again slow, at 9:35.*)

Now. Take for example probable event X. This so-called probable event or action will be experienced by the various portions of the self in their own way. When it is experienced by the ego you call it an actual physical event. When the event is perceived or experienced by other layers of the self, the ego does not know of it.

The event is actual all the same, and is experienced in variation. The whole self therefore perceives and is affected by <u>probabilities</u>, and experiences these as action, regardless of whether or not the ego has chosen to accept any given event as a physical occurrence.

The time sequence varies also as you have seen. That is, events are experienced in different sequences. However past, present and future has reality <u>only</u> to the ego. Now there is some bleed-through. The ego is certainly aware to some extent of the subconscious. The subconscious is certainly aware of the ego. The portion of the self, or rather the portions of the self, that experience action in terms of what the ego would term probability, is further divorced from the ego, however, and this probability reality appears to the ego very rarely, and only very occasionally.

When this does happen it usually occurs as a bleed-through from the subconscious from the dream state, for the subconscious is somewhat acquainted with probabilities, and to some degree experiences these in a problem-solving manner. It views various probabilities with the <u>purposes</u> of the ego in mind, and therefore aids the ego in its decisions as to which probable events it should choose for its own experience.

Now, the time in which the inner ego exists is, as you know, the spacious present. The spacious present is the basic time in which the whole self has its existence, but the various portions of that self have their experience in their own time systems, which are the results of their characteristic methods of perception.

Now. It should be obvious that the psychological framework must be different when the time system of experience is different. You can see easily for yourself the individual psychological variations that exist simply between the ego and the subconscious, but these portions of the self are very close. Other portions of the self, that deal in what you would call probable realities, are very different in their psychological makeup.

There is a chameleonlike characteristic, a continuity, not in terms of successive moments, but a continuity in terms of <u>design</u>. Events are perceived in what would seem a most alien manner to the ego. The probabilities are <u>traveled</u> through, so to speak. Identity or continuity of the self is retained and strengthened in a series of <u>simultaneous</u> events, with value fulfillment foremost insofar as purposeful action is concerned.

The probable events are experienced in such a way that any given action or probable action is followed through in its various and almost infinite varieties.

I have been slow in giving you this data, since it is so divorced from your normal experience that it is difficult to put the concept into words. You do not have sufficient words to clearly explain what I mean. We will end up making this quite clear, however.

(Jane now took a long pause. Her pace had again become very slow. although her eyes were opening rather often.)

The ego maintains much of its stability by looking backwards, so to speak, into its experience of its past, and finding something of itself there. Now the past may be an illusion, but it is not illusion to the ego. The portions of the self that deal in probabilities do not have such an experience with a past, to give them their feeling of identity or continuity.

Permanence as the ego thinks of it would be an alien concept to these portions of the self, and to them a highly distasteful concept, adding up to rigidity. Flexibility is the key here, a voluntary changing or alteration of the self as it is allowed to change freely with each probability that is explored. Experience here therefore is of a plastic nature. Some thought concerning your own dream state may give you an intimate key to understand what I mean here.

The identity, the basic identity, of these portions of the self, are carried by what you could compare to the subconscious that you know. This is difficult, but listen: in these portions of the self it is the <u>subconscious</u> that carries the burden of identity, and it is the ego whose experiences are of a dreamlike, plastic nature. I use these terms to make the point clear. Do not let them confuse you. These portions of the self would seem topsy-turvy to you for this reason.

You may take your break.

(Break at 10:07. Jane had been dissociated as usual. Her eyes had opened often and been very dark. She had spoken slowly but with emphasis, and said she could almost feel Seth wanting her to get just the right words. Her manner had been intent, as though she worked much harder than usual for the material. She had not smoked.

(It was now time for the 37th Dr. Instream experiment. Jane's pace remained broken by many rather short pauses. She sat with her head down, her hands raised to her closed eyes. She did not smoke. Resume at 10:12.)

Now. Give us a moment, please. *(Pause.)*

Something resembling a bench, but small and lighter in weight. Old-fashioned, it is old-fashioned. *(Pause.)* I have the impression of a miniature antique, of Victorian style, and it is scrolled. *(Pause.)* The legs, I believe, are scrolled. This is our object.

I believe it has a back on it, covered with a fabric, perhaps of satin.

Now, generally. *(Pause.)* Some kind of misrepresentation. Dr. Instream feels that something has been misrepresented to him professionally, I believe, on the part of the university or in connection with his work there. *(Pause.)*

A scramble of communications is connected with this, and perhaps of letters crossed in the mail.

Near him now, a miscellany of objects, small ones, some of them white, that look like marble. Perhaps figurines, but they are not marble. *(Pause.)* A knock on the door. *(Pause at 10:20.)* This is at his home, and a caller, a male, younger than he, a fairly young male, perhaps a student. *(Pause.)*

Now, do you have a test for me? I will from here on in ask if you have an envelope instead.

("Yes."

(It was 10:21. As usual Jane took the experimental envelope, the 31st, from me without opening her eyes. We had decided to call these studies envelope experiments instead of tests. Now Jane sat quietly for a moment; she held the envelope to her forehead as she spoke briefly, then lowered it to her lap.)

There are impressions.

Some connection with a magistrate of some sort.

The numbers three and twelve, and an occurrence that was not repeated.

An afternoon. Many colors. Two men, one taller than the other. Both of them here at one time or another.

Connection with a note, and money. A sweeping out. The color gray. Strong uprights. Other designs, and numbers in some sort of pattern.

You may take a break.

(Break at 10:28. Jane was dissociated as usual during both experiments. Her eyes had remained closed. She said she wasn't worried about the results of the experiments, and that nothing she said about them had any personal meaning to her at all.

(See the tracings of the object on page 258-59, and the notes on page 260. Most of the data was at once clear to us.

("Some connection with a magistrate of some sort." When Jane and I went to the Elmira Bureau of Motor Vehicles to inquire as to why I hadn't received the license plates I had ordered several weeks prior to mid-January, we found the office very crowded. We stood in line for perhaps fifteen minutes. Then a man I thought to be a policeman entered. I succeeded in talking to him, and saw by his shoulder patch

that he was a sheriff.

("The numbers three and twelve." I had ordered my 1966 license plates by mail, on December (twelve) 3rd (three), and had the money order stub with me in case it was necessary to show a record of payment.

("and an occurrence that was not repeated." The sheriff told us the bureau was flooded by mail requests for plates and was very much behind; indeed they had just begun filling mail orders a day or so before our visit. The sheriff advised us to return a few days later if we did not receive our plates. Although we didn't receive the plates by the day he mentioned, we did not return to the bureau as he said to do, but chose to wait a little longer; the plates arrived the next week.

("An afternoon." Jane and I made our visit to the motor vehicle bureau in the afternoon.

("Many colors." We can think of connections here but do not have enough data. I neglected to ask Seth to elaborate when he resumed.

("Two men, one taller than the other. Both of them at one time or another." This I felt to be a rather far-removed connection involving myself and the service manager of the Ford garage in town that keeps our car running. He is a friend; visiting us over the Christmas holidays, he urged Jane and me not to wait too long before making personal inquiries at the bureau, to check and see if they had received my application. I am the taller of the two referred to.

("Connection with a note, and money." As stated I ordered the plates by mail, enclosing a money order in payment, on December 3, 1965. Since they had not arrived as the holidays approached, I wrote a short letter of inquiry just before Christmas to the bureau. I asked them to answer the letter only if they had not received my application. To help the bureau check I enclosed the number from the money order stub, mentioned the amount of the money order, etc.

("A sweeping out." Again, we can think of connections but feel the data too general. I did not ask Seth to elaborate.

("The color gray." As can be seen from the tracings on page 258-59, the envelope object is half gray on the front, and over two-thirds gray on the back.

("Strong uprights. Other designs." The leaflet is designed effectively in a simple bold upright or vertical format. The lines of type indicated in a pen line on the tracing are actually printed in a heavier, boldface block lettering. We suppose other designs is a reference to the various signs shown on the leaflet; in the past Seth has referred to lettering or type as designs, also.

("and numbers in some sort of pattern." In the lower right hand corner of the back of the leaflet is a series of numbers, code numbers referring to date of printing, etc.

(Jane was pleased with the test results. As stated, the envelope object had good emotional connections for both of us, with the added connection of the dream material mentioned on page 260. The dream material was not specifically mentioned by Seth, however. It will be noted that his data moved between the fact of our being strongly concerned about the license plates, and the experimental object itself, which was picked up as the _focal point_ of our concern.

(_Jane's eyes began to open when she resumed, while smoking, at a faster pace at 10:32._)

I will close the session for your convenience.

You may give Ruburt a pat on the back, for all in all he deserves it.

Now I will continue with the session if you request me to do so, or I will close it to give you a rest.

(_"You might as well continue then."_)

Since we covered some of our own material quite well this evening, I will add a few comments here on other matters.

(_Seth now refers to the unscheduled 230th session of February 6, in which Jane gave the predictions for the ages of death for herself, the Gallaghers, and me._)

Now, Ruburt's subconscious simply got in our way at last evening's session. Now and then it is to be expected, but I regret the particular circumstances deeply. He was _subconsciously_ but never consciously aware that next month marked the time of his grandfather's death, and subconsciously he knew his grandfather's age at death.

When I gave my material it was meant to be reassuring. This was my intent. But when I tried to give information regarding Ruburt, the subconscious activity interrupted. We had his identification with his grandfather momentarily, and the subsequent distortion.

(_Jane's grandfather died at the age of 67. During last night's session she gave this age for her own life span, and said I would live to be 87. The Gallaghers are also to live into their eighties. Later Seth corrected the distorted data, telling us Jane too would live that long._)

All the particular information given was indeed based upon probability. However, unless drastic changes occur in all of your _characteristic_ ways of handling stress, then the relatively old ages mentioned should stand up well.

I would apologize to Ruburt, but the distortion was not my own. I do deeply regret it however. I also think that you will find his attitude from now on an improvement over his past attitude, as far as our experiments are concerned, and this will be of benefit to all of us.

It will also mean that the experimental results will be of like quality, to some degree. That is, after a vacation from experiments he will not be nervous and distort data.

The yoga discipline is helping him more than he realizes. He need not try to force himself into any sort of strained spirituality. He is intuitively aware of more than he knows.

Do you have any questions for me?

("Will you explain the references to the two men, in the envelope experiment tonight?")

That was indeed our weak point, and since we were doing well I did not press it. You were the taller man, and your garage man was the short one. I let this go since we were doing well enough without pressing Ruburt.

This has been an excellent session in many respects. My heartiest good wishes to you both.

Ruburt should trust and rely upon his intuitional nature, for it is sturdier and more reliable than he knows.

("Good night, Seth.")

(End at 10:47. Jane was dissociated as usual. The last line of the session sums up pretty well Jane's new attitude concerning the sessions, experiments, etc. Actually the attitude is not new; both of us have been aware of the point made for a long time. The recent difference seems to be that Jane is evidently able to put the realization into effect more efficiently now.)

SESSION 232 267

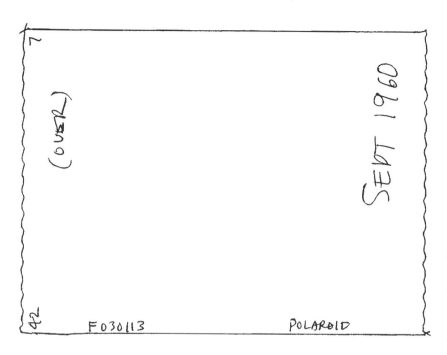

(Tracings of the black & white Polaroid photo of myself used in the 32nd envelope experiment, in the 232nd session for February 9, 1966.)

SESSION 232
FEBRUARY 9, 1966 9 PM WEDNESDAY AS SCHEDULED

(The 32nd envelope experiment was held during the session. The object was a black and white Polaroid photo, taken of myself by a coworker in September 1960, at my desk at the Artistic Card Co. in Elmira. The older individual in the left background of the photo, Ezra Havens, figures in the envelope data, also. The friend who took the photo caught me by surprise during a lunch hour; hence my position in the act of stretching, and the startled expression.

(I placed the photo between the usual two pieces of Bristol and then sealed it in the usual double envelope. This photo had laid in my files for several years. Jane had seen it a long time ago, I knew, but certainly not recently. Since it was a photo of me I felt it would have an emotional attraction for her.

(For the record: In the 227th and 228th sessions Seth discussed the book of poetry Jane produced so quickly by using suggestions for abundant energy, and told us the book would be published. Jane had also finished the first third of her book on the Seth material itself, and felt it ready to send out.

(On Tuesday, February 8, she telephoned her publisher, Frederick Fell, in New York City. She read a few of the poems from the book to Mr. Fell over the phone and outlined her ideas for its humorous format, etc.; to her surprise he requested that she send him the manuscript for consideration. Jane had not been aware that he would consider poetry. Mr. Fell also asked to see the manuscript on the Seth material, and told Jane some of the plans he had for publicizing her ESP book, due to be published this May. The publicity may include adds in the New York Times Book Review; surveys taken by the publisher show the book should have a good reception and sale. Mr. Fell also told Jane she may appear on some radio and/or TV shows; this has been Jane's idea also. Summing up, the publisher told Jane that once the ESP book is on the market and her name begins to be known through publicity, it will help the sales of future books considerably—namely the Seth material.

(Mr. Fell asked Jane to make a tape of her poems to send along with the manuscript, since he enjoyed her telephone reading. This was done this afternoon. The tape, the poetry book, and the Seth material will be mailed Thursday. Jane will be waiting to hear.

(Last Friday Jane received a letter from Fate Magazine, to the effect that they would like to see, on speculation, an article dealing with Seth and the envelope experiments.

(The session was held in our front room. Jane began speaking rather slowly, with pauses. Her hands were raised to her closed eyes and she was not smoking.)

Good evening.

SESSION 232

("Good evening, Seth.")

Now, I wanted to make a few remarks concerning the unscheduled session which occurred.

(This would be last Sunday's unscheduled 230th session, during which Jane gave data on our life spans and those of Bill and Peggy Gallagher. It developed that some of this material was distorted.)

There is a fine discrimination used in our sessions. There is indeed a tuning into, a reception of frequencies. Now it is <u>extremely</u> difficult to lock in here. There is a pulsation always occurring. It is difficult for Ruburt to maintain <u>steadily</u> that particular reception of frequency, and within certain limits there is sometimes a slipping in and out, so that now and then Ruburt's personal subconscious is allowed to intrude. This is what happened the other evening.

I am going to ask you to wait a moment while the kitchen window is closed, as the traffic is disturbing Ruburt.

(Break at 9:06. Jane's eyes opened and she was out of trance. I too had been aware of the traffic noise, although I had pulled our kitchen window closed, I thought, before the session. I now latched it tightly, which helped, and pulled the curtains over it to further deaden the sounds.

(Seth began talking about pulsations in the very early sessions, the 12th among others. He added more material on such frequencies along with the data on the inner senses, by the 50th session; then elaborated further in the material on the electrical universe, given in the sessions from 122 on. See Volumes 1 through 3.

(Jane now resumed, still with pauses, at 9:07.)

The information which you have been receiving, and which you will continue to receive, will be of great benefit, not only to yourselves but to others. Ruburt's present book on the subject, on our Seth material, will indeed be published, and meet with success.

He is obviously drawing upon knowledge that is beyond his own conscious abilities. Now much of it would, and is, theoretically available to each human being; but practically of course things simply do not work that way. He is reaching beyond his own personal subconscious, for while the personal subconscious does have definite knowledge unknown to the conscious mind, it also has definite limits.

Information received must however be sifted <u>through</u> the subconscious. We are managing now in such a way that our material survives without undue coloration from the subconscious. The whole process is a complicated one, but the very act of holding the sessions is of great benefit to the organism as a whole. For the vibrations and frequencies which are received in order to make our communications possible, are also most beneficial in <u>themselves</u> to the human and psychic system.

They are quite literally healing. I mention this in particular to explain to Ruburt the reason for our Jesuit's comments the other evening. I had intended however to make the point clear earlier in any case.

(*Before the unscheduled 230th session of last Sunday, Bill Gallagher had surprised Jane by telling her he thought she possessed healing ability. Seth discussed this ability in the 185th session, and he referred to it briefly in a few others.*)

The book of poetry which Ruburt has just completed can also be taken as tangible proof that he is in the process of learning how to use energy in such a way that it can be most beneficially used psychically, but also with very practical results. He will find that this ability will grow.

It will also be developed on your part as you let it develop, Joseph, and in your own work. Spontaneity must be allowed for in this respect. You should give yourself the suggestions that I mentioned earlier, consistently. Do you recall the suggestions?

("*Yes. I've already started using them.*")

(*See the 228th session.*)

They are potent. They will help you, not only to do the excellent painting that you desire, but to do so in such a way that others will be benefited, and <u>you</u> be financially rewarded.

In his previous poetry, as a <u>rule</u>, Ruburt was not reaching deeply enough. I wanted to make these comments, and do suggest that at least a portion of a session a month be concerned with the state of your psychic and physical circumstances, for there are possibilities here from which you are not yet fully benefiting.

("*How about the first session following the first of each month?*")

That will be fine.

Now. Some of the information that I gave you in our last session, concerning the portions of the self, seem rather alien, I am sure. Do not forget however that you are not even aware of many portions of the self that you know intellectually do exist. So it is not so strange to imagine other portions of the self with which you are not at all familiar in any conscious way.

The workings of any cell within your physical body would strike you as quite alien. Its ways of perception are different. Each cell is an intimate part of your reality, and yet consciously you are not as familiar with it as you are with the rug upon your floor.

The self enclosed within the physical system is indeed only a small portion of the whole self. The portion that deals with probabilities is as much a part of <u>you</u> as any cell within your physical body. It simply deals with different kinds of reality, and so does the cell.

I will suggest a brief break and we will continue.

(*Break at 9:30. Jane had been dissociated as usual. The traffic noise had not bothered her any more. Her pace had picked up; her eyes had opened briefly, quite often, and had been very dark. She had smoked a cigarette after the interruption.*

She resumed in the same manner at 9:41.)

Now. This system of probabilities is quite as real and actual as the system with which you are familiar, and <u>you exist in</u> it whether or not you realize it.

You simply are not focused within it, or your <u>attention</u> is not focused within it. You sometimes become aware of it when you are in the dream state. Now I have told you that these images have a reality, beside an imaginative reality.

(*This discussion began in the 41st session. See Volume 1.*)

Now, probabilities exist in the same manner. They simply are not concrete for you, as dreams are not <u>concrete</u> for you. You may dream for example of holding an apple, then wake up and the apple is gone. This does not mean that the apple did not exist. It simply means that in the waking state you are not aware of its reality. You do not experience it, or perceive it. In the same manner you do not perceive or experience physically the actuality of probable events.

Now a <u>portion</u> of you may be quite involved in these probable events. Another portion of yourself therefore is concerned here, and a portion with which you are not ordinarily familiar.

The system of probabilities is not as easily perceived even as those events that exist within the dream state, for with these you are familiar, while you are in the dream state. Often the ego is even made aware of dream events. Now the self that is the I of your dreams can quite legitimately be compared to the self that experiences probable events.

(*Jane's pace had become much slower by now. She used many pauses, some of them quite long as she sat quietly with her eyes closed.*)

For that matter, some intuitive understanding of the inverted time system can be achieved through a study of time as it appears to the dreamer.

Let us consider the following. The individual within your system—and this is quite simplified—an individual finds himself with a choice of three actions. He chooses one of these and experiences it within the physical field. The other two actions <u>are</u> experienced however, but not within the physical system. The results of the other two actions are perceived by the inner ego.

The results are then checked by the inner ego against the action that was chosen for actuality within the physical system. These results are then sent to certain portions of the subconscious, where through this information knowledge is gained as to whether or not the ego and the subconscious made the best decision under the circumstances.

The results are retained, to be checked against future decisions, and to be used by the physical self as an aid in making future decisions. The probable actions were definitely perceived and experienced however, and these experiences make up the existence of this other portion of the self, as indeed dream actions make up the experience and existence of the dream self, or of the I as it exists within the dream state.

Now through hypnosis it has been ascertained that this dreaming I has memory of its past existence, which is made up of past dreams. You may call this the dreaming personality if you prefer, but it amounts to another self. Now the I who experiences probable events, not chosen for experience in the physical universe, has the same kind of identity and memory as this dream self. There is a constant subconscious interchange of information between these portions of the self.

If you must think in layers to make this clearer, then this probable self would exist on the other side of the subconscious from the ego.

Now I suggest your break.

(*Break at 10:00. Jane was dissociated as usual. Her pace had picked up once more, her eyes had begun to open, and she had smoked a cigarette. The traffic noise hadn't bothered her.*

(*It was now time for the 38th Dr. Instream experiment. Once more Jane sat with her hands raised to her temples; her eyes were closed. She spoke with many short pauses, but her pace was not too slow in actuality. Resume at 10:05.*)

Now. Give us a moment, please.

A chest of drawers (*pause*), it seems of grandiose design, and of dark wood. (*Pause.*) Full size, with a frilly shaded lamp on top. The shade may be pink and fairly transparent.

An oval rug in front of it, not smooth in texture. A dark-colored wooden bed with high posts. A desk, and a chair by it, at which Dr. Instream sits. (*Pause.*)

A letter by his hand. The letter is either from somewhere in Nebraska, or has some connection with Nebraska in the contents. (*Pause.*) It is from a man but there is also a connection with a woman. There is an April date, I believe April 11, in connection with the letter. (*Pause.*) Having to do with a meeting of many men, and concern over what could be an upsetting element (*pause*), to upset the meeting.

Some child known to Dr. Instream has measles. Dr. Instream's throat has been sore.

SESSION 232

273

Do you have an envelope for me?

("Yes.")

(*It was 10:15. I handed Jane the envelope for our 32nd experiment. As usual she took it from me without opening her eyes, and held it against her forehead throughout. She spoke with many short pauses.*)

Give us a moment, please. These are impressions.

A connection with four people, and with February. And with something circular. And here also with an unknown element.

I do not know to what <u>this</u> refers, but a twist, or something twisted. A four. A five six.

A lifting up. Something rising.

(*Ruburt's impression is of a table next, and you may put this in parenthesis. Also Ruburt's impression, rounded objects and colored.*)

A mine. Two people coming upstairs. Perhaps <u>your</u> stairs.

I suggest your break.

(*Break at 10:20. Jane was dissociated as usual. Her eyes had remained closed, her pace not too slow. While she was giving the envelope data some snow broke loose from a steep third floor roof of the house, and came crashing down on a porch roof not far from our living room; the house shook. Jane heard this, she said, but was not bothered by it. But she now said the earlier interruption caused by the traffic had disturbed her, and she felt she hadn't been at her best afterwards.*

(See the tracings of the envelope object on page 267, and the notes on page 268. Jane and I could make connections with the object and Seth's data, and these are noted below as usual. Seth later adds to our interpretations.

("A connection with four people," I felt to be a vague reference to others I worked with at Artistic Card Co., when the photo was taken in 1960. Not specific enough.

("February." I thought another vague reference, to the fact that I had just found the envelope object in my files on this day in February 1966.

("And with something circular." to me represented the round bottle of ink showing in the photo on the table beside my drawing board, and to the standard color mixing tray on the drawing board itself; this contains four circular wells.

("And here also with an unknown element." referred, in my opinion, to the death of Ezra Havens, shown in the background of the photo. Ezra died of a heart attack in September 1964. Jane of course knew of Ezra's death although she had never met him; she agreed with me that "an unknown element." could be a reference to death.

("I do not know to what this refers, but a twist, or something twisted." referred I thought to myself, caught in the act of stretching in the envelope photo.

("A four." Jane said this was a reference to the 4 in 42, on the back of the photo in the upper left corner.

("A five six." Note that Jane, or Seth, pronounced these numbers as five six, rather than fifty-six. Nevertheless I felt five six referred to the age of Ezra Havens when the photo was taken in 1960. As stated, Ezra died in 1964. Inquiring at the plant the day after this session, I learned that he had been 60 when he died; this of course made him 56 in 1960. Ezra had a history of heart trouble and his death from this was not unexpected.

("A lifting up. Something rising." Both of us thought this a clear reference to the action of my stretching arms in the envelope photo.

("Ruburt's impression of a table...and rounded objects and colored." In the photo I am sitting at a drawing table. Rounded objects and colored I thought another reference to "something circular." listed above. The table data brings up another instance of the fine discrimination necessary to Jane in giving such experimental data. She said she had an impression of a table while speaking for Seth; not only this, but of a white table. In the envelope photo it can be clearly seen that my drawing table is covered with white paper, for cleanliness while working. This is still my habit.

(However, we also have a small coffee table in our apartment, and it is painted white. Jane said she thought of this table while speaking for Seth, yet knew it wasn't the right table. To avoid confusion in speaking the data she omitted the adjective white.

("A mine." This is interesting also. Speaking this word, Jane said, she had an impression of being underground, while not being specifically in a location such as a coal mine for instance. She was aware of sides of rocky earth, with the rocks visible. The sides were rather close together. Consciously of course Jane knows Ezra Havens is dead and buried. But while giving the data she had no impressions of Ezra. Looking back, she thinks she might have been trying to get at the impression of a grave while skirting around it. She remembers that she was going to elaborate on the mine impression by using the word underground; but instead of doing so she went on to the next impression.

("Two people coming upstairs. Perhaps your stairs." No one came up the stairs of our apartment house while this data was being given. The art room at Artistic, where the envelope photo was taken, is located on the second floor. Since the photo was taken at noon it is possible people were using the stairs at the end of the hall. But the impression is too vague.

(Jane now said she puts herself "in the hands of whoever or whatever possesses these abilities" during such experiments, and tries to stay out of the way of what will happen.

(She was now smoking, and her eyes began to open at brief intervals, when she resumed at 10:37.)

Now we will shortly end our session.

Ruburt was correct. He was not at his best this evening. However he did very well for me. In the past when he was not at his best, we simply could not get this much legitimate information through. He is operating in a more efficient manner, and his attitude of late is of great benefit to us.

The mine was a case where he was not quick enough. I gave him the underground impression, but he did not translate this into grave, simply because he does not like graves.

(Jane's eyes opened and she smiled.)

The fifty-six did refer to the man's age.

Ruburt's explanation of the table was correct. I did give him the white table, but he confused it with the white table in your room, knew that this was not the table to which I referred, made the correct distinction, but thought that the white indication did not belong.

My heartiest wishes to you both, and I hope, Joseph, that you make a habit of giving yourself the suggestion which I advised. If you do this regularly you will be amazed, as Ruburt was, at the results.

Your fortunes are taking a turn for the better, as I told you that they would. The turn however is a result of development on your parts, and the development will accelerate now that it has reached a certain level, with of course continued application on your parts.

And now good evening. You are making your lives much more pleasant for yourselves.

("Yes. Good night, Seth."

(End, presumably, at 10:45. As we sat talking I told Jane that Seth had discussed some of the points mentioned in the envelope data, but that since he said good night I didn't press for more information. Yet I had the feeling Seth would continue, if Jane were willing. She said she was, and resumed at 10:46.)

Very well then, we shall. The twisting was distortive, having to do with the motion of the body. Ruburt translated this into a dancing motion, you see.

The February was simply insufficient data, for it did refer to your coming across the item, and that was all. Ruburt's new attitude here will allow much clearer perception.

("What about the connection with four people?")

There were, shortly before, four people in the room.

("Just before the picture was taken?")

(Remember, the envelope photo was taken in 1960.)

Indeed. And two others, who had been in the room, were on the stairway.

(This is a reference to the last bit of envelope data.

("What about the reference to an unknown element?")

The unknown element did refer to the man's imminent death, that was not known of course at that time.

(Note that Seth's idea of our time is quite different from our own at times. The photo was taken in 1960, and Erza died in 1964; we do not call a four-year wait imminent. At various times Seth has told us his idea of time may not coincide with ours. Without going into details I recall a prediction of his that was to materialize "soon." It did materialize, but six months later.

("What did you mean by the something circular reference?")

That was explained later in the data. Later on we made that clear.

(This involved my ink bottle, the mixing tray for color on my desk in the photo, etc.

("That takes care of that then, Seth."

(Jane now took a long pause at 10:51. Her eyes were closed.)

I would add here, once more, that during our sessions your physical organism is automatically allowed greater healing abilities. It is easier for the physical organism to utilize energy in order to make any desirable adjustments.

("Why do I sometimes feel sleepy during sessions?")

For several reasons. For one thing, obviously your attention is detached to some degree from other activities.

There is even in your case some lowering of blood pressure, for example.

("I've often wondered if I go into a light trance myself.")

Also. You make certain automatic adjustments in order to perceive what little of my presence that you do perceive. And I also have a calming effect on you, which is most beneficial to you.

("Does this effect apply to anyone witnessing sessions?")

Under most circumstances, and according to their attitude. The benefits would always be there, whether or not they were taken advantage of. To some extent this effect lingers, and is part of your psychic framework, or rather environment.

Now I shall close the session or continue as your prefer.

("I guess we're ready to close.")

Once again then my heartiest wishes to you both.

("Good night, Seth.")

(End at 10:58. Jane was dissociated as usual. Her eyes had remained closed. Her pace had been average.)

> Mr. and Mrs. Loren D. Butts
> announce the marriage
> of their daughter
> Linda Estelle
> to
> Dennis R. Murray
> United States Air Force
> on Saturday the twenty-second of January
> Nineteen hundred and sixty-six
> Brooklyn, New York
>
> Brooklyn, New York 11225

(Tracing of the wedding announcement used in the 33rd envelope experiment, in the 233rd session for February 14, 1966.)

SESSION 233
FEBRUARY 14, 1966 9 PM MONDAY AS SCHEDULED

(The 33rd envelope experiment was held during the session. I trimmed down the front page of the wedding announcement of my niece, placed it between two pieces of Bristol and sealed it in the usual double envelope. It is printed in black and the reverse side is blank. It has a blind embossed border as indicated.

(On the evening of February 2, during the 229th session, Seth said: "You will

get no <u>appreciable</u> amount of snow, I believe for ten days or so..." See page 254. Seth was correct. Indeed, we began to receive our first appreciable snow within three hours after the ten days were up. This was a very heavy wet snow that began shortly before 1 AM Sunday, February 13; it continued until dawn, accumulating about an inch, then turned into a very heavy soaking rain that lasted all day Sunday and on into the night. Jane and I were quite conscious of the prediction Sunday because we had to be traveling. I had been keeping track of it in the meantime, however, and noted that we received a few very light dustings of snow during the ten day interim. Actually, the weather has been so warm that most of the heavy snow received two weeks ago has melted.

(Saturday night, February 12, Jane had a vivid dream that she believes to be significant, and hoped Seth would discuss it this evening. It is included later in the session.)

(The session was held in our front room. All windows were shut tightly, and the traffic noise was not a problem, although it was audible to some degree. Jane began speaking while sitting down, at 9:01. Her eyes were almost immediately open. Today was Valentine's Day. Jane had been in a good mood, and so was Seth. Jane smiled broadly as she opened the session.)

Now good evening, my Valentines.

("Good evening, Seth.")

You did get it in the record that I called you my Valentines, did you not?

("Yes.")

It will be evidence that I am a sympathetic sort occasionally, and that I can show high humor.

(Jane's eyes now closed. She sobered, and began to speak at a slower pace.)

Now. We shall indeed discuss Ruburt's dream in good time, when he is not expecting it. For now, I would like to add somewhat to our discussion concerning inverted time and probable events.

If you recall, we mentioned the fact that the dreaming self has its own memories. It has memories of <u>all</u> of its dream experiences. To you this might mean that it has memory of its past, and indeed to you memory itself is dependent upon the existence of a past, or it is meaningless.

To the dreaming self however, past, present and future as such do not exist, and yet it has what you term memory. How can this be?

All experience as I have told you is basically simultaneous, and the dreaming self is simply aware of its experiences in their entirety.

(Seth began to talk about the simultaneity of basic reality in the 41st session, which dealt with the spacious present. see Volume 1.)

<u>You</u> are not aware of your experiences in their entirety, for you experience

events in a consecutive manner. You are therefore aware of your dreams only in a consecutive manner. You are hardly familiar with all of the dream experiences of your dreaming self, and barely familiar with any of their implications. The dreaming self is to some considerable degree conscious of the self which we shall here term the probable self. The probable self is somewhat like a twin self to the dreaming personality, for neither the experiences of the dreaming self nor the probable self occur within the complete radius of physical reality.

(Jane's voice now began to grow somewhat heavier.)

There is a constant give and take between the probable self and the dreaming self, for much data is received, particularly by the dreaming personality from the probable self, or the self that experiences what the ego would term probable events.

This data is often wound by the dreaming self into a dream drama, which informs the subconscious of dangers, <u>or</u> of the probable success, of any given event which is being <u>considered</u> by the subconscious as suitable for physical actuality.

In other words the ego is not familiar with the probable self, but certain portions of the subconscious are. For the subconscious, like the probable self, is aware of its existence in the inverted time system. The subconscious is aware of many realities which are not accepted by the ego as actual physical events, and it reacts to many stimuli of which the ego is completely unaware.

Again past, present and future are definite realities only to the ego. Memory to the ego presupposes the existence of a past that no longer exists within physical reality. When I say that the dreaming self has memory, therefore, of its dream experiences, I mean that it scans its present existence. It is a simultaneous self.

The same can be said for the <u>probable</u> self. Were it not for the experience of this probable self and for the information which it gives, via the dreaming self to the subconscious, then it would be most difficult for the ego to come to any kind of a decision within the physical universe.

The ego does not realize the data that is constantly feeding into it. It cannot afford to, generally, since all its focused energy must be used in the maintenance and manipulation of physical actuality.

It will take us many years before all of this information on this particular subject is clear. You must take it for granted also, you see, that this probable self has operated in each incarnation, in each materialization of the whole personality, and has therefore at its command literally millions of probable situations and conditions upon which to make value judgments.

(For an idea of the complexity implied here, in Volume 3 see the 88th session,

in which Seth goes into the structure of the subconscious to some degree.)

Of itself however it does not make these judgments in those terms. The decision as to whether or not a particular probable event should be perceived as a physical one depends, of course, upon the nature of the ego which would then experience it. The probable self does not make the decision, but merely passes on the data which it has received through its own experience with the event.

The information is sifted often through the dreaming self to the subconscious, which has intimate knowledge of the ego with which it is closely connected. The subconscious makes its own value judgments here, and passes these on to the ego. But then the ego must come to its own decision.

In some cases the decision is made by the subconscious. However, for various reasons often the ego will simply refuse to make the decision. Occasionally when a decision has been made by the ego, the subconscious will change it, because the decision is obviously such an unwise one.

The self is far from a simple psychological structure, and your psychologists are barely beginning to have any understanding of what it is.

I suggest your break.

(*Break at 9:29. Jane was well dissociated for a first break, she said. Her voice was heavier than usual, and her pace had finally become very fast. After the humorous opening her eyes had remained closed. She had not smoked.*

(*Ordinarily, Jane said, she would have had a cigarette during the delivery; but this time she "got the message" that she was not to smoke. It came on a parallel level while she was speaking other words aloud. She felt no force preventing her hand from reaching for a smoke, yet she didn't feel free to reach for one.*

(*In the 222nd session Seth asked Jane not to smoke during tests. Sometimes seriously but more often humorously, he has gone into the reasons behind Jane's smoking in these sessions: 31, 32, 147, 148, 149, 150, 151, 222.*

(*Jane was smoking when she began speaking again. Now her eyes began to open frequently; they were very dark. Her pace was slower, her voice average. Resume at 9:39.)*

Now. This probable self can be reached through hypnosis, but only with excellent subjects and an excellent operator.

It will often not be recognized for what it is, however, for there will be no evidence in the physical universe to back up its statements. There will not be much of a problem however, since it will not be reached often. It lies, so to speak, on the other side of the subconscious.

Its data will agree when taken within its own framework, but this will be the only clue visible at first sight. The probable self, as far as I know, has not yet been reached in any hypnotic experiments. It has been glimpsed however, but not recognized as a separate part of the self, in dream recordings given in analytic sessions.

It must be recognized also that these portions of the self exist in each incarnation. In the materialization of personality through various incarnations, only the ego and the layers of the personal subconscious adopt new characteristics. The other layers of the self retain their past experiences, identity and knowledge.

The ego receives, in fact, much of its stability because of this subconscious retention. Were it not for past experiences in other lives on the part of deeper layers of the self, the ego would find it almost impossible to relate to other individuals, and the cohesiveness of society would not exist.

Learning to some extent is indeed passed on through the genes, biochemically, but this is a physical materialization of inner knowledge achieved and retained from past lives. Human beings learn mainly through experience, and the experience is derived from past experience in other existences.

The human organism does not spring full blown, erupt into existence at birth, and laboriously then begin its first attempt to gain experience. If this were the case you would still be back in the stone ages.

Now there are indeed waves of energy, and waves of reincarnational patterns, for there have been many stone ages on your planet, where new identities began their first experience with physical existence, and changed the face of the earth as they progressed.

They changed it in their own individual ways, and not in your ways. But this will be discussed at a much later time. Yet all of this occurs, basically, within the blinking of an eyelid, so to speak, yet all with purpose and with meaning, and based upon achievement and responsibility. Each portion of the self, while <u>independent</u> to some considerable degree, is nevertheless responsible to every other portion of the self, and each <u>whole self</u>, or individuality, is responsible to all others while it is still largely independent as to activity and decision.

For as many layers of the self compose the whole self, so many selves form a gestalt of which you know relatively little, and of which I am not yet prepared to tell you.

You may take your break.

(Break at 9:55. Jane was quite well dissociated, she said. She wasn't aware of much except the voice. Her pace had on the whole been good, her voice average. Her eyes had opened occasionally, and she had smoked.

(Seth has mentioned psychic gestalts before, and has given bits and pieces of information on them, along with data on the general heading of the God concept, in these sessions: 31, 66, 81, 95, 96, 97, 146, 147, 149, 135, 151, etc.

(It was now time for the 39th Dr. Instream experiment. As usual Jane sat with

her eyes closed, her right hand raised to them. Her voice was quiet, with many short pauses. Resume at 10:08.)

Now give us a moment please for our Instream material.

A chandelier, with four large bulbs, and small bulbs between them. Now. A green object. Rectangular in shape, as a book shape. The fourth book on a shelf, having to do with mediums. Page 98. And a description of a particular seance attended by Lodge and two others. *(Pause.)*

The seance given by a woman, as described in the book, with dark hair, parted in the middle. Some connection here also with Dr. Instream's book on spiritism; that is, his own book.

He has recently corresponded with a colleague, or the man has written him. Or Dr. Instream has been strongly thinking of the colleague.

A disagreement here somewhere, in connection with two men. This is not the disagreement that Dr. Instream spoke of to you and Ruburt when you met. *(Pause at 10:15. See Session 169 in Volume 4.)*

A spectacular-enough result in certain tests conducted by Dr. Instream since his last letter to you.

If he did not conduct them, the tests, himself, then he is strongly aware of them. They are not trivial, the results.

A March 2 date in his mind for a planned event.

The substance of a letter, colon: "I will meet with you on March 2, if there is no change in plan." The meeting to be in Oswego. The letter from a man to Dr. Instream concerning a series, now, of tests. The hypnosis experiments I believe.

Now. Do you have a test for me, Joseph?

("Yes."

(It was 10:17. I handed Jane the envelope for our 33rd experiment; as usual she took it without opening her eyes. She sat with it pressed to her forehead for a few sentences, then lowered it to her lap.)

Give us a moment, please. It takes me a moment to change focus.

These are impressions. Strips of color. A connection with a photograph, and some sort of <u>grand</u> affair, such as a ball.

An entrance, and a schedule. A connection with three people, and a fourth who is not present. An initiation, and a bringing together of fragments. Four, the number four. A connection with an older man.

A disturbance that was not unexpected, and a result that <u>was</u> expected and hoped for.

These are still impressions: two houses separated by grass. The numbers three, four, five, six. Six being significant.

Too many too soon. November six three, and a letter that did not meet your approval. A connection with something twice, and five in a circle.

I suggest your break.

(*Break at 10:25. Jane was dissociated as usual. Her eyes had remained closed throughout both experiments. She said she had tried to block out all personal associations in connection with the envelope data.*

(*I read the data to her before she opened the envelope. Jane pointed out three instances in it where she had personal associations with Seth's data, and as it turned out all three would have been in error had she voiced them.*

(*See the tracing of the envelope object on page 278. As stated, the object is the front page of the announcement of the marriage of my brother Loren's daughter, Linda, to Dennis Murray of Brooklyn, NY. Once again Seth goes over the data with us, so immediately below is listed, first, the connections Jane and I made ourselves.*

(*"Strips of color." This meant nothing in particular to us.*

(*"A connection with a photograph", referred we thought to the fact that my brother took color pictures of the wedding. We visited him last Sunday at my parents' home, in Sayre, PA, and he had expected to have the color prints with him; however they had not arrived from the processor yet, to our disappointment and his.*

(*"and some sort of a grand affair, such as a ball." A reference to the wedding, but hardly to a ball.*

(*"An entrance," Linda, a Protestant, married a Catholic in a Brooklyn church. Jane said she felt the reference to an entrance concerned the recent decision by the Ecumenical Council in Rome, to the effect that Protestants could now be allowed to enter the altar enclosure to be married. My brother Loren told us Sunday that this decision is so recent that his daughter was the first to be married in such a fashion in this church.*

(*"and a schedule." My brother and his wife traveled to Brooklyn by bus to attend the marriage. They were so pressed for time on this particular weekend that the day of the wedding was changed from Sunday, January 23, to Saturday, January 22, so that they could return to their home in time for work Monday, January 24. Fortunate that this was so, for they narrowly missed being stranded in the first heavy snowstorm of the winter. The announcement is a schedule of events.*

(*"A connection with three people, and a fourth who is not present." We thought this a too-vague reference to my brother and his wife, and their daughter, and the groom.*

(*"An initiation, and a bringing together of fragments." We thought this of course a reference to Linda's marriage. The use of the word fragments here, by Seth, led us to think that reincarnational motives might be involved in the marriage; but I did not think to quiz Seth about this when he resumed. In the very early sessions*

Seth began to use fragment as a reference to each physical personality manifested by the entity.

("Four, the number four. A connection with an older man." This was perhaps a vague reference to the father of the groom; he is quite a bit older than my brother, who is Linda's father. Later, Jane told me that this <u>was</u> a reference to brother Loren, Linda's father.

("A disturbance that was not unexpected", we thought a reference to the disapproval with which Linda's maternal grandmother greeted the news of the marriage. She definitely was not in favor of it, as everybody knew.

("and a result that <u>was</u> expected and hoped for." Linda did want to get married, of course.

("two houses separated by grass." This was too general.

("The numbers three, four, five, six. Six being significant." We did not make anything out of this particularly.

("Too many too soon. November six three", are very accurate references to Linda, but are here not explained because of personal reasons on her part. The data are available however to anyone making a study of these experiments. The numbers refer to November 1963; during this month Linda was involved in a strong emotional experience that was unique for her.

("and a letter that did not meet your approval." This is a reference to the letter written to Jane and me by Linda's mother, on January 24, telling us about Linda's marriage on January 22.

("A connection with something twice" is another quite accurate reference by Seth to personal matters involving Linda, and data on this are withheld here for the same reason announced above. The three pieces of data that are not explained in this experiment are the best, incidentally, that Seth gave in connection with the object.

("and five in a circle." meant nothing to Jane and me.

(We were discussing the data when Seth resumed. The first couple of sentences of his discussion concerned the three items noted above. He seemed in the mood to continue for a while, and to discuss the envelope data, so I began to ask questions. Jane resumed with her glasses on, and with her eyes opening occasionally, at 10:40.)

...The six, which was significant. This was simply not given clearly. I merely meant that two sixes did appear, as 66.

(1966 appears on the wedding announcement.

("Did we correctly interpret the data about a letter?")

The letter referred to the original note of the girl's marriage, which Joseph didn't meet, with your approval, incidentally; nor for that matter with Ruburt's.

(Here now Seth elaborated further on the three points not explained: Too many too soon; November six three; and A connection with something twice.

("What about the 'five in a circle' data?")
I beg your pardon?
(I repeated my question.)
These were simply distortions, or rather material from Ruburt's own subconscious.

The "strips of color" represented however, I believe you call it, confetti. This was in many colors and in small strips.

This was not our best. However, on the average we are doing much better. Ruburt is loosening up some.

("Were we correct concerning our interpretation of the photograph data?")
You were indeed.

("And concerning your reference to an entrance?")
Indeed. This referred to the altar arrangement. The "initiation" referred to the marriage of course, but also to the beginning of a new tradition in the particular church where for the first time a Protestant was allowed into the altar section.

The "something twice" also referred to the sixty-six, or sixes twice. I picked this up quite literally, I'm afraid.

("What about your reference to an older man?")
The older man represented the groom's father, simply because of the discussion concerning him Sunday. *(But see Jane's comment on page 285.*

("And the number four?")
The four people. The parents of the girl and the groom, mentioned in the announcement.

("Were we right about the 'disturbance?'")
You were.

The "grand affair" and the "ballroom" implication, you see—the connection somewhat distorted here was the formality of the wedding—clothes, the wedding clothes, which did lead Ruburt to think of a ball.

("Were we correct about 'two houses separated by grass?'")
You were.

(I did not write it down earlier, but we thought Seth had referred to the home of my parents and the house next door. The connection is far-out: My brother, father of the Protestant bride who married a Catholic, was at my parents' home Sunday; the people who live next door are Catholic.

("What about the numbers, three, four, five?")
This was simply to lead me up, or to lead Ruburt up, to the number six. I saw the number six twice, which led me to think it was significant. With numbers I use this device, and have in the past, counting aloud to the number

that I want.

("You did that once with John Bradley.")

(See the 204th session, page 39. In this case Seth used the method to pinpoint a raise John received from his company.)

I did indeed. It is of a help to Ruburt, but soon we shall not need it.

Now. The Fate article will be sold, providing Ruburt follows the way which has been set out for him.

(As mentioned in the notes for the 232nd session, page 269, Fate Magazine wrote Jane concerning an article on the envelope experiments. She has now written the first draft for the article. We suppose Seth's rather cryptic note above means the article will sell if Jane sticks to the way she has planned.

(There follows a copy of Jane's dream of Saturday, February 12, as taken from her dream notebook. Jane believes the dream to be a significant one, and had hoped Seth would discuss it this evening:

("I dreamed I was on a bed, Rob on one side of me and another man also. No pain, movement in pelvis and I delivered a baby. Someone, a doctor, holds up two babies, twins, and I thought, somewhat humorously: 'Oh no, twins! Really, this is too much.' By this I meant, after having no babies all these years, now to have two at once! Then, though I'm not sure, I think that the doctor reassured me, that only one baby was involved. The hospital, or whatever it was, was near Lizzy Roohan's old house, in my childhood neighborhood in Saratoga Springs, NY. I was pleased that the delivery was so easy and painless for me.")

His dream represented several layers of information; on a superficial layer it represented his knowledge that fear of physical childbirth is not a deterrent to him. On another level it represented a knowledge that a future endeavor would at first appear to be two separate endeavors, two separate accomplishments not connected to each other; but on later examination it will be seen that they are unified.

These have not yet come to pass, and they represent a rebirth, or a new birth, from the subconscious. This spring will be the time.

I am one of those represented in the dream, and you are another. The affair will be most beneficial from many viewpoints, and represents a creative endeavor.

He will think that two endeavors are involved, and will realize that one united product has been achieved instead. He <u>saw</u> a female child because the product will be intuitive, and psychic, rather than born from logic.

He will be reborn about the time of his own birth date. This is another reason why the birth symbolism was used.

("How do you mean, reborn?")

(The term made me wonder if Seth referred to another physical life for Jane; in the past he has reiterated that our present physical lives are the last for both of us.

(We are not sure whether Seth refers to the publication of Jane's ESP book, or perhaps the start of another in some fashion. The ESP book is due May 16; Jane's birthday is May 8. Also, Seth and I are mentioned often in the book. Jane was speaking rather rapidly now, and I did not think to interrupt and ask Seth to clear up this point. She is 38. I am 47.)

The product will not come from pain, and so he felt none in the dream. It will come from psychic motion. This simply represents another creative project which he shall deliver, with our help.

Now. My fondest regards to you both from your own Valentine.

("The same to you.")

And if we are not all hearts and flowers, let it be said that hearts and flowers as a steady diet could become quite boring.

("Yes. Good night, Seth."

(End at 11:01. Jane was well dissociated, she said. Her eyes had opened often, and halfway through the delivery she had opened her glasses, as if to put them on. Her pace had been good but her voice had sounded tired. Now she said she did feel tired at the end of the session.)

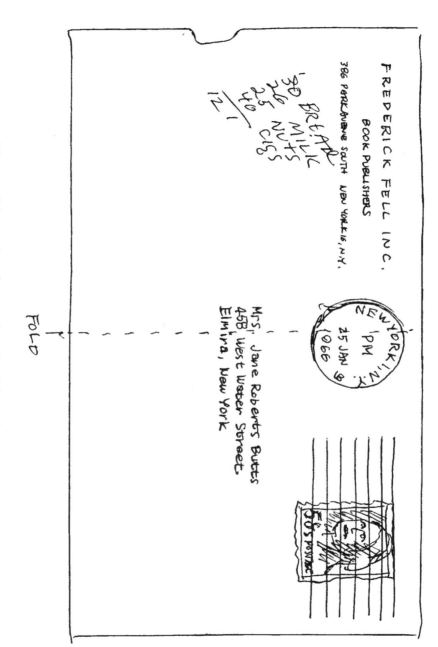

(Tracing of the envelope front used in the 34th envelope experiment, in the 234th session for February 16, 1966.)

SESSION 234
FEBRUARY 16, 1966 9 PM WEDNESDAY AS SCHEDULED

(*The 34th envelope experiment was held during the session. The object was the front of a recent letter to Jane from her publisher's secretary. I folded it once, put it between two pieces of board and sealed it in the usual double envelope. Jane did not know I had saved it. I thought this object simple enough, while containing some good emotional charges, but as will be seen Seth picked up many connections. The experience turned out to be a complicated one. There were unexpected hits, and one not used.*

(*Jane was visited by the wife of our landlord after supper this evening. Marian Spaziani is a good friend. It will be remembered that Seth dealt with her husband's financial activities in some detail in the 229th session. Seth has also called Marian an excellent telepathic receiver, and has dealt with some of her experiences, concerning the death of her husband's father, in past sessions. See the notes on page 248; and the 100th and 101st sessions in Volume 3, for example.*

(*Marian had an interesting experience to tell Jane. Recently Marian's daughter wrote what Marian considered to be an excellent composition on the poet Donne; the quality was exceptional, according to Marian, and she typed up the paper for her daughter to take to school. To their surprise the English teacher marked the paper with a D minus.*

(*Marian and her husband went to school to see the teacher, a middle-aged woman. The teacher was much embarrassed, appeared to be very upset, and finally said she thought the daughter had copied the paper from other sources. She did not change the mark she had given however, so Marian and her husband went to the school principal; this individual said he was powerless in such cases.*

(*A few days later, before a class which contained Marian's daughter, the same teacher burst into tears without apparent cause, and fled the room. The daughter told Marian. Shortly afterward, while working at home, Marian felt what she called a compulsive urge to telephone this teacher and make peace with her; Marian found herself picking up the telephone before she realized what she was doing. She talked with the teacher for half an hour, and the two women made their peace. Marian had felt she had hurt the teacher unduly, and had no wish to do this. She felt much better for making the call. Four days after this, the teacher dropped dead.*

(*Marian now wondered if she had been subconsciously aware of the woman's impending death, etc., and had tried to offer solace. Marian knows of the sessions but has not witnessed any; she has read some of the early material.*

(*The session was held in our front room. Jane began speaking while sitting down, and her eyes opened briefly almost at once. Her pace was fast; she sipped wine occasionally and was smoking.*)

Now, good evening.

("Good evening, Seth.")

It did Ruburt good to talk with his friend, for he has been concentrating with too much <u>vigor</u> of late.

It is not the time he spends working, necessarily. He should understand this by now, but the effort, energy and concentration that is expended. Now, it is to be expected that he expend energy and that he concentrate with some thoroughness, but at times he becomes <u>emotionally</u> weary as a result of expending huge amounts of energy within a small amount of time, comparatively speaking.

When he does so he forgets to draw from subconscious energy and uses nervous energy, and is therefore somewhat depleted. This time however we mention it when the trend only begins, and so nip it in the bud. The social interlude was therefore most beneficial.

I have mentioned this before, and do not intend to hammer you both over the head with it. Nevertheless an evening a week spent out of your own quarters, a social evening, reaps many benefits which you may not as yet understand, and is, all in all, quite necessary for overall well-being on your parts.

Proper balance is not maintained otherwise. For one thing the change of environment is necessary—and I am speaking for you, Joseph, as well as for Ruburt; and here we shall let the matter rest.

As far as the experience recently encountered by Ruburt's friend, it was quite legitimate. Subconsciously the teacher realized that she was about to die, and communicated this realization to Ruburt's friend, who is indeed, as I have said before, an excellent receiver.

Now. Back to our probabilities.

The field of probable events exists as a reality. From it the self chooses those actions which shall become a part of physical reality. Here indeed free will enters into the matter. This is a pun. I would be disappointed if it were missed. It is a good one.

(Jane, her eyes wide open, stared at me, smiling broadly.

("Yes.")

Now. Often clairvoyant information will appear to be wrong. In some cases this is because a different probable event has been chosen by a self for physical materialization. I have access to the field of probabilities and you do not—egotistically, you do not. I have access to your so-called past. I can view your present. To me your past, present and future merge into one.

(This reminds me that on page 58 of the 206th session, Seth briefly described what he usually "sees" of us, or any witnesses, during a session. Unless he narrows his

focus and concentration to concentrate upon the present individual during a session, Seth told us he sees a composite image, an energy reality that is composed of past personalities, and in many cases also of future personalities that will be adopted by the inner self.)

On the other hand as I have told you, your past continually changes. It does not <u>appear</u> to change to <u>you</u>, for you change with it. You are not aware of the changes that have come about. The question of clairvoyance however is not at issue with information given concerning your past. Your <u>future</u> changes as your past changes. But clairvoyant information deals with the future, that is, precognitive clairvoyant information, and it is here that the issue shows itself.

We shall consider an example. Suppose that in the past you sat behind a John X in grade four. At the time you sat behind him, you liked him very much. He was then an agreeable fellow, and you considered him as such.

In grade six, let us suppose that you had a severe disagreement with this same John X, and then you disliked him thoroughly. He was a disagreeable fellow in your perceptions.

In twelfth grade you become fast friends. He is once again an agreeable fellow. You know him for several following years. Someone who is supposed to have psychic abilities looks into your past, and tells you that you sat behind a most disagreeable child. Most unlikeable in the earliest grade, and mentions the name John X.

You think that the information is wrong, for John X, you are convinced, is a friend of yours, has always been a friend of yours, and consciously you are convinced that you have always found him agreeable. Consciously you have forgotten the past, and you have remade it.

In most cases however it is the future in which you are interested. The future changes. <u>You</u> change it, in the same manner that you have changed the past. In such cases it is necessary that the <u>correct</u> channel of probable events be perceived, correct meaning the channel which shall ultimately be chosen. And the choice is dependent upon your choices in both past and present.

These choices however are based upon your changing perceptions of past and present. Because I have a larger scope of perception than you, I can with much greater facility predict what may happen. But this is dependent upon my prediction as to which <u>choice</u> you will make, and the choice is still your own.

Predictions, per se, do not contradict the theory of free will, though free will is dependent upon much more than any freedom of the ego alone. If the ego were allowed to make all the choices, with no veto power from other layers of the self, you would all be in a sad position indeed.

You may take your break.

(*Break at 9:29. Jane said she was dissociated as usual for a first delivery. Her pace had been generally fast, slowing a bit in the middle. Her eyes had opened often, her delivery had been emphatic.*

(Seth has spoken on free will at various times. Much of this has been incorporated in discussions on the God concept and psychic gestalts. See the following sessions among others: 3, 4, 31, 35, 49, 66, 81, 95-97, 135, 146-49, 151. Volumes 1 to 4.

(Jane was again smoking when she resumed in the same manner at 9:42.)

I can therefore perceive far more than you can of your own future.

I am hardly omnipotent, however. Nor, strictly speaking, is such omnipotence possible. Now. Ruburt, <u>generally</u> speaking, has been doing very well in utilizing the energy available to him from other portions of the self, and in so doing he has indeed picked up clairvoyant information of which he is not aware on a conscious level.

He does now and then need a rest from such matters however, and the <u>release</u> of purely physical stimuli and enjoyments. He needs to throw himself occasionally into other activities. When he does not do so he tries too hard, and the very attempt throws him back on his own nervous energy.

I will endeavor to warn him of the <u>beginning</u> of such episodes, as of now, so that they will never become extended. Such depletions minimize the ability of the inner self to draw upon all the available information from other layers of the self, concerning the field of probabilities.

The <u>available</u> events are not fully perceived on a subconscious level, and therefore choice is limited. When he is operating at his best he remembers his dreams very easily, and this can be a guide point for you both.

(*True, Jane has had trouble remembering her dreams lately, and for that matter so have I. She had also been quite tired at the end of sessions, as noted; whereas she usually feels better than at the beginning.*)

Once more, the field of probabilities does not consist of imaginative fancy, nor of nebulous activity. It is quite as real as the physical universe. The experiences that are encountered there by other portions of the self are used by the whole self, and the knowledge thus gains is invaluable. Not only in terms of overall experience, but also as a means of training the ego, <u>and</u> the subconscious, to choose between various activities.

All of this data is instantly available to layers of the self, and only the ego is not aware of this field. It would be snowed under completely. Now, this field of probabilities has existed in your past, and <u>formed</u> your present.

It constantly expands, as does your own universe. It is never static. From it you choose those patterns of thought which you will weave into the physical matter of your universe. The dreaming self sees both fields, and operates in each.

It should be realized that the probable self <u>also</u> has its dreams.

This probable field <u>seeds</u> many other systems beside the one physical system with which you are familiar. The probable field is strongly composed of thought images, not physically materialized, but extremely vivid and actual storehouses of energy. Here is the material from which all pasts and presents and futures are made.

It is far from a closed system in any way. Not only does it feed the physical universe, but in it many aspects of your own dreams become actual. Do you dream of an apple? Do you dream of a child, who has no existence in physical reality? Often these exist in the field of probability.

You may take your break.

(It was now time for the 40th Dr. Instream experiment. Jane sat with her right hand raised to her closed eyes. She used many short pauses but her pace was average in between. She was not smoking. Resume at 10:09.)

Now. Give us a moment please.

I have the impression of a group of miscellaneous objects, bearing no particular relationship to each other: a stone, a pencil, a grape, something that looks like a twig. Another, a banana shape. All of these in a circular arrangement. *(Pause.)*

A paper clip also, and a small grain, g-r-a-i-n, something small and granular.

The items have been kept in a box. Also the impression of a small ceramic sculpture, of two people, and colored. The figures upright, with some gadget on top. This is only an example now, but a gadget like a handle, for example.

The above is to be taken as my impressions concerning an object, or objects.

Now. In connection with Dr. Instream himself, a splendid occasion of some kind, occurring recently. *(Pause at 10:15.)* Something movable and round. These are separate impressions, you understand; the movable and round does not necessarily refer to the splendid occasion.

(Here Jane made a gesture, her eyes still closed, as if she could somehow distinguish between the above impressions.)

A willingness to make a journey despite other considerations. A store where he was recently overcharged two dollars and fifty cents on a purchase. *(Long pause at 10:17.)*

Twelve people in a group, listening to him. A special group in which he is highly interested. A letter from an F W. Findings that are surprising to him, involving somehow X's and Y's. Perhaps on the third, thirteenth or twenty-third of this month. I am sure of the three but not of the other figures.

Do you have an envelope for me, Joseph?

("Yes."

(*It was 10:20. I handed Jane the sealed double envelope; as usual she took it without opening her eyes, then resumed her former position, with her right hand raised to her eyes.*)

Give us a moment.

A connection with twine. With the numbers four three, and an automotive establishment.

A connection with a grand view. A package. (*Jane gestures.*) Ruburt's association is with something that did not arrive on time, but let that one pass.

An achievement and a scarcity. Three people in particular.

A note—there is some confusion here—that was not <u>sent</u>, or did not arrive. This leads Ruburt to think of a note <u>he</u> wrote but did not send, to Father Martin. I mention this for your information.

The impression of cleverness, several children, and a dismissal. A long passage of time, and then a meeting.

A willingness to achieve. Paws, and netlike shapes, and triangles.

I suggest your break.

(*Break at 10:28. Jane was dissociated as usual. Her eyes had remained closed. She had spoken at a fair pace broken by many short pauses.*

(*Jane said she felt that she was trying too hard during the experiment; she wanted Seth to name the object exactly, and when she realized this she tried to relax. She now went on to explain that when I handed her the envelope she had "shifted gears" in order to give herself suggestions that she do very well on the experiment.*

(*Jane said she felt her awareness "rising" as she did this; she believes she came part of the way out of her trance state, then sank back into it when she made her effort to relax. In retrospect she does not believe such tactics to be good ones, and will not repeat them.*

(*See the tracing of the envelope object on page 289. I had used this for the object on the spur of the moment, more or less, without being concerned with whether Jane might know, or have on file, the letter the envelope had contained. Some of the data we could connect with the object, some we could not. When Jane began to go through her file of correspondence with her publisher, F. Fell, we began to see what complications could evolve from what seemed to be a simple envelope object.*

(*In order to understand the data it was necessary to write out a schedule of events; most of this was done after the session. As it was we spent about half an hour during break in an effort to begin to sort out the impressions. It developed that four letters were involved with the envelope object, and that one of these was enclosed in the experimental object. The common denominator here is that the date, January*

25, 1966, is somehow involved with all four letters. Seth uses this as a springboard for his impressions.

(First, a brief description of the four letters, including the dates written:

(Letter #1: Written January 20. Jane wrote Frederick Fell giving approval of the title given to her ESP book. She also offered her help in writing copy for mail order ads, and offered her small collection of ads for various ESP books which she has collected, as a guide. She told F. Fell copy for the ESP field is hard to write without experience in the field.

(Letter #2: Written January 25. This acknowledged Jane's letter of January 20, and was written by F. Fell's secretary, Rhoda Monks. She informed Jane that F. Fell was out of town for two weeks, and that he would be back in town—NYC—on February 7. F. Fell was out of town from Monday January 24, to Monday February 7. It developed that he was in Florida on a selling trip and vacation.

(Letter # 3: Written January 25. This too was from the offices of F. Fell, written the same day as letter # 2, and was a simple note from an Emma Hesse, of the bookkeeping department, requesting that Jane send in her social security number for tax purposes. Actually the letter was a form letter and Jane was addressed as "Gentlemen:".

(Letter # 4: Written January 25 by Jane, before the receipt of the two letters from F. Fell on the same day. Our mail arrives late in the day. In this letter Jane discussed the 200 pages she has finished on her first book on the Seth material itself. She also discussed the title for the ESP book, again offered her help on publicity ideas re this book, and told F. Fell that she was ready to help in any way she could.

(Both letters of January 25 from F. Fell to Jane, although on different-sized paper, bore fold marks that revealed either one could have been enclosed in the experimental object, which is an envelope front from F. Fell, postmarked January 25. Since the data obtained from the experiment this evening refers to both letters, as will be shown, we have no way of knowing which letter was actually mailed in the experimental object. I did not realize until after the session that it would have helped to ask Seth this.

(It should be noted here that Jane spent most of the day working on the article for *Fate Magazine*, dealing with Seth and the envelope experiments. In the 233rd session, Seth said the article would be sold. In order to do the article. Jane spent much time going over past envelope experiment results. It was tiring work in its own way, and Seth gives this activity as one of the reasons the envelope experiment results were not better. He has also said in the past that this kind of work on Jane's part can lower the level of her results.

(During the half hour that break lasted we made what connections we could, but most of our time was spent puzzling out the four letters, etc. Seth discusses the *experimental results to some extent. On some points we did not see or get explanations.*

("A connection with twine." We thought this general, since Jane's book manuscripts are usually bound with twine.

("With the numbers four three", was also general. Jane speculated that it could refer to the age of either the publicity director of F. Fell, or to Rhoda Monks, the author of letter # 2. Jane telephoned Frederick Fell on February 8th, and in so doing spoke first to Rhoda Monks; to Jane she sounded as though she could be about that age.

("an automotive establishment." elicited no response from us.

("A connection with a grand view." Again this was too general.

("A package." A package was mailed to F. Fell on February 10. It contained the manuscript for the book on the Seth material, plus that of the poetry book. See page 269 of the 232nd session for Frederick Fell's request to see the book plus the tape recording Jane made of some of the poems. The connection here with the envelope data is the January 25 postmark on the experimental object; Jane discusses the book on the Seth material in letter #4, written on January 25. Also, the tape was mailed to F. Fell on February 10 in a separate package.

("Ruburt's association is with something that did not arrive on time, but let that one pass." After break Seth tells us he hoped to make this clearer, but could not. Jane and I thought this was a reference to the fact that F. Fell left for Florida on January 24, Monday, before reading Jane's letter #1, of January 20, the previous Thursday. Letter #1 would not have arrived at his office by the next morning, Friday. Thus letter #1 was acknowledged in letter #2, written by F. Fell's secretary, Rhoda Monks, on Tuesday, January 25.

(We think also that Seth's statement above might refer to letter #4, written by Jane on January 25. At the time she wrote this letter Jane had yet to receive letter #2, and thus did not know F. Fell would be out of NYC until February 7. Actually Jane's letter #4 was never answered by mail. It was discussed in the telephone call between Jane and F. Fell on February 8. This is the call discussed in the notes on page 269 of the 232nd session. And again, the connection here with the envelope object is the January 25 date on which Jane wrote letter # 4, and the January 25 postmark on the object.

("An achievement and a scarcity." We think this a reference to letter # 1, written by Jane on January 20. Achievement being a general reference to her ESP book, and scarcity being a more specific connection in that Jane offers her own small collection of ESP ads to F. Fell's office for use as a guide in writing copy. The connection with the envelope object being that this letter #1 was answered on January 25, by letter #2, and that it is quite possible this is the letter contained in the object used in this evening's experiment.

("Three people in particular." Three people wrote the four letters involved. Jane wrote letters #1 and #4, Rhoda Monks wrote letter #2, Emma Hesse was responsible for letter #3. But I did not ask Seth for clarification and so we are not certain.

("A note—there is some confusion here—that was not <u>sent</u>, or did not arrive. This lead Ruburt to think of a note <u>he</u> wrote but did not send, to Father Martin. I mention this for your information." There is an interesting example of association at work here. Jane saw it before I did. Father Martin is a monk in a nearby monastery close to Elmira, and the author of letter #2, possibly enclosed by the envelope object, is Rhoda Monks.

(Jane did write Father Martin a letter on December 2, 1965 that she never mailed. In the 212th session for November 29, 1965 Seth discussed various measurements that could be taken from Jane just before, during, and after sessions by a doctor. Father Martin was a doctor before entering the religious life; he knows of the sessions but has not witnessed any or read the material. We considered asking his help in the matter of getting some data on Jane's physiological states, but did not go through with the idea because of lack of time.

("The impression of cleverness", meant little in particular, other than that Jane received the impression that F. Fell is the shrewd businessman type, through her telephone talks with him.

("several children, and a dismissal." rang no bells with us.

("A long passage of time, and then a meeting." This is a connection growing out of letter #4, written by Jane on January 25, which is the postmark date on the experimental object. As stated, F. Fell did not answer letter #4 by mail. The letter was answered by telephone in the call of February 8, between Jane and F. Fell. Jane said the passage-of-time reference grows out of Mr. Fell's questions as to when she was coming to New York, and her reply that she saw no use in it until the ESP book was out; then, in May, she wanted to be in NYC to help with publicity. Thus a year or so is involved from the time F. Fell agreed to publish the book and Jane began her final draft of it. The "meeting" grows out of Mr. Fell's reference that in this telephone call of February 8, he felt he was getting acquainted with Jane as a person, meeting her personally; also that he looked forward to their meeting in May.

("A willingness to achieve." In both letters #1 and #4, Jane expresses her willingness to do all she can to help with publicity re the ESP book—write copy, appear on radio or TV shows, etc. In the February 8 phone call, F. Fell told Jane he would try to get her on some shows to publicize the book.

("Paws, and netlike shapes, and triangles." These are very good references to letter #3, and take the form of doodles executed by Jane. She remembers making these on February 8, just before her telephone call to F. Fell. Letter #3, again, was written

January 25, and the date connects this letter with the January 25 postmark on the envelope experimental object. Either letter #2 or letter #3 was enclosed in the experimental object.

(Jane has the habit of making such doodles, but as it happens letter #3 is the only one of the four letters involved that has doodles on it. Nor, for the record, does Jane's unmailed letter of December 2, 1965 to Father Martin contain any doodles. The doodles from letter #3 are reproduced below as tracings from the originals, and are not in the same position as on the original, standard-size 8½ x 11 inch typing paper; the doodles are scattered over the page.

(I interpreted the portion indicated of the one doodle as bearing a resemblance to the imprint of a paw, although Jane intended this design as flowers. The netlike shapes and triangles are obvious.

(The "10 times" is the only other doodle appearing on the letter.

(We now come to an impression that Jane had while giving the experimental data this evening, but to which she did not give voice. Naturally, she was considerably vexed to learn that it was a legitimate one, and pertained directly to the object. See the tracing of the experimental object on page 289. Note that the word "bread" is *written upon it as part of a grocery list. As soon as she opened the sealed double envelope and saw the object, Jane realized she had had an impression of bread. She did not have an image of a loaf of bread, for instance, but the words "a loaf of bread," rather quickly. She does not know why she didn't give voice to them, other than that the next impression came along quickly. This has happened before, she said. Then succeeding impressions crowd out memory of what has been left unsaid, until later. In this instance, Jane could not recall very accurately what part of the data she was giving voice to when she had the bread impression, except that she was sure it wasn't toward the end.*

(*Jane resumed with her eyes closed, but opening occasionally, at 11:01.*)

Now. We have various circumstances operating here, merely because of the several letters connected with the same date. The fact, also, that Ruburt was indeed overextended.

With good circumstances it would have been quite an achievement to separate all the impressions connected with these letters.

The four three refers to the age, <u>either</u> of Rhoda Monks, or the man who sent the request for the social security number. They are both approximately of the same age.

(*Seth slipped up here, we believe. Rhoda Monks did author letter #2, but letter #3 was written by a woman, also; it is this letter that concerns Jane's social security number.*

(*Seth's next comment refers to a remark I made during break.*)

While it is true that any conceivable item can be used, it is indeed simpler at present if an item without so many associated impressions is used.

The three letters of the same date brought about the difficulty, though the difficulty would have been far less had our circumstances this evening been better. There is no need to go into the meanings for other impressions which were not clear.

Most of them are legitimate enough, but far from specific enough. Ruburt's concentrated work on our test data today simply resulted in his strained efforts on my behalf. This is all right, and sometimes to be expected.

Now, unless you have any questions for me, we shall close our session with my heartiest regards to you both.

(*"Just one then. Are we right about the connections between Father Martin and Rhoda Monks?"*)

The impressions which you caught were indeed legitimate. I asked you to let the one impression pass because I hoped to make it clearer, but was unable to. Even when conditions are not the most beneficial, we are not too far off, you see.

The twine was nearest I could get Ruburt to come. I was seeing however

300   THE EARLY SESSIONS

the January 25 letter <u>Ruburt</u> wrote, and was trying to get across the idea of a book to be mailed out. There was some small discussion, if you recall, when it was mailed, as to whether or not twine should be used.

(Seth is correct, and after he mentioned the twine connection Jane and I remembered it. This took place not on January 25, however, but on February 10, when the manuscript on the Seth material and the poetry book were mailed together. But Jane wrote letter #4, concerning the Seth material, on January 25. We did not use twine on the package, incidentally, but did use it on the package containing the tape recording Jane made of some of the poems in the poetry book. This was also mailed February 10. See page 269 of Session 232.)

The "grand view", I am afraid, was not nearly specific enough, and referred to Mr. Fell's view of the ocean in Florida.

("Good night, Seth."

(End at 11:14. Jane was dissociated as usual. Her pace had been average, her eyes had opened occasionally. Once again she said she was tired after the session.)

(Tracing of the coaster used as the object in the 35th envelope experiment, in the 235th session for February 23, 1966.)

SESSION 235
FEBRUARY 23, 1966 9 PM WEDNESDAY AS SCHEDULED

(The regularly scheduled session for Monday, February 21, was not held. Jane and I felt the need to rest and vary our routine. As a result we felt much refreshed for tonight's session. We wanted to make up for the Dr. Instream experiment we missed on Monday, however, so before tonight's session we mentioned aloud that we hoped Seth would deal with this.

(The envelope object for tonight's 35th experiment was a beer coaster that I picked up from our table last Saturday evening, at our favorite dining and dancing establishment here in Elmira. It was the one I had used. Jane and I met two young couples there by prearrangement, and we had much fun dancing. The coaster is made of heavy absorbent cardboard, so I peeled the top layer of paper from it. This contained the design, printed in red, without any unusual thickness to furnish Jane unwitting clues. It was sealed in the usual double envelope between two pieces of Bristol.

(The two young couples, Marilyn and Don Wilbur, and Ann Diebler and Paul Sinderman, witnessed the unscheduled session of November 5, 1965. See the notes for the 206th session. The Wilburs and Ann Diebler also witnessed the unscheduled session for December 3, 1965; see the notes for the 214th session.

(The session was held again in our front room, and was not interrupted. The windows were closed to dampen traffic noise. Jane began speaking while sitting down and with her eyes closed, but they soon began to open for brief intervals. Her pace was rather slow, and she was smoking as the session began.)

Good evening.

("Good evening, Seth.")

And welcome after your vacation. Certainly I have nothing against your taking some time off occasionally. You have been most faithful. Then, so have I.

(Jane smiled.

("Yes.")

Ruburt did well to relax the last few days, and he will now find that he applies himself to his various endeavors with renewed energy. I am glad that he put his dream book aside for a while, merely because he will have much more data for it within a short time. He can be working out his ideas however in the meantime, as this will be most beneficial. Even though some of his <u>ideas</u> will change, he will still need these present ideas as a basis.

Now. If you would have some idea of what the probable universe system is like, then examine your own dreams, looking for those events which do not have any <u>strong</u> (underline) resemblance to physical events in your own conscious existence. Look for dream individuals with whom you are not acquainted in your waking life. Look for landscapes that appear bizarre or alien, for all of these exist <u>somewhere</u>.

You have perceived them. They do not exist in the space which you know, but neither are they nonexistent, merely imaginative toys of the dreaming mind, without substance.

You may not be able to make sense from what appears to be a chaotic jumble of disconnected images and actions. The main reason for your confusion is your inability as an egotistical identity to perceive an order that is not based upon continuity of moments.

The order within the probable system is based upon something that could be compared to subjective associations, or intuitive flashes of insight, that can combine elements that would appear to the ego as quite disconnected, into whole and integrated patterns of action.

Now. In reality the possible system does <u>not</u> achieve its order through subjective association, but the term, subjective association, is the nearest that I can come in approximating the basic causes for this order.

The word subjective, to you, implies immediately that which is not objective. However the events and actions of the probable system are <u>indeed</u> objective and concrete <u>within</u> their own field of reality. Your own physical system, you should remember, is only real and concrete within <u>its</u> own field. It is for this reason mainly that the physical system is so little perceived by you when you sleep.

You withdraw yourself to a large extent from the physical field of actuality, but you do not only withdraw from the physical system. You <u>enter</u> other fields of actuality. Sleep is far from a negative state. In the sleep state there are as you know several stages. Some of these you call dream states, because the ego is aware upon awakening that some kind of mental activity has occurred.

But there are <u>other</u> states which the ego does not recall, states of activity that are presently beyond the reach of current scientific endeavors, and these states we shall discuss rather thoroughly.

You may however take a break, and we shall deal with these, and also with Dr. Instream for Monday, and for this evening.

(*Break at 9:23. Jane was dissociated as usual for a first delivery. Her eyes had opened and her pace had finally become rather good. She was not smoking when she resumed, in an even more emphatic manner, at 9:36.*)

Now. First of all, some of these states of activity take place so far beneath the ego or the subconscious that you simply do not know of them.

Some of these states take place above the ego or the subconscious, although I am using the terms above or below simply for your convenience. <u>You</u>

think of the ego as the center of the self, therefore I am forced to use these terms. You think the other portions of the personality revolve about the ego.

(*Jane's eyes now began to open widely. They were very dark. Her delivery was most emphatic, and she used many gestures, speaking rapidly.*)

The ego is only <u>one</u> layer of the self that has self-consciousness. Being self-conscious, the ego attempts to be conscious <u>only</u> of itself. Self-consciousness results in an intense, but necessarily limited focus. It necessitates boundaries. It depends upon some sort of inner psychological decision as to what will be considered self, and therefore accepted by consciousness, and that which will be considered notself, and not accepted by consciousness.

Now, my dear friends, <u>your</u> self-consciousness is the self-consciousness of the ego which you know, and which you consider <u>your self</u>. But where this self-conscious self ends, another self-conscious self begins. The two selves, being self-conscious selves, cannot be aware of any reality but their own.

They cannot be <u>consciously aware of each other</u>. Now the ego interprets all it perceives mainly in terms of its self. <u>Other</u> portions of the self, also self-conscious, interpret what <u>they</u> perceive in terms of themselves.

Each layer, or each area of the whole self, imagines that it is the center of awareness, and that the whole self revolves about it. So far you have had little experience with these other "centers"—you may put that in quotation marks—but before too long we shall give you some ideas so that you may become at least slightly acquainted. Initially this will be done through suggestion on a subconscious level.

Now. You have become somewhat aware of the subconscious. This means that your ego has enlarged <u>its conception</u> of the self, of <u>itself</u>, to include certain activities of which it is now aware. Progress in the development of personality in the long run will be determined by the ability of the whole self to recognize and become aware of all of its self-conscious portions.

The subconscious is a <u>self-conscious portion</u> of the whole self. It is called subconscious because the ego as a rule is not conscious of it.

The subconscious, so-called, is aware to some extent of the ego, regarding it as an extension of itself, over which it does not have as much control as it would like. This is precisely however the way the ego views the subconscious, as a rule. These two self-conscious portions of the self simply happen to coincide or to coexist with some proximity, psychologically speaking.

There are other self-conscious portions of the self however, with which the ego is not at all familiar, but of which the subconscious has intuitive knowledge. These self-conscious portions of the self exist in <u>different</u> reality systems. Before we go into our Dr. Instream material, let me remind you however that there <u>is</u>

a whole self, composed of these various self-conscious selves, and that a <u>portion</u> of the self is indeed <u>aware</u> of the unity that exists to form the whole psychological gestalt.

Now, a very brief break and we shall continue.

(Break at 9:58. Jane said she was dissociated more than usual. Her pace had slowed somewhat but been very emphatic, and her eyes opened many times. She had smoked, and sipped wine occasionally.

(It was now time for what we thought would be the 41st and 42nd Dr. Instream experiments. As usual Jane sat with her hands raised to her closed eyes. She was not smoking. On the whole her pace was not slow, although broken by many short pauses. Resume at 10:05.)

Now, give us a moment, please—some moments—for this.

These are impressions. Something that resembles a <u>shield</u> in shape, with inscriptions on it. Made I believe of metal, an insignia. Either the inscription or the insignia is of red color. The object itself of a <u>metal</u> color.

Fairly heavy in weight for its size. The edges of the object would ordinarily be <u>sharp</u>, it seems, but they are somewhat blunted. I get the numbers one eight eight eight, in connection with this.

Also a connection with flowers. Either they are represented somewhere on the object, or somehow connected with it, and small leaves. The flowers could be violets. The object is not full size. That is, it is not a soldier's shield of full size, but a representation. And a connection with jewelry.

Give us another moment, please.

First, a connection with a scroll for the above object. The object which we have dealt with is Monday's object. *(For February 21.)*

(Jane paused at 10:12, took a sip of wine without appearing to open her eyes, then gave voice to the last sentence above. She resumed her previous position. I have seen her reach out for objects often without seeming to look at them. She appears to have no memory of opening her eyes on such occasions; if she does slit them open I cannot tell, even from my position across a narrow table from her.

(Jane spotted it at break at 10:28 before I did: part of the above data seems to pertain to this evening's envelope object. This was interesting to me especially. I prepared tonight's envelope sometime after supper, then forgot about it in the press of other business. When the time for the envelope experiment arrived, I then had the idea the envelope contained another object, one I had thought of earlier in the day. So my surprise was considerable, consciously, when Jane opened the envelope and revealed the coaster.)

Now. Something round for this evening's object.

It has a connection with a clock, but is not a clock. It has hands but it does not tell time. The numbers four, three, six are connected here, and also a <u>schoolhouse</u>, and a <u>bell</u>, such as one that is rung to some children to school.

A vest. *(Pause at 10:16.)* The object is smooth, with moving parts. Twice, something on it twice, or two times.

Did I tell you this is this evening's object?

("Yes.")

Now, a turnabout for Dr. Instream of some sort, I believe professionally, or in his professional life. Ten students in particular. Tuesday at eight. An acclimation, acclaim.

A mission that worked out differently than he expected.

Do you have a test for me, Joseph?

("Yes."

(At 10:20 I handed Jane the 35th double envelope and she took it without opening her eyes. She held it against her forehead with her right hand.)

Please give us a moment.

Four, the number four, having to do with several of a kind. An enclosure. A specific event, which is anticipated. These connected with the item.

Writing. A rectangular shape, with an indentation that could suggest a border. A paper item. Connected with the initials J R.

<u>Terwilliger</u>. This is not correct, but take it down, the Terwilliger.

(Jane rather blurted out the word Terwilliger, as though somewhat surprised herself, then gestured impatiently, her eyes still closed.)

A connection with grassy land, and strings, such as apron strings. Four, five, no, six, the number six. February. Someone runs away. A connection with round colored objects, and a person who was not familiar to you personally.

Also a <u>grading</u>. Ten, September. Perhaps six three.

I suggest your break.

(Break at 10:28. Jane was dissociated as usual. Her eyes had remained closed except for the possible instant noted during her pause at 10:12. In spite of the many brief pauses her pace had been good. On the average it is now much faster during these experiments than it used to be.

(See the tracing of the envelope object on page 301. As stated, Jane was the first to notice that some of the data given for the Instream object of Monday, February 21, appeared to apply to our own envelope object for this evening, February 23.

(How much of this data on page 305 might pertain to the Instream object we do not know, but Jane had intuitive feelings that a bleed-through had occurred involving the envelope object. I go along with her in that such feelings are legitimate, since the basis of these experiments, as Seth has told us many times, is emotional.

(Jane felt that the following impressions on page 305 could very well apply to

the envelope object:

("Something that resembles a shield in shape, with inscriptions upon it." We suppose that since shields are of many shapes, this can apply to the shape of the envelope object. The printed copy on the coaster can be inscriptions. Our dictionary does not distinguish as to whether inscriptions need be lettering or designs, such as the three glasses on the coaster, or can be both.

(I was interested to note that our dictionary lists the word inscroll also, following inscriptive, and that the last line of the data for the Instream object for Monday contains this reference: "a connection with a scroll for the above object."

("Either the inscription or the insignia is of red color." Our envelope object, the coaster, is printed in a bright red. The color of the porous paper or board is a typical light beige or tan, not resembling metal, and certainly not heavy in weight for its size. Seth also mentioned these last two points in connection with the Instream data for Monday.

("The edges of the object would ordinarily be <u>sharp</u>, it seems, but they are somewhat blunted." Jane was perhaps more definite concerning this impression, than any of the others. She feels the sharp edges is a reference to the beer glasses depicted on the coaster: one can think of glass ordinarily as sharp-edged, but to be useful as a drinking vessel the material would have its edges smoothed, or blunted.

("I get the numbers one eight eight eight, in connection with this." My own idea here is that Seth/Jane picked up the three-ring design shown on each of the three glasses depicted on the coaster, and translated or converted this data into the number 8, three times. There is a graphic resemblance here. The numeral 1 appears in the code number, in small type, next to the bottom border.

(Seth goes over the envelope results with us to some extent this evening, and answers a few questions pertaining to such experiments. First however there follows the connections Jane and I made with the envelope object, and Seth's data on page 306.

("Four, the number four, having to do with several of a kind." There is a connection here but we did not see it at the time. Seth reminds us of it later in the session.

("An enclosure." We thought this a reference to the dining and dancing establishment we visited last Saturday evening, February 19, where I picked up the envelope object. Not to the establishment itself, but to the particular table we sat at with the other two couples. Its location, in one corner of the place, is unique; it sits on a raised platform perhaps two feet higher than the other tables; the dance band is on the left, the fireplace on the right, with an excellent view of the dance floor in between. The table itself is round, and backed up by a wide circular leather-covered divan-type of seat. In short, it's the best seat in the house.

("A specific event, which is anticipated. These connected with the item." This is a reference to the Saturday evening of dancing, which was planned in advance by us with the other two couples, Marilyn and Don Wilbur, and Ann Diebler and Paul Sinderman. Certainly it was anticipated with pleasure.

(Note above that Seth first gives data connected with the object; next he tries to become more specific about the object itself. Later in the session he has something to say about this method.

("Writing." The object bears printed copy.

("A rectangular shape", does not obviously apply, in that the coaster measures square within $1/32$ inches.

("with an indentation that could suggest a border." The object has a border, as can be seen in the tracing. In actuality the border is indented, or debossed, into the porous paper or cardboard material of the coaster, to the extent that it can be easily felt with the ball of the finger. This is a common effect obtained easily enough by the printer, through control of the pressure the printing plate applies to the object, and one which I work with often on my job. Jane however is not familiar with the term, debossed.

("A paper item." The envelope object is a paper item. As stated, it originally was quite thick, so I peeled the top layer from it, containing the design printed in red, to insert into the double envelopes. This reduced it to the thickness of rather heavy writing paper. When this thin layer was enclosed between the regular two pieces of Bristol, then sealed in the usual double envelope, it was not possible to judge by feel, or weight, that it was in any way somewhat different from the usual envelope object.

("Connected with the initials J R." Jane said she felt this was a reference to the entity names Seth has assigned to us, Joseph and Ruburt. Of course this kind of data could apply to many envelope objects.

("Terwilliger.", etc. This meant nothing to us, although Seth explains it later. At the moment Jane could only say that she had also found herself writing the word down in her daily predictions a few times lately, without knowing why.

("A connection with grassy land", led Jane to say a connection could be seen with the envelope object after all. When she gave this impression, she had the mental impression of grain; thus her voicing the word grassy came from the mental grain. Jane had the idea, now, that the envelope object advertised beer, made from grain.

(This interpretation is not correct, as will be seen. Instead Seth leads us to recall the rather hilarious incident Saturday evening that did give rise to this impression.

("and strings, such as apron strings." We did not see any connection right away.

("Four, five, no, six, the number six." Here again Seth leads Jane by his method of counting. There were six of us in our gathering last Saturday evening, when I obtained the envelope object.

("February.") I picked up the object on February 19, but this is too general.

("Someone runs away.") I thought this a reference to the fact that Don Wilbur and his wife Marilyn left the dancing establishment somewhat earlier than the rest of us did, because he was very tired after putting many hours of overtime work for the county, in connection with the snow we have been getting this month. This was not correct.

("A connection with round colored objects,".) I thought this might be a vague reference to the fact that Marilyn found in her handbag, Saturday night at the establishment, a group of miniature plastic castings of animals that she had made for her two-year old son. They were translucent, of different colors, tiny horses that were not round as a marble is round, but with rounded simple lines. We toyed with them throughout the evening.

(I did not think to query Seth about this impression later, so do not know if my interpretation is correct.

("and a person who was not familiar to you personally.") The connection here is tied in with the "grassy lands" data, but Jane and I did not see it during break.

("Also a grading.") We did not see anything here.

("Ten, September. Perhaps six three.") If this referred to the date, September 10, 1963, we were unable to make any immediate connection. Nor did any other interpretation occur to us.

(Jane's eyes began to open at times when she resumed, at an average pace, at 10:50.)

Now. We shall shortly end our session.

The date is pertinent, but I will let you figure this one out for yourself.

(I can offer a connection, but cannot verify it with Seth until next session. After this session I remembered that the Wilburs are reading what we call Book One of the Seth material. This consists of the first 26 sessions. The first formal session was held December 2, 1963. My introductory notes contain a reference to Jane and me borrowing a Ouija board from our landlord "in the fall of 1963," which compares with the date given by Seth this evening, of September 10, 1963. The notes refer to our attempts to use the board early in November 1963 also, without success.)

The initials J R were to refer to you both.

By the person not familiar to you, I meant to refer to someone not a <u>friend</u>—this being your obnoxiously pleasant Rice—<u>and this was the grain</u>. Now, you see.

(Jane paused and smiled broadly. See the reference to "A connection with grassy land," and "and a person who was not familiar to you personally." in the envelope data. At once I recalled an incident that took place at the dancing establishment last Saturday evening; the six in our party had watched it with much amusement.

(It involved a man I see very occasionally at my job. He works in another department, and is named Hack Rice. Jane and I see him more often when out dancing that I do on the job. He is always accompanied by his wife. Early Saturday evening, we saw Hack Rice and his wife dancing, and said hello as we usually do. At this time Hack was quiet and smiling.

(For a while the couple then disappeared from view and we forgot about them. Much later, around midnight, when the floor was crowded, Jane and I saw Hack again. Now he was obviously feeling good, and dancing with another woman. Hack is what they call a slow and smooth dancer. To the amusement of most people, Hack and the woman, whom we did not know, put on quite an exhibition of exaggerated, sinuous, close-contact dancing.

(So Jane, while voicing the impression of "grassy land", had the mental impression of grain, which referred to a man named Rice, who was present in the place where I obtained the envelope object. The connections are as far out as Hack Rice's funny behavior.)

The apron strings referred to your Marilyn, who holds her son on her apron strings.

(This reminded Jane and me that during Saturday evening, Marilyn had described to us how her young son had discovered what fun there was to the universal game of hanging by his mother's apron strings, as she tried to go about her duties in the trailer home in nearby Wellsburg, NY.

("What about your reference to the number four?")

The four in the beginning was merely my effort to lead Ruburt further, in counting as I did do later on, ending up with our correct six. The number, as a <u>beginning</u> number, was chosen because it does appear, though minutely, on the item itself. Also, there were four, initially, and then six. <u>I came in</u>, so to speak, when there were four.

(The number 4 does appear in the small code number printed on the envelope object, inside the bottom border. We missed noting this during break. We had also forgotten that we met Marilyn and Don Wilbur first at the dancing establishment, and had time for our first drink before Ann Diebler and her escort, Paul Sinderman, arrived.

("Do you want to say something about the Terwilliger reference?")

This had no connection. The Gallaghers were at a party that evening. They were somewhat on Ruburt's mind, and the name Terwilliger is a subconscious designation <u>he</u> uses for them. A distortion of the words Tim and Gallagher, simply because Tim has a particularly Gaelic connotation for him. More so than Bill, which is our Jesuit's first name.

A distant connection here, you see, with Dickens, and little Tim of the

Christmas Carol, and other connections hardly worth mentioning here.

Do you have any other questions?

("How about clearing up the reference to grading?")

(Jane smiled. Her eyes were opening now, and she lit a cigarette.)

The grading was, I am afraid, a poor reference to the parking lot, which was <u>paved</u> recently.

(True. The large parking lot at the dancing establishment, once consisting of the usual rather loose gravel, had been paved with amacite late last fall.

("What do you think of me asking you a question once in a while during an experiment?"

(I had been wondering lately if an occasional question might not produce more specific results. At times I'd had the distinct feeling that such questions would provide enough of a nudge to bring forth more data, but had hesitated because I didn't want the questions to be considered leading.)

It would be better if you asked me a question at the immediate ending of a test, rather than interrupt the data. Simply say, I have a question for you, or I will have a question for you.

A simple one-word question would probably not be harmful, but it is best for now to wait until the end.

Now. On those occasions where there is some bleeding through, I attempt to make some specific points in any case, that <u>are</u> identifying.

("Did that happen tonight?")

To some degree. This merely involves my efforts to teach Ruburt to focus more specifically. It is a learning process.

(Now see my notes on page 305, concerning my consciously forgetting the contents of the double envelope used in this evening's experiment. I was sure that subconsciously however I knew the contents well.

("Well, it seems the data on the Instream object for last Monday became entangled with tonight's envelope object data. Did you pick this up from me, telepathically, or clairvoyantly from the envelope object itself?")

No, this was a clairvoyant activity.

("From the envelope object itself, some time before we got to the envelope experiment?")

(In the 180th session, after the second envelope experiment, Seth told us he worked well clairvoyantly with objects, although at times telepathy could enter into such experiments.)

Yes. From the color red, which has strong connotations. The strongest elements are perceived more easily, as emotional elements are always perceived more easily. Initially with objects, I pick up shapes, and <u>emotional</u> connections, and then try to get Ruburt to let me narrow these down more specifically.

Ruburt, you see, does not perceive shapes as I do. Also he does not deal with details, as far as his overall perceptive patterns are concerned, and I am teaching him to do so psychically in these tests.

("Then did your 'Someone runs away.' envelope data have a strong emotional color?")

(See page 306.)

This had to do with the quick and too-speedy journey of one of the young men. I perceived a fast journey.

(This referred to Ann Diebler's escort, Paul Sinderman. Paul holds a job in Norfolk, VA. He makes the 1200-mile round trip to Wellsburg, a small town just outside Elmira, to see Ann every other weekend. We were discussing the amount of driving this involved, during our evening at the dancing establishment last Saturday. Paul has been in at least one auto accident that we know of.

("Did you make any of that journey, to or from Norfolk?")

No I did not. Our progress will be clear to those who read our records. There will be fluctuations. As larger areas are perceived more training is needed on Ruburt's part, to give us specifics. But we shall get a hold of these specifics.

("Is there any training involved here for you also?")

No. There is _effort_ involved, as I learn, indeed, the best ways of giving Ruburt data, and try to guide him in discriminating between, or rather among, the many personal associations that any one legitimate impression may bring to his mind.

On occasion he is in somewhat deeper a trance state, and our results are better, but this does not teach him what I want him to learn. The light trance state is ideal for _my_ purposes. For with this training he will be able to give specific information, but he will also have some knowledge of how this comes about. Do you have any more questions?

("No, not for tonight.")

I will then close our session.

("It's been very good.")

Ruburt will find, and you will find, that his latest endeavors have born fruit, and not lemons.

("Good. I'm sure he's interested. Good night, Seth."

(End at 11:15. Jane was dissociated as usual, her eyes open often. She ended the session with a smile. Presumably Seth refers to the writings she has sent out recently. Her publisher, F. Fell, has written expressing interest in her book on the Seth material and on the poetry book described in the 232nd session, page 269. Jane has also received a letter concerning some of these poems from Playboy Magazine, *regarding their consideration for publication as a book. All of this is tentative. In addition Jane mailed her article to* Fate Magazine *recently. See page 287 in Session 233. Seth said the article would sell.*

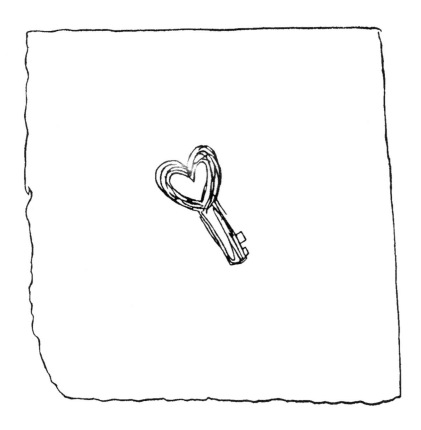

(Tracing of the pencil drawing on white paper, used as the object in the 36th envelope experiment, in the 236th session for February 28, 1966. Drawing executed by my boss, Harry Gottesman, at the Artistic Card Company in Elmira, NY.)

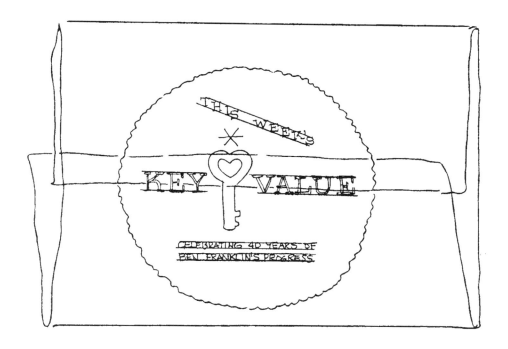

(Reduced tracing of my pencil sketch on transparent tracing paper. There are pencil rubbings on the back, so the sketch can be traced. The object is folded, and enters into the envelope data.)

SESSION 236
FEBRUARY 28, 1966 9 PM MONDAY AS SCHEDULED

(A short unscheduled session took place last night, Sunday, February 27, after our guests, the Gallaghers, had left. It was held in our living room and lasted from 11 PM to about 11:35 PM. I took no notes; this account is written from memory the following day.

(The evening's conversation had largely concerned matters other than Seth, but his name had been mentioned. After the Gallaghers left Jane said she could feel Seth "buzzing around." Shortly after this she began speaking as Seth, in an average voice;

she was smoking; she gestured often, and eventually her eyes began to open. She spoke without a break until the session ended. It was a question and answer affair for the most part. I will summarize the main points covered. I did not ask Seth the type of question I would prefer being answered in writing.

(Seth began by discussing a very emotional dream I had on the night of Thursday, February 24, involving what seemed to be the death of my father. I had not asked him to go into the dream yet, but had considered it, as Jane knew. Seth explained how the dream was built around my subconscious fears concerning my father. His interpretation of the dream was detailed, and in the manner of those he dissected in the 216th and 217th sessions. The conclusions were somewhat similar, and contained Seth's assertions that the death of my father is not imminent, although he is 75. Seth went into one of the basic problems behind the dream, the lack of an easy communication between my father and myself. He said this particular problem is more my father's fault than mine, and went into some methods concerning how I could begin to bridge this gap.

(Seth reiterated that Jane's book on the Seth material would be published, and that the poetry book would be published. He did not say who would publish them, and I did not ask. See page 269 of the 232nd session for background material and other references. Jane's publisher F. Fell, has written asking for photographs pertaining to the Seth book; in connection with this and in answer to my question, Seth said he would be amused to see a reproduction of my painting, purporting to be Seth, in the book. I'd done my oil of Seth in May/June of 1965.

(I discussed with Seth the surprise with which Jane and I have watched young people take to his ideas on time, dreams, clairvoyance, telepathy, etc.; with this I speculated as to the reaction of Jane or myself had we been introduced to such ideas at the age of 20 or so. Seth said there was no cause for surprise here, that young people are intuitively aware of much more than one gives them credit for, and that when Jane and I meet young people who express interest we should help them by recommending books, giving our own ideas, etc.

(Seth also said we have helped the Gallaghers, and that they have helped us. He said I have been particularly benefited, since they have the ability to open me up, whereas I had always thought Jane benefited most, because of her very warm relationship with Peggy. Jane is more outgoing than I am.

(Seth had some interesting things to say about using suggestion. The kernel of thought here is that it is important to use whatever suggestions we want to, daily; he stressed the importance of not missing a day. He explained that in a given period of say, thirty days, the suggestions on perhaps but three or four days within that period would be really effective, and that as of now we have no way of knowing the best days. So if we miss a day, we run a chance of missing out on a particularly effective day for suggestion. Seth said that on occasion suggestion will reach all levels of the personality, that our voice will be heard throughout the personality, and that effective action will follow. There was more here but the above is the main point made.

(I asked no questions about other major topics, such as the envelope experiments, Dr. Instream, etc., preferring to have such answers in writing. Our exchange was leisurely and quiet, and Jane was dissociated as usual.

(Two additional notes to add to the above account: Seth told me we might have witnesses to the session scheduled for Wednesday, March 2, but he did not say how many and I did not ask. He also said Jane should use suggestion to teach herself to sleep without a pillow. This would benefit her as an individual greatly, he said, and promised to go into the reasons later. When I remarked that I often woke up to notice that Jane _was_ sleeping without a pillow, having pushed it aside in her sleep, Seth said this was an indication that her subconscious knew what it was doing. I sleep with a heavier pillow than Jane uses, and sometimes use two; Seth said my reasons were different than Jane's and that in this case the pillows were not a hindrance.

(Seth used Jane's pillow data to go on to explain that she had a habit of sleeping with her hands tensed, or sometimes clenched, and that this allowed tension to move up her arms, across her shoulders and into the upper back and neck. Sometimes upon arising Jane will notice a stiffness in her upper back and neck, which wears away as she becomes active. Suggestion re the hands would help, according to Seth.

(The 36th envelope experiment was held tonight. See the tracings on pages 313-14. The drawing on 313 is the actual envelope object. The drawing on 314 is executed by myself, after my boss's drawing and instructions, and enters into the envelope data in the manner in which the four letters became involved with the envelope object in the 234th session. The relationship tonight is simpler, however.

(Today Jane received the galley proofs of her ESP book, along with the original manuscript, from her publisher by special delivery. We noted that most of the typed pages of her script bore handwritten comments in the margins and on the back. They were made evidently either by a psychologist or parapsychologist, probably at the invitation of the publisher before he accepted the book. We had considered this possibility, although the publisher had not mentioned it to us.

(Someone had then laboriously used a magic marker to try to cross out the notes so they couldn't be read; we were much amused to read them rather easily by holding the pages up to a light. The comments run the gamut from scorn to approval, and tell us as much about their author as they do about Jane's book. Jane plans to ask her publisher, F. Fell, for the name of the author of the notes, and for a copy of the covering letter he refers to. We have initials. Seth also comments on the events, although we did not ask him to.

(Jane was pleased at the choice of type for the book, and the manner in which

Seth's quotes have been distinguished from her own copy. The arrival of the galleys had excited her, but she felt the excitement stemmed from not from this alone, but from the manner in which they arrived from New York City. She apparently had the situation covered in her daily predictions for the two previous days.

(Without going into details her predictions involved a lost package and other pertinent forecasts having to do with delays. The post office fouled up here, misplacing the special delivery notice, then failing to make delivery, etc. Finally when Jane went to the post office just before closing time today to claim the package, it proved to be lost again, this time on the premises. It was found after a lengthy search.

(Previous to obtaining the package, Jane spent several hours in a strong state of worry and anticipation, and feels this state was a clairvoyant/telepathic attempt to give her conscious self information concerning the package. She believes her tension prevented her understanding what she was trying to tell herself. Her publisher had not advised her the galleys were on the way, incidentally.

(Tonight's session was held in our large front room. Jane felt good as session time arrived, and perhaps for this reason Seth spoke at a somewhat slower pace than usual. There were many very brief pauses. Jane's eyes opened almost at once, briefly, closed, then began their usual fluctuation. Her voice was average. She lit a cigarette soon after she began.)

Good evening.

("Good evening, Seth.")

May I join the party?

("Yes.")

(Jane smiled.)

Now, we shall <u>say</u> what we shall say in our own good time. The ESP book will be very widely read, and well noticed. There will be some controversy, and Ruburt will simply learn to relax, and not to upset himself.

The book will be, in its field, the most controversial of the year. This is quite all right, and to be expected.

By the time we are finished, we will have some excellent evidential material. By the time critics' voices become noisy we will be ready to show what we can do. We will have progressed enough for that.

The less complicated portions of my material have been used in the ESP book, but there is enough there to give serious question to many learned gentlemen, and they will look forward to the Seth book, for the further developments that will be given.

(Jane now took a pause that lasted a full minute, sitting quietly with her eyes closed.)

The inverted time system should be at least briefly explained in the Seth book. I do not want to dictate to Ruburt, or tell him how to write this book. It occurs to me however that it would be advantageous to include in the middle section my ideas concerning the construction of physical matter, the inverted time system, moment points, a discussion concerning the dream universe, and the system of probability. All of this in direct quotes from the material itself. The last section of the book could then deal with what evidential material we have, and you shall have more. I am certain that Ruburt could so organize the center portion of the book so that stress could still be given to the personal story line.

In this manner a tantalizing sample of the material in several aspects would be given. Questions would be raised in the minds of the readers, and in other books the various ideas could be expanded from the material, and these questions answered. In this way you would be presenting an overall picture that would later be filled in.

(Jane took another long pause. We had just about decided to finish the book in the above manner. Jane has been thinking over what material to include in the center section so as to maintain reader interest, and some time ago decided to finish the book with what evidential material we have so far. The first section is now in the hands of her publisher.)

The first section would then remain as it is, basically, except for any changes Ruburt wishes to make in small matters. I would like, you see, the overall picture presented as much as possible. The <u>overall</u> picture will capture the imagination, and the specifics will follow.

(Another long pause. Jane sat with her head down as she leaned forward, hands clasped, eyes closed.)

The material on reincarnation will appear consistent and logical only within the whole framework. The objections of many will be offset only when the reincarnational data is seen in the light of a full understanding of the spacious present and the inverted time system.

I believe you will hear from Dr. Instream himself shortly.

Now, I have a few comments concerning your own activities.

You did indeed tune in on your dancing establishment, and hear the music. It is of course no coincidence that you were between waking and sleeping when this occurred.

Ruburt's experience in psychological time today represented a legitimate attempt to dissociate his awareness from physical matter, and was a sign that he is embarking upon another fruitful period of activity.

There are certain self-regulating devices at work here, psychologically speaking, that insure necessary periods of passivity and rest. In any <u>well-balanced</u> personality these operate automatically, as in Ruburt's case.

Now I suggest a brief break.

(Break at 9:30. Jane was dissociated as usual. "Seth," she said, "is being tricky tonight." Because of her excitement in the day's events, she felt Seth was using a more deliberate manner than usual in order to "lull" her psychologically. Jane said she was fully aware of Seth's tactics. She announced also that she was cooperating in case Seth wanted to say anything about the notes on her ESP manuscript.

(There follows the account from my notebook describing my adventure in hearing music while almost asleep: "February 27, Sunday night, actually 12:30 AM: As I lay in bed half asleep I heard very clearly music in chords, played by an electric guitar. The sound was very harmonious, neither too fast or slow, and quite beautiful, almost with an echoing quality. I realized I had been listening to it for some little time, perhaps a minute, before I consciously realized what was happening. I then came awake and described the effect to Jane, who had not yet fallen asleep."

("A little later, while in the same state, I heard the music again to a reduced degree, for a few seconds. I then fell asleep. It is interesting that the evening before this experience, Saturday, February 26, Jane and I had an excellent time dancing to a new band at our favorite dancing establishment in town. I believe the guitar music I heard in bed was very much like one of the guitars in the band. I had watched this particular musician often during the evening, admiring his playing. The band plays until 1 AM each evening, when the establishment closes. Since I had my experience at 12:30 AM, when presumably the band would still be playing, did I perhaps tune in on it there?"

(I have had several other suggestive experiences recently, and keep a list of these in my dream notebook. One involved voices; another and more striking one involved my naming the exact item of clothing Jane purchased for me, unknown to me while I was at my job.

(Jane said there is little to say about her psychological time experiences, other than that she felt she was making a guarded attempt to lift out of her physical body.

(Break proved to be a little longer than usual. Jane began speaking in the same rather slow manner, and for the most part her eyes remained closed. Resume at 9:45.)

Now. A few general remarks before our Instream material.

You will both meet the gentleman to whom you refer. The man whose writing appears on Ruburt's original manuscript.

(Jane now took a one-minute pause. She sat with her hands raised to her closed eyes.)

These are impressions concerning that gentleman.

A connection with Harvard about the year 1934. He lived for a long time near water, but I believe inland water. If it was near the ocean, it was where the ocean was quiet, for example a bay location.

SESSION 236

The initials M S connected with him. A stomach disorder. A mole, fairly noticeable, on the face, perhaps in the region of the nose. He is cautious about money, but prides himself upon an open mind. He holds on to his ideas however, as he holds on to money.

A connection with a cottage on the water, perhaps not on a year-round basis. A connection with a large organization. Now a young man. Sometimes given to wearing checkered <u>vests</u>, or jackets. I believe vests.

A connection with <u>cold</u>. I am not sure to what this refers. Perhaps somehow the sounds of his name suggest ice, or the letters. We shall see.

A downtown location, in which he sometimes works. For a scientist he is himself rather long-winded, and can hardly afford to take me to task on that particular point.

I shall give you a very brief break at this time, and then for the Instream material. There is a connection here in the above impressions with Priestley, yes.

(*Break at 9:59. Jane was dissociated as usual. Earlier in the evening we had noted a similarity in some of the comments on her manuscript with J.B. Priestley's ideas on time. Jane had the idea that Priestley and our unknown commentator were contemporaries. Priestley we believe to be 70. Jane said she had the personal association of Norway when she heard herself giving the data on ice, regarding the name.*

(Jane's pace had been slow for the most part all evening. It was now time for the 43rd Dr. Instream experiment, and once again her pace was broken by pauses. As usual she sat with her head down, her hands raised to her closed eyes. Her pace picked up a little as the data proceeded. Resume at 10:05.)

Now. Give us a moment, please.

A page, I presume from a book, that somehow deals with history. I do not know if it is a history book, but it deals either with events in the past, or with ideas of the past.

Some allusions to Rome, about 30 AD. Some to the Middle Ages, and some to the previous century—that is, to the century before this one.

A brown or <u>red</u> binding. Perhaps leather. That is, the cover is rather heavy or thick. Something to do with Descartes also, in the copy. A medieval scene depicted, with romantic overtones. Romantic not necessarily in terms of love interest, but in terms of imaginative fancy.

A book marker. The number three two eight. A philosophical exchange in terms of a classic dialogue.

Something ground up or tattered. I do not know to what this refers. A woman in old-fashioned clothing, a representation rather than a person. The color red, large flowery first letters, open sentences or paragraphs.

A mention of a much-maligned historical figure, also I believe from the

past. A title of four words I believe.
  Do you have a test for me, Joseph?
  ("Yes.")
  (*At 10:16 I handed Jane the 36th double envelope; as usual she took it from me without opening her eyes, then sat holding it to her forehead with her right hand. Her eyes were still closed.*)
  Give us a moment, please. These are impressions.
  An establishment, or something established. Something turned up.
  A connection with a marvelous occasion, though the word marvelous may be too strong.
  I get a connection with a missionary, or religion, and the number 8, and something rising. But as a <u>geyser</u> rises, rather than something simply lifting up. An explosive type of motion.
  A small round object, with some inscriptions resembling a postmark. A connection with something unclaimed, with the number 12, perhaps also with six three, and with <u>ribbon</u>like shapes. That is, long lines that are straight, perhaps two of these, and of dark color I believe, or dark red. Black on red. Horizontal rather than vertical, in the position in which I hold this.
  (*Without opening her eyes, Jane held the envelope before her in a horizontal position, and moved it from side to side to show horizontal movement. She then rested her elbow on the arm of her rocker and kept holding the envelope up as she continued.*)
  A connection with a machine, and locomotion, and some people you do not know, and some you do know.
  December. A connection with a willingness to go somewhere. Star shapes. The color white background, and a paper item, folded like a card, the center being a rectangular shape.
  Somehow <u>cluttered</u>, or full, and empty toward the outsides. Dark and shadowy in the center, with suggestions of motion, and late afternoon.
  A connection with a house and a white border.
  You may take a break. Also a hat.
  (*Break at 10:27. Jane was dissociated as usual Her eyes had remained closed, her pace had been slow, she hadn't smoked, etc.*
  (*See the tracing of the envelope object, and its accompanying drawing, on pages 313-14. We did not ask Seth to clear up each point in the data, so give below our own interpretations. As stated, the key drawing made by my boss was the actual envelope object. This is on thin white paper. The drawing on tracing paper was made by me, from instructions given to me by my boss, and is a schematic drawing to be traced onto Bristol board for final artwork.*

(My drawing was actually a recreation of artwork that had been lost at Artistic Card Co. As often happens the original art was later found after I had duplicated it. The drawing was for a gummed sticker to be applied to a line of packaged cards of various kinds—religious, Christmas, Valentine's Day, etc., and was for a large old department store in Philadelphia, PA, that goes under the cavalier name of John's Bargain Store. As the copy of my tracing shows these stickers are applied to the appropriate merchandise at various times of the year.

("establishment, or something established." My thought was that both drawings were produced at an establishment, namely my place of employment. But this could also refer to the customer in Philadelphia.

("Something turned up." As stated, the lost artwork was found after I had spent time duplicating it.

("A connection with a marvelous occasion, though the word marvelous my be too strong." The word marvelous is too strong, we suppose, but the stickers are made for special occasions through the year, as explained above.

(As can be seen, much of the envelope data given by Seth was transposed from the actual object to my own tracing-paper drawing. It might be noted that during the session, while Jane held the envelope in her hand, my tracing-paper drawing was in the same room with us, although I was unaware of this until after the session. It reposed in my jacket pocket in our front room closet; I had brought it home several days ago, then forgot about it, not having worn the jacket since. Both drawings were made about two weeks ago. Jane hadn't known they even existed.

("I get a connection with a missionary, or religion", is a reference to the fact that the stickers were to be used on boxes of religious cards, as well as other categories. While I was making the drawing the four or five boxes of different cards were laid out before me so that I could refer to them, and the religious box was among them.

("and the number 8", offers no connections that we can see.

("and something rising. But as a geyser rises, rather than something simply lifting up. An explosive type of motion." This is an associative bit of data on Jane's part and will be explained later.

("A small round object, with some inscriptions resembling a postmark." Jane said she saw within a small round object, with horizontal lines running across it; she thought of a postmark on an envelope, with the cancellation lines, but knew this wasn't it. When she looked at my tracing-paper drawing, she said this was evidently what she was trying to arrive at subjectively; my drawing is of a round object, although much larger. Jane said the straight-across lettering, Key Value, is in the position of the horizontal lines she saw within. There are also ruled-in horizontal lines on the drawing.

("A connection with something unclaimed, with the number 12, perhaps also with six three", brought no connections to mind. Then later Jane thought of the lost artwork at Artistic—"something unclaimed"?

("and with <u>ribbon</u>like shapes. That is, long lines that are straight, perhaps two of these, and of dark color, I believe, or dark red. Black or red. Horizontal rather than vertical, in the position in which I hold this." As stated on page 321, Jane held the rectangular double envelope up with its long edge parallel to the floor, and moved it back and forth to indicate most definitely her insistence upon the horizontal attribute. This is most interesting, for the envelope object itself contains neither vertical or horizontal lines or masses. Once again her actions and data seem to be an attempt to get at my tracing-paper drawing, which bears a close connection to the envelope object.

(My drawing contains lines that are horizontal and straight. There are two sets of these horizontal lines, across the top and the bottom of the words Key Value, and when one turns the drawing over on the back—not shown here—is seen the dark smudges of my pencil as I prepared the drawing for tracing onto paper. Jane said these lines and the dark smudges beneath them are what she believes she was referring to, more so than the other two horizontal sets of lines below the end of the key.

(When she saw the smudges on the back of the tracing-paper drawing, Jane said this was what gave her the idea of "<u>ribbon</u>like shapes." The "dark color" and "dark red" references were her attempts to further refine this data.

("A connection with a machine", could refer to the fact that I did some of the work on my tracing-paper drawing on a darkroom machine that is called a Lacey-Luci. This is a bulky contraption containing floodlights, a ground glass, and a magnifying-reducing lens for fast juggling of copy or artwork to proper size. A machine of this type is a standard in most art departments.

("and locomotion", is to me a personal association of Jane's derived from the machine data above.

("and some people you do not know, and some you do know." Too general. I do not know the people who operate John's Bargain Store, but neither do I know many other of Artistic's clients. Obviously there were people around the art room whom I do know.

("December. A connection with a willingness to go somewhere." We saw no connections here.

("Star shapes." This is related to the geyser data on page 321, and out of it grows a personal association of Jane's. Note that my tracing-paper drawing bears a formalized six-pointed star. Jane said she had an image of a star of sorts, and that this gave her the idea of fireworks shooting into the sky—thus the idea of a geyser, and something rising and explosive, etc.

("The color white background", might be taken as a reference to the white paper the envelope object was drawn on, but Jane said that once again this referred to the tracing-paper drawing I made. Tracing-paper is a pale translucent gray or off-white color, but not really white as this typing paper is white.

("and a paper item, folded like a card", also referred, Jane said, to my drawing rather than the envelope object. Jane said she had a vague image of a small round object upon a rectangular folded object that was like a card, yet the circle was not placed as neatly in the center of the rectangle as my drawing is. It was more offset toward the upper right corner, hence her postmark reference on page 321 also. On page 314 note that my tracing-paper drawing is folded roughly like a card.

("the center bring a rectangular shape." Jane said this is another reference to the rectangular area taken up across my drawing by the words Key Value.

("Somehow <u>cluttered</u>, or full, and empty toward the outsides." On the original tracing-paper drawing my pencil smudging on the back shows through easily, and gives the drawing a cluttered or crowded look in the center. By contrast it looks bare toward the edge of the circle. This is an effect I noticed at work while making the tracing, but the illusion disappeared on the finished art.

("Dark and shadowy in the center", Jane said, is another reference to my smudges on the back of the drawing, and refer back to the ribbonlike shapes on page 321. She had a fairly good image of this darkened area, and its horizontal disposition.

("with suggestions of motion", again refers to my drawing rather than the actual envelope object; the motion, Jane said, of my pencil smudges across the back of the drawing, and to the slant of the words This Week's above the key and star.

("and late afternoon." Jane said this is another impression taken from the smudges on the back of my drawing. Note that this pencil smudging on the back of the tracing affected Jane probably more than anything else. This late afternoon impression stemmed from the feeling of dusk or evening falling, as suggested by the dark smudges. Jane was quite aware of this feeling subjectively.

("A connection with a house and a white border." This is interesting, in that Jane said she had an image of a card shape with a house and foliage on it. It was not very clear, yet she knew that much about it. The boxes of cards for which the sticker was made are large, large enough to contain reproductions of four cards, arranged in a rectangular pattern on the box top, and on a printed gold background. Each card design is surrounded by a rectangular white border, perhaps an eighth of an inch wide. Some of the boxes laid out before me, as I made my drawing for the sticker, contained reproductions of cards bearing houses, trees, flowers, etc.; the standard kind of subject material for greeting cards.

("Also a hat." I saw no connection here.

(Jane said that out of all the connections we made, practically all of them referred to my tracing-paper drawing rather than to the actual envelope object itself. My boss made the envelope object. Jane knows him of course, and likes him; yet the fact that I made the tracing-paper drawing evidently exerted a stronger pull emotionally. Perhaps this diverted Seth/Jane's focus from the envelope object to a closely related object. As stated, Jane didn't know the two drawings existed.

(*Jane resumed, still at a somewhat slow pace, at 10:45.*)

Now we will end the session very shortly. You have had a busy day.

Ruburt is just coming out of what can be called a rest period. It is true that five months earlier it would not have been possible to get this much valid information through during such a period.

(*The first envelope experiment was held on August 18, 1965, almost 8 months ago.*)

The interpretations he gave when you discussed the impressions were correct. All of them.

You may ask me questions at the <u>end</u> of my delivery of impressions, and before the break.

(*Seth had mentioned this in the last session; and again tonight we had talked about it during break.*)

("*Well, I think it natural that I want to ask questions during these experiments, but I don't want to lead Ruburt on.*")

They may indeed. It will help you clarify some data perhaps, <u>before</u> Ruburt sees it, and this will be to our advantage.

(*I believed Seth's answer showed a mild misunderstanding between us.*)

("*What I mean is, will I be accused of giving him clues if I ask questions about the envelope data? Suppose I ask him to be more specific about a certain point, say a shape? Won't he take the question as a sign that the point needs to be clarified?*")

You will have to be careful, but we are learning also.

(*Now Jane lowered her head. She raised her hands to her closed eyes once more.*)

Now wait a moment.

Some distant connection with the name Margo. This concerns our impressions of the man who made notations on the manuscript. Two other females also. <u>Younger</u> than he.

My heartiest regards to you both, and good evening. Unless you have any questions.

("*Just one. Will we have any witnesses to Wednesday's session?*")

(*Seth had mentioned this possibility during the unscheduled session of last Sunday, February 27. Jane smiled.*)

You <u>may</u>.

SESSION 236

("Why the smile?")

You may have <u>two</u> sets of witnesses.

("How many people?")

The possibilities exist for four, perhaps even five.

("It sounds like a busy time, then... Good night, Seth."

(End at 10:55. Jane was dissociated as usual. Her eyes had remained closed since break, her pace rather slow. She said she felt sure about the impressions concerning my tracing-paper drawing. She was aware, she repeated, of the circular shape upon the rectangular shape formed by the folded tracing paper; she felt it was folded when Seth said so.)

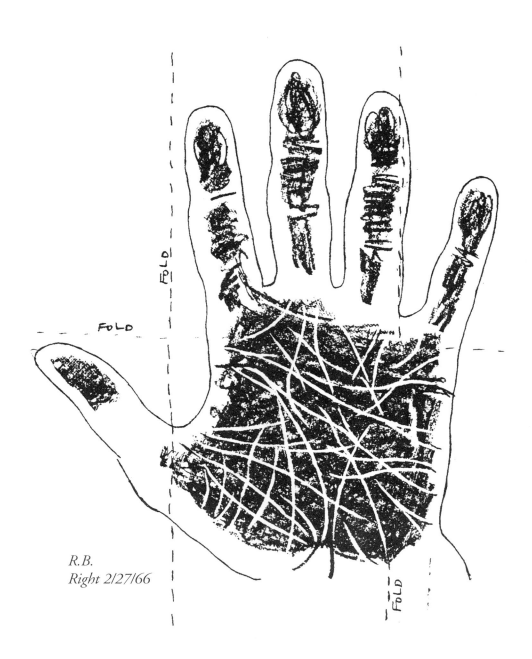

(Reduced copy of the print of my right palm, used as the envelope object in the 37th envelope experiment, in the 237th session for March 2, 1966. Made on February 27, 1966.)

SESSION 237
MARCH 2, 1966 9 PM WEDNESDAY AS SCHEDULED

(*The 37th envelope experiment was held during the session. See the tracing of the envelope object on page 327. It is a print of my right hand, made with black stamping ink on paper. I made it on February 27, 1966. Jane had picked up a book on hands at the library recently, and this got us interested in making such prints.*

(*The print is on the whole darker than my pencil indication on the preceding page, and of much better quality. The lines in the palm, indicated by black lines, are in actuality in white on the original print, so that the effect is the interesting one of a hand in reverse, or perhaps a map or plan printed in reverse. The fingerprints show with fair clarity also. This is but one of many prints I made that evening; I discovered it is not easy to obtain a full print that has good overall detail.*

(*Jane of course saw this particular print, along with perhaps twenty others I made at the same time. There is nothing about this one to distinguish it from many of the others. Following the instructions in the book, I traced the outline of my hand in pencil while pressing the inked surface against the white paper. The print was sealed in the usual double envelope between the usual two pieces of Bristol.*

(*In the last session Seth said the possibility existed that we would have four or five witnesses for the session tonight. He had also mentioned such a possibility during Sunday's unscheduled session of February 27. However no witnesses appeared.*

(*Prior to the session Jane and I had a discussion as to the exact profession of the person who had written the many notes on the manuscript of her ESP book. See pages 319-20 for notes on this, in the 236th session, and Seth's comments. Neither of us thought the person in question a psychologist. I favored a parapsychologist, Jane a psychiatrist. In his comments he referred rather often to his own theory of spherical time. Neither of us have heard of this, nor can we find a reference to it in our books.*

(*The session was held in our front room. Jane spoke while sitting down and with her eyes closed, and once again her pace was slow; at times during this first delivery it was as slow as I can remember during any session. Jane was not smoking. She sat for some time with her head down, her hands raised to her temples. Begin at 9:02.*)

Good evening.

("Good evening, Seth.")

I enjoyed your little discussion.

Our friend of the manuscript thinks of himself as a liberal-minded man, but he will not take any giant steps away from the lines of academiclike safety.

He takes <u>prissy</u> tiptoeing steps, always looking backward with worried caution. He does not carry his precious spherical time idea far enough to begin with. His spherical time is like the surface of a sphere only.

The spacious present and the inverted time system deal with the insides of the sphere.

(Jane now took a long pause. The above material had been broken by many pauses.)

There are a few points I would like to make. They will take us a bit away from our main lines of discussion, and they have to do with communication between essence personalities and those still within the physical system.

(Seth enjoys calling himself an energy personality essence.)

Now. When the communicator is still strongly tied emotionally to your own system, and when he is still acclimating himself to his new conditions, then his communications will be extremely garbled, as a rule.

His control over the nervous system of the person through whom he communicates will be faulty and erratic. His interests will largely be those he had during physical existence. This is generally true.

He will be mainly concerned in an effort to prove his survival. His messages will be full of trivial but significant data that will make his survival plain to those he has left behind.

Our communications are not of this type. As an overall personality, I have always been concerned with ideas. I am not emotionally in strong connection with any personalities known to Frank Watts, for example. He is a part of, or a fragment of, my whole self, and an independent one.

(These sessions began when we contacted the Frank Watts personality through the Ouija board, in December 1963. The Frank Watts personality was replaced in the 4th session by Seth. Seth has dealt with Frank Watts to some degree in the following sessions: 4, 8, 11, 14, 15, 16, 21, 25, 29, 31, 51, 85, 88, 173, 184, 189, 224. See Volumes 1 through 5.)

My field of reality is not the same as it is for those who have recently left your system. It is not necessary for Ruburt to adopt the deep trance state for our sessions, since I am able to speak through him without shutting out most aspects of his consciousness.

Of course I get help from him. One of my main purposes is to instruct, and to do so with all the available equipment operating at least to some degree. The light trance state is ideal for this.

(Jane's pace was now very slow, as slow as it has ever been, I believe. Some of her pauses lasted well over a minute. Yet at times her eyes opened briefly.)

Now. Emotional intensities are still our guidelines however, and they have meaning and significance within all systems. It is by their light that you see.

(See the sessions on the electrical universe in Volume 3.)

One of the reasons, incidentally, for Ruburt's good performance for me is precisely his ability to use words well. We are building up a foundation here, in which words are important, and for which incidentally subconscious shorthand symbols would be of little use.

You may take a short break.

(*Break at 9:32. Jane was dissociated as usual for a first delivery. She knew Seth was being deliberate, she said, but was not aware that half an hour had passed. Her pace had been very slow, and she did not have too good an idea of what she had said.*

(*Jane said she thought Seth might have gone into the survival material because of some of the marginal notes made on her ESP manuscript by our unknown friend, particularly on the chapters dealing with reincarnation.*

(*She thought the last paragraph came about because our same friend had made some notes about authentic survival messages being given in "shorthand," the letter "U" for the word you, etc.*

(*Jane still used pauses, but her pace was much faster when she resumed. She was not smoking. Her eyes remained closed. She sat quite still for at least a minute after closing them, before resuming at 9:44.*)

Now, back to our main discussion.

When the inverted time system is understood clearly, then the inadequacy of the cause and effect theory will be clear. If your psychologists and scientists would begin a study of <u>their own dreams</u>, they would learn much through personal experience.

They would tackle realities that cannot be measured with physical instruments. Since psychologists deal with psychological activity, it is all the more amazing that they have not concentrated upon psychological activity, observing it first hand as it exists in their own various stages of consciousness.

If such a study is conducted however with preconceived ideas, then each experimenter will find only what he has been looking for, for all else will appear meaningless to him.

But the dreaming state presents any experimenter with original and varied material, and the opportunities involved are tremendous. The inverted time system will appear plainly, if any examination is made as to the relationship between time and the dream state.

This may not be the <u>time</u> to make this remark, but quite literally, <u>tomorrow's</u> dream can change yesterday. All of the experiments that you are conducting are in themselves beneficial simply because of the training involved, and the expansion of consciousness.

I am not <u>de</u>-emphasizing consciousness. I am trying to teach you to focus your consciousness in many directions, even to carry a portion of <u>egotistical</u>

consciousness into the dream state.

Clues as to the existence of inverted time appear also in the waking condition however, and soon I shall have much to say on this matter. It <u>is</u> the existence of inverted time that is mainly responsible for clairvoyance.

Now, give us a moment please, before the Instream data.

(Jane paused at 9:56. Seth dispensed with the usual break before our experimental material. When break finally did arrive Jane said Seth was going to give a break at this time but decided to go ahead because she was in a good state. Usually, Jane said, she reaches a better state as time passes.

(Now, her head down, her hands raised to her closed eyes as usual, she began the material on the 44th Dr. Instream experiment.)

He is in a building several stories high, and he is not on the first floor. The building is modern. He has matches in his hand, and lights one. He stares at the matches, a small packet of ordinary matches.

(Jane took a longish pause at 10:00. Her pace was broken by many short pauses, but was still good.)

The cover has a representation of a building on it. Howard Johnson. Two other men in particular, standing up as if to leave. One taller than the other, and both seem hatless.

There is a coffee urn, or a silver-colored urn. A button loose—that is, a button is loose. *(Jane gestured, her eyes still closed.)* The color orange used as a decoration. Glass doors, and many voices from the other side.

One of the other men mentioned has a mustache, a dark one, though he is not necessarily a young man, and pointed features. The chin small but pointed. *(Jane touched her own chin.)*

One of the men carries a brown cardboard large envelope, or folder, with strings on it, and records inside.

Some connection with the initials C S. Also a connection with a young boy—that is, young <u>man</u>, I believe, but not an adult male.

Some talk of money for a project, or the lack of it, and an immediate plan considered. A framework, or something framed. *(Jane shook her head.)* The matches are the object.

Do you have a test for me, Joseph?

("Yes."

(Jane paused at 10:09. I handed her the envelope for our 37th experiment, and as usual she took it from me without opening her eyes. Then she sat with it held against her head. She gave the material on the envelope with many short pauses.)

Now give us a moment, please.

Five. Something for a consideration. A floor plan, or diagram.

I have the impression of a steeple shape, or upside-down V shape, that is rather prominent.

A connection with many people, and with something like a basement—low, that is. This leads Ruburt to think of your Myhalyk's, his impression.

Something low and something high, in contrast, to do with an understanding reached. I pick up five again, and a connection with a man who wears glasses. Not you, Joseph. And with walls, and an interior.

That will be all before we take our break, unless you have any questions.

(*Jane paused at 10:14. Her eyes were still closed and she still held the envelope to her forehead. This was my first opportunity to ask a question during such experiments; I picked what I thought was a safe one, meaning that I didn't think it would give Jane any clues.*

("*Well, do you want to say something about colors involved with the object, if any?*")

Give us a moment.

A violet. Red, and a grading to yellow. Plus white, and very dark.

The darks horizontal, the verticals bright. Also let me add initials, or symbols.

(*Break at 10:16. Jane was dissociated as usual, she said, and her eyes had remained closed. My question had not upset her. It will be recalled that this asking of questions during experimental material, or immediately afterward, has been led up to gradually in very recent sessions. As will be seen, the question bore fruit.*

(*See the tracing of the envelope object on page 327. Jane and I made most of the connections between the envelope object and the data easily enough, and did not ask Seth to clear up any points. The connections tonight were predominantly related with the envelope object itself, and not displaced onto another as they had been in the last session, and in the 234th, which involved the episode of the four letters.*

("*Five.*" *My handprint of course shows five fingers.*

("*Something for a consideration.*" *The print was made to be read, or considered, after the manner outlined in the book on hands.*

("*A floor plan, or diagram.*" *Note here how Jane narrowed the meaning down to a diagram. The original print used as the object, with the white lines apparent, is a diagram. See the detailed description on page 328.*

("*I have the impression of a* steeple *shape, or upside-down V shape, that is rather prominent.*" *To Jane the shapes of my fingers as outlined in pencil on the print, were steeple shapes. There are several V shapes on the print, and a prominent one between the thumb and forefinger. We are not sure why the upside-down reference to a V shape however. During the experiment I noticed that Jane held the rectangular* test envelope to her forehead with its long axis roughly parallel to the floor; perhaps the folded object inside gave rise to the upside-down impression.

(Personal association also operated with this impression. It wasn't until after the session ended that Jane realized that the "steeple shape," and the "many people" data to follow, had reminded her of a childhood poem she hadn't thought of in years. After the session she recited the little poem to me; it is done with hand gestures accompanying, the fingers of both hands interlocking in various positions. This is the poem: "Here is the church, here is the steeple. Open up the doors, and see all the people."

("A connection with many people, and with something like a basement—low, that is. This leads Ruburt to think of your Myhalyk's, his impression." Jane believes her impression here is correct. Myhalyk's is our favorite dancing establishment in Elmira. On Saturday, February 19, Jane and I met Marilyn and Don Wilbur and some others at Myhalyk's for an evening of dancing. This was shortly after we had obtained the book on hands, and during the evening Jane asked the Wilburs if they would cooperate in having handprints made. The Wilburs, who have witnessed several unscheduled sessions, consented. Arrangements were made to obtain their prints on Friday, February 25, but were not carried out because of the difficulty in getting good prints. My print, made on February 27, was an experiment in an effort to learn just how to make a good print.

("Something low and something high, in contrast, to do with an understanding reached." We think this is a reference to part of the technique in reading a hand; as described in the book it is not only necessary to consider the lines, but the "mounts", which are the high points of flesh at the base of the fingers, the thumb, the heel of the hand, etc. Also the low spots or depressions are considered significant.

("I pick up five again", If this is not a reference to the handprint, we do not see the connection, unless it is tied in with the next data.

("and a connection with a man who wears glasses. Not you, Joseph." Don Wilbur wears glasses. I do also. So does Bill Gallagher. Peggy Gallagher was visiting Jane on the evening I made the print used as the envelope object, on Sunday, February 27. After I was through with my efforts Bill arrived. As we recall he was not wearing his glasses on that particular evening. Don Wilbur wears his all the time, as I do.

("And with walls, and an _interior_." Although this is too general Jane thinks it is another reference to the aforementioned evening at Myhalyk's, where references to handprints were made.

("A violet. Red, and a grading to yellow." This is very interesting to me personally; Jane also recalls these details. After spending a couple of hours trying to make a good handprint, I gave up and began cleaning the ink from my hand. This proved to be a job. As I applied scouring powder I was surprised to see the black ink on the *palm turn what might be termed a red with violet undertones. This effect at once reminded me of reading that the quality of a black ink can be judged by its behavior when diluted: If a red color develops it means the ink is of inferior quality. The ink I had used was stamp-pad ink purchased at a 5-and-10 downtown.*

(The ink might have been of poor quality but it was difficult to remove. The red color was pronounced and I called Jane's attention to it. She too had had the experience, since she had tried prints of her own a few days earlier. A lot of scrubbing reduced the red stain to a yellowish cast finally, but here I had to let it wear off. This took several days. Thus we have a progression here from black to violet to red to yellow.

(Bear in mind that Jane had this experience as well as I. Perhaps her own experience reinforced whatever data she had picked up from my involvement with the actual envelope object. Jane said she cannot distinguish between the two, if this took place.

("Plus white, and very dark." I made the handprint on white paper identical with this page, and the print itself is very dark.

("The darks horizontal," Note the fold marks on the copy of the envelope object on page 327. When the object was folded and then held in a roughly horizontal position in the rectangular double envelope, the dark patterns of the fingers would be horizontal within the envelopes.

("the verticals bright." If this is a reference to the white spaces between the fingers of the print, then these would be horizontal also. We do not know why the vertical designation then.

("Also let me add initials, or symbols." As indicated on the copy on page 327, my initials, right hand designation, and the date were noted by me when I made the print. This was in black pen.

(When she began speaking Jane used short pauses often. Her eyes remained closed. Much of the time she cradled her cheek on her crossed arms, supported by the table. She was not smoking. Resume at 10:32.)

Now. We shortly end our session.

Ruburt has been intellectually involved in a strong manner with <u>our</u> whole relationship and experience, as he studied the galleys for his book. This is not particularly conducive to his intuitional activities, so I did not give him a break before our tests, but let the trance state continue. This worked to our advantage. This period just passing, of comparative rest on his part, from psychic activities, makes one point at least plain: our results, all in all during this period, have been good.

It was in a similar period in the past that the test data were very poor. The improvement will show itself more clearly as he becomes psychically more active again. My best regards to you both. If you have no questions I will end the session.

("What happened to the witnesses we were supposed to have?"
(Jane raised her head, eyes still closed, and smiled.)

I was being cagey. I merely said their attendance was possible. My time elements were simply off here, unfortunately.

("Good night, Seth."

(End at 10:40. Jane was dissociated as usual. See page 326 for the data on the expected witnesses for this evening's session.)

SESSION 238
MARCH 4, 1966 11:45 PM UNSCHEDULED FRIDAY EVE

(An unscheduled session was held this evening. It was witnessed by four people, and interrupted by a fifth. This account is written the following morning after a review of the main points with Jane. No notes were taken at the time of the session.

(It will be remembered that during the unscheduled session on last Sunday, February 27, and during Monday's regular session for February 28, Seth had mentioned the possibility of witnesses for last Wednesday's session, March 2. Moreover he mentioned the possibility existed for two sets of witnesses, and for four people, perhaps even five. When no witnesses appeared for Wednesday's session Seth said in answer to my question: "I was being cagey. I merely said their attendance was possible. My time elements were simply off here, unfortunately." Jane had smiled broadly while giving this answer.

(Two sets of witnesses did attend tonight's unplanned session, the Gallaghers and Marilyn and Don Wilbur. Jane began speaking as Seth at 11:45 PM, continued until about 12:15 AM, took a break during which the Gallaghers left, then resumed briefly, from about 12:30 to 12:45 AM with the Wilburs present. The session might have continued but was interrupted by the visit of a friend who does not know of them. We do not often get visitors after midnight; this friend has visited us perhaps three times in the last year, so we can say his arrival was unexpected.

(It can be said that since the Gallaghers and the Wilburs both know of the sessions, and that they visit us regularly, an unscheduled session is hardly unusual with these two sets of witnesses. It can also be said however that we do not easily hold unscheduled sessions, although from the record it might seem they are held rather often. Jane and I usually go out of our way to avoid them because of the extra work involved, etc. Hence the late starting hour for this one.

(Seth made some interesting points which I will attempt to summarize. Earlier in the evening Bill Gallagher spent perhaps three-quarters of an hour contemplating the oil painting of an elderly man which I executed in July 1965. Seth on various *occasions has claimed this painting, along with one other, to be likenesses of him. I did these two without models. This evening Bill commented often that the painting in question had a peculiar alive quality for him. I told him the lighting was flattering, but Bill insisted there was a different quality in the work, and that he did not believe it was due solely to suggestion.*

(Since the conversation revolved around matters psychic and nonpsychic, the stage was set rather effortlessly for Seth's appearance, although as stated neither Jane nor I actively encouraged the session. Everyone was in an excellent mood however. Soon after she began speaking for Seth, in a quite low and pleased voice, Jane launched into the reasons for Bill's response to the painting. It marked Bill's emotional perception, according to Seth, of Seth's presence in the painting, earlier in the evening. Hence Bill's feeling of an extra quality of life in the work. This event thus meant that for the first time Bill felt an emotional rapport with Seth, although previously he had been intrigued intellectually by the material.

(Seth went on to explain that with the exception of me everyone else in the room, including Jane, still had doubts as to what he was, that I accepted his explanation of his personality, and that this was a help in the sessions. This led to an exchange concerning secondary personalities. Seth said that in the future we would have many exchanges with psychologists and other scientists. Seth told us he knew how "their minds worked," and that when they thought they had him pinned down as a secondary, he would have a surprise for them, a demonstration. He did not go into detail here and I did not press for particulars because I was not making notes. I believe such events lay quite well ahead of us however.

(The surprise, Seth went on, would embarrass scientific personnel, but would also lead to clearer understanding of the Seth phenomenon. None of this information was given in a superior, or smug or sarcastic manner. It was a warm evening and our living room windows were open. Traffic noise even at this hour was audible; when I told Seth he was in danger of being drowned out by the traffic noise, the voice immediately rose in strong volume, humorously, for a few sentences: "I will never be drowned out by traffic..." etc.

(Earlier in the evening our conversation had turned on the subject of death and related topics in a rather humorous way, and Seth pointed out that he had listened in on us at this time. He was not disapproving, but neither did he approve.

(Peggy Gallagher has been bothered in recent weeks by what she calls bursitis in her left shoulder. In the last few days the discomfort has moved down into her left arm; periodically she said the arm tingles, in a sensation similar to that felt when a limb has gone to sleep. The feeling is not that drastic though. Seth, without being asked, told Peggy that she had a disturbance in the area of the third to fifth vertebrae, and that this, basically, was the cause of her back and arm disturbances. Peggy had

thought circulation was at the seat of the trouble. Seth said the circulation was healthy, but interfered with somewhat by tension.

(Seth proceeded to suggest several things Peggy might do; if she followed the suggestions the trouble should disappear. She should give herself suggestions before sleep that she not sleep on her left side, but her right side instead. This would remove the pressure on the afflicted side of the body. Peggy said she didn't think she slept on her left side; Seth said she did after going to sleep, and that suggestion would prevent this. Seth told Peggy not to lean on her left elbow during the day, especially at work. Even as he spoke, we saw Peggy leaning on her left elbow. Peggy said she may have the habit of leaning on her desk at the newspaper office with her left arm or elbow; she will check.

(Seth told Peggy to stand up and stretch her arms over her head frequently during the day. He told her to use suggestion that her circulation in the afflicted areas be more than adequate until the condition subsided; she should do this frequently during the day. He went into some detail here, explaining that the tension caused a slowing of the blood flow in the shoulder and arm making the blood's normally easy flow much more difficult. He told Peggy there was nothing wrong with her circulation.

(In connection with the above, Seth told Peggy not to take aspirin. The aspirin, he said, aggravates the problems caused by tension in this particular instance. A congestion builds up in the back and arm. Seth then told Peggy to drink two cups of coffee at breakfast. Peggy drinks one as a habit. Seth said the extra caffeine in her case would stimulate circulation, whereas the aspirin would hinder it. He was definite on this.

(We now come to a surprising development. Seth proceeded to tell Peggy that she was doing her yogic neck rolls much too fast in the morning. This is an exercise, Peggy told us at break, that she does each morning. Like Jane, she works out with yoga each day, but rushes the exercises in the morning while dressing for work. Jane did not know this, and Peggy said she had never mentioned it. Seth was right here, according to Peggy, for lately she felt she had been hurrying the exercises too much. Seth told Peggy the rapid neck rolls, which are an exercise supposed to be done slowly, were actually being detrimental to her. In addition, Peggy should be careful at the end of this exercise, when she drops her head forward, supposedly in a relaxed manner. Seth said the sudden dropping put a strain on the third to fifth vertebrae. Peggy agreed that she ended the exercise in this manner; and again, she had not thought to mention this to Jane previously.

(Seth told Peggy the yoga exercises were basically excellent for her if done at the proper tempo, and to keep them up. He said Peggy should surmount the problem setting up the tension in her back, which was leading in turn to the other physical symptoms, for if she did not there was a danger that any habits of rigidity would grow worse in the future. Seth did not go into any emotional causes this evening, and *was not asked to. Peggy agreed to try the routine suggested, and will report on results.*

(Seth took a break at 12:15 AM, during which the Gallaghers left. He resumed at about 12:30, until interrupted at 12:45. The interruption marked the end of the session.

(The Wilburs have witnessed a few unscheduled sessions. Their first experience is mentioned in the notes for the 206th session, of November 8, 1965. Their next is mentioned in the notes for the 214th session, of December 6, 1965. The unscheduled session was held on November 5, 1965; see page 57.

(During that session Seth gave Don Wilbur a little information concerning a job change he was contemplating. I made no notes during the evening, but Don took down the data pertaining to him. It amounted to perhaps a medium-long paragraph, and included a description of a building he would visit, its offices, and a man to whom he would apply for employment. Don's wife carried the notes in her handbag for some weeks. Don never did see about the job he was thinking of, in December, because his present employment kept him too busy during the winter months. He and his wife lost track of the notes, and Jane and I had forgotten them long ago.

(Last week, the first week in March 1966, Don Wilbur began making the rounds in Elmira in his quest for a better job. Answering an ad in the local paper, he drove to the location given for a construction firm. He had forgotten consciously about Seth's data, but as he drove into the firm's property he was immediately struck by the similarity there with Seth's predictions. He had not been to the location before. The description of the building matched, as well as the description Seth had given of the man Don would talk to about work. Marilyn, Don's wife, believes she still has Seth's notes at home and will look for them.

(Don Wilbur's parents are against his changing jobs. The Wilburs did not ask Seth for advice, nor did Jane and I. Seth volunteered that it was better for Don to make his own decisions. He did say that Don would leave his present job because it offered no opportunities for advancement, and that he would try three other positions before he settled into one he really liked. But Seth did not say when. Don himself has not decided what to do. The place he visited that matched Seth's description has made him an offer of employment.

(Seth was going into the relationship between predictions and probabilities when the session came to an end because of the mentioned interruption. As stated, two sets of witnesses had been present. A fifth person had also appeared, causing the end of the session after one set of witnesses had left. See page 326.

(Jane's eyes had been wide open much of the time, and very dark. Her voice for the most part had been very quiet, her pace average. Her delivery at times had been humorous.)

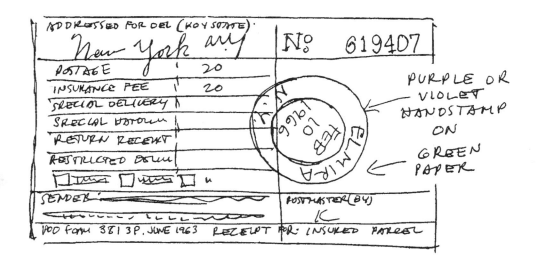

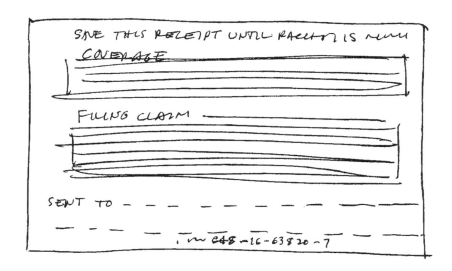

(Front and back tracings of the insurance slip used as the envelope object in the 38th experiment, in the 239th session for March 7, 1966.)

SESSION 239
MARCH 7, 1966 9 PM MONDAY AS SCHEDULED

(The 38th envelope experiment was held during the session. The object, sealed in the usual double envelope, was the insurance slip for the two manuscripts Jane mailed to her publisher on February 10, 1966. These were the poetry book and the first section of her book on the Seth material. This material is discussed in the 234th session, among others.

(Jane was not feeling at her best, and did not do as well as she wanted to on the experiment. I had suggested earlier in the day that she skip the session but she declined. She also wanted to have the envelope experiment. John Bradley, our salesman friend from Williamsport, PA, was a witness, and I believe this contributed to the envelope results, in some way I cannot define. Previously Jane has done well with envelopes before witnesses.

(John's entity name is Philip. He has witnessed a number of sessions, the last being the 226th. John's presence usually calls forth some telepathic and/or clairvoyant material from Seth, and so it developed this evening. The form of the material is a little different however this time, and involves John and his wife for the most part.

(The session was held in our front room. Jane began speaking while sitting down and with her eyes closed. She was smoking, and opened her eyes but the one time to put out her cigarette. Her pace was average, her voice a little more active than usual.)

Good evening.

("Good evening, Seth.")

([John:] "Good evening, Seth.")

Welcome to our friend Philip. We shall have some remarks later that will pertain to him.

There are some additions, Joseph, that I would like to make concerning our inverted time system. An understanding of this system will serve to explain to the psychologists certain things that are not now plain to them.

For one thing, association is not clearly understood by any means. It cannot be clearly understood simply because at present psychologists believe that association works only in connection with past events.

They also underestimate <u>dream</u> events, for many associations in your present are the result of events which have occurred in the dream state. The mind is hardly shut off when you dream. It continues to use its associative processes. Therefore any given personal association may originate from a dream event as well as from a past waking event.

Psychologists, generally speaking, have not accepted the latest theories of your own physicists, however. They continue to consider time as a series of moments, one following the other.

The inverted time system recognizes the actual nature of time, however. There is room in this system for a rather complete explanation of the mind's associative processes.

Now. The mind as opposed to the brain, perceives time in terms of the spacious present. It is true that the mind works on associative principles. Therefore these associations are drawn not only from the past, but also from the future.

Take an example here. Frederick Y. becomes ill whenever he smells a certain perfume. He does not know the reason. A psychologist would explain this reaction by presuming some kind of unpleasant event occurred in the past. An event that was connected with his sensual perception of this particular perfume.

The explanation is a good possible one. However, it is the only one that your psychologists would consider, and at least two other possible explanations exist. Frederick may be reacting to an unpleasant event experienced within the dream state, where in the dream the upsetting situation was accompanied by the odor of a particular perfume.

Frederick however could also be reacting to the same sort of event that has not yet occurred, however, to his perception—that is, to an event in the future. For the mind does not divide time into a series of moments. This is done by the physical brain and the physical senses.

The ego is not as a rule aware of this broader time experience. The subconscious however is so aware, and the associative processes of the mind can, and do, react to a future event, while the ego is closed off to it. Therefore it is possible for Frederick, this year, to become ill at the smell of a particular perfume because subconsciously he knows that in 1980 his mother will be wearing that perfume when she dies.

The associative processes work both backwards and forwards. An understanding of this will help in a study of the associative processes in general.

You may take a brief break and I shall continue.

(Break at 9:20. Jane was dissociated as usual, she said, for a first delivery. Her delivery had become rather active and fast.

(A long break now ensued. It was brought about because John began talking about his family relationships; the subject came up when we discussed some of the sessions John has witnessed, and the data Seth has given in them pertaining to John, his family, his job, etc. Some of the predictions are long-range. See 166th, 190th, 204th, 226th, for example; in Volumes 4 and 5.

(John said it was all right for the personal material to be included in this

record, and it is a good example of the way Seth handles such data. Jane and I, incidentally, have never met John's wife. Most of the family material is self-explanatory. During break John gave us some information; briefly, it has to do with his restlessness in his job, his wife's reactions, his wife's parents, his own strong need to assert his independence, etc. John is also active politically in Pennsylvania, as a conservative. He is an excellent medical representative for Searle Drug, but feels he is not being extended enough in his work; he wants more challenge. Seth has advised patience here; John said this is difficult for him but that he is carefully considering the advice. Searle itself is going through a difficult time managerially and financially.

(Jane finally resumed, her eyes closed even though she was smoking, at 9:48.)

Now. I did not resume the session for rather obvious reasons.

We will however shortly begin our Instream material, and then we will be involved with our own envelope, if you have one for me, Joseph.

However I will discuss this later in the session, and make a few comments now. Give us a moment however.

(Jane now paused. As when giving experimental material, she sat with her head down, a hand raised to her closed eyes.)

Ruburt is not particularly pleased with what he knows I am about to say, but I am not held by the same social rules that hold him in this particular matter, and I know Philip perhaps better than he does.

This discussion will be begun now but ended later this evening.

Now. We have fear and rage on the part of the girl, for despite the children she is yet a girl, and a very nice one. However the relationship between her own parents has been destructive. The father has wanted domination, and to some extent has forced his wife into a position of dominance which she strongly resents. Because of this she lashes out at her husband. I am speaking now, you understand, of the parents of Philip's wife.

(John and his mother-in-law do not get along.)

Now, the girl respects Philip because he will not be dominated. On the other hand the woman image that she understands, because of her mother, is a dominating woman image. To her she fails as a female if she cannot hold him in line. At the same time her personality is far different than her mother's, and less focused.

Also she loves Philip, and would not consciously want to dominate him if she could. He senses this subconscious need of hers however to hold him, and resents it vigorously. She attempts to dominate him in her own way, and on a subconscious basis, and it is indeed by appealing to him through helplessness. At the same time she does not want him to give in to her.

She tries to dominate in more feminine ways. Her mother's domination had more masculine aspects. We will have more to say concerning this, and I hope some helpful comments after our other material.

Now, please give us a moment for the Instream data.

(Jane paused at 10:01. She sat with her head down, her hands raised to her closed eyes. She began speaking with many short pauses, but overall her pace could not be called slow. This is the 45th Instream experiment.)

A dark corner of a room, with wooden paneling. It is a right corner. He stands facing it. In front of him there is a large and very bulky chair.

It is covered with leather or plastic, rather than cloth. A table with a lamp sits beside it. The initials R H connected here. Perhaps the initials of the man who lives here.

Two other people in the room, I believe a woman and a man, and another man has been present but is now out of the room. There is also another wall adjacent to this one, with a long window now covered by a closed cloth drapery. The drapery is short, that is, it does not reach all the way to the floor.

A desk beneath this window, of dark wood. The floor covered with a light-colored, textured rug. In the light it looks green. Two doorways to the room. There is an office close by in the same dwelling place, that also belongs to the owner, the man who Dr. Instream visits.

This room, the office, has a large <u>light</u>-colored wooden desk, set out from a window—that is, not in the center of the floor—the chair between the window and the desk.

This window also covered by a short closed drapery. A photograph on the desk, taken in 1936, of a woman. An earlier party this evening for Dr. Instream. This dwelling I <u>believe</u> is on another level but the first level of a building. The street faces north and south, runs north and south. The numbers 312 connected here.

Now. Do you have an envelope for me?

("Yes."

(As usual Jane took the double envelope from me without opening her eyes. On impulse I almost told Seth there was to be no envelope, but decided to go ahead in the presence of a witness. Jane appeared to feel all right, also. She held the envelope against her forehead.)

Please, give us a moment. These are impressions.

The numbers 4, 6. An unknown element. A connection with a man and a woman. A paper item.

Black and white, a border, I believe of white. A light strip on this item. Perhaps wider at one end, and in the lower portion.

Again the impression of lights. A 4 and 9. A connection with a <u>shovel</u>, or something dug up. Something that you wish to know.

The paper item having to do with a gathering. Now. Ruburt's connection here with your acquaintances, the Smiths. Handwriting, or writing, lettering, on it.

I pick up also some connection with flag shapes and colors, and with a connection with Wisconsin.

Do you have any questions, Joseph?

(*Jane paused at 10:17, without opening her eyes. She now held the envelope in her lap. This was the second time Seth had given me the chance to ask a question after an experiment. I could not be sure, without checking with Seth in detail, but I thought Jane had been wandering about on the above data. Because we had a witness I didn't think we would spend too much time checking details. Earlier in the day I had wondered what would happen if I asked Seth/Jane to go over all of the data again; I supposed Jane would take this as a sign that the first data wasn't much good, and at break Jane said this was her thought at the time.*

(*"Do you want to try again?"*)

We can. 4. A square. 3, diagonal, 2, 1. A connection with a rush, or hurry. An engagement. A framework and a variety of incidents leading up to an important development.

Purple, the color. A connection with a ring, and with a time schedule. Four separate blocks, or divisions of color. Connection with a missionary and a turnstile.

More numbers, and I suggest your break.

(*Break at 10:25. Jane said that toward the end of the delivery she was more dissociated as usual. When I asked her to try again she took it as a sign that the first attempt with the envelope wasn't good.*

(*See the tracing of the object on page 339. The object is the insurance slip for the manuscripts of Jane's poetry book, and the first section of the Seth material, mailed to her publisher on February 10, 1966. This material is discussed to some extent in the 234th session, among others.*

(*Seth offered to go over the test material but we went on with more material for John Bradley, the witness. Jane and I made a few connections, which will be noted. In the first group of impressions Jane said the data "A light strip on this item. Perhaps wider at one end, and in the lower portion." pertained to a mental image she had at the time. She saw a wedge-shaped light strip, horizontally, but could tell no more than this.*

(*Since most envelope objects are paper items, we usually discount such data. The numbers 4, 6 and 9 however do appear on the object, as mentioned in the first data.*

(*My question proved to have some value, for in some manner it spurred Seth,* or Jane, to a better effort. Listed below are the connections we could make without asking Seth.

("4." The number 4 appears on the receipt. There could be other connections.

("A square." Jane said this probably referred to the tape recording that was mailed along with the manuscripts. The tape was one Jane made reading some of the poems for her publisher. It was wrapped in a thin box that was square in area.

("A connection with a rush, or hurry. An engagement. A framework and a variety of incidents leading up to an important development." Jane felt emotionally good about this data, she said. It involved her efforts in getting the tape made, and the two manuscripts in question, ready for the mail. All of it was done in quite a hurry, at the request of her publisher. Jane called her publisher on February 8, as noted in the envelope material in the 234th session, then hurried to get the scripts and tape ready for the mail on February 10. A variety of incidents were involved while Jane made the tape recording of the poems, etc.

(The important development for Jane was making the tape, and sending in the script on the Seth material. We are not sure of the reference to a framework however.

("Purple, the color. A connection with a ring, and with a time schedule." As stated, the handstamp applied to the insurance receipt is in purple or violet, and is in the shape of a ring. The time element is also apparent in the above material.

("More numbers." There are several sets of numbers on the front of the receipt, and a string of them along the bottom on the back.

(Thus there are four pieces of data we made no connections for: 3, diagonal, 2, 1; A framework; Four separate blocks, or divisions of color; Connection with a missionary and a turnstile.

(John Bradley said that as far as he knew Seth was correct in his analysis of his wife's parents, and correct concerning the relationship between John and his wife.

(Break had again been fairly long. Jane resumed at a comfortable pace; her eyes were closed and she was smoking. After she had been speaking for a while her eyes, very dark, began to open occasionally. Resume at 10:45.)

Now. The test results were fairly poor.

We have gone into the reasons for such results in the past. I would prefer to make some remarks to Philip now, rather than discuss the tests in the time available. I will discuss them if you wish.

("No, that's all right.")

(Once again Jane bowed her head and raised her hand to her closed eyes.)

Give us a moment.

With the girl's background it is natural enough that an independent male would both frighten and fascinate her. It was this way from the beginning of their relationship.

(Jane pointed at John, her eyes still closed.)

What he does not understand is the rage that she is containing. There is considerable strength to it, and he should recognize this. She does not <u>want</u> to dominate him through feminine wiles, and yet subconsciously she feels driven to do so.

She feels <u>threatened</u> by serious conversation, Philip, for she fears the unknown. She <u>feels</u> like a child when a parent says "Now, we must discuss this seriously." Such a discussion threatens the status quo.

The trivial conversations which you were all discussing would be helpful here, as reassurance. Your own ideas concerning various issues could be profitably inserted when you are not emotionally upset over them.

Your anger is interpreted simply as violence, and she fears it. Ideas expressed at such occasions will be strenuously fought by her. You must make an emotional bridge, for she will not understand an intellectual one. But the emotional bridge must not be of a violent nature.

This is all you have achieved so far in that regard.

She fears, for one thing, that you could run the house more efficiently than she can, and basically that you do not need her. She is not certain of her own merit, and achieves her self-approval through your auspices.

She is not a partner and you are indeed in difficulties. She can <u>become</u> a partner however, but anger will only minimize her importance in her own eyes, and therefore in yours.

One of the children is suffering to some extent psychologically because of the dilemma, and you are too much the autocrat with this child, a female.

This is merely a question of relationships, where any thought of blame is meaningless. The situation can be salvaged.

Now, give us a moment again.

(Jane now took a pause lasting over a minute. Her eyes had been opening occasionally but they were now closed. Her hands were once again raised to her face.)

Her father has been more destructive to her psychological health in some respects than her mother, for he gave her the image of males as weak.

The strong male is therefore a threat, while he also represents security. There seems to be some situation arising particularly on Wednesdays, that is important emotionally to her. I am not certain as to what this refers.

She does not realize basically, subconsciously, her importance to you. If you can make her see this you will be able to maintain that sense of independence that is important to you. If you cannot she will be driven to snatch it away.

If you cannot communicate important ideas, then you must communicate trivial ones. The big conversation, in which you attempt to communicate your ideas, only frightens her. The idea should be communicated when you are not emotionally upset, and you should not adopt the tone of a parent speaking to a child.

I suggest a brief break. We cannot have Joseph's hands falling off at every session.

(*Break at 11:13. Jane was dissociated as usual. Her pace had been good; my hand was feeling some fatigue. Her eyes had remained closed except when she put out her cigarette and took a sip of wine.*

(*John said he agreed with Seth's material. He verified that a situation does arise on Wednesdays in his home. Every other week a cleaning woman works at his home on Wednesdays, helping his wife with heavier chores. John's wife is named Mary-Ellen, the cleaning woman is Lois. Lois, John said, is around 40 years old, and she has her own personal problems. Mary-Ellen is not the type to talk with others about personal affairs, John said, but he has had the thought that she may get satisfaction listening to others talk about their troubles. Lois is a talker.*

(*Again the break was rather long. Jane resumed while smoking, in a faster manner, and her eyes began to open more often, at 11:34.*)

Now. I am rather an old man to be speaking in such terms.

However, in the main you are doing two things wrong. You are treating her primarily as a woman rather than an individual person; but you are not treating her as a <u>desirable</u> woman rather than an individual person.

If you treat her as a desirable woman, you will find a difference in your home atmosphere. If you <u>cannot do this</u>, then you must treat her primarily as an individual person. But if you treat her as a woman primarily, it must be as a desirable woman, or she will find no content as a woman or as an individual.

And if you treat her as a desirable woman, she will become one. You are treating her as a <u>wife</u> and mother, primarily. With this particular individual this is not adequate. She wants to be regarded as a desirable woman who happens to be your wife and a mother.

She will be much more content and pliable to reason if you can manage, regardless of your intellectual tendencies, to approach her in that light. She needs drama, within the framework of the home, and she wants this from you. It will take some effort on your part, but if she feels that you spend time with <u>her</u> simply because you want to be with her, this will go a long way in solving your difficulties.

And if you cannot do this honestly, then your difficulties are more serious than you realize. The effort will be more than worth your while, but the effort must be an honest one, or she will sense the hypocrisy.

Do you have any questions, Philip?

([John:] "No, not specifically.")

I realize that you feel as if you are in a vicious circle. In many cases however you do not ask, but have a tendency to command her. Not in words so much as in attitude. She does not feel truly desirable. You can do much to change this.

If your relationship is as important to you as I believe it is, then you will make the effort. The simple fact is that you do need her, and you have not communicated this. Obviously there are reasons for <u>her</u> behavior, and changes also that she can and should make, but I am speaking to you and not to her.

There seems to be someone, three houses away, a woman with whom your wife could make friendly and profitable contact. Either the woman is younger, or seems so.

The adjustments necessary are not all on your part, but your adjustments can initiate hers. You are concerned, and have made efforts, but you are better equipped, simply because of your personality structure, to make these efforts. She is at this point like a child in the woods, but the potentialities are there for an excellent relationship. We will take a break or end the session, as you prefer.

("We'll take a short break then."

(11:59. I thought John wanted more information, but we were tired by now, and this proved to be the end of the session. Jane had been dissociated as usual. Her rapid pace had been broken by some rather long pauses, and her eyes had remained closed.

(John again agreed with Seth. He also verified Seth again, in that he remembers a younger girl living three houses away. This girl is perhaps five years younger than John and his wife; they know her only to say hello to. John said a younger woman lives but two houses away, also. Jane knew nothing of these two women, just as she knew nothing of the Wednesday incidents.)

THE SETH AUDIO COLLECTION

RARE RECORDINGS OF SETH SPEAKING through Jane Roberts are now available on audiocassette. These Seth sessions were recorded by Jane's student, Rick Stack, during Jane's classes in Elmira, New York, in the 1970's. The majority of these selections have never been published in any form. Volume I, described below, is a collection of some of the best of Seth's comments gleaned from over 120 Seth Sessions. Additional selections from The Seth Audio Collection are also available. For information ask for our free catalogue.

Volume I of The Seth Audio Collection consists of six (1-hour) cassettes plus a 34-page booklet of Seth transcripts. Topics covered in Volume I include:

- Creating your own reality – How to free yourself from limiting beliefs and create the life you want.
- Dreams and out-of-body experiences.
- Reincarnation and Simultaneous Time.
- Connecting with your inner self.
- Spontaneity—Letting yourself go with the flow of your being.
- Creating abundance in every area of your life.
- Parallel (probable) universes and exploring other dimensions of reality.
- Spiritual healing, how to handle emotions, overcoming depression and much more.

FOR A FREE CATALOGUE of Seth related products including a detailed description of The Seth Audio Collection, please send your request to the address below.

ORDER INFORMATION:
If you would like to order a copy of The Seth Audio Collection Volume I, please send your name and address, with a check or money order payable to New Awareness Network, Inc. in the amount of $59.95 plus shipping charges. United States residents in NY, NJ, PA & CT must add sales tax.

Shipping charges: U.S. - $5.00, Canada - $7, Europe - $15, Australia & Asia - $17
Rates are UPS for U.S. & Airmail for International - Allow 2 weeks for delivery
Alternate Shipping - Surface - $8.00 to anywhere in the world - Allow 5-8 weeks

Mail to: NEW AWARENESS NETWORK INC.
P.O. BOX 192,
Manhasset, New York 11030
(516) 869-9108 between 9:00-5:00 p.m. Monday-Saturday EST

Visit us on the Internet - http://www.sethcenter.com

Books by Jane Roberts from Amber-Allen Publishing

Seth Speaks: The Eternal Validity of the Soul. This essential guide to conscious living clearly and powerfully articulates the furthest reaches of human potential, and the concept that each of us creates our own reality.

The Nature of Personal Reality: Specific, Practical Techniques for Solving Everyday Problems and Enriching the Life You Know.. In this perennial bestseller, Seth challenges our assumptions about the nature of reality and stresses the individual's capacity for conscious action.

The Individual and the Nature of Mass Events. Seth explores the connection between personal beliefs and world events, how our realities merge and combine "to form mass reactions such as the overthrow of governments, the birth of a new religion, wars, epidemics, earthquakes, and new periods of art, architecture, and technology."

The Magical Approach: Seth Speaks About the Art of Creative Living. Seth reveals the true, magical nature of our deepest levels of being, and explains how to live our lives spontaneously, creatively, and according to our own natural rhythms.

The Oversoul Seven Trilogy (The Education of Oversoul Seven, The Further Education of Oversoul Seven, Oversoul Seven and the Museum of Time). Inspired by Jane's own experiences with the Seth Material, the adventures of Oversoul Seven are an intriguing fantasy, a mind-altering exploration of our inner being, and a vibrant celebration of life.

The Nature of the Psyche. Seth reveals a startling new concept of self, answering questions about the inner reality that exists apart from time, the origins and powers of dreams, human sexuality, and how we choose our physical death.

The "Unknown" Reality, Volumes One and Two. Seth reveals the multidimensional nature of the human soul, the dazzling labyrinths of unseen probabilities involved in any decision, and how probable realities combine to create the waking life we know.

Dreams, "Evolution," and Value Fulfillment, Volumes One and Two. Seth discusses the material world as an ongoing self-creation—the product of a conscious, self-aware and thoroughly animate universe, where virtually every possibility not only exists, but is constantly encouraged to achieve its highest potential.

The Way Toward Health. Woven through the poignant story of Jane Roberts' final days are Seth's teachings about self-healing and the mind's effect upon physical health.

Available in bookstores everywhere.